Awkward Silence

Story and Art by Hinako Takanaga

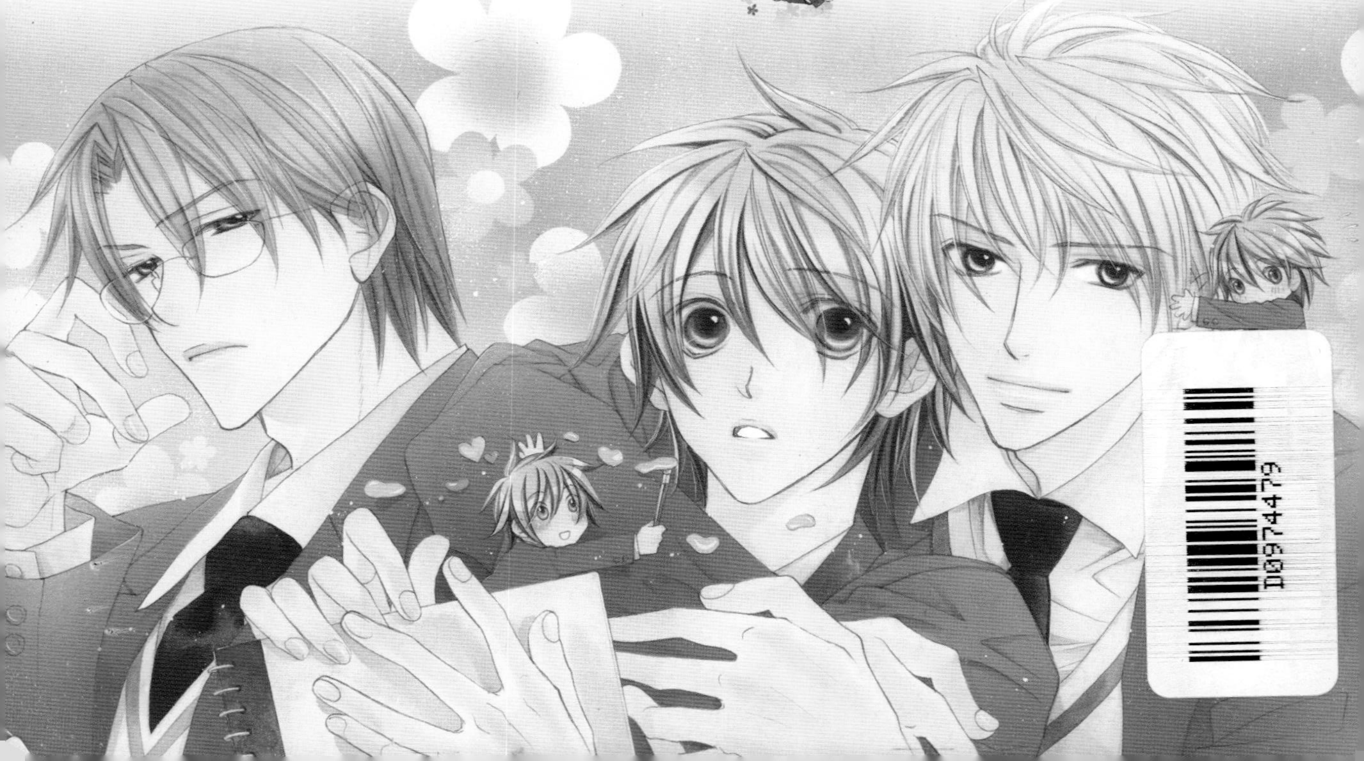

Awkward Silence

Story and Art by **Hinako Takanaga**   volume **2**

CONTENTS

SUBLIME
SuBLime Manga Edition

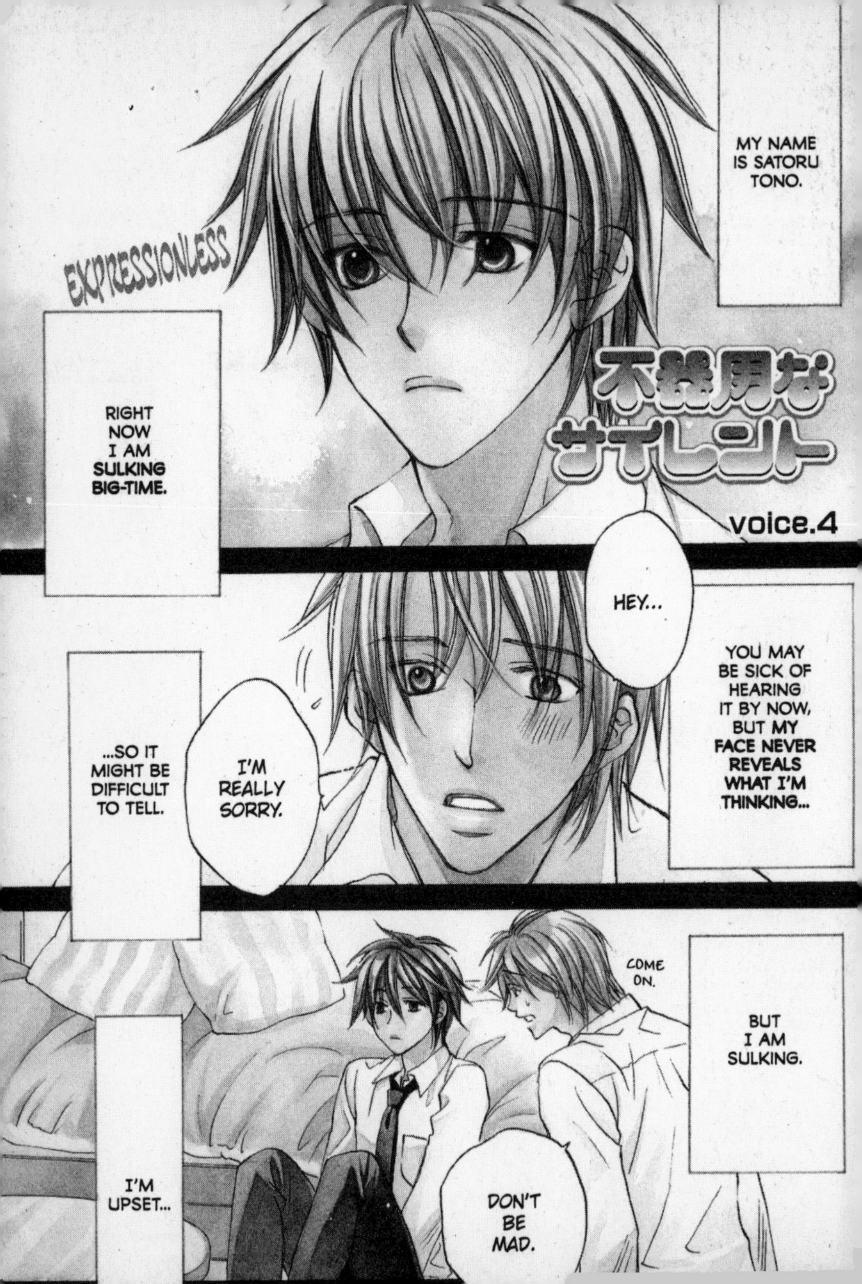
MY NAME IS SATORU TONO.
不器用なサイレント
voice.4
EXPRESSIONLESS
RIGHT NOW I AM SULKING BIG-TIME.
HEY...
YOU MAY BE SICK OF HEARING IT BY NOW, BUT MY FACE NEVER REVEALS WHAT I'M THINKING...
I'M REALLY SORRY.
...SO IT MIGHT BE DIFFICULT TO TELL.
BUT I AM SULKING.
COME ON.
DON'T BE MAD.
I'M UPSET...

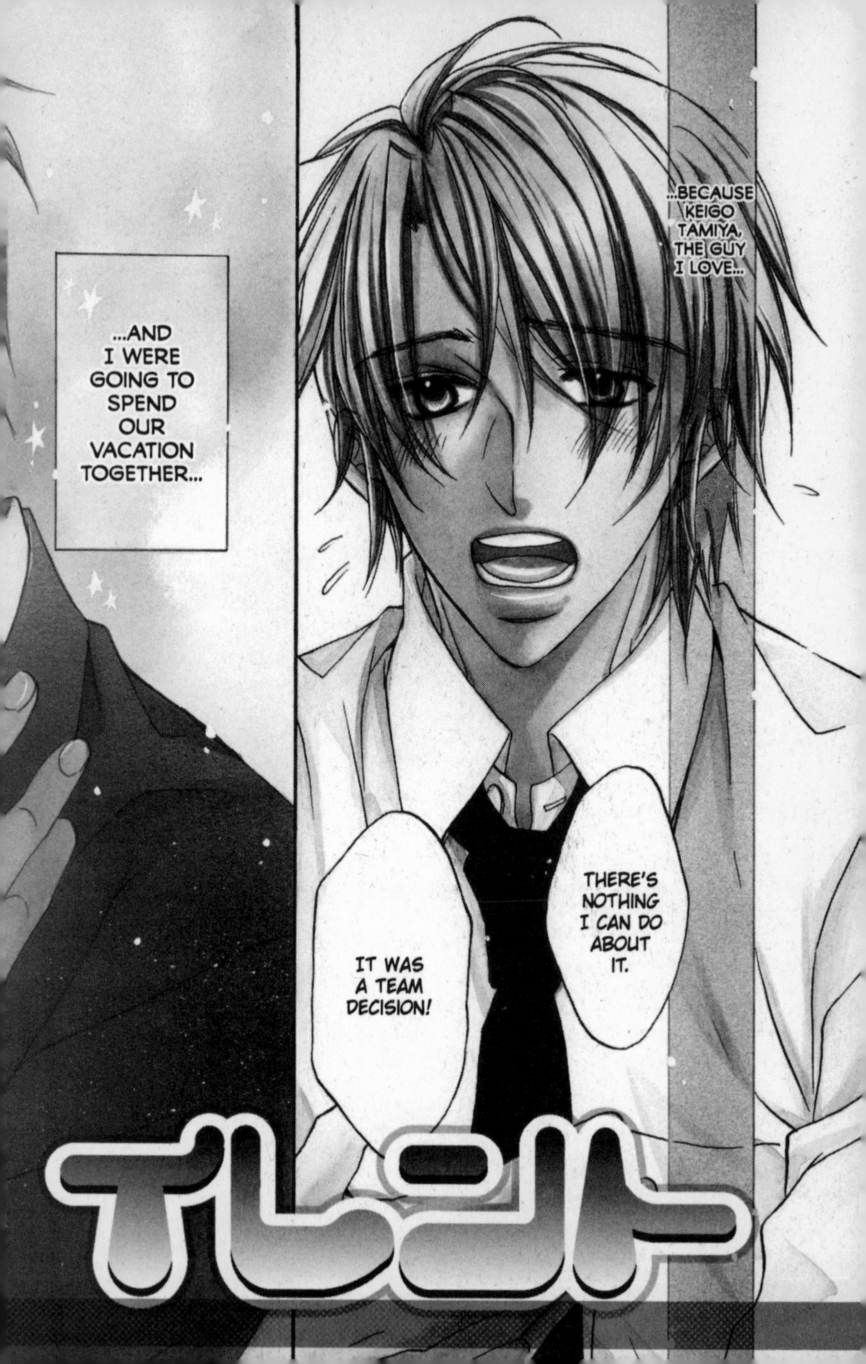
...BECAUSE KEIGO TAMIYA, THE GUY I LOVE...
...AND I WERE GOING TO SPEND OUR VACATION TOGETHER...
THERE'S NOTHING I CAN DO ABOUT IT.
IT WAS A TEAM DECISION!

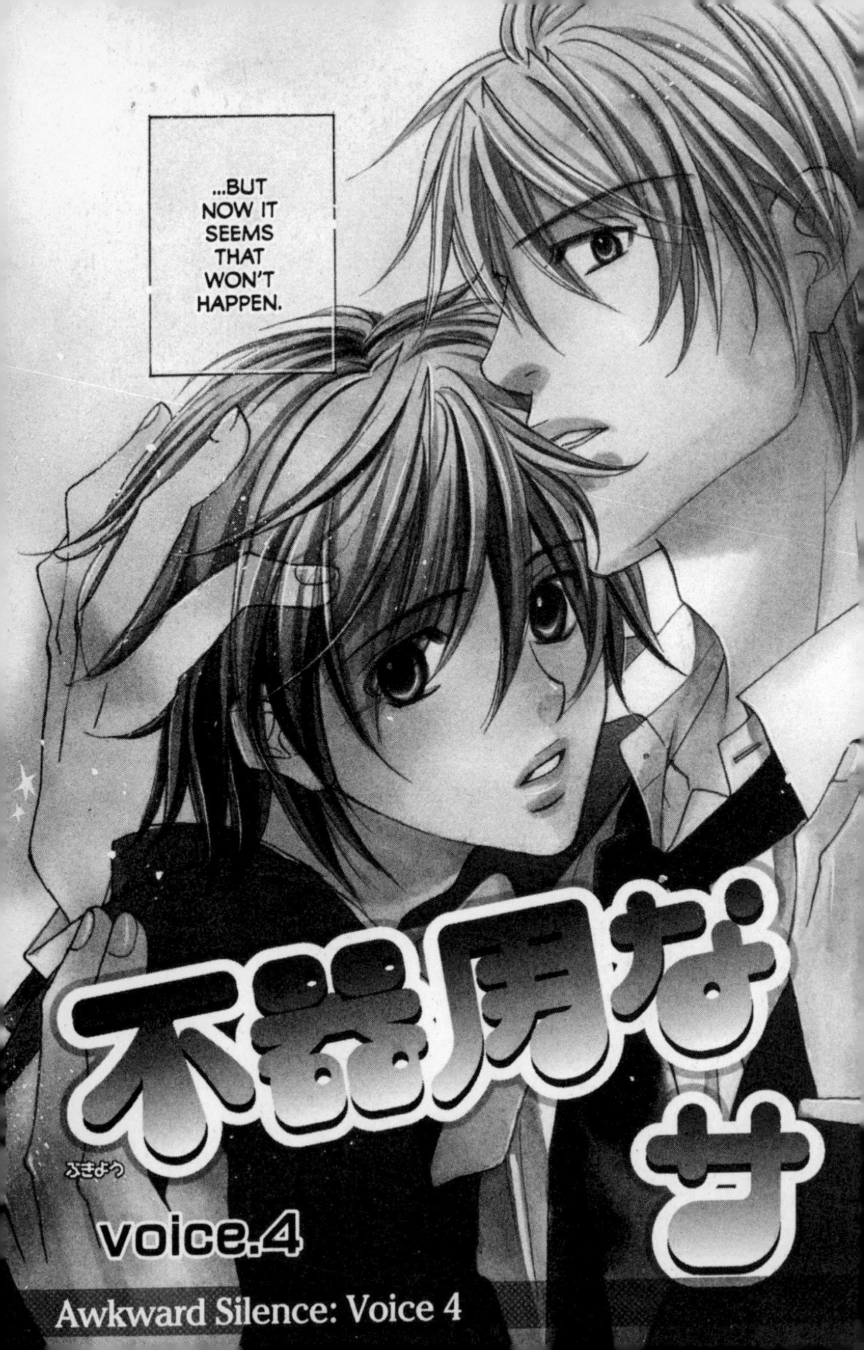
...BUT NOW IT SEEMS THAT WON'T HAPPEN.
不器用な男
ぶきよう
voice.4
Awkward Silence: Voice 4

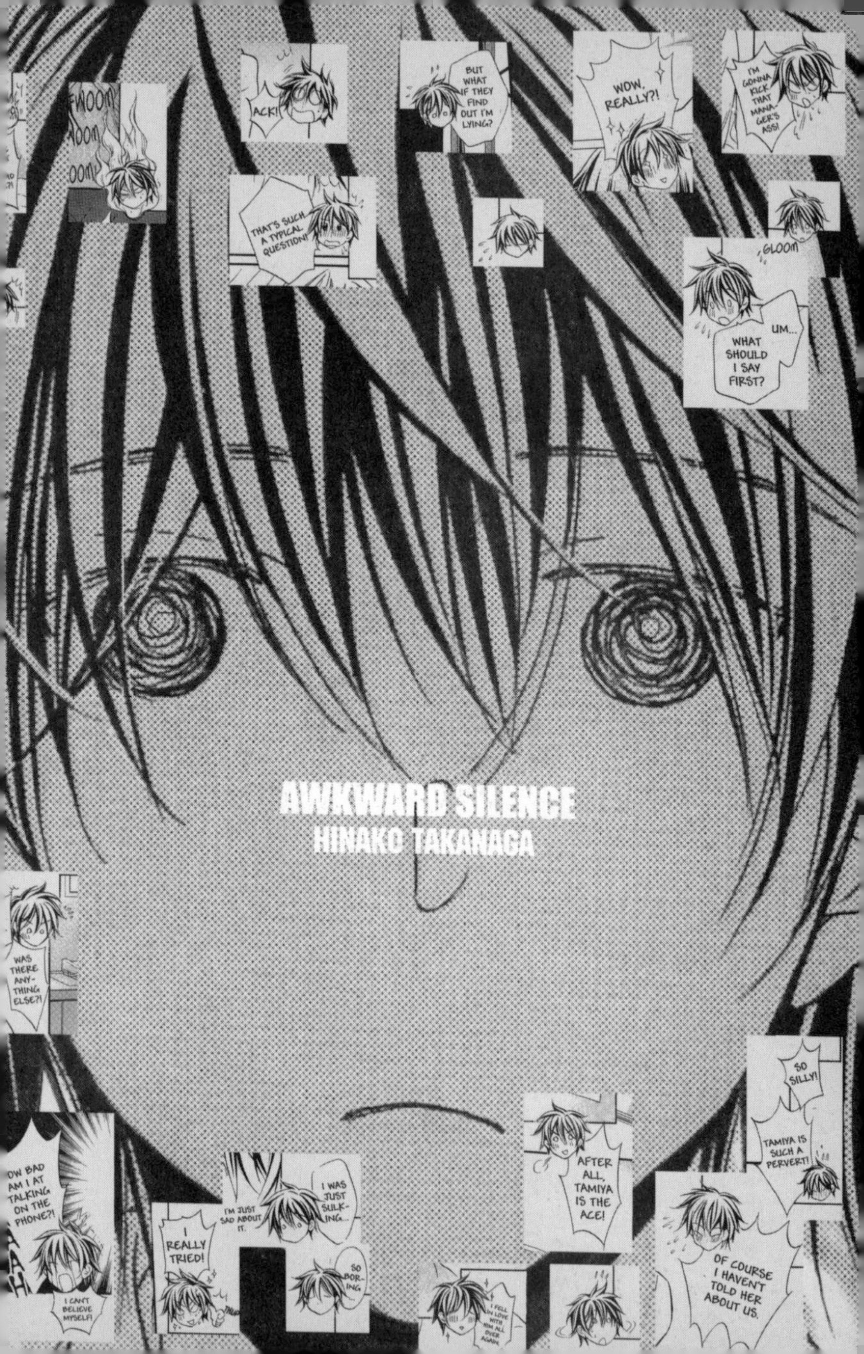
I'M GONNA KICK THAT MANA-GER'S ASS!
WOW, REALLY?!
BUT WHAT IF THEY FIND OUT I'M LYING?
ACK!
FWOOM
FOOM
OOM
GLOOM
UM...
WHAT SHOULD I SAY FIRST?
THAT'S SUCH A TYPICAL QUESTION!
AWKWARD SILENCE
HINAKO TAKANAGA
WAS THERE ANY-THING ELSE?!
SO SILLY!
TAMIYA IS SUCH A PERVERT!
OF COURSE I HAVEN'T TOLD HER ABOUT US.
AFTER ALL, TAMIYA IS THE ACE!
I FELL IN LOVE WITH HIM ALL OVER AGAIN.
I WAS JUST SULK-ING...
SO BOR-ING...
I'M JUST SAD ABOUT IT.
I REALLY TRIED!
OW BAD AM I AT TALKING ON THE PHONE?!
I CAN'T BELIEVE MYSELF!

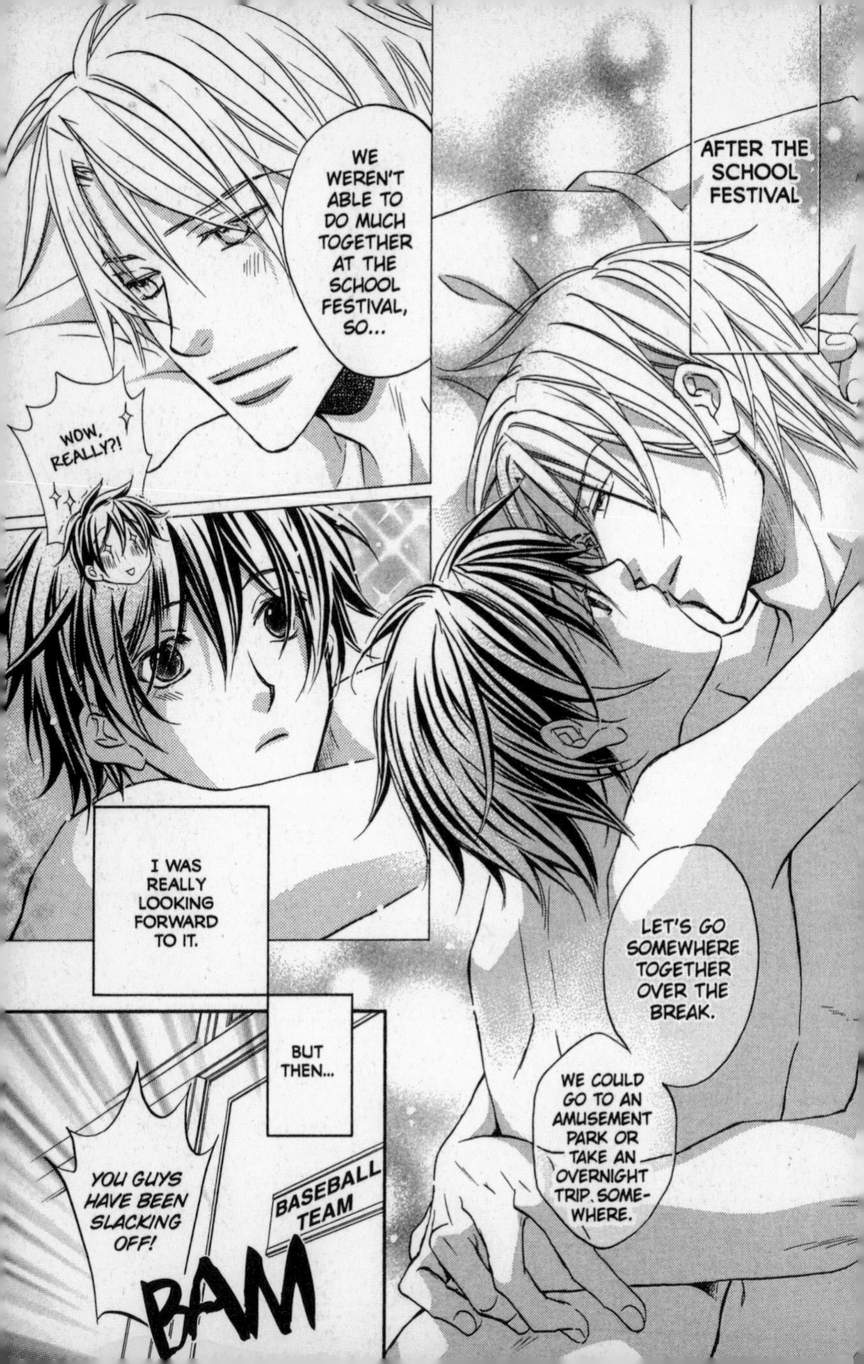
AFTER THE SCHOOL FESTIVAL
WE WEREN'T ABLE TO DO MUCH TOGETHER AT THE SCHOOL FESTIVAL, SO...
LET'S GO SOMEWHERE TOGETHER OVER THE BREAK.
WE COULD GO TO AN AMUSEMENT PARK OR TAKE AN OVERNIGHT TRIP SOME-WHERE.
WOW, REALLY?!
I WAS REALLY LOOKING FORWARD TO IT.
BUT THEN...
YOU GUYS HAVE BEEN SLACKING OFF!
BASEBALL TEAM
BAM

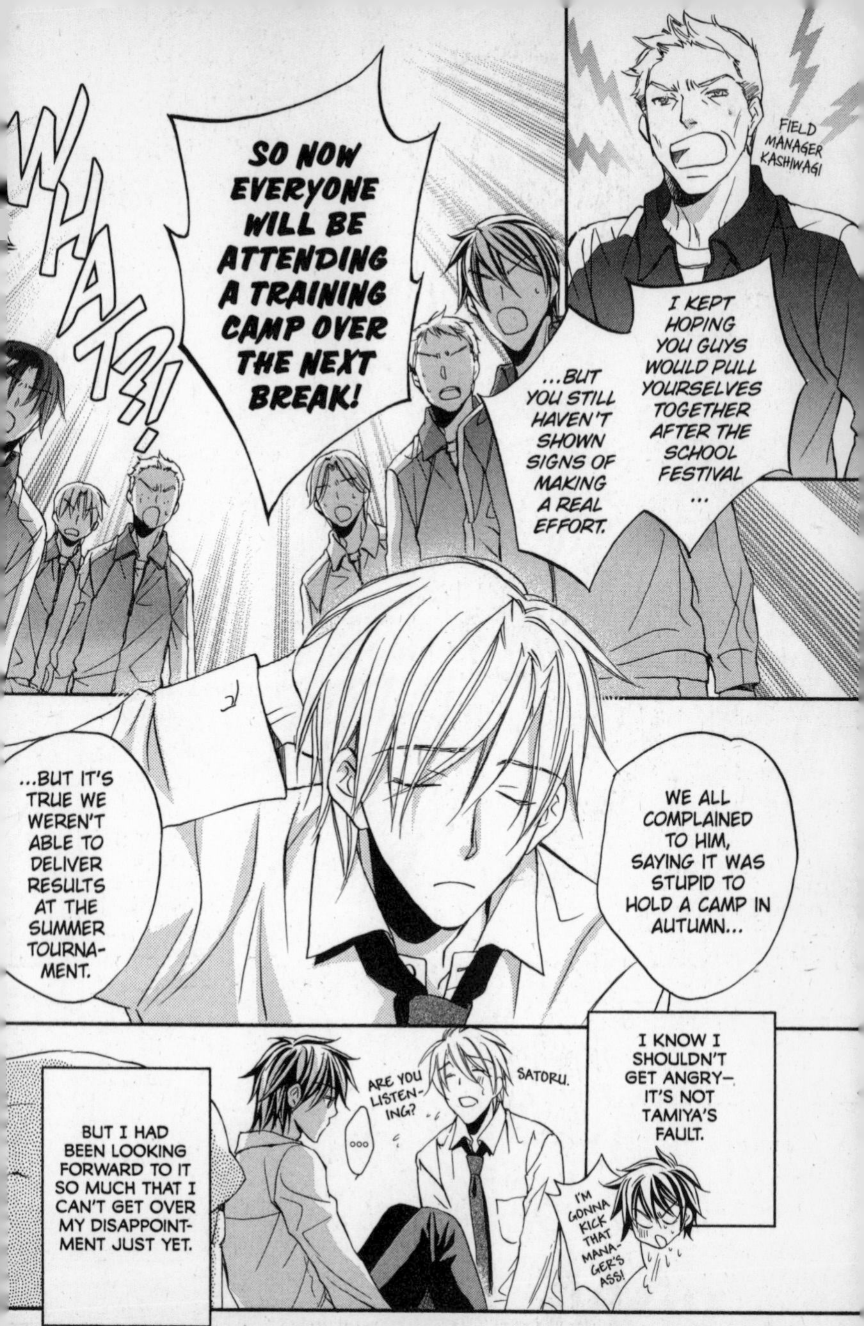
FIELD MANAGER KASHIWAGI
I KEPT HOPING YOU GUYS WOULD PULL YOURSELVES TOGETHER AFTER THE SCHOOL FESTIVAL...
...BUT YOU STILL HAVEN'T SHOWN SIGNS OF MAKING A REAL EFFORT.
SO NOW EVERYONE WILL BE ATTENDING A TRAINING CAMP OVER THE NEXT BREAK!
WHAK!!
WE ALL COMPLAINED TO HIM, SAYING IT WAS STUPID TO HOLD A CAMP IN AUTUMN...
...BUT IT'S TRUE WE WEREN'T ABLE TO DELIVER RESULTS AT THE SUMMER TOURNAMENT.
I KNOW I SHOULDN'T GET ANGRY— IT'S NOT TAMIYA'S FAULT.
I'M GONNA KICK THAT MANAGER'S ASS!
SATORU.
ARE YOU LISTENING?
...
BUT I HAD BEEN LOOKING FORWARD TO IT SO MUCH THAT I CAN'T GET OVER MY DISAPPOINTMENT JUST YET.

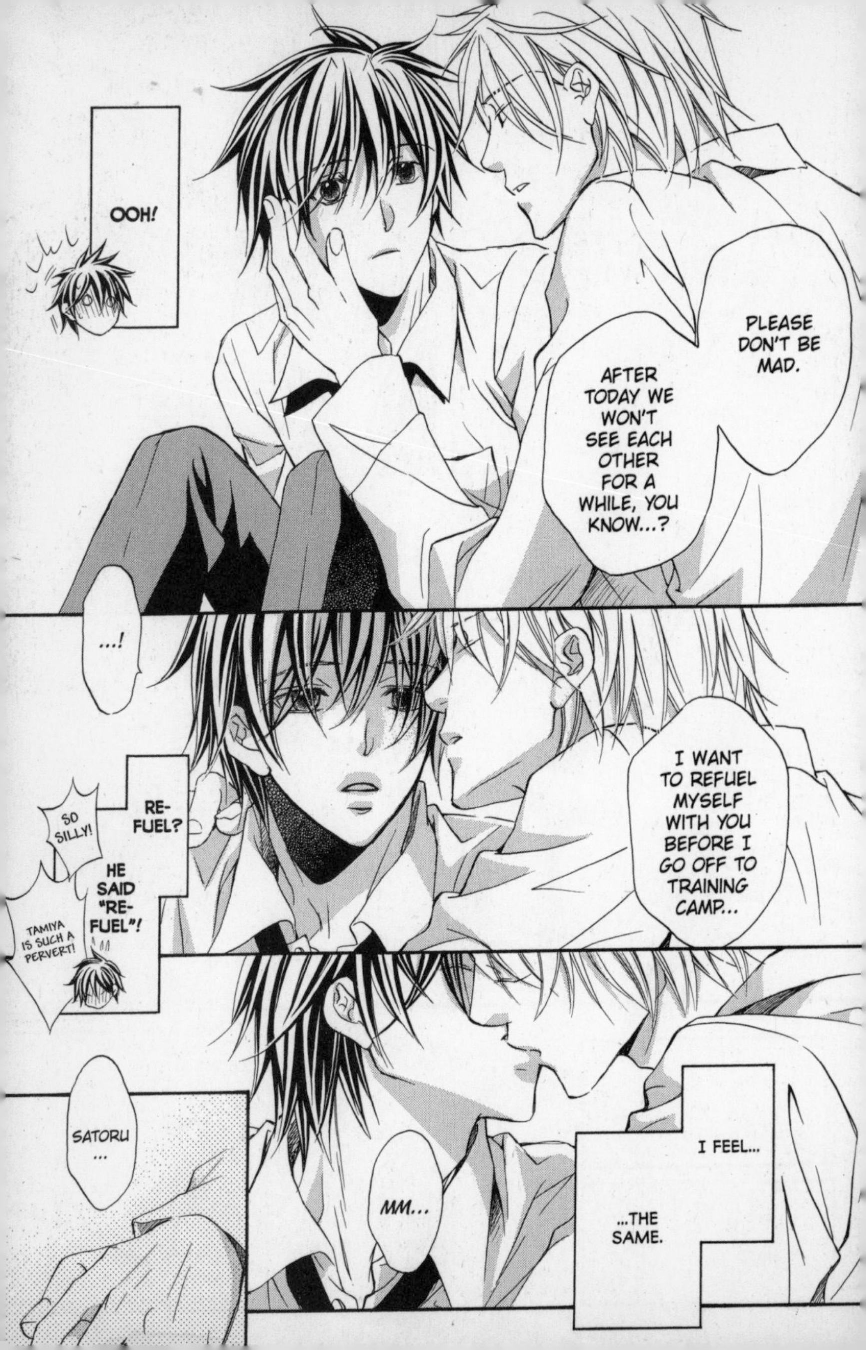
PLEASE DON'T BE MAD.
AFTER TODAY WE WON'T SEE EACH OTHER FOR A WHILE, YOU KNOW...?
OOH!
...!
I WANT TO REFUEL MYSELF WITH YOU BEFORE I GO OFF TO TRAINING CAMP...
RE-FUEL?
HE SAID "RE-FUEL"!
SO SILLY!
TAMIYA IS SUCH A PERVERT!
I FEEL...
...THE SAME.
MM...
SATORU
...

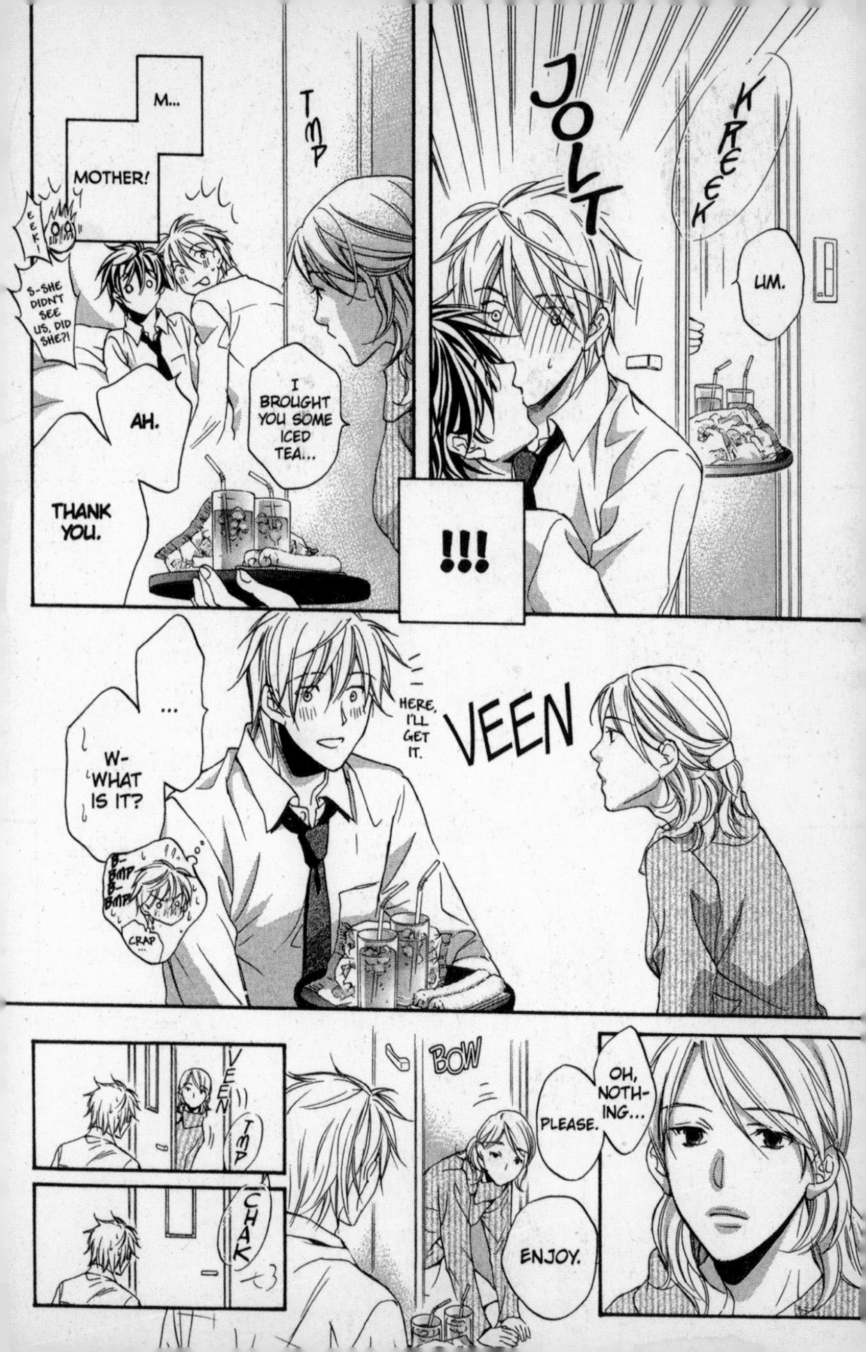
KREEK
UM.
JOLT
!!!
TMP
M...
MOTHER!
I BROUGHT YOU SOME ICED TEA...
EEK!
S-SHE DIDN'T SEE US, DID SHE?!
AH.
THANK YOU.
VEEN
HERE, I'LL GET IT.
...
W-WHAT IS IT?
B-BMP B-BMP
CRAP...
OH, NOTHING...
BOW
PLEASE.
ENJOY.
VEEN
TMP
CHAK

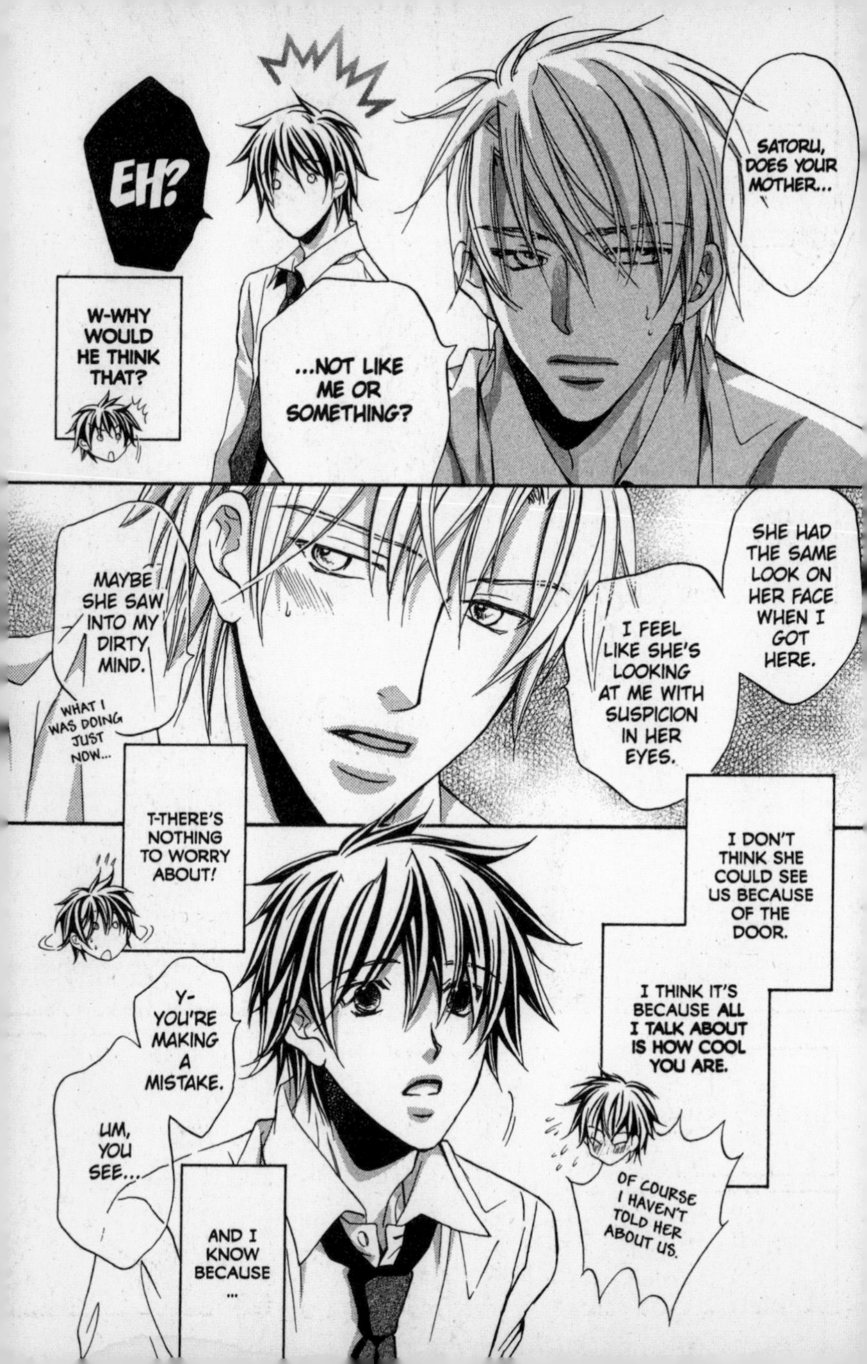
SATORU, DOES YOUR MOTHER...
...NOT LIKE ME OR SOMETHING?
EH?
W-WHY WOULD HE THINK THAT?
SHE HAD THE SAME LOOK ON HER FACE WHEN I GOT HERE.
I FEEL LIKE SHE'S LOOKING AT ME WITH SUSPICION IN HER EYES.
MAYBE SHE SAW INTO MY DIRTY MIND.
WHAT I WAS DOING JUST NOW...
I DON'T THINK SHE COULD SEE US BECAUSE OF THE DOOR.
T-THERE'S NOTHING TO WORRY ABOUT!
I THINK IT'S BECAUSE ALL I TALK ABOUT IS HOW COOL YOU ARE.
OF COURSE I HAVEN'T TOLD HER ABOUT US.
Y-YOU'RE MAKING A MISTAKE.
UM, YOU SEE...
AND I KNOW BECAUSE ...

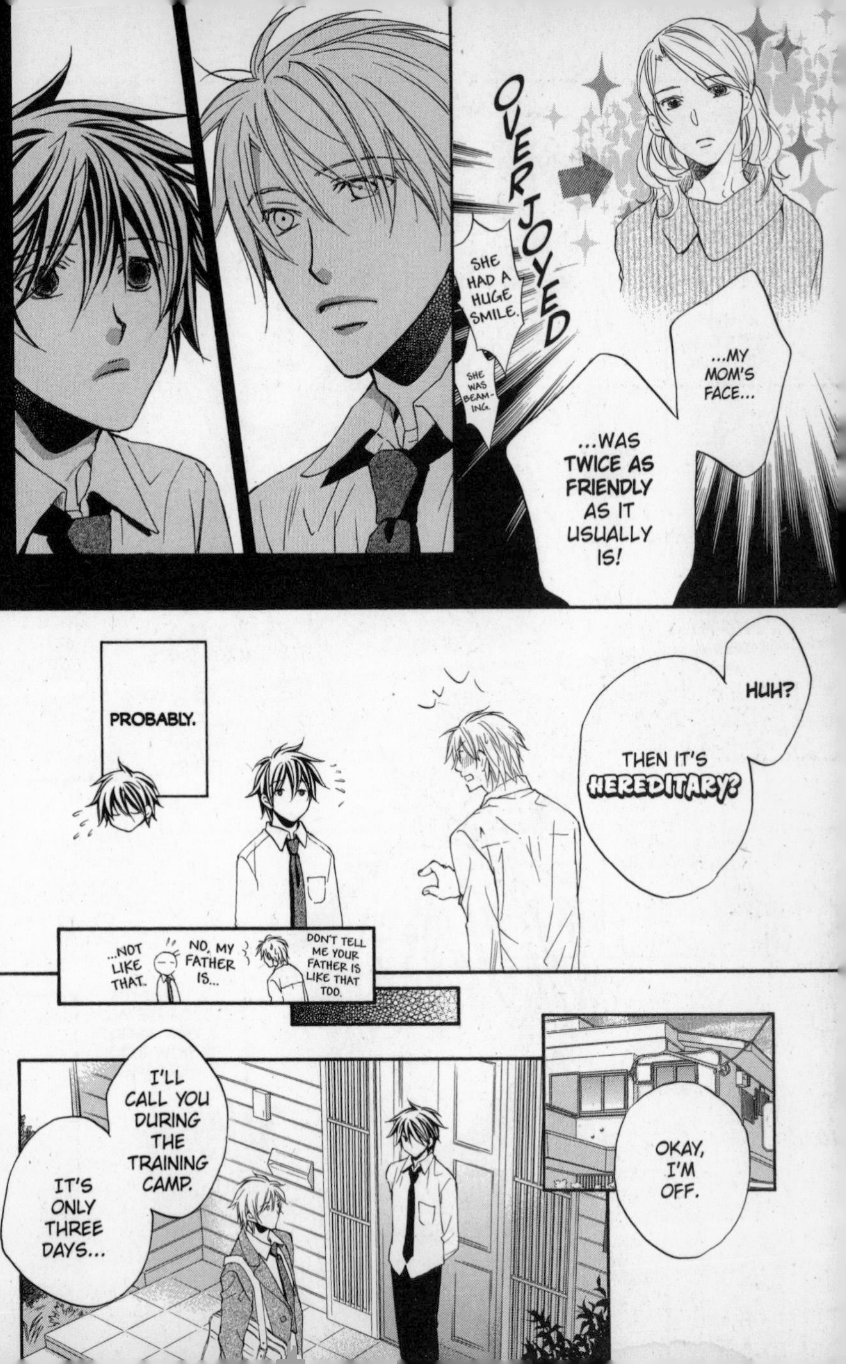
...MY MOM'S FACE...
...WAS TWICE AS FRIENDLY AS IT USUALLY IS!
OVERJOYED
SHE HAD A HUGE SMILE.
SHE WAS BEAM-ING.
HUH?
THEN IT'S HEREDITARY?
PROBABLY.
DON'T TELL ME YOUR FATHER IS LIKE THAT TOO.
NO, MY FATHER IS...
...NOT LIKE THAT.
OKAY, I'M OFF.
I'LL CALL YOU DURING THE TRAINING CAMP.
IT'S ONLY THREE DAYS...

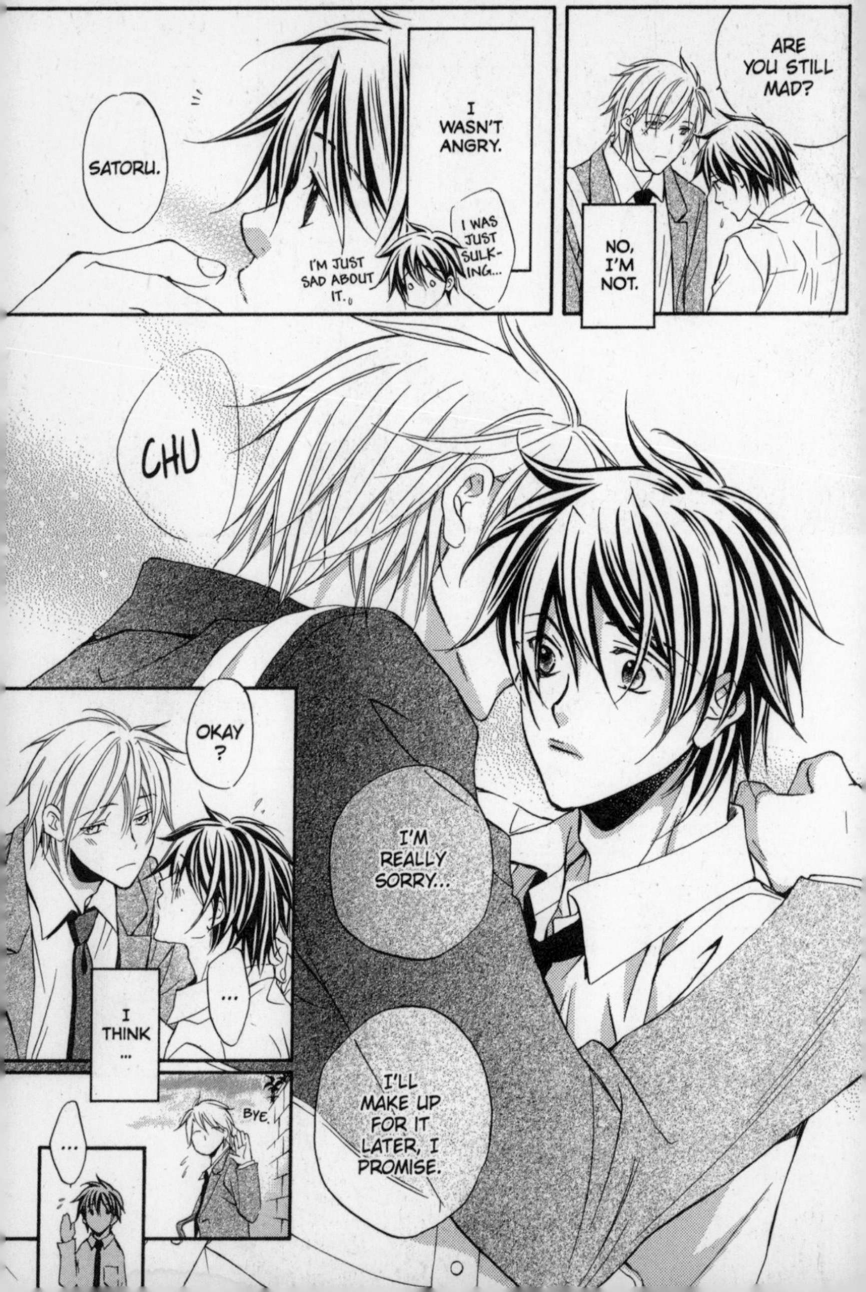
ARE YOU STILL MAD?
NO, I'M NOT.
I WASN'T ANGRY.
I WAS JUST SULKING...
I'M JUST SAD ABOUT IT.
SATORU.
CHU
I'M REALLY SORRY...
I'LL MAKE UP FOR IT LATER, I PROMISE.
OKAY?
...
I THINK...
BYE.
...

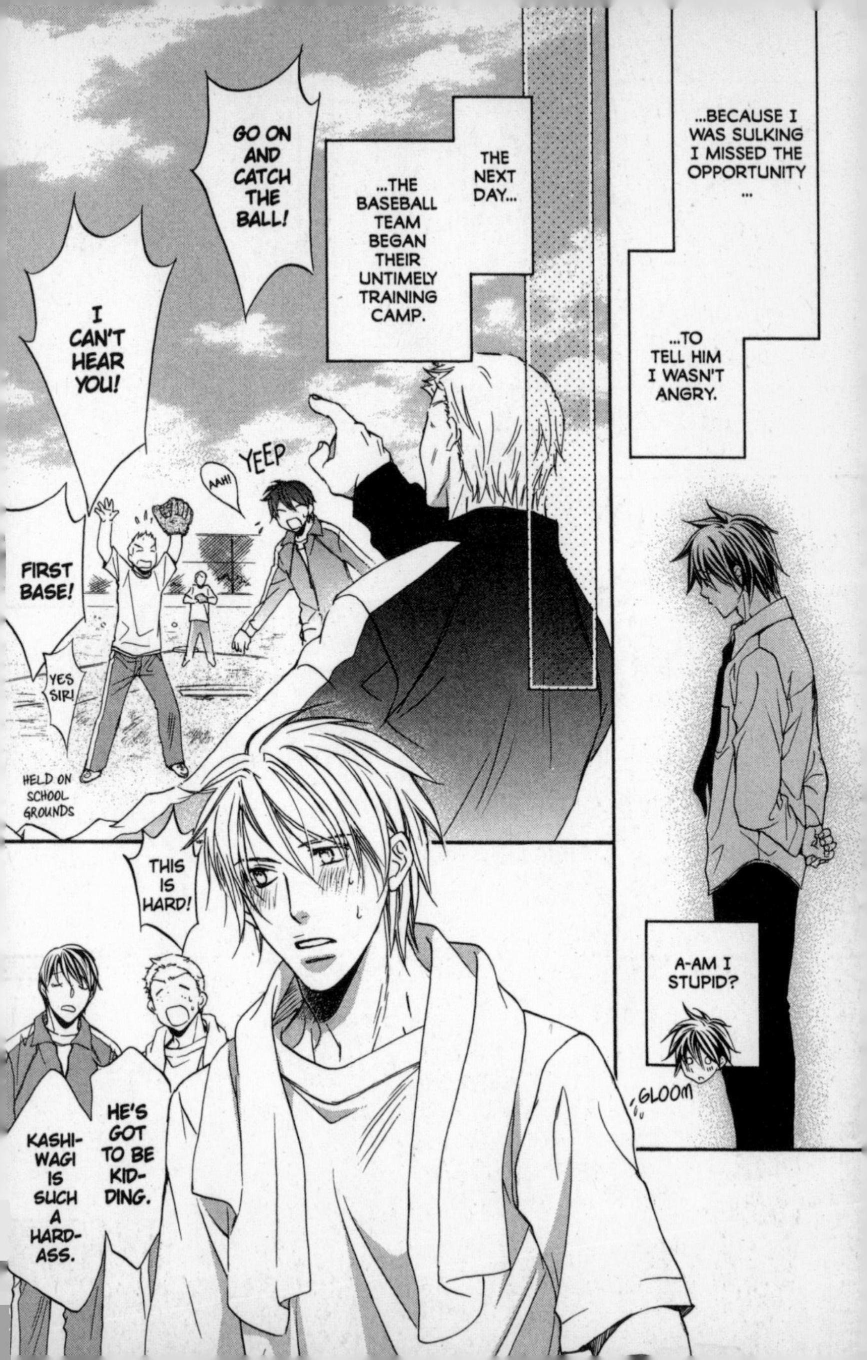
...BECAUSE I WAS SULKING I MISSED THE OPPORTUNITY ...
...TO TELL HIM I WASN'T ANGRY.
A-AM I STUPID?
GLOOM
THE NEXT DAY...
...THE BASEBALL TEAM BEGAN THEIR UNTIMELY TRAINING CAMP.
GO ON AND CATCH THE BALL!
I CAN'T HEAR YOU!
YEEP
AAH!
FIRST BASE!
YES SIR!
HELD ON SCHOOL GROUNDS
THIS IS HARD!
HE'S GOT TO BE KIDDING.
KASHIWAGI IS SUCH A HARD-ASS.

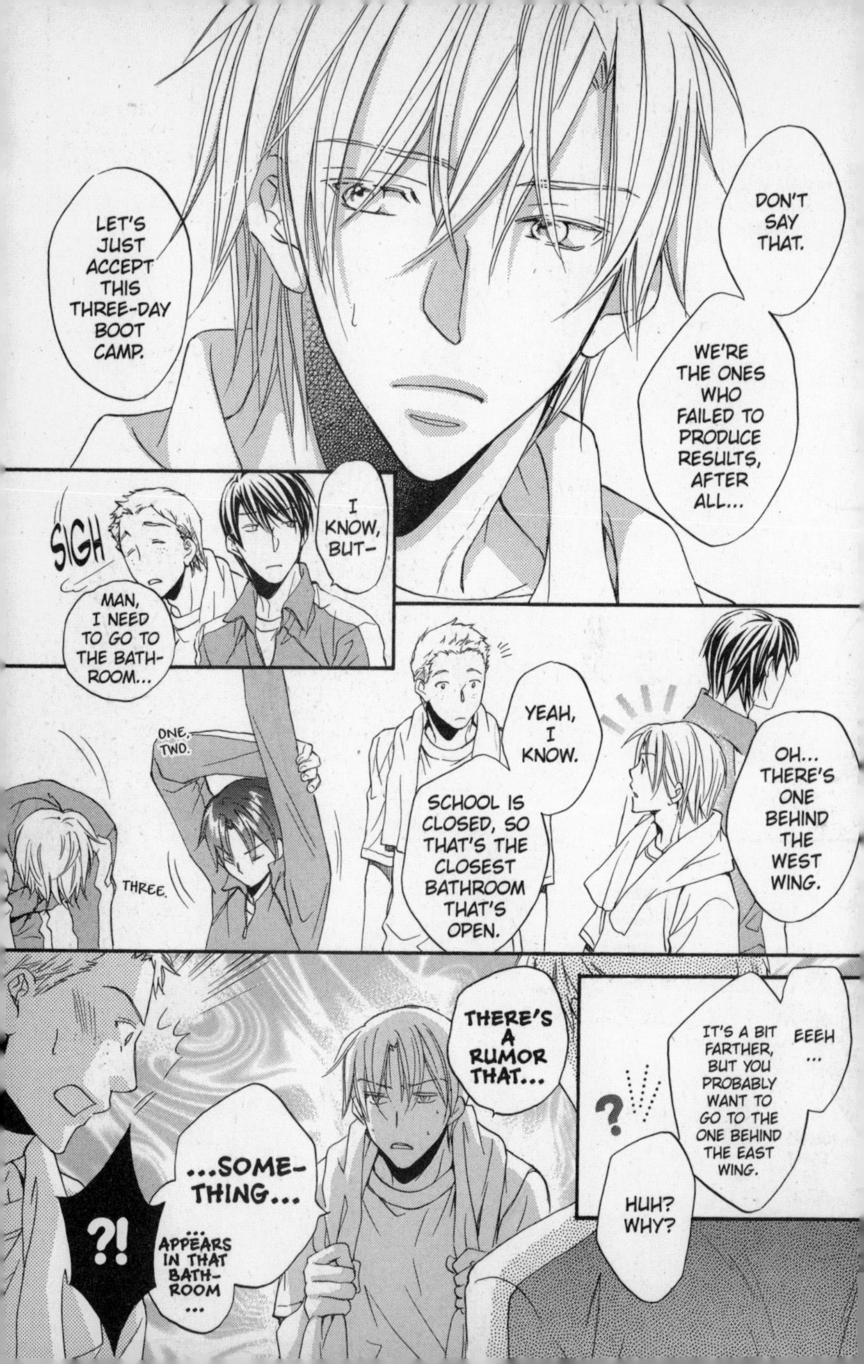
DON'T SAY THAT.
WE'RE THE ONES WHO FAILED TO PRODUCE RESULTS, AFTER ALL...
LET'S JUST ACCEPT THIS THREE-DAY BOOT CAMP.
I KNOW, BUT-
SIGH
MAN, I NEED TO GO TO THE BATH-ROOM...
OH... THERE'S ONE BEHIND THE WEST WING.
YEAH, I KNOW.
SCHOOL IS CLOSED, SO THAT'S THE CLOSEST BATHROOM THAT'S OPEN.
ONE, TWO.
THREE.
EEEH ...
IT'S A BIT FARTHER, BUT YOU PROBABLY WANT TO GO TO THE ONE BEHIND THE EAST WING.
?
HUH? WHY?
THERE'S A RUMOR THAT...
...SOME-THING...
?!
... APPEARS IN THAT BATH-ROOM ...

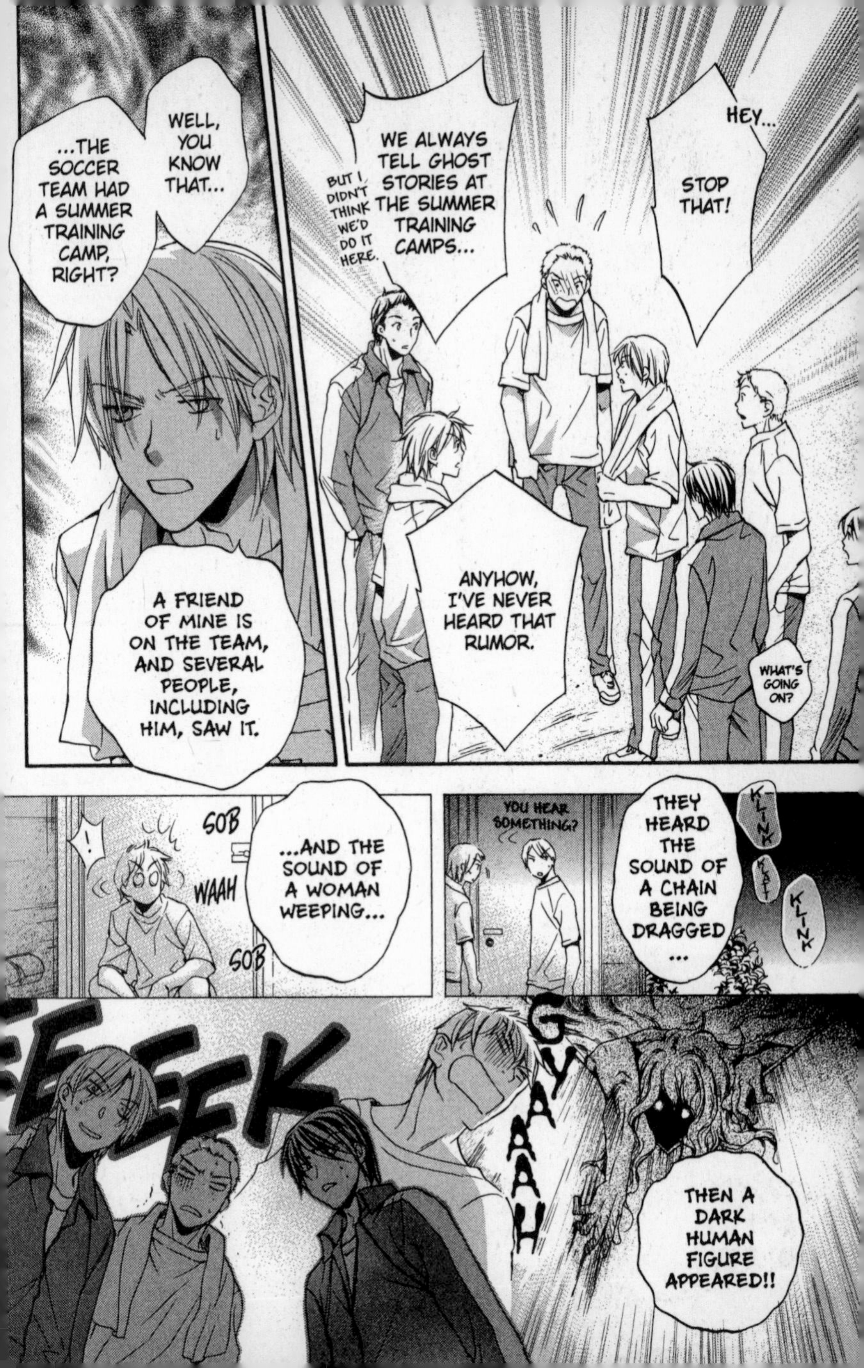
HEY...
STOP THAT!
WE ALWAYS TELL GHOST STORIES AT THE SUMMER TRAINING CAMPS...
BUT I DIDN'T THINK WE'D DO IT HERE.
ANYHOW, I'VE NEVER HEARD THAT RUMOR.
WHAT'S GOING ON?
WELL, YOU KNOW THAT...
...THE SOCCER TEAM HAD A SUMMER TRAINING CAMP, RIGHT?
A FRIEND OF MINE IS ON THE TEAM, AND SEVERAL PEOPLE, INCLUDING HIM, SAW IT.
KLINK
KLAT
KLINK
THEY HEARD THE SOUND OF A CHAIN BEING DRAGGED...
YOU HEAR SOMETHING?
...AND THE SOUND OF A WOMAN WEEPING...
SOB
WAAH
SOB
!
THEN A DARK HUMAN FIGURE APPEARED!!
GYAAAAH
EEEK

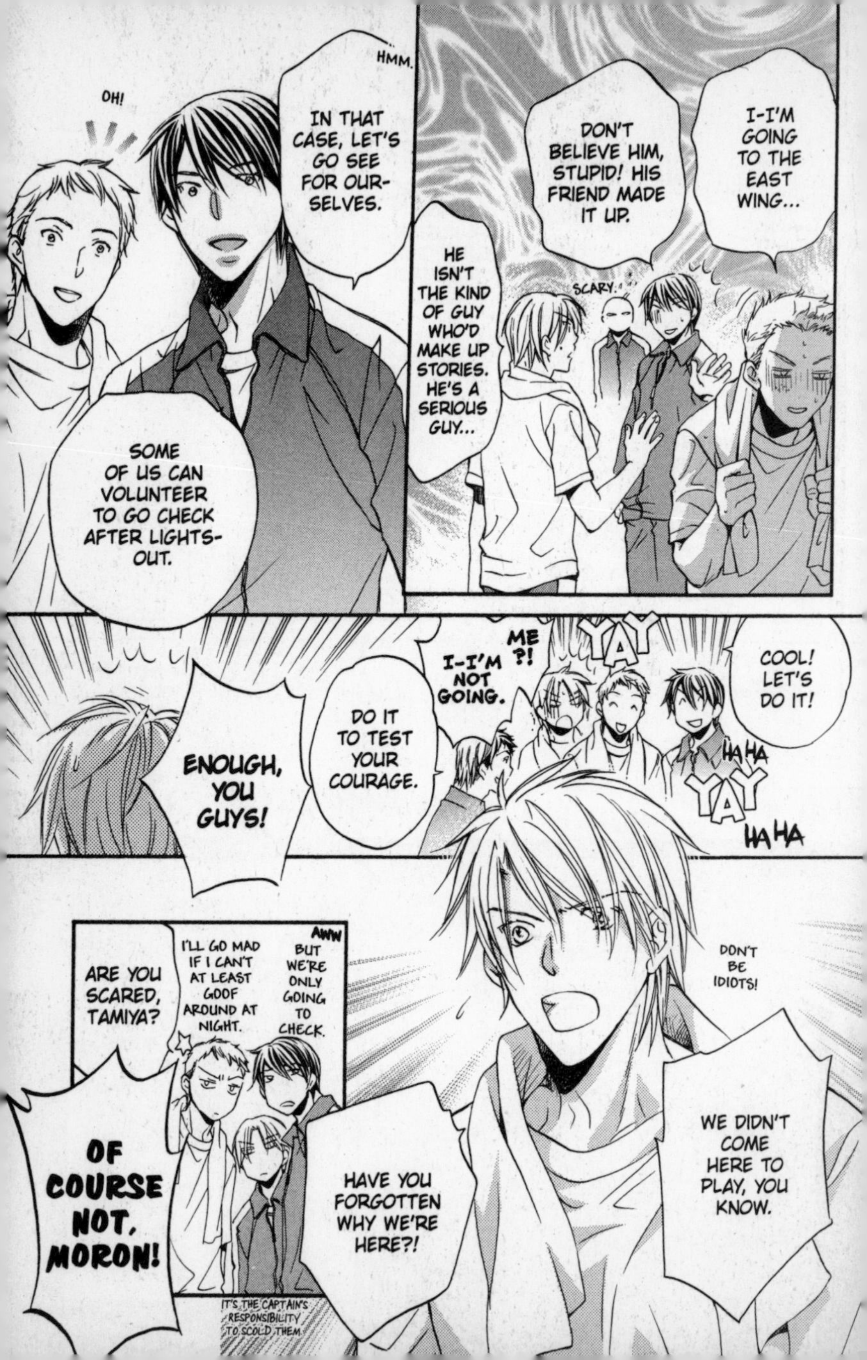
I-I'M GOING TO THE EAST WING...
DON'T BELIEVE HIM, STUPID! HIS FRIEND MADE IT UP.
SCARY.
HE ISN'T THE KIND OF GUY WHO'D MAKE UP STORIES. HE'S A SERIOUS GUY...
HMM.
IN THAT CASE, LET'S GO SEE FOR OUR-SELVES.
OH!
SOME OF US CAN VOLUNTEER TO GO CHECK AFTER LIGHTS-OUT.
COOL! LET'S DO IT!
YAY
HA HA
YAY
HA HA
ME ?!
I-I'M NOT GOING.
DO IT TO TEST YOUR COURAGE.
ENOUGH, YOU GUYS!
DON'T BE IDIOTS!
WE DIDN'T COME HERE TO PLAY, YOU KNOW.
HAVE YOU FORGOTTEN WHY WE'RE HERE?!
AWW
BUT WE'RE ONLY GOING TO CHECK.
I'LL GO MAD IF I CAN'T AT LEAST GOOF AROUND AT NIGHT.
ARE YOU SCARED, TAMIYA?
OF COURSE NOT, MORON!
IT'S THE CAPTAIN'S RESPONSIBILITY TO SCOLD THEM

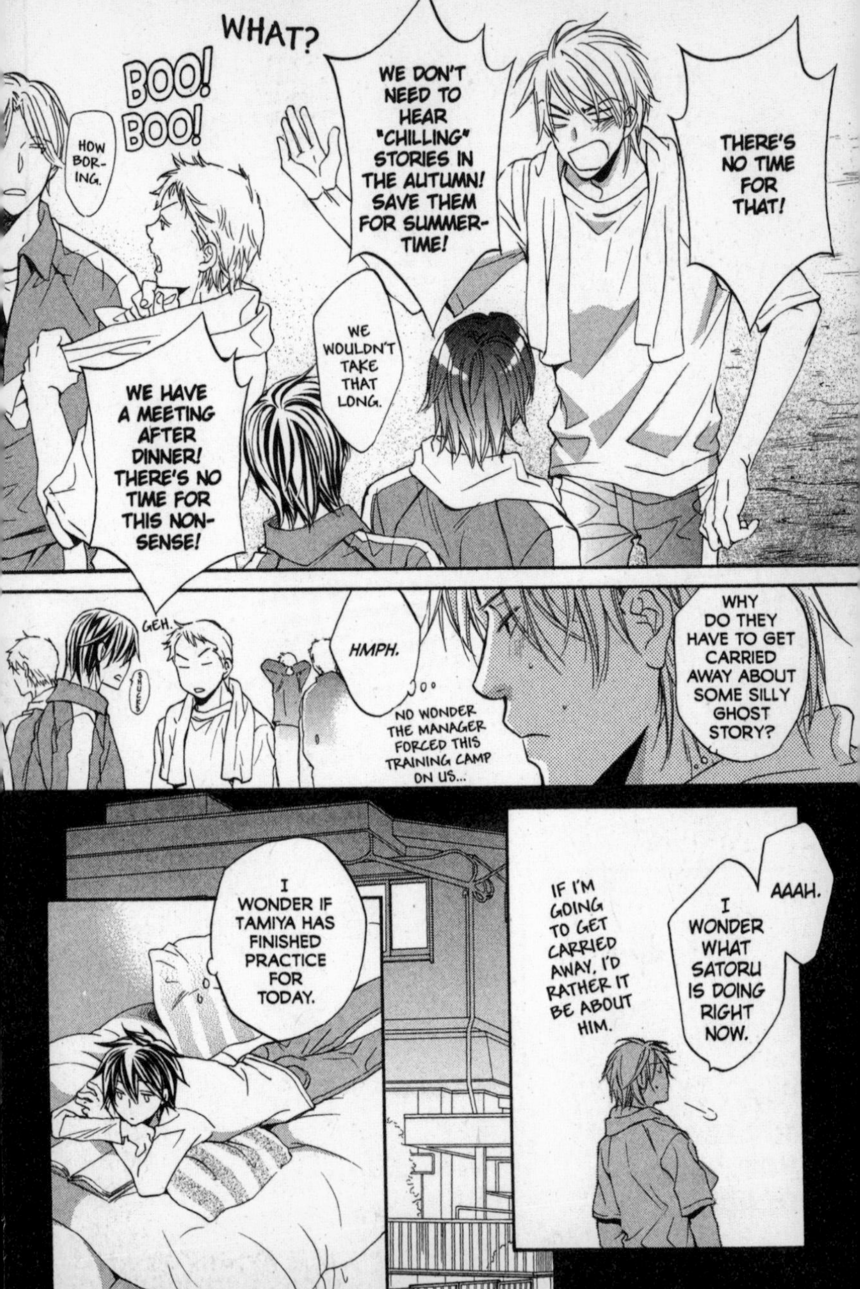
THERE'S NO TIME FOR THAT!
WE DON'T NEED TO HEAR "CHILLING" STORIES IN THE AUTUMN! SAVE THEM FOR SUMMERTIME!
WHAT?
WE WOULDN'T TAKE THAT LONG.
BOO! BOO!
HOW BORING.
WE HAVE A MEETING AFTER DINNER! THERE'S NO TIME FOR THIS NONSENSE!
WHY DO THEY HAVE TO GET CARRIED AWAY ABOUT SOME SILLY GHOST STORY?
HMPH.
NO WONDER THE MANAGER FORCED THIS TRAINING CAMP ON US...
GEH.
AAAH.
I WONDER WHAT SATORU IS DOING RIGHT NOW.
IF I'M GOING TO GET CARRIED AWAY, I'D RATHER IT BE ABOUT HIM.
I WONDER IF TAMIYA HAS FINISHED PRACTICE FOR TODAY.

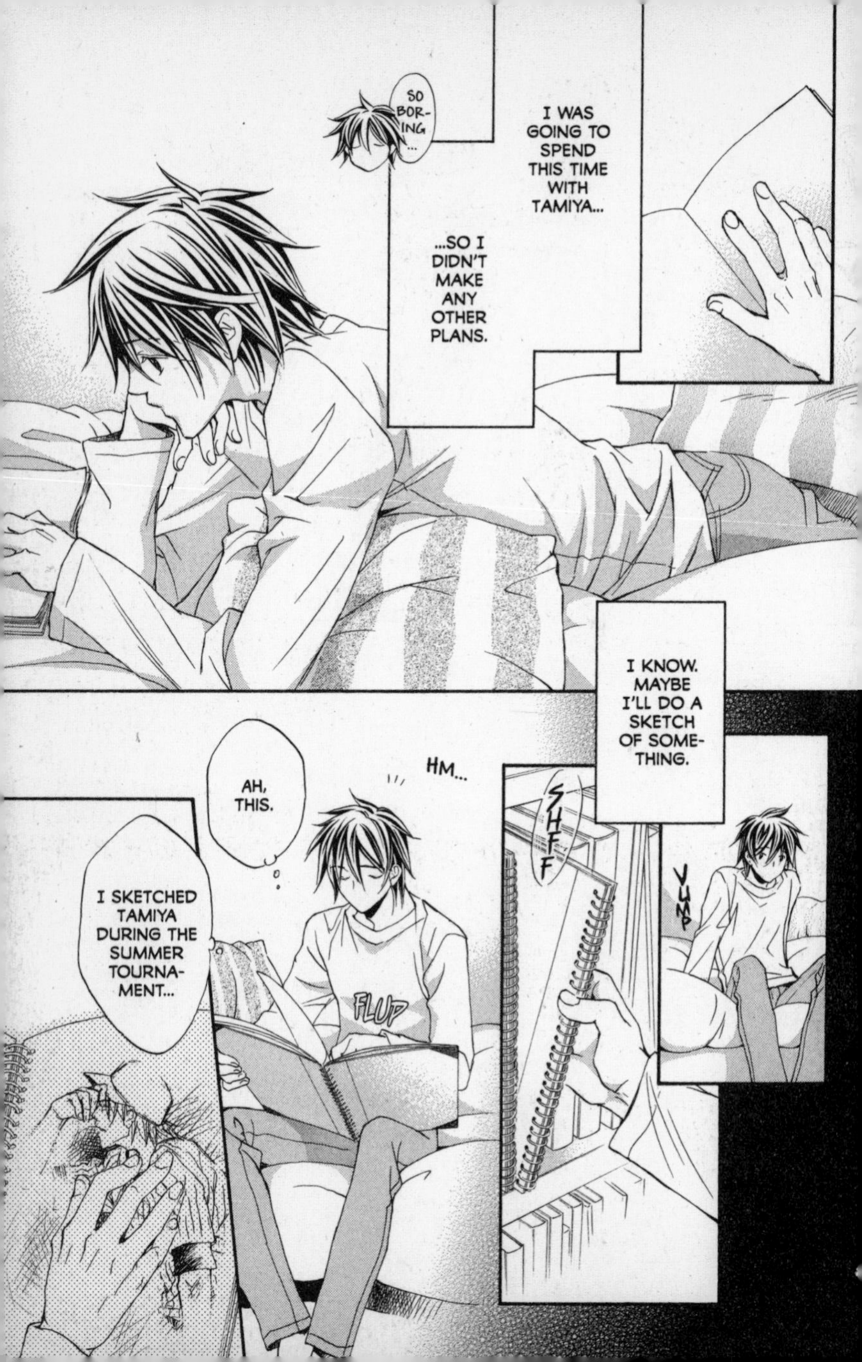
I WAS GOING TO SPEND THIS TIME WITH TAMIYA...
...SO I DIDN'T MAKE ANY OTHER PLANS.
SO BOR-ING...
I KNOW. MAYBE I'LL DO A SKETCH OF SOME-THING.
VUMP
SHFFF
HM...
AH, THIS.
FLUP
I SKETCHED TAMIYA DURING THE SUMMER TOURNA-MENT...

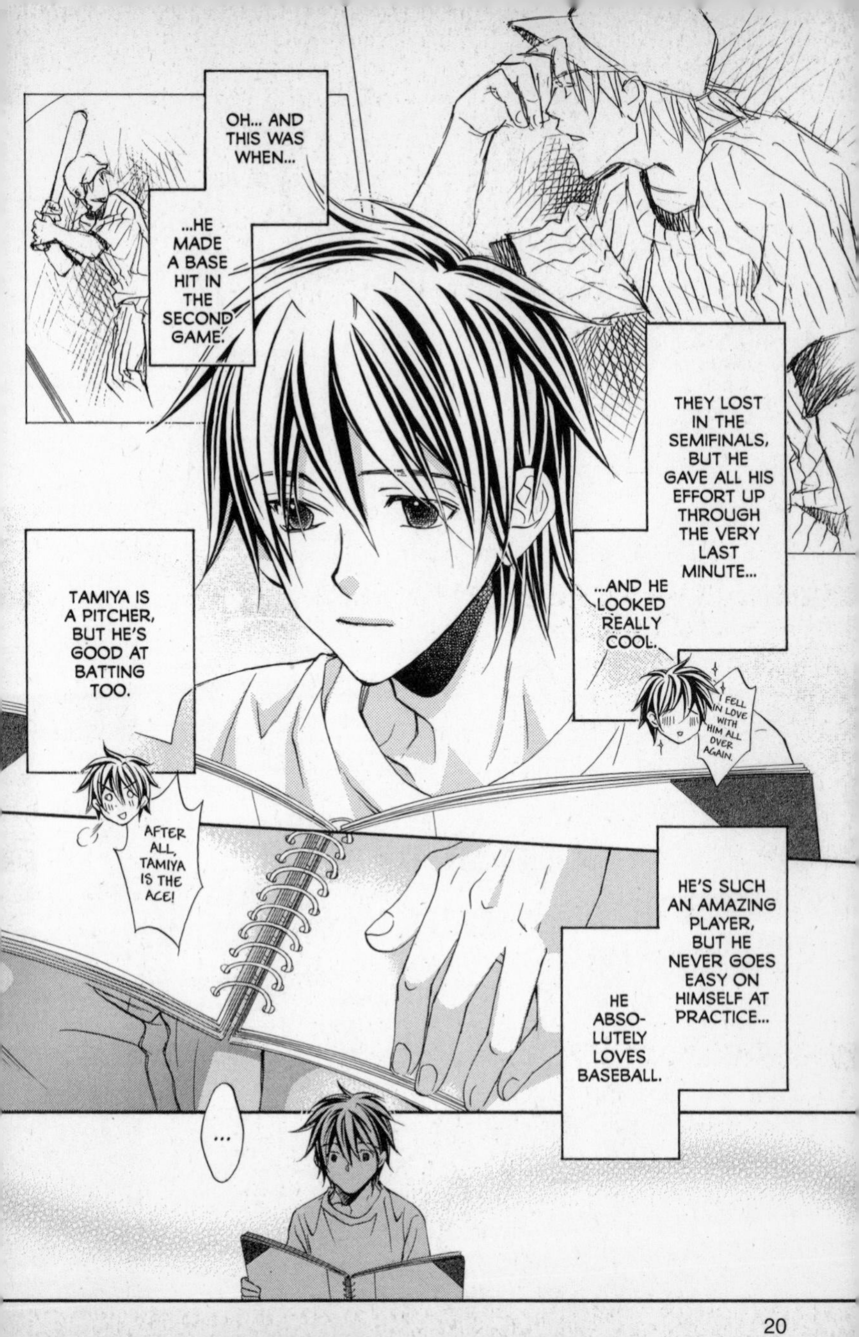

OH... AND THIS WAS WHEN...
...HE MADE A BASE HIT IN THE SECOND GAME.
THEY LOST IN THE SEMIFINALS, BUT HE GAVE ALL HIS EFFORT UP THROUGH THE VERY LAST MINUTE...
...AND HE LOOKED REALLY COOL.
I FELL IN LOVE WITH HIM ALL OVER AGAIN.
TAMIYA IS A PITCHER, BUT HE'S GOOD AT BATTING TOO.
AFTER ALL, TAMIYA IS THE ACE!
HE'S SUCH AN AMAZING PLAYER, BUT HE NEVER GOES EASY ON HIMSELF AT PRACTICE...
HE ABSO-LUTELY LOVES BASEBALL.
...

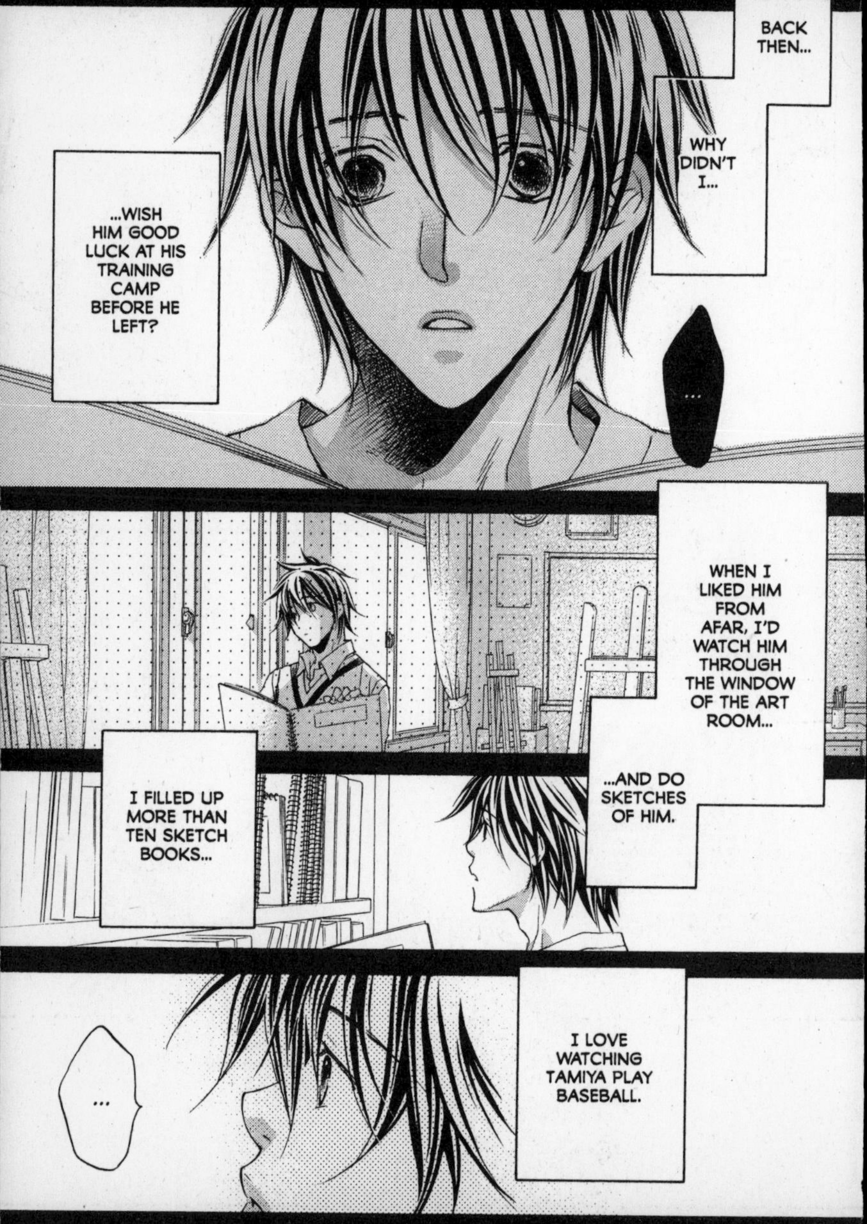
BACK THEN...
WHY DIDN'T I...
...WISH HIM GOOD LUCK AT HIS TRAINING CAMP BEFORE HE LEFT?
...
WHEN I LIKED HIM FROM AFAR, I'D WATCH HIM THROUGH THE WINDOW OF THE ART ROOM...
...AND DO SKETCHES OF HIM.
I FILLED UP MORE THAN TEN SKETCH BOOKS...
I LOVE WATCHING TAMIYA PLAY BASEBALL.
...

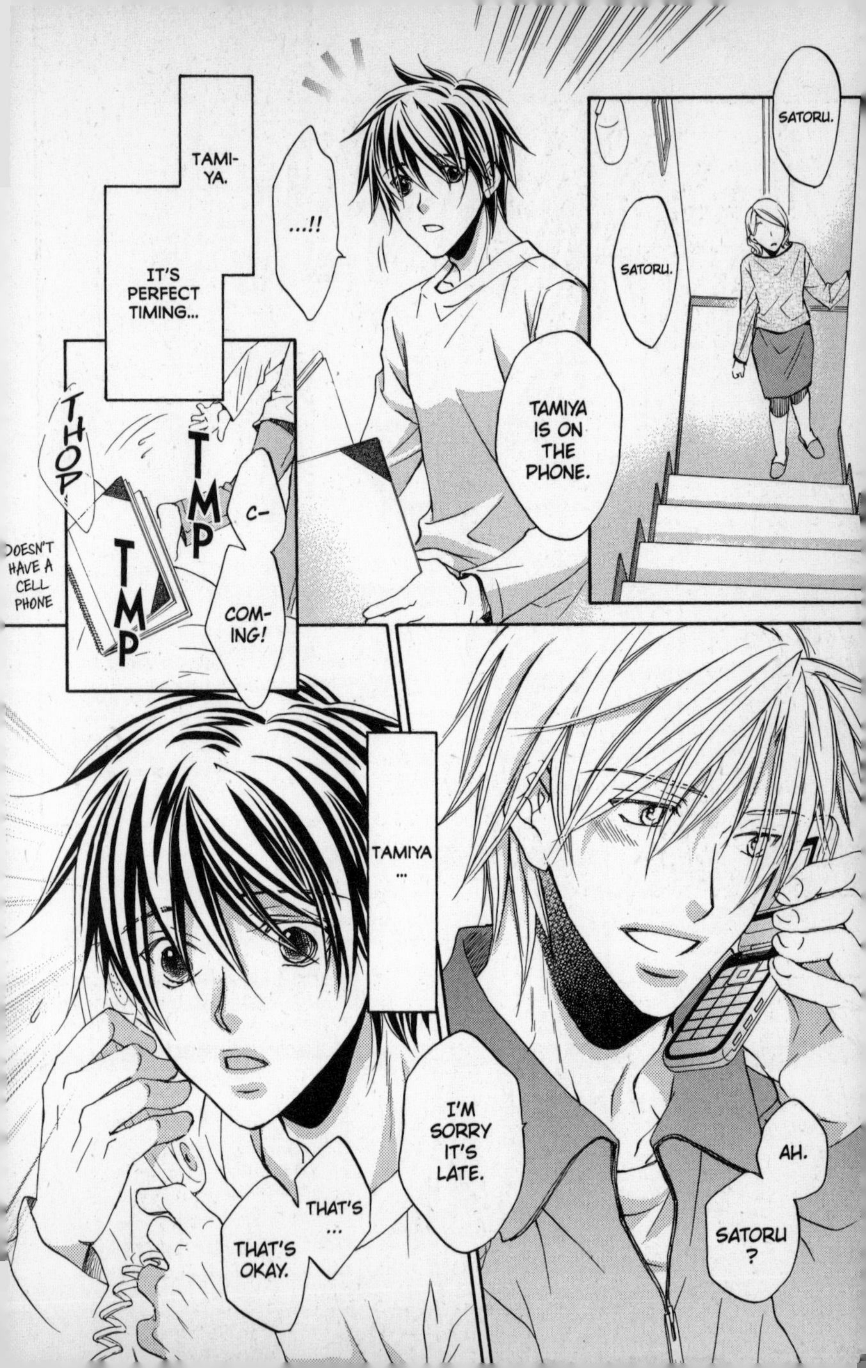
SATORU.
SATORU.
TAMIYA IS ON THE PHONE.
...!!
TAMIYA.
IT'S PERFECT TIMING...
C-
COMING!
THOP
TMP
TMP
DOESN'T HAVE A CELL PHONE
AH.
SATORU?
I'M SORRY IT'S LATE.
TAMIYA...
THAT'S...
THAT'S OKAY.

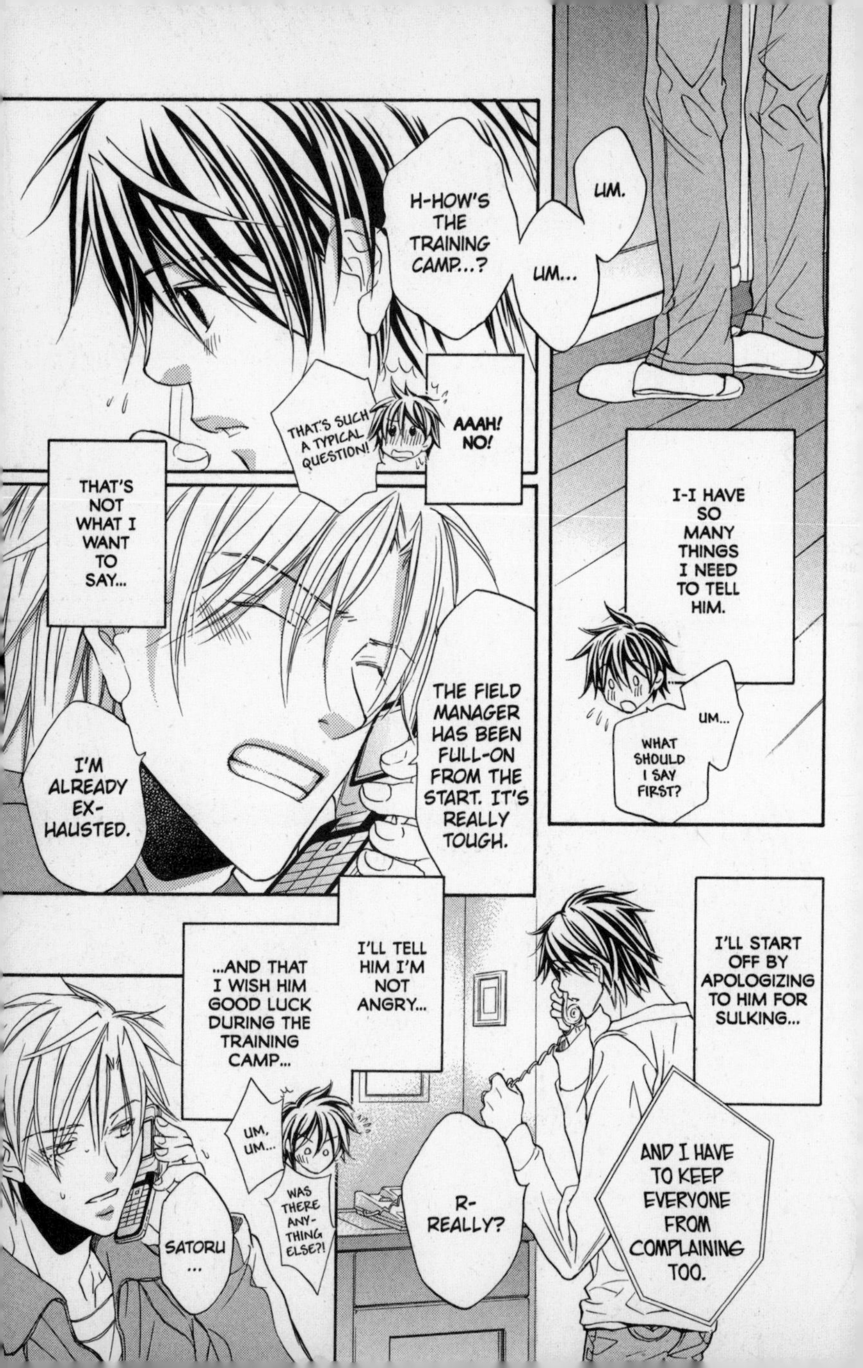
UM.
UM...
I-I HAVE SO MANY THINGS I NEED TO TELL HIM.
UM...
WHAT SHOULD I SAY FIRST?
H-HOW'S THE TRAINING CAMP...?
AAAH! NO!
THAT'S SUCH A TYPICAL QUESTION!
THAT'S NOT WHAT I WANT TO SAY...
THE FIELD MANAGER HAS BEEN FULL-ON FROM THE START. IT'S REALLY TOUGH.
I'M ALREADY EX-HAUSTED.
I'LL START OFF BY APOLOGIZING TO HIM FOR SULKING...
AND I HAVE TO KEEP EVERYONE FROM COMPLAINING TOO.
R-REALLY?
I'LL TELL HIM I'M NOT ANGRY...
...AND THAT I WISH HIM GOOD LUCK DURING THE TRAINING CAMP...
UM, UM...
WAS THERE ANYTHING ELSE?!
SATORU ...

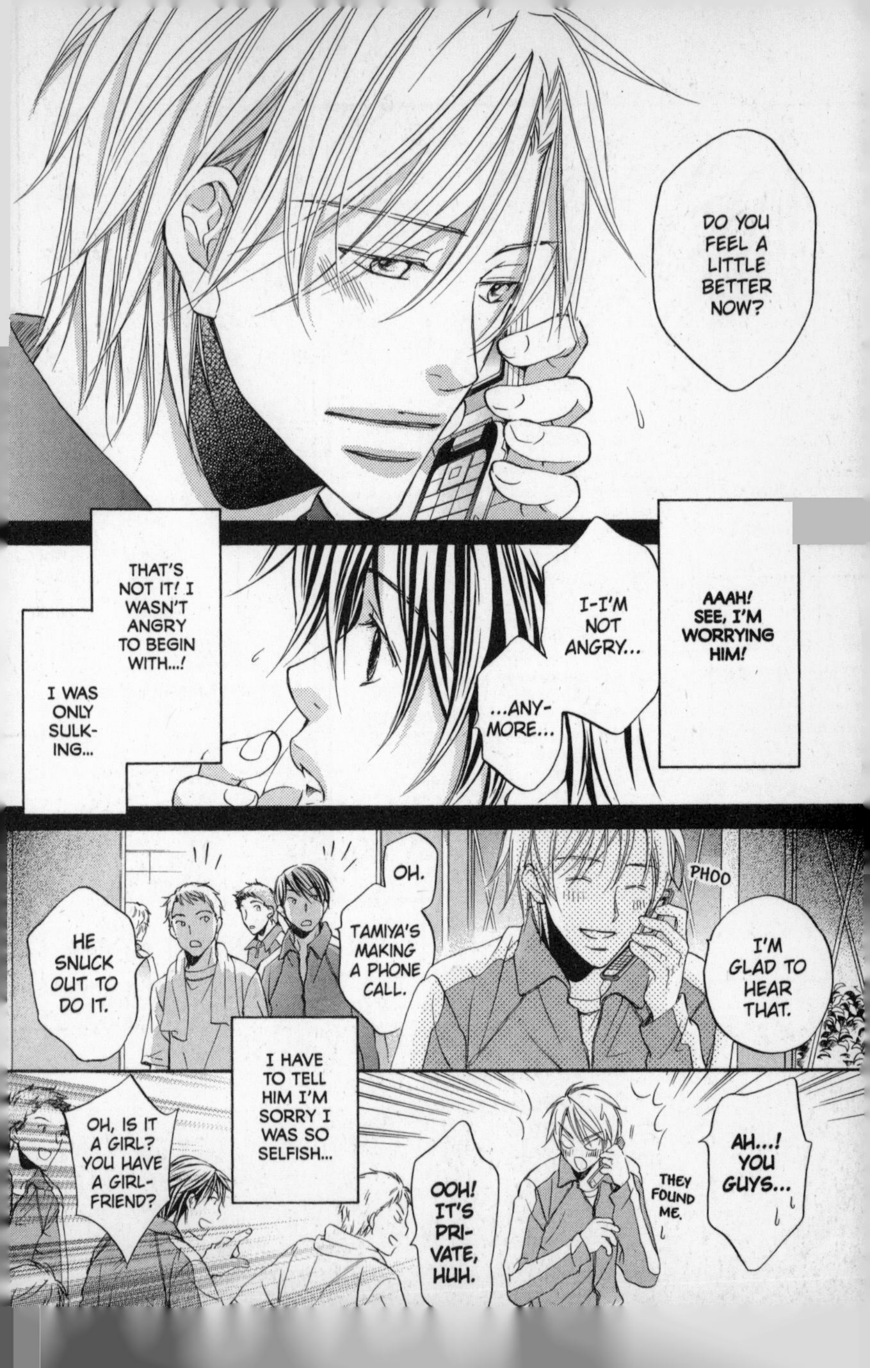
DO YOU FEEL A LITTLE BETTER NOW?
AAAH! SEE, I'M WORRYING HIM!
I-I'M NOT ANGRY...
...ANY-MORE...
THAT'S NOT IT! I WASN'T ANGRY TO BEGIN WITH...!
I WAS ONLY SULK-ING...
PHOO
I'M GLAD TO HEAR THAT.
OH.
TAMIYA'S MAKING A PHONE CALL.
HE SNUCK OUT TO DO IT.
I HAVE TO TELL HIM I'M SORRY I WAS SO SELFISH...
AH...! YOU GUYS...
THEY FOUND ME.
OOH! IT'S PRI-VATE, HUH.
OH, IS IT A GIRL? YOU HAVE A GIRL-FRIEND?

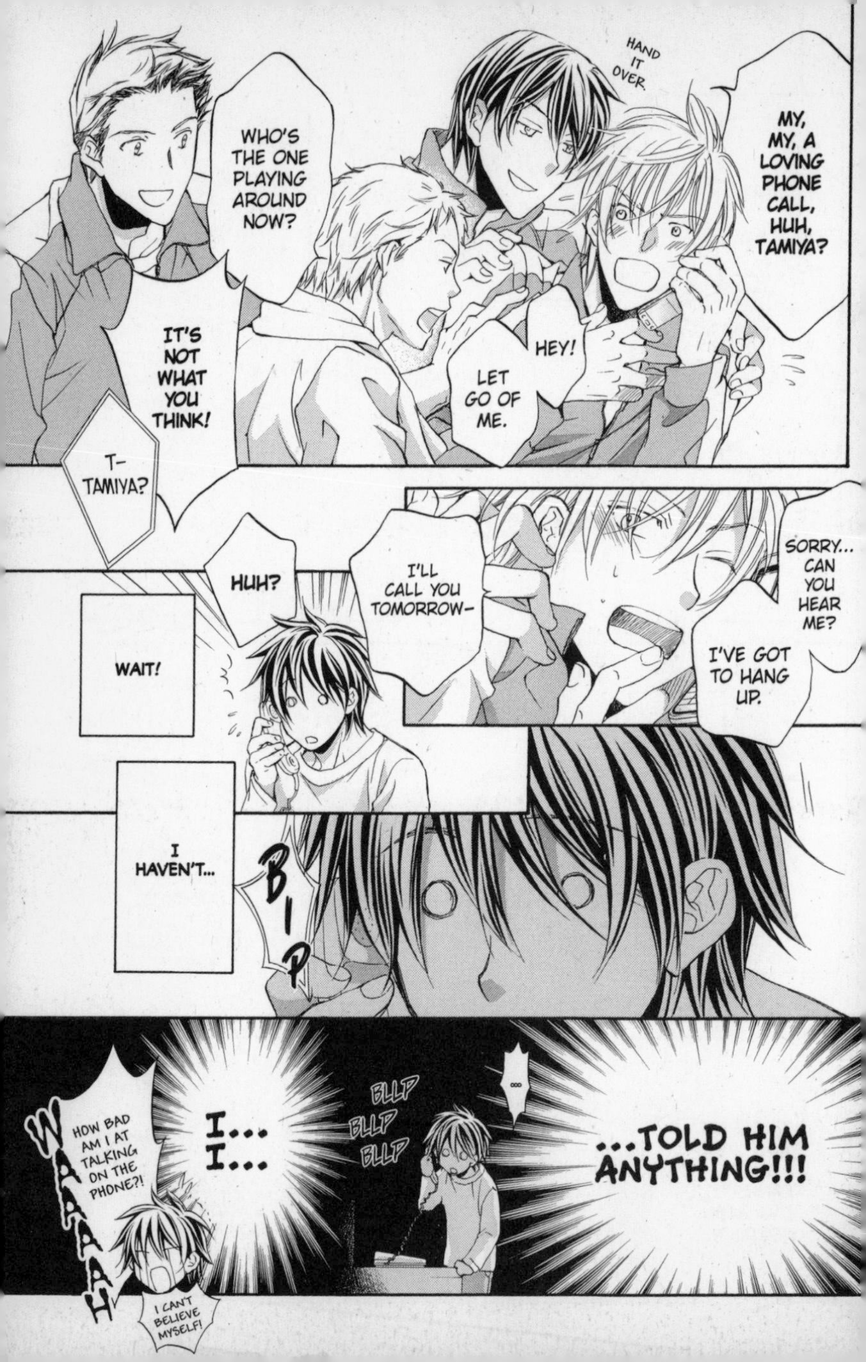
MY, MY, A LOVING PHONE CALL, HUH, TAMIYA?
HAND IT OVER.
HEY!
LET GO OF ME.
WHO'S THE ONE PLAYING AROUND NOW?
IT'S NOT WHAT YOU THINK!
T- TAMIYA?
SORRY... CAN YOU HEAR ME?
I'VE GOT TO HANG UP.
I'LL CALL YOU TOMORROW-
HUH?
WAIT!
BIP
I HAVEN'T...
...TOLD HIM ANYTHING!!!
...
BLLP BLLP BLLP
I... I...
HOW BAD AM I AT TALKING ON THE PHONE?!
WAAAAAH
I CAN'T BELIEVE MYSELF!

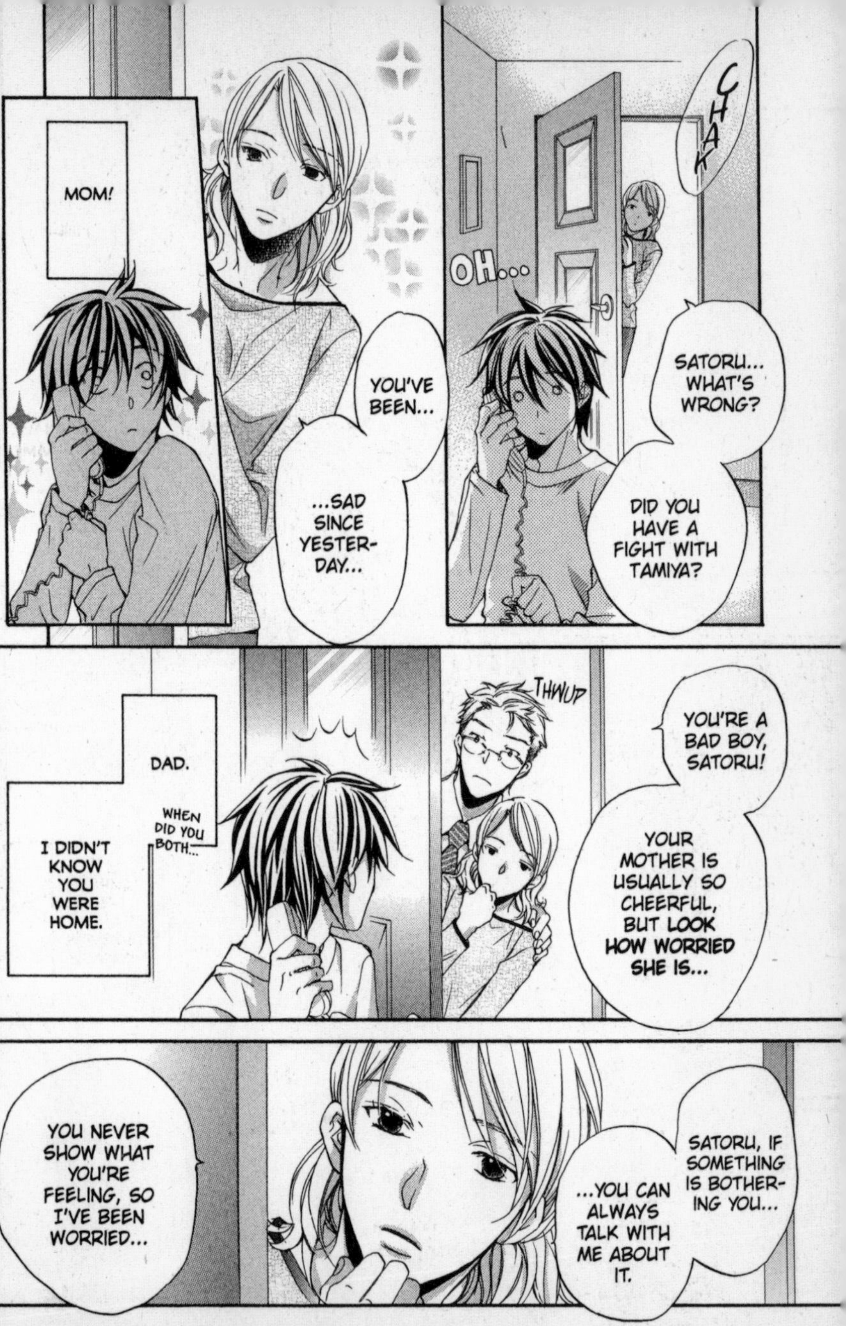
CHAK
OH...
SATORU... WHAT'S WRONG?
DID YOU HAVE A FIGHT WITH TAMIYA?
MOM!
YOU'VE BEEN...
...SAD SINCE YESTER-DAY...
THWUP
YOU'RE A BAD BOY, SATORU!
YOUR MOTHER IS USUALLY SO CHEERFUL, BUT LOOK HOW WORRIED SHE IS...
DAD.
WHEN DID YOU BOTH...
I DIDN'T KNOW YOU WERE HOME.
SATORU, IF SOMETHING IS BOTHER-ING YOU...
...YOU CAN ALWAYS TALK WITH ME ABOUT IT.
YOU NEVER SHOW WHAT YOU'RE FEELING, SO I'VE BEEN WORRIED...

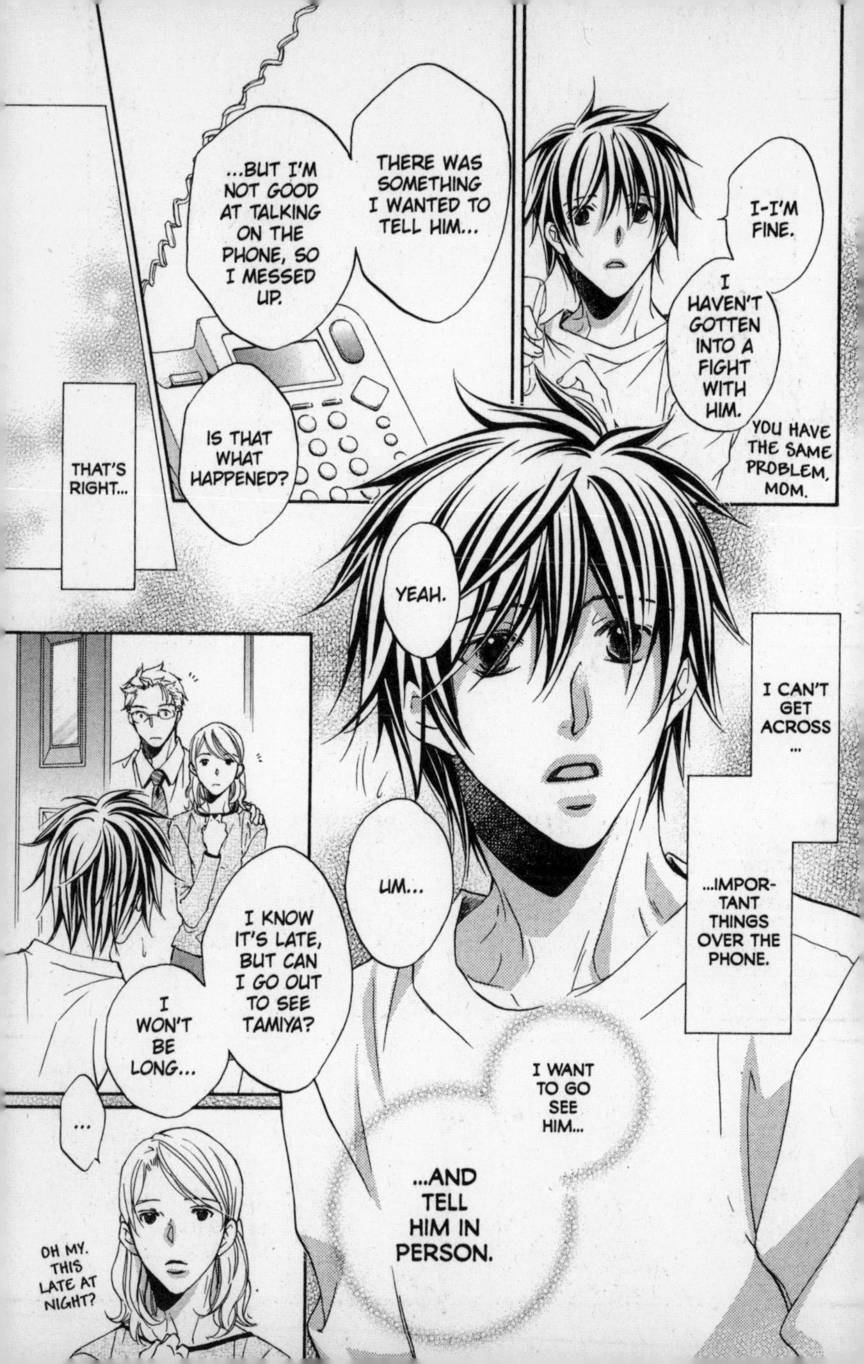
I-I'M FINE.
I HAVEN'T GOTTEN INTO A FIGHT WITH HIM.
YOU HAVE THE SAME PROBLEM, MOM.
THERE WAS SOMETHING I WANTED TO TELL HIM...
...BUT I'M NOT GOOD AT TALKING ON THE PHONE, SO I MESSED UP.
IS THAT WHAT HAPPENED?
THAT'S RIGHT...
YEAH.
I CAN'T GET ACROSS...
...IMPORTANT THINGS OVER THE PHONE.
UM...
I KNOW IT'S LATE, BUT CAN I GO OUT TO SEE TAMIYA?
I WON'T BE LONG...
I WANT TO GO SEE HIM...
...AND TELL HIM IN PERSON.
...
OH MY. THIS LATE AT NIGHT?

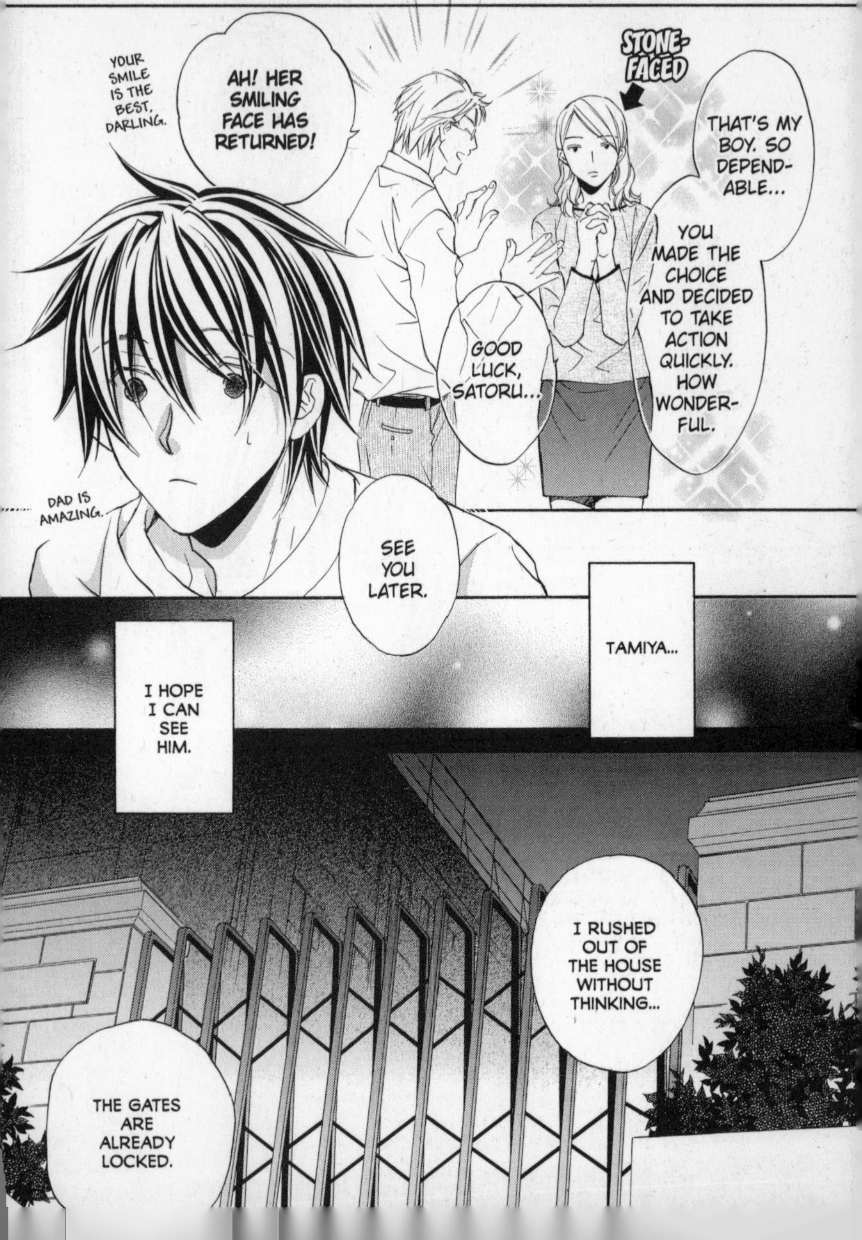
STONE-FACED
THAT'S MY BOY. SO DEPENDABLE...
YOU MADE THE CHOICE AND DECIDED TO TAKE ACTION QUICKLY. HOW WONDERFUL.
GOOD LUCK, SATORU...
AH! HER SMILING FACE HAS RETURNED!
YOUR SMILE IS THE BEST, DARLING.
DAD IS AMAZING.
SEE YOU LATER.
TAMIYA...
I HOPE I CAN SEE HIM.
I RUSHED OUT OF THE HOUSE WITHOUT THINKING...
THE GATES ARE ALREADY LOCKED.

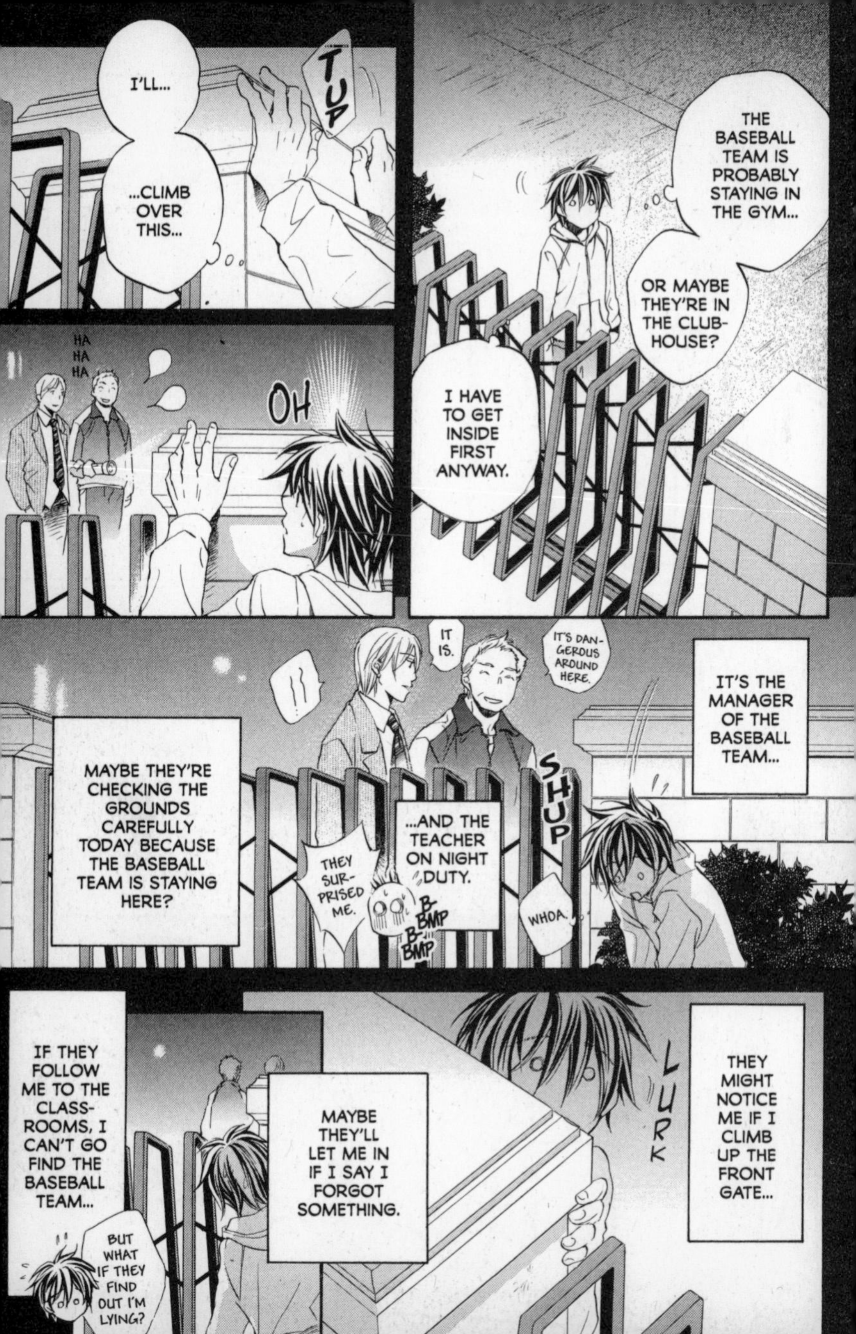
THE BASEBALL TEAM IS PROBABLY STAYING IN THE GYM...
OR MAYBE THEY'RE IN THE CLUB-HOUSE?
I HAVE TO GET INSIDE FIRST ANYWAY.
I'LL...
TUP
...CLIMB OVER THIS...
HA HA HA
OH
IT'S THE MANAGER OF THE BASEBALL TEAM...
SHUP
WHOA.
IT'S DAN-GEROUS AROUND HERE.
IT IS.
...AND THE TEACHER ON NIGHT DUTY.
THEY SUR-PRISED ME.
B-BMP B-BMP
MAYBE THEY'RE CHECKING THE GROUNDS CAREFULLY TODAY BECAUSE THE BASEBALL TEAM IS STAYING HERE?
THEY MIGHT NOTICE ME IF I CLIMB UP THE FRONT GATE...
LURK
MAYBE THEY'LL LET ME IN IF I SAY I FORGOT SOMETHING.
IF THEY FOLLOW ME TO THE CLASS-ROOMS, I CAN'T GO FIND THE BASEBALL TEAM...
BUT WHAT IF THEY FIND OUT I'M LYING?

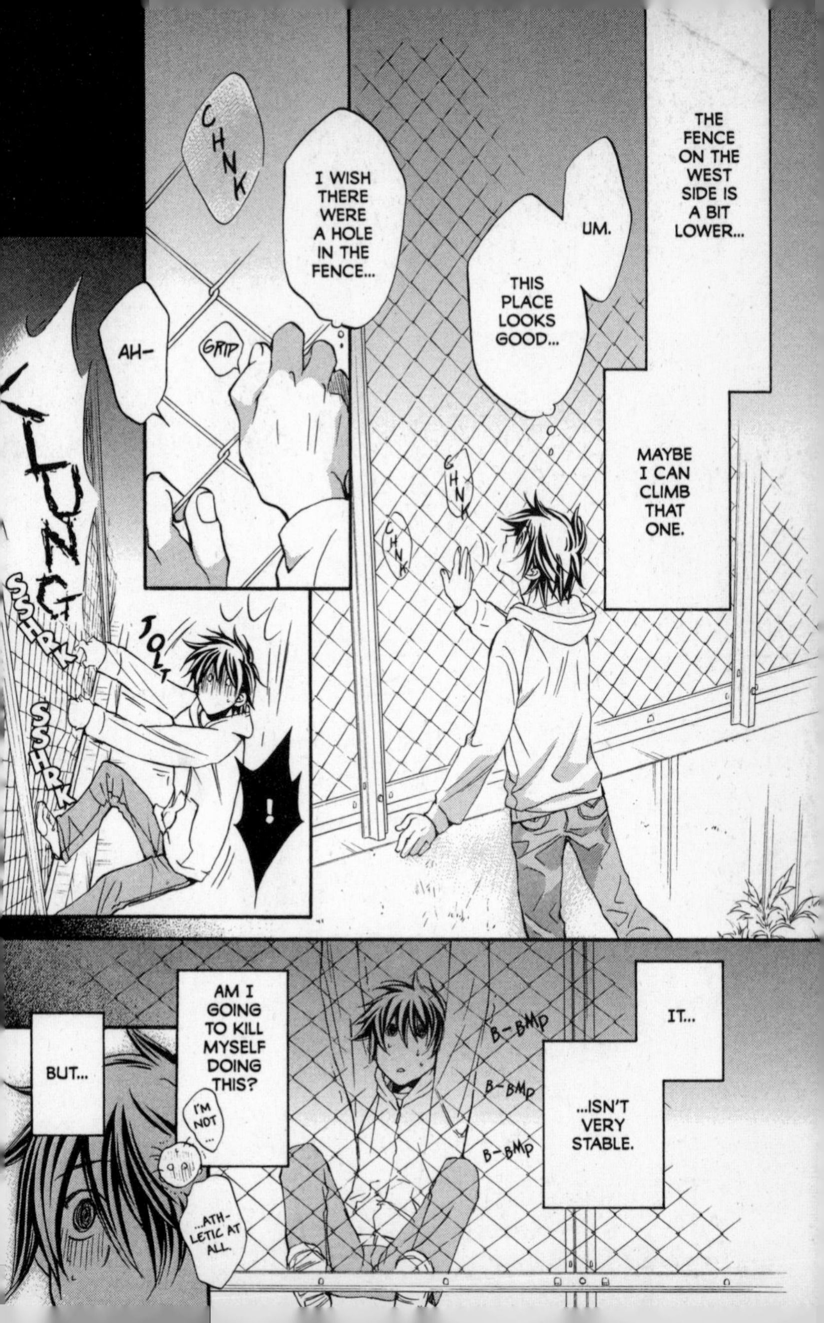
THE FENCE ON THE WEST SIDE IS A BIT LOWER...
UM.
THIS PLACE LOOKS GOOD...
MAYBE I CAN CLIMB THAT ONE.
CHNK
CHNK
I WISH THERE WERE A HOLE IN THE FENCE...
CHNK
GRIP
AH-
!
JOLT
CLUNG
SSHRK
SSHRK
IT...
...ISN'T VERY STABLE.
B-BMP
B-BMP
B-BMP
AM I GOING TO KILL MYSELF DOING THIS?
BUT...
I'M NOT...
...ATH-LETIC AT ALL.

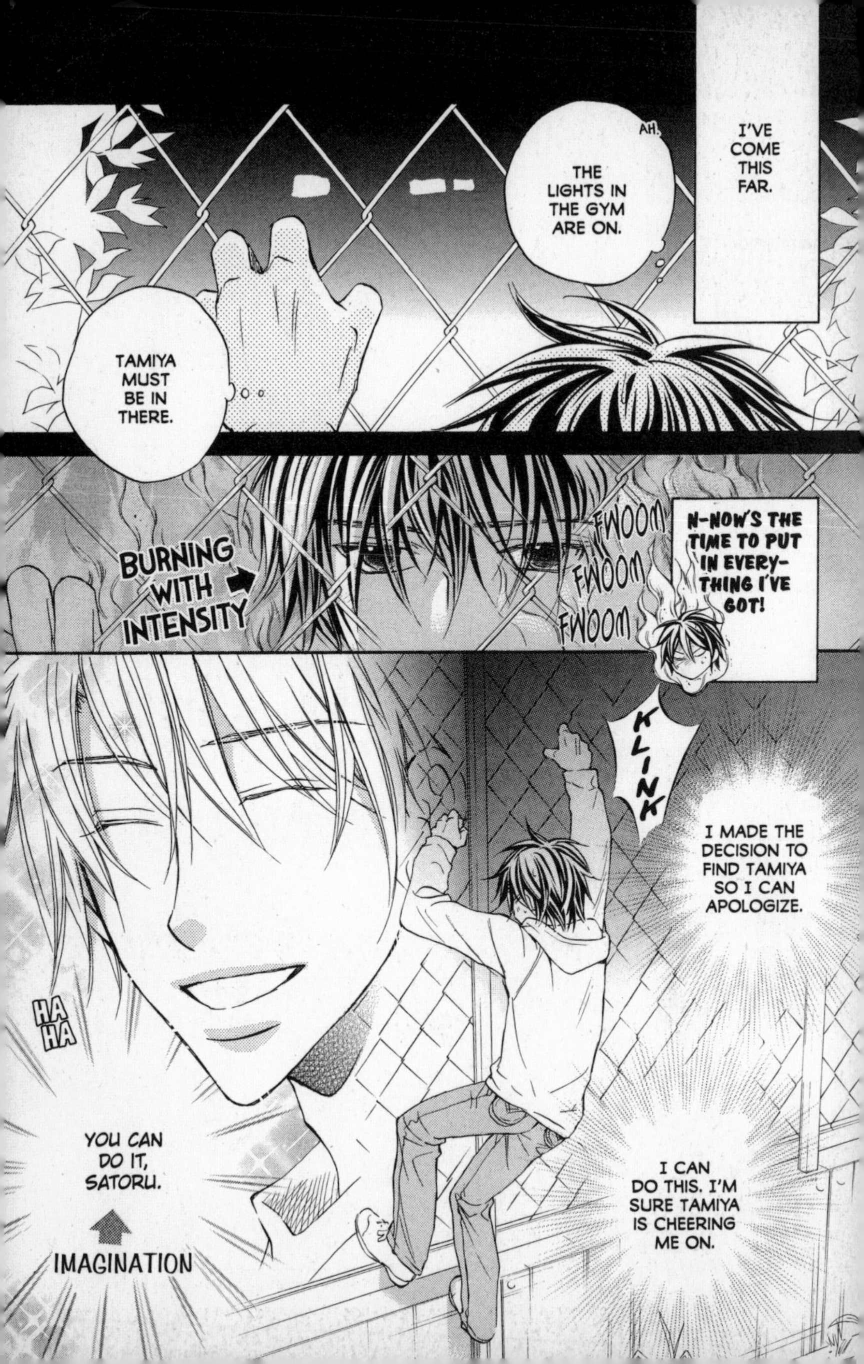
I'VE COME THIS FAR.
AH, THE LIGHTS IN THE GYM ARE ON.
TAMIYA MUST BE IN THERE.
N-NOW'S THE TIME TO PUT IN EVERY-THING I'VE GOT!
FWOOM FWOOM FWOOM
BURNING WITH INTENSITY
KLINK
I MADE THE DECISION TO FIND TAMIYA SO I CAN APOLOGIZE.
I CAN DO THIS. I'M SURE TAMIYA IS CHEERING ME ON.
HA HA
YOU CAN DO IT, SATORU.
IMAGINATION

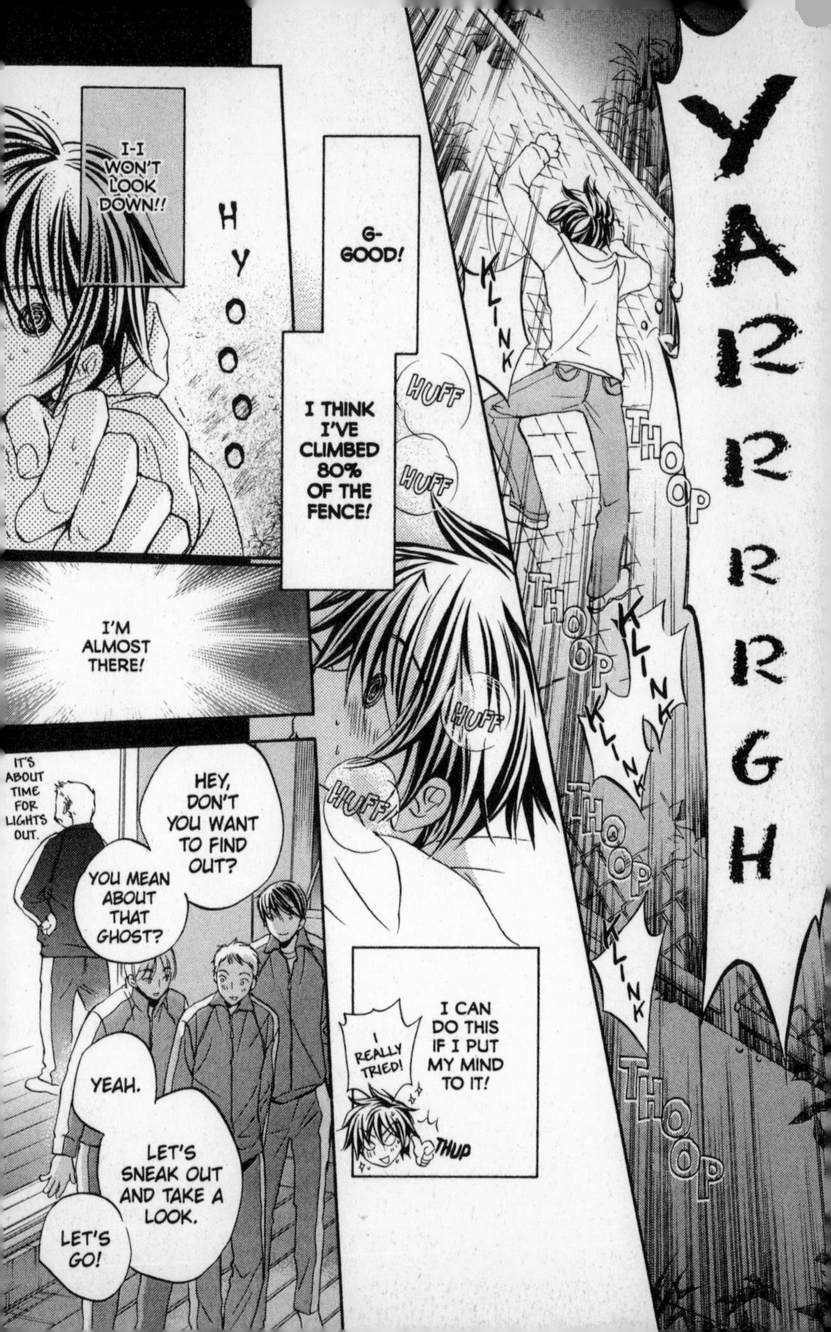
YARRRRGH
KLINK
THOOP
THOOP
KLINK
KLINK
THOOP
KLINK
THOOP
G-GOOD!
HUFF
HUFF
I THINK I'VE CLIMBED 80% OF THE FENCE!
HUFF
HUFF
I CAN DO THIS IF I PUT MY MIND TO IT!
I REALLY TRIED!
THUP
HYOOOO
I-I WON'T LOOK DOWN!!
I'M ALMOST THERE!
HEY, DON'T YOU WANT TO FIND OUT?
IT'S ABOUT TIME FOR LIGHTS OUT.
YOU MEAN ABOUT THAT GHOST?
YEAH.
LET'S SNEAK OUT AND TAKE A LOOK.
LET'S GO!

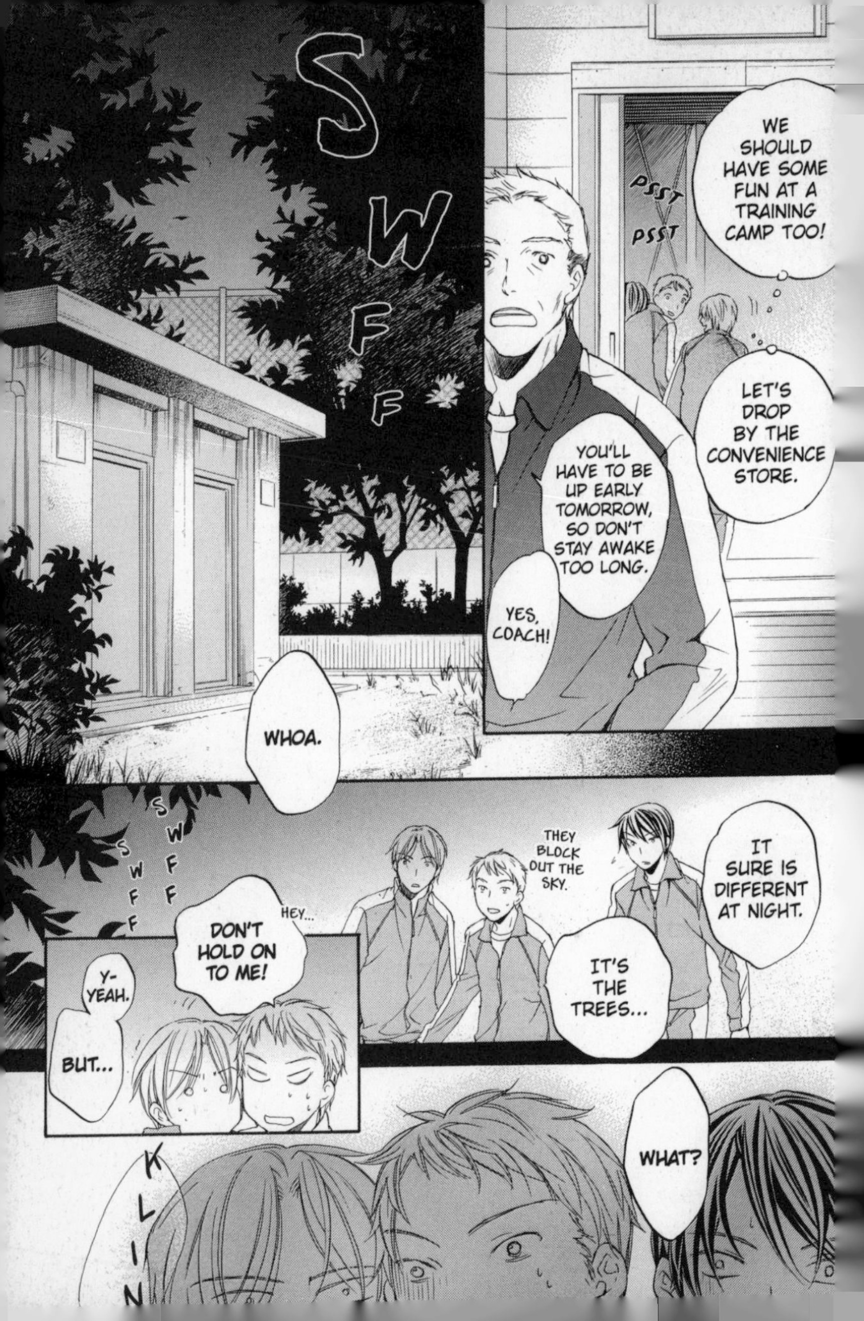
WE SHOULD HAVE SOME FUN AT A TRAINING CAMP TOO!
PSST
PSST
LET'S DROP BY THE CONVENIENCE STORE.
YOU'LL HAVE TO BE UP EARLY TOMORROW, SO DON'T STAY AWAKE TOO LONG.
YES, COACH!
SWFF
WHOA.
IT SURE IS DIFFERENT AT NIGHT.
THEY BLOCK OUT THE SKY.
IT'S THE TREES...
HEY...
SWFF
SWFF
DON'T HOLD ON TO ME!
Y-YEAH.
BUT...
WHAT?
KLIN

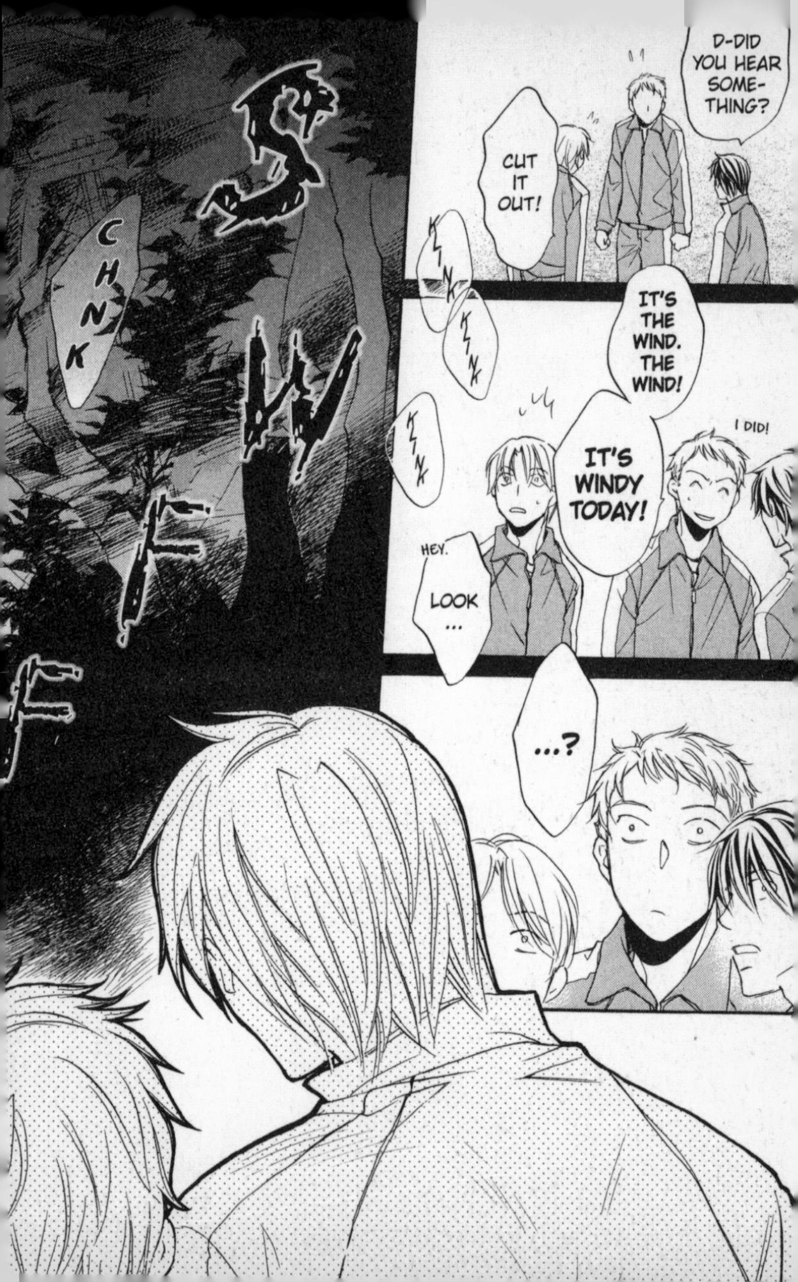
D-DID YOU HEAR SOME-THING?
CUT IT OUT!
KLINK
KLINK
IT'S THE WIND. THE WIND!
I DID!
IT'S WINDY TODAY!
KLINK
HEY.
LOOK ...
...?
CHNK

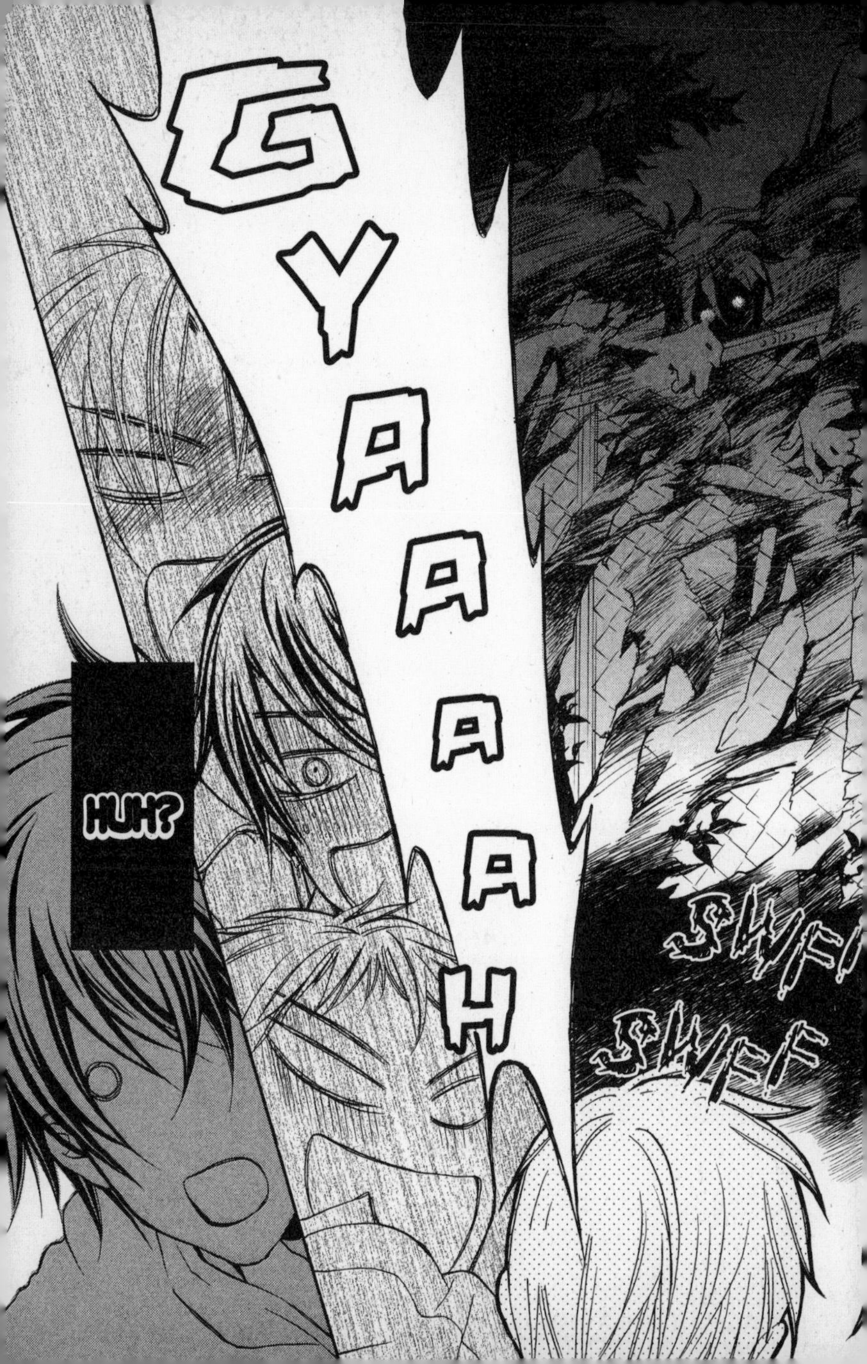
GYAAAAH
SNFF
SNFF
HUH?

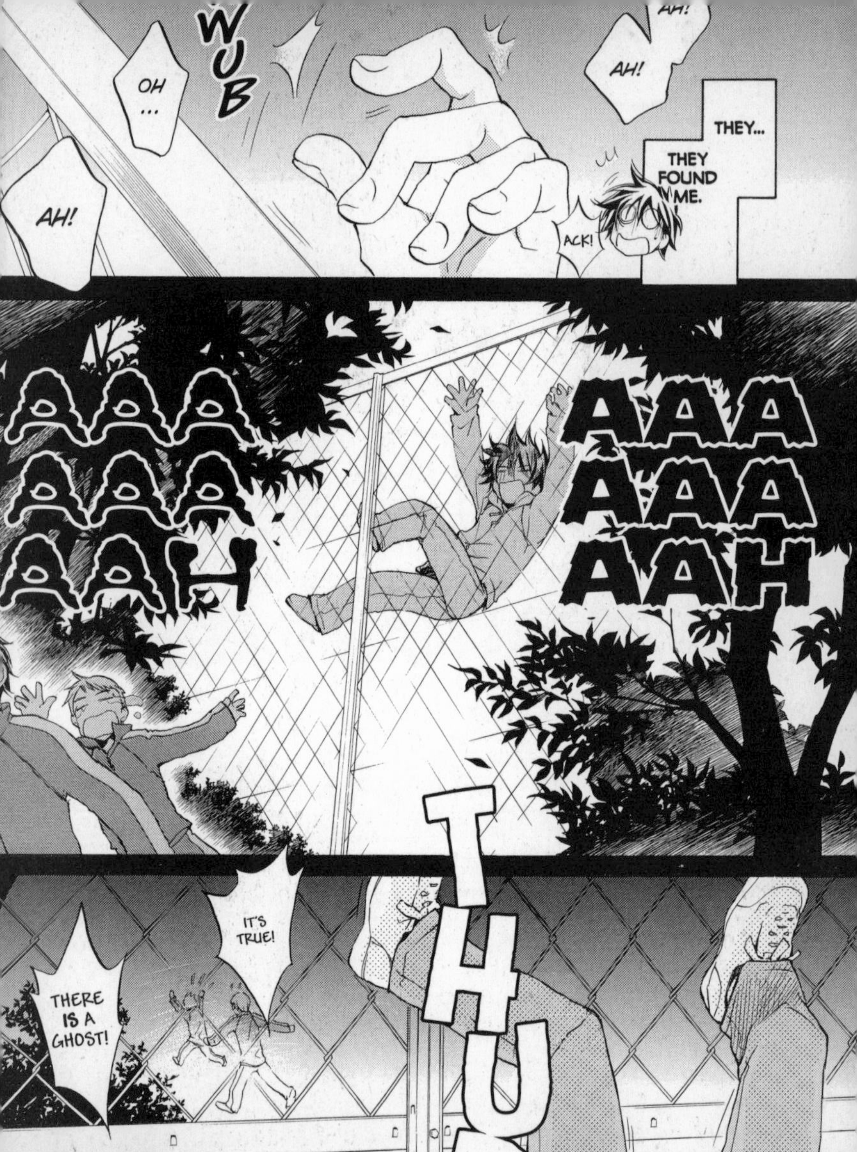
AH!
AH!
THEY...
THEY FOUND ME.
ACK!
WUB
OH ...
AH!
AAAAAAAAH
AAAAAAAAH
THUD
IT'S TRUE!
THERE IS A GHOST!

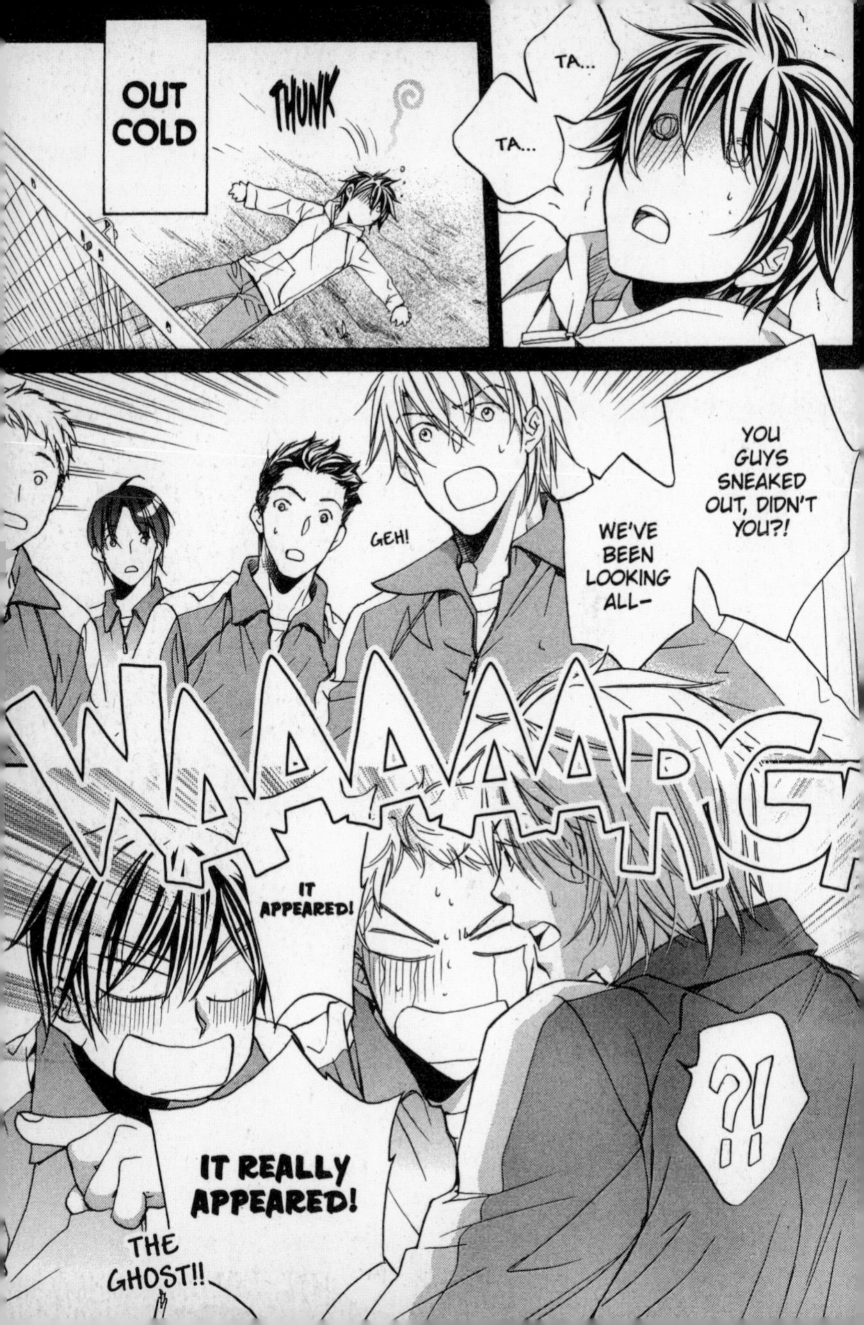
TA...
TA...
OUT COLD
THUNK
YOU GUYS SNEAKED OUT, DIDN'T YOU?!
WE'VE BEEN LOOKING ALL-
GEH!
WAAAARG
?!!
IT APPEARED!
IT REALLY APPEARED!
THE GHOST!!

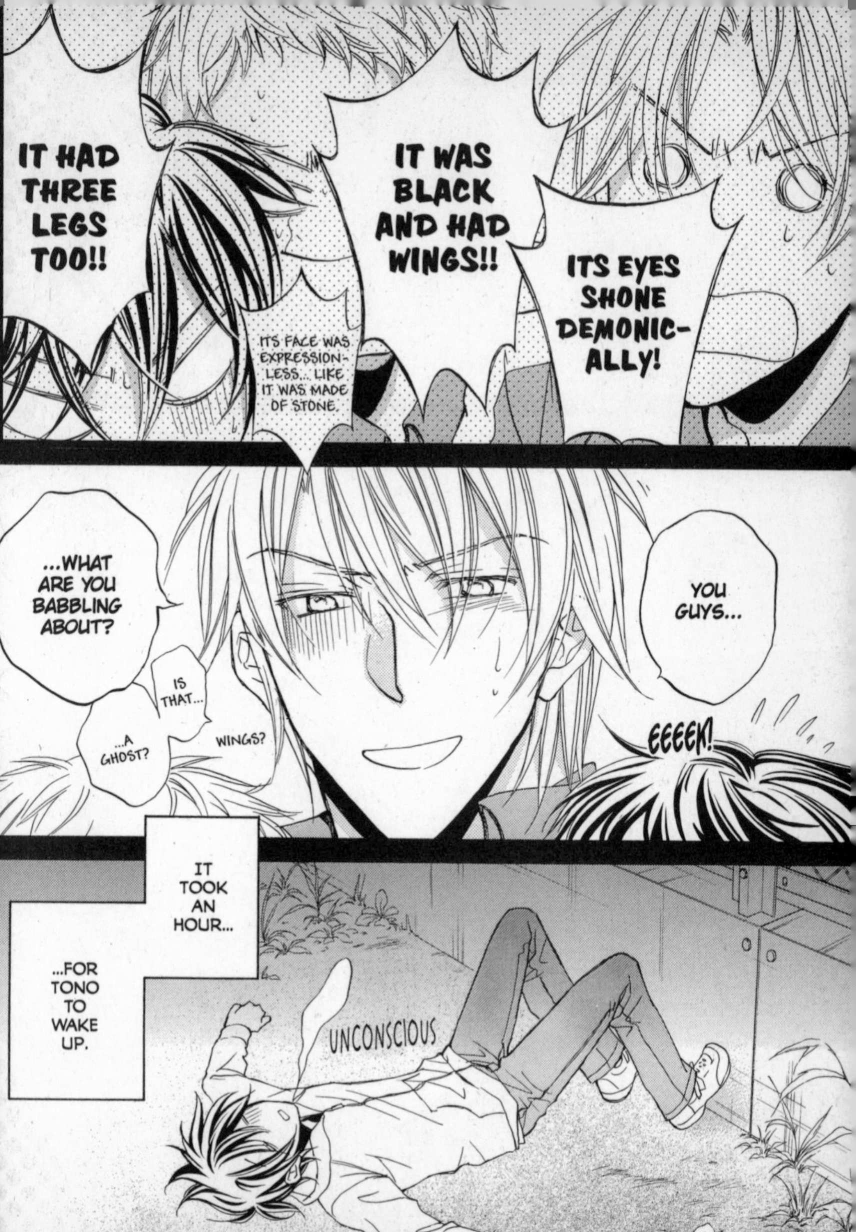
ITS EYES SHONE DEMONIC-ALLY!
IT WAS BLACK AND HAD WINGS!!
IT HAD THREE LEGS TOO!!
ITS FACE WAS EXPRESSION-LESS... LIKE IT WAS MADE OF STONE.
YOU GUYS...
EEEEK!
...WHAT ARE YOU BABBLING ABOUT?
IS THAT...
WINGS?
...A GHOST?
IT TOOK AN HOUR...
...FOR TONO TO WAKE UP.
UNCONSCIOUS

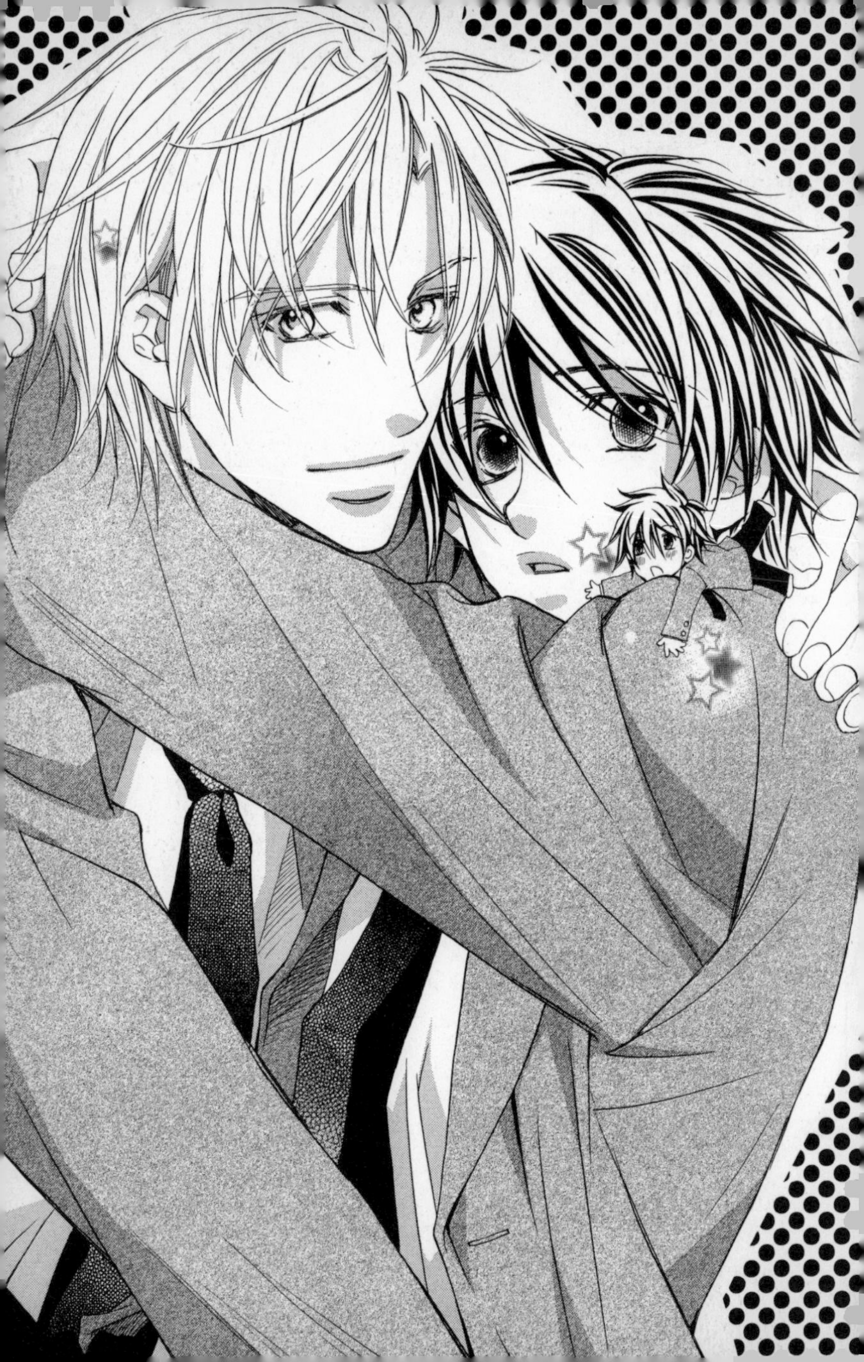

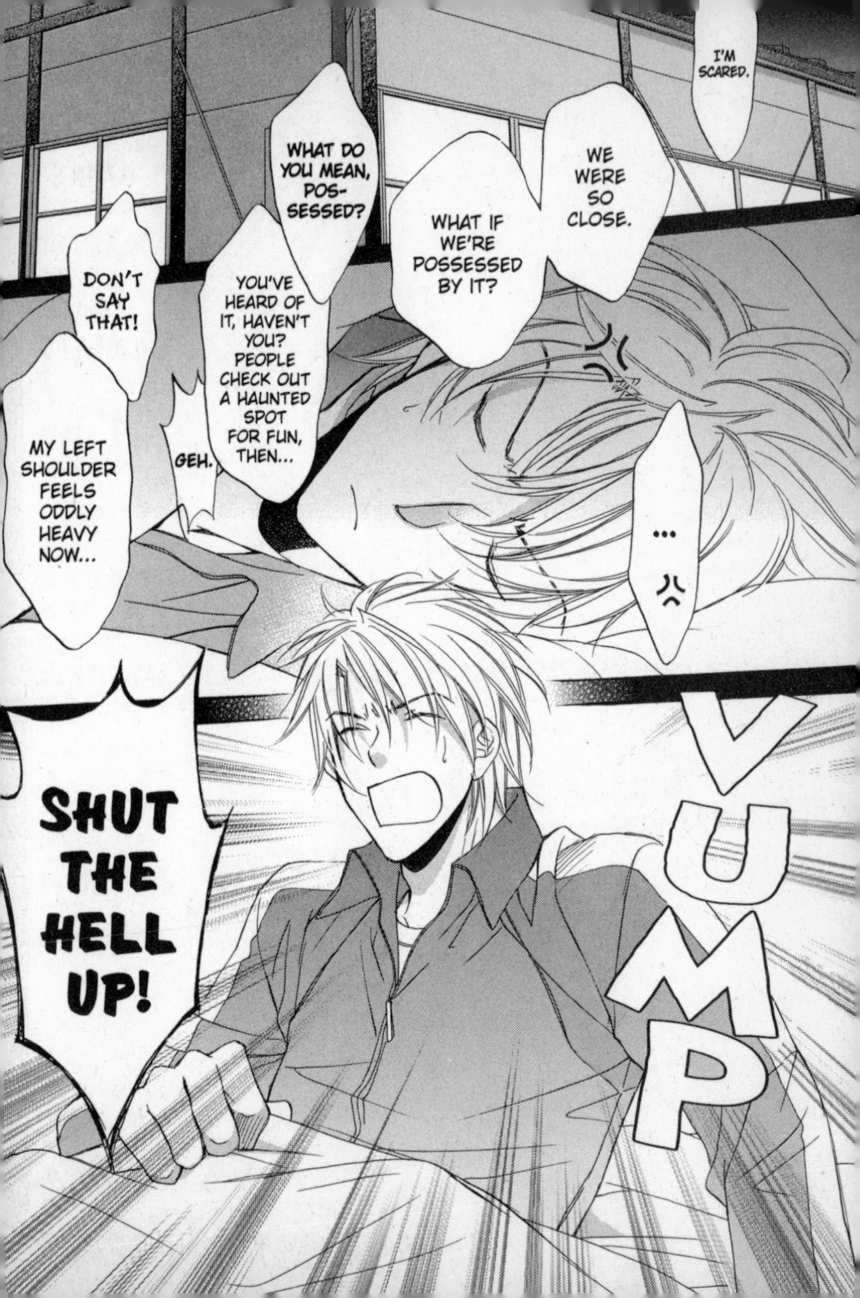
I'M SCARED.
WE WERE SO CLOSE.
WHAT IF WE'RE POSSESSED BY IT?
WHAT DO YOU MEAN, POS-SESSED?
YOU'VE HEARD OF IT, HAVEN'T YOU? PEOPLE CHECK OUT A HAUNTED SPOT FOR FUN, THEN...
DON'T SAY THAT!
...
GEH.
MY LEFT SHOULDER FEELS ODDLY HEAVY NOW...
VUMP
SHUT THE HELL UP!

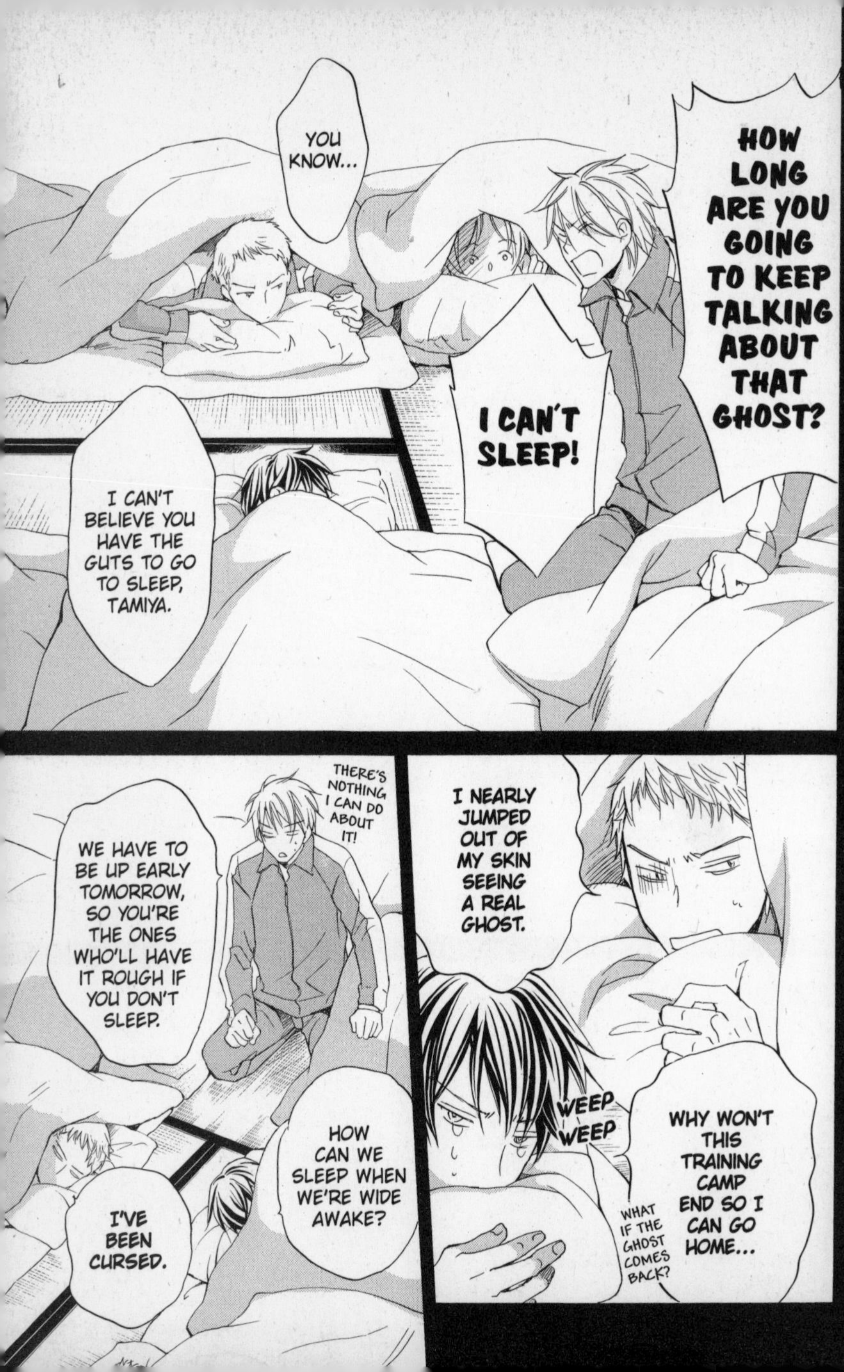
HOW LONG ARE YOU GOING TO KEEP TALKING ABOUT THAT GHOST?
I CAN'T SLEEP!
YOU KNOW...
I CAN'T BELIEVE YOU HAVE THE GUTS TO GO TO SLEEP, TAMIYA.
I NEARLY JUMPED OUT OF MY SKIN SEEING A REAL GHOST.
WEEP WEEP
WHY WON'T THIS TRAINING CAMP END SO I CAN GO HOME...
WHAT IF THE GHOST COMES BACK?
THERE'S NOTHING I CAN DO ABOUT IT!
WE HAVE TO BE UP EARLY TOMORROW, SO YOU'RE THE ONES WHO'LL HAVE IT ROUGH IF YOU DON'T SLEEP.
HOW CAN WE SLEEP WHEN WE'RE WIDE AWAKE?
I'VE BEEN CURSED.

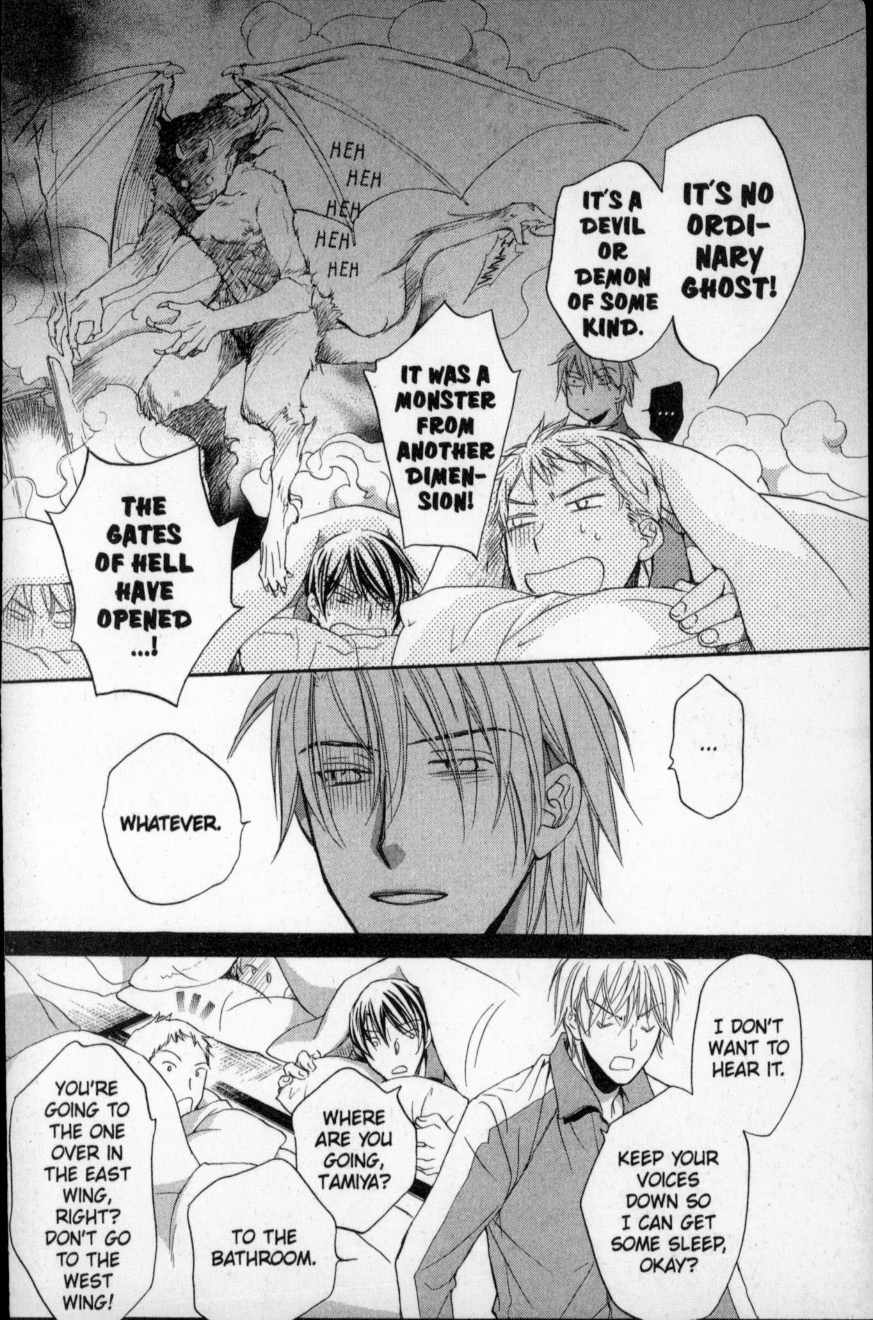
IT'S NO ORDINARY GHOST!
IT'S A DEVIL OR DEMON OF SOME KIND.
...
HEH HEH HEH HEH HEH
IT WAS A MONSTER FROM ANOTHER DIMENSION!
THE GATES OF HELL HAVE OPENED ...!
...
WHATEVER.
I DON'T WANT TO HEAR IT.
KEEP YOUR VOICES DOWN SO I CAN GET SOME SLEEP, OKAY?
WHERE ARE YOU GOING, TAMIYA?
TO THE BATHROOM.
YOU'RE GOING TO THE ONE OVER IN THE EAST WING, RIGHT? DON'T GO TO THE WEST WING!

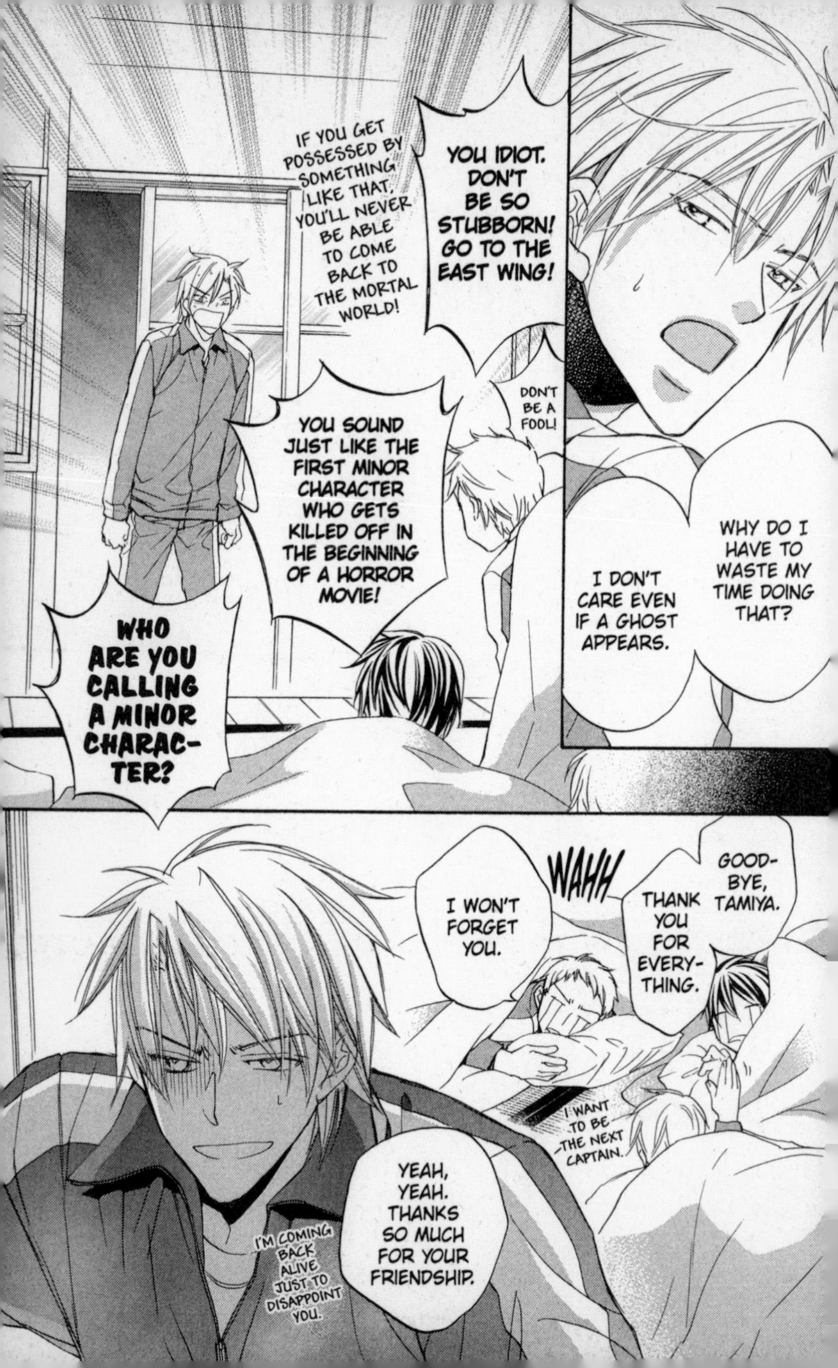
WHY DO I HAVE TO WASTE MY TIME DOING THAT?
I DON'T CARE EVEN IF A GHOST APPEARS.
YOU IDIOT. DON'T BE SO STUBBORN! GO TO THE EAST WING!
IF YOU GET POSSESSED BY SOMETHING LIKE THAT, YOU'LL NEVER BE ABLE TO COME BACK TO THE MORTAL WORLD!
DON'T BE A FOOL!
YOU SOUND JUST LIKE THE FIRST MINOR CHARACTER WHO GETS KILLED OFF IN THE BEGINNING OF A HORROR MOVIE!
WHO ARE YOU CALLING A MINOR CHARAC-TER?
GOOD-BYE, TAMIYA.
THANK YOU FOR EVERY-THING.
WAHH
I WON'T FORGET YOU.
I WANT TO BE THE NEXT CAPTAIN.
YEAH, YEAH. THANKS SO MUCH FOR YOUR FRIENDSHIP.
I'M COMING BACK ALIVE JUST TO DISAPPOINT YOU.

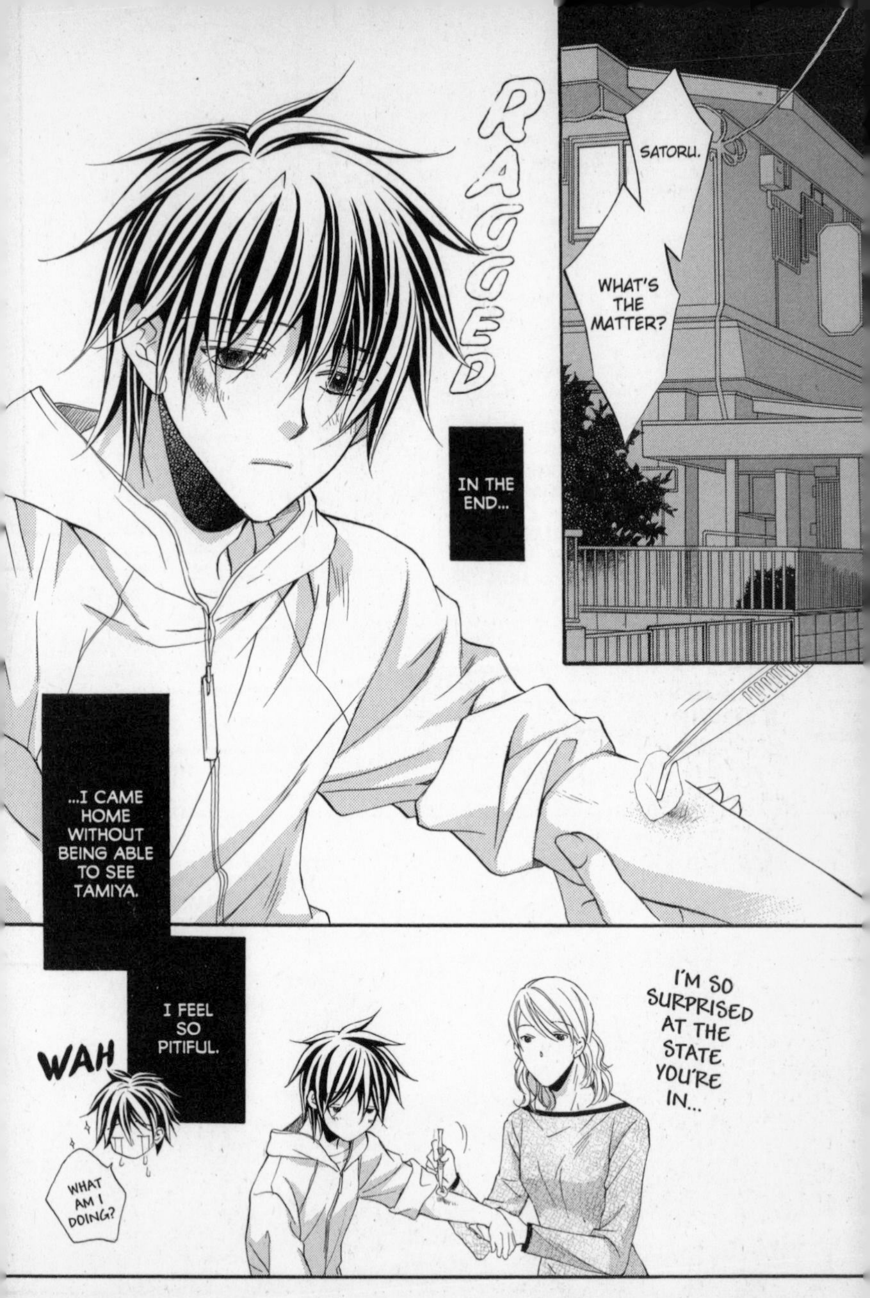
SATORU.
WHAT'S THE MATTER?
RAGGED
IN THE END...
...I CAME HOME WITHOUT BEING ABLE TO SEE TAMIYA.
I FEEL SO PITIFUL.
I'M SO SURPRISED AT THE STATE YOU'RE IN...
WAH
WHAT AM I DOING?

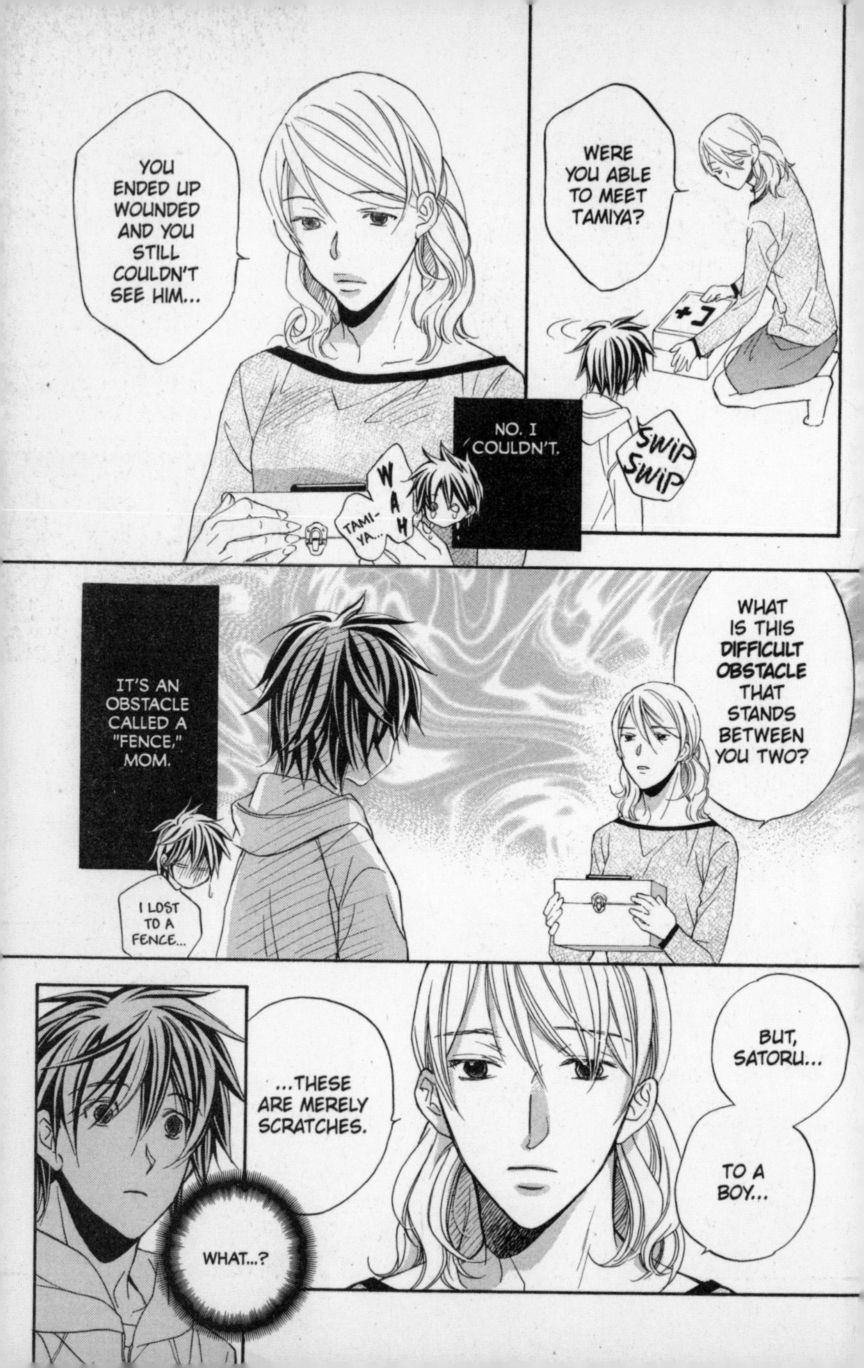
WERE YOU ABLE TO MEET TAMIYA?
SWIP SWIP
YOU ENDED UP WOUNDED AND YOU STILL COULDN'T SEE HIM...
NO. I COULDN'T.
WAH
TAMI-YA...
WHAT IS THIS DIFFICULT OBSTACLE THAT STANDS BETWEEN YOU TWO?
IT'S AN OBSTACLE CALLED A "FENCE," MOM.
I LOST TO A FENCE...
BUT, SATORU...
TO A BOY...
...THESE ARE MERELY SCRATCHES.
WHAT...?

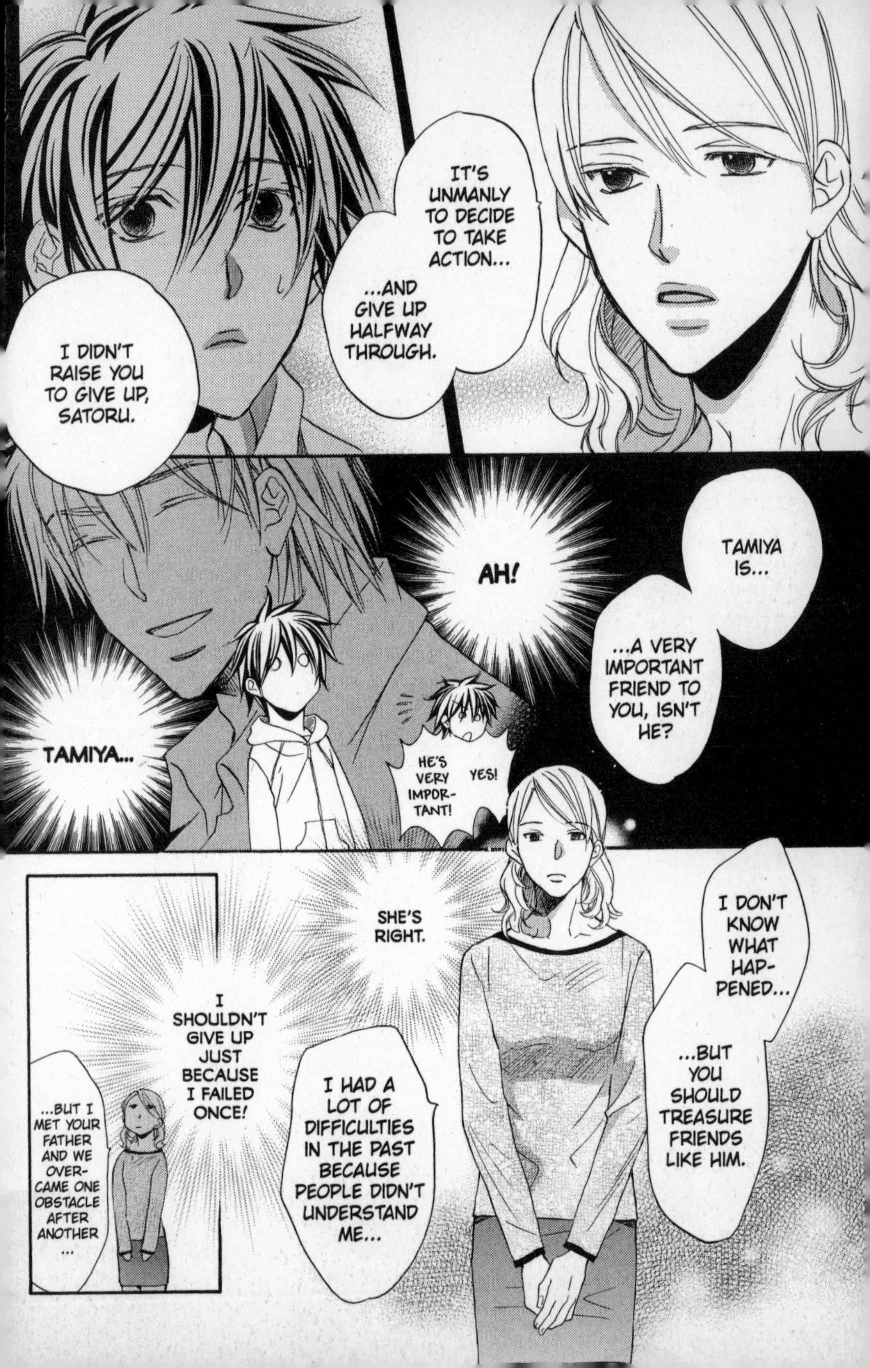
IT'S UNMANLY TO DECIDE TO TAKE ACTION...
...AND GIVE UP HALFWAY THROUGH.
I DIDN'T RAISE YOU TO GIVE UP, SATORU.
TAMIYA IS...
...A VERY IMPORTANT FRIEND TO YOU, ISN'T HE?
YES!
HE'S VERY IMPOR-TANT!
AH!
TAMIYA...
I DON'T KNOW WHAT HAP-PENED...
...BUT YOU SHOULD TREASURE FRIENDS LIKE HIM.
I HAD A LOT OF DIFFICULTIES IN THE PAST BECAUSE PEOPLE DIDN'T UNDERSTAND ME...
...BUT I MET YOUR FATHER AND WE OVER-CAME ONE OBSTACLE AFTER ANOTHER ...
SHE'S RIGHT.
I SHOULDN'T GIVE UP JUST BECAUSE I FAILED ONCE!

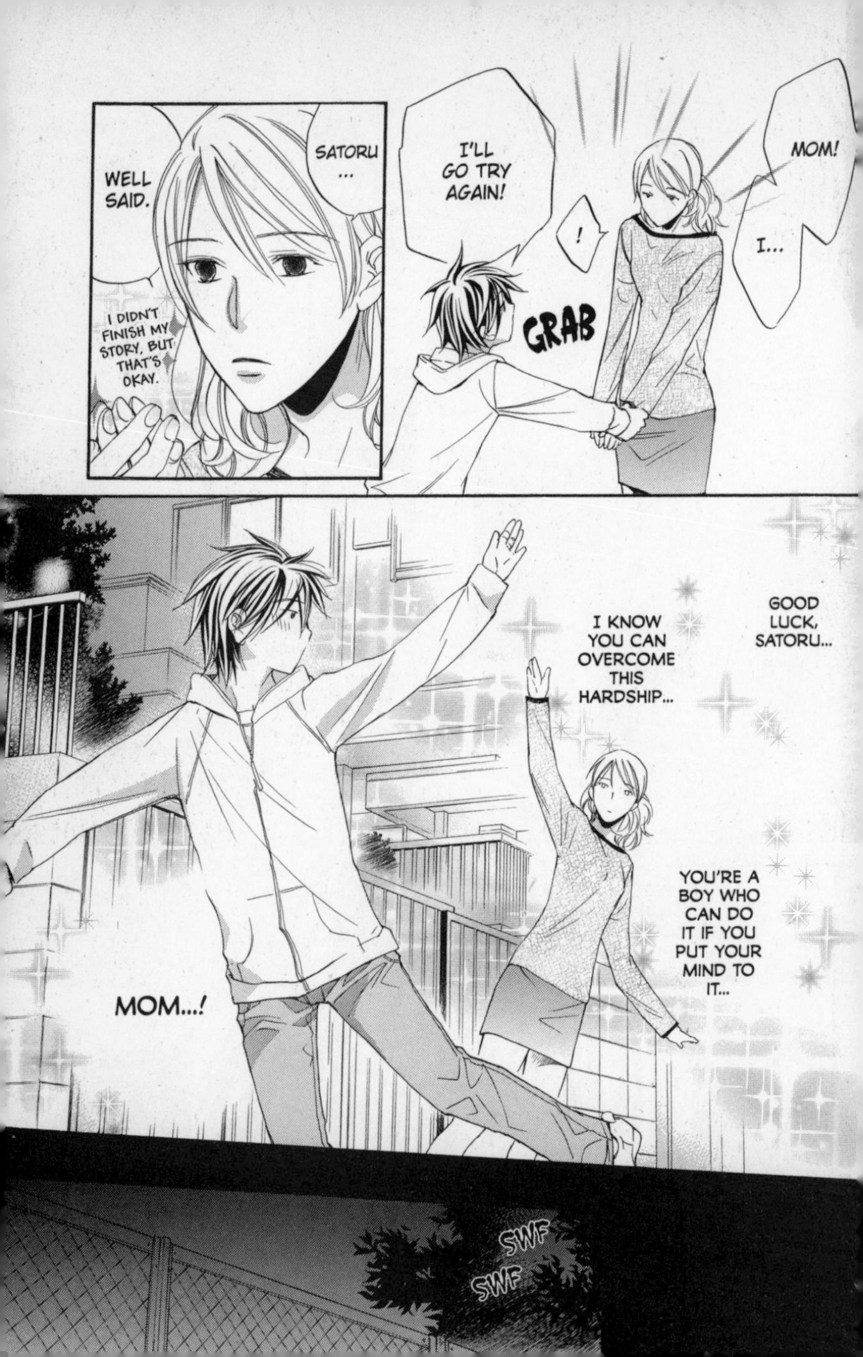
MOM!
I...
!
GRAB
I'LL GO TRY AGAIN!
SATORU ...
WELL SAID.
I DIDN'T FINISH MY STORY, BUT THAT'S OKAY.
GOOD LUCK, SATORU...
I KNOW YOU CAN OVERCOME THIS HARDSHIP...
YOU'RE A BOY WHO CAN DO IT IF YOU PUT YOUR MIND TO IT...
MOM...!
SWF
SWF

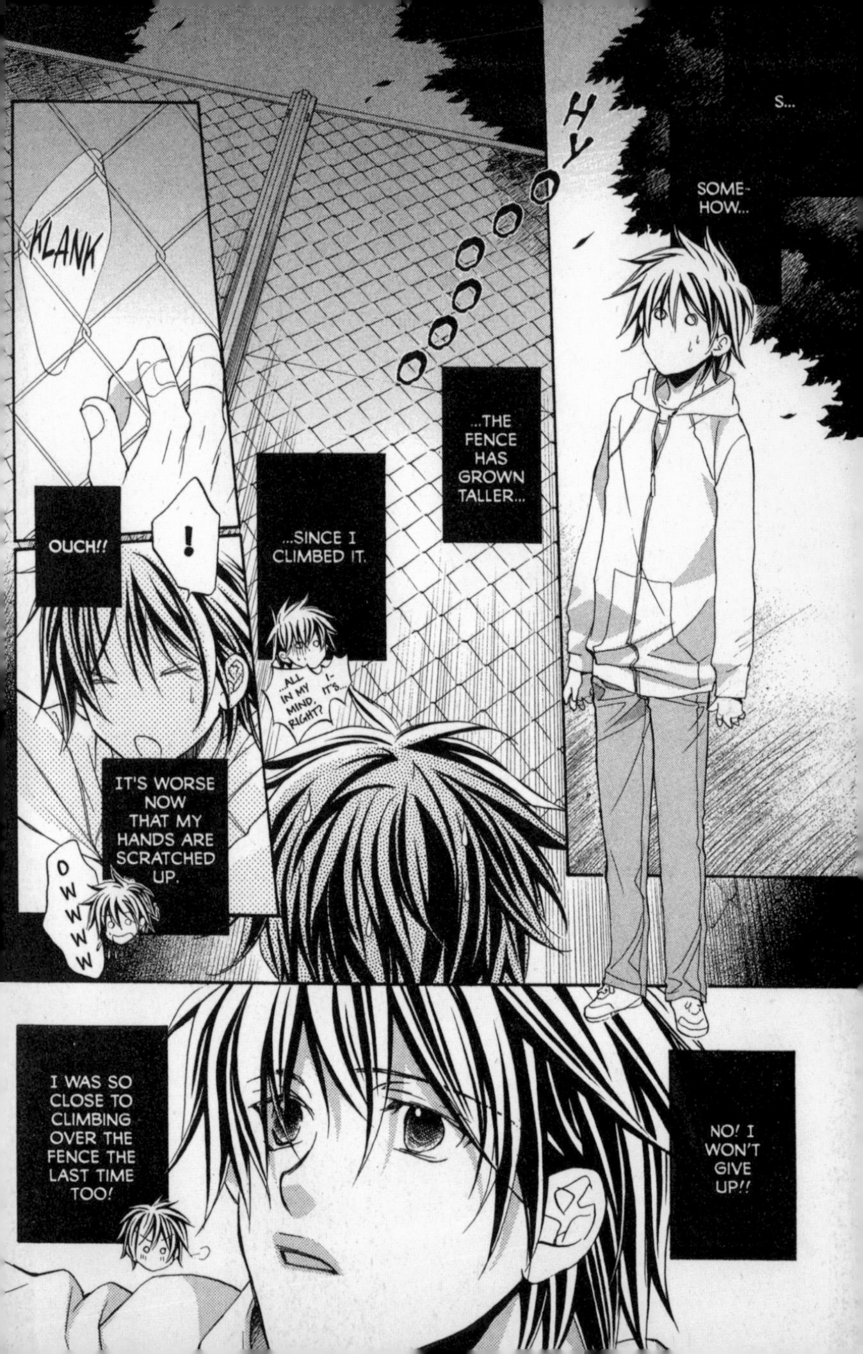
S...
SOME-HOW...
HYOOOOOOO
...THE FENCE HAS GROWN TALLER...
...SINCE I CLIMBED IT.
I-IT'S...
...ALL IN MY MIND, RIGHT?
KLANK
!
OUCH!!
IT'S WORSE NOW THAT MY HANDS ARE SCRATCHED UP.
OWWWW
NO! I WON'T GIVE UP!!
I WAS SO CLOSE TO CLIMBING OVER THE FENCE THE LAST TIME TOO!

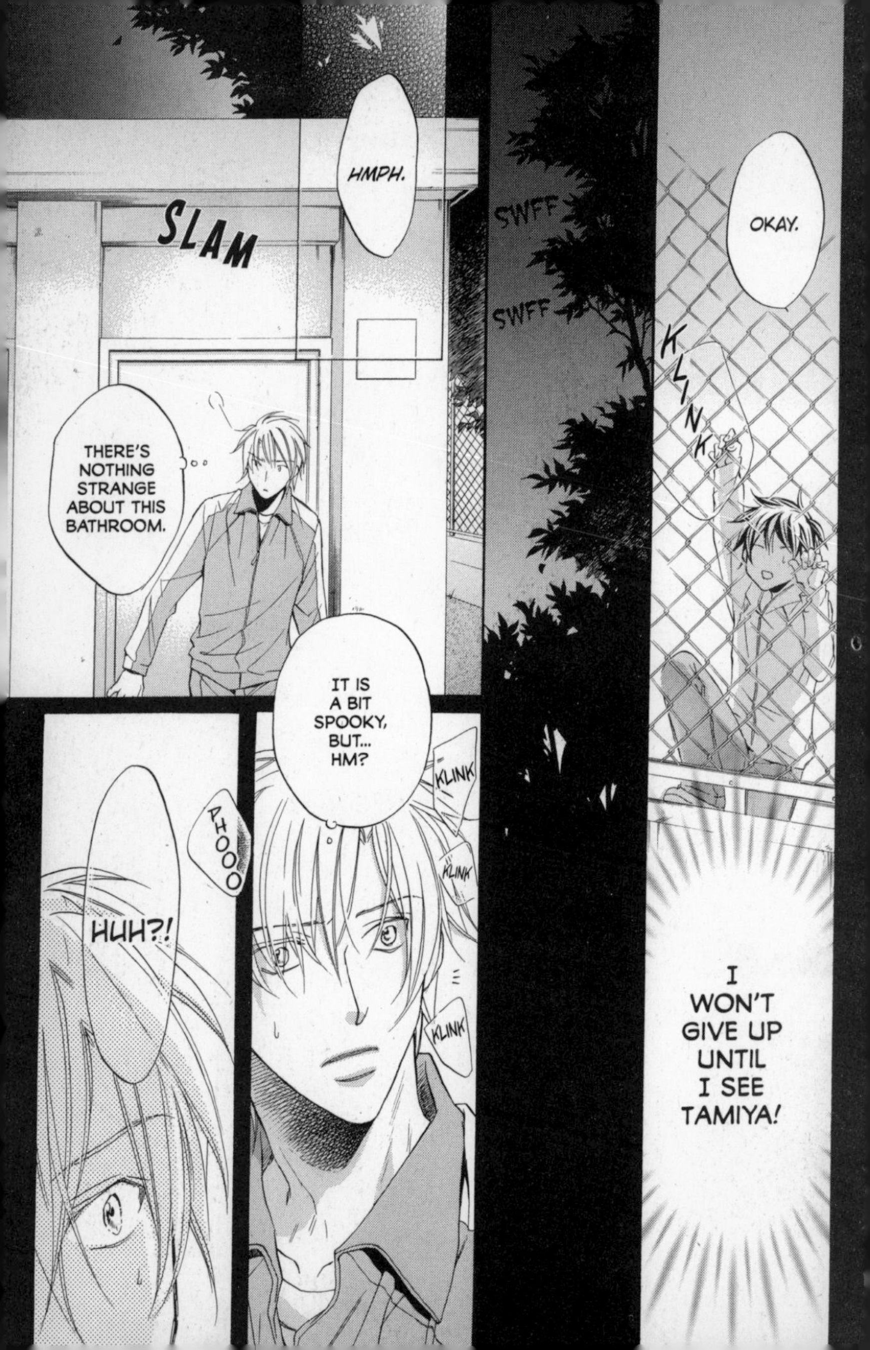
OKAY.
KLINK
I WON'T GIVE UP UNTIL I SEE TAMIYA!
SWFF
SWFF
HMPH.
SLAM
THERE'S NOTHING STRANGE ABOUT THIS BATHROOM.
IT IS A BIT SPOOKY, BUT... HM?
KLINK
KLINK
KLINK
AHOOO
HUH?!

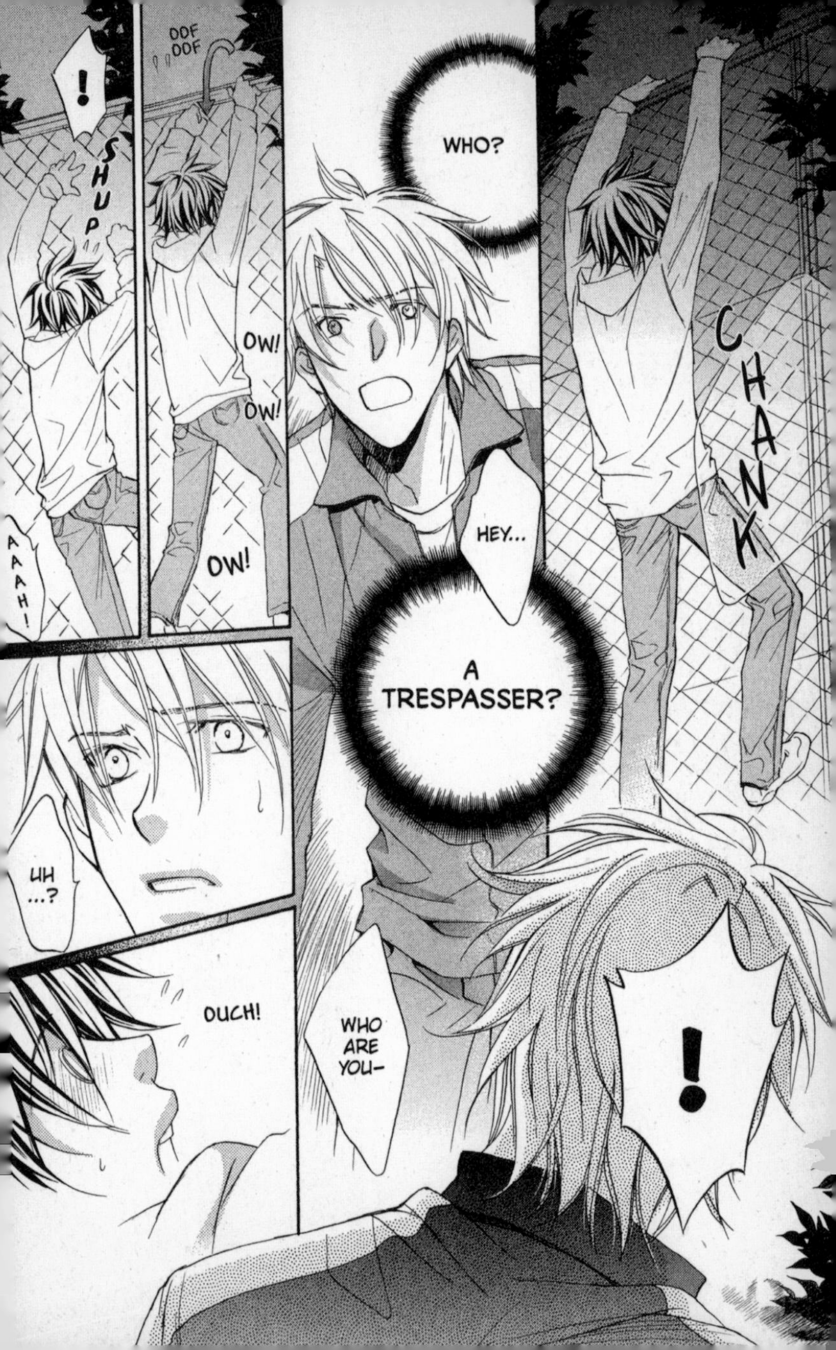
CHANK
WHO?
HEY...
A TRESPASSER?
WHO ARE YOU-
!
DOF DOF
OW!
OW!
OW!
!
SHUP
AAAAH!
UH ...?
OUCH!

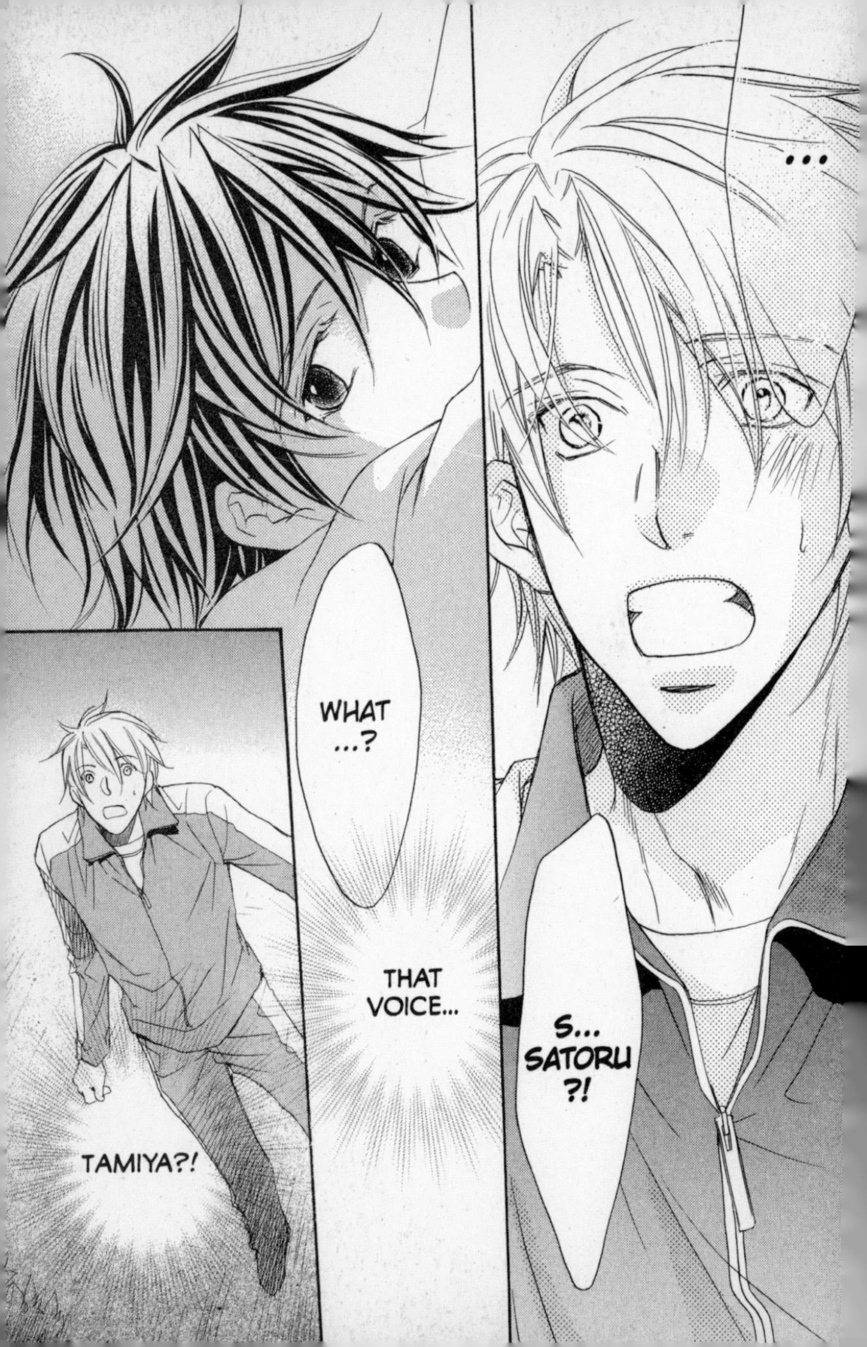
...
S... SATORU ?!
WHAT ...?
THAT VOICE...
TAMIYA?!

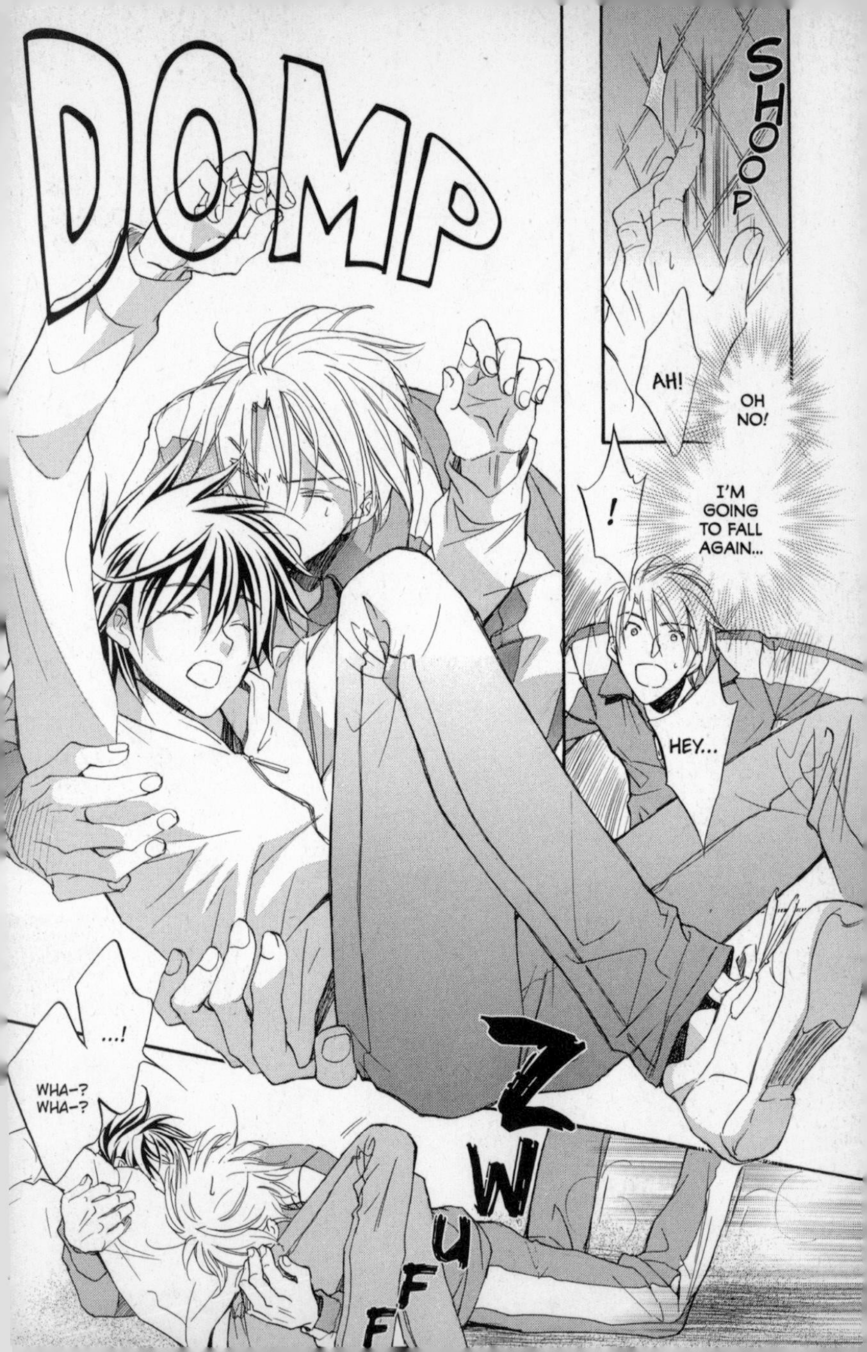
SHOOP
AH!
OH NO!
I'M GOING TO FALL AGAIN...
DOMP
!
HEY...
ZWUFFF
...!
WHA-? WHA-?

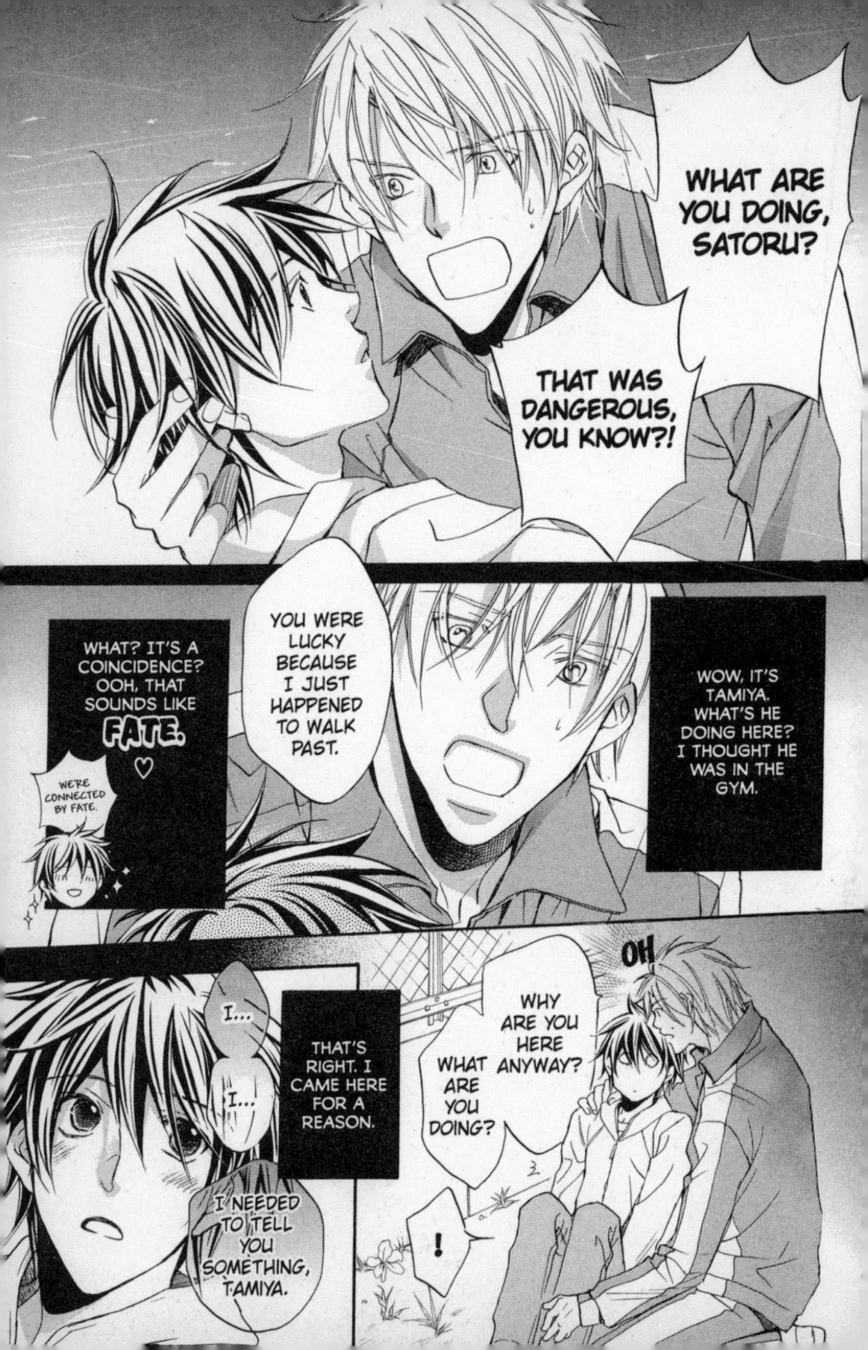
WHAT ARE YOU DOING, SATORU?
THAT WAS DANGEROUS, YOU KNOW?!
WOW, IT'S TAMIYA. WHAT'S HE DOING HERE? I THOUGHT HE WAS IN THE GYM.
YOU WERE LUCKY BECAUSE I JUST HAPPENED TO WALK PAST.
WHAT? IT'S A COINCIDENCE? OOH, THAT SOUNDS LIKE FATE. ♡
WE'RE CONNECTED BY FATE.
OH
WHY ARE YOU HERE ANYWAY? WHAT ARE YOU DOING?
!
THAT'S RIGHT. I CAME HERE FOR A REASON.
I...
I...
I NEEDED TO TELL YOU SOMETHING, TAMIYA.

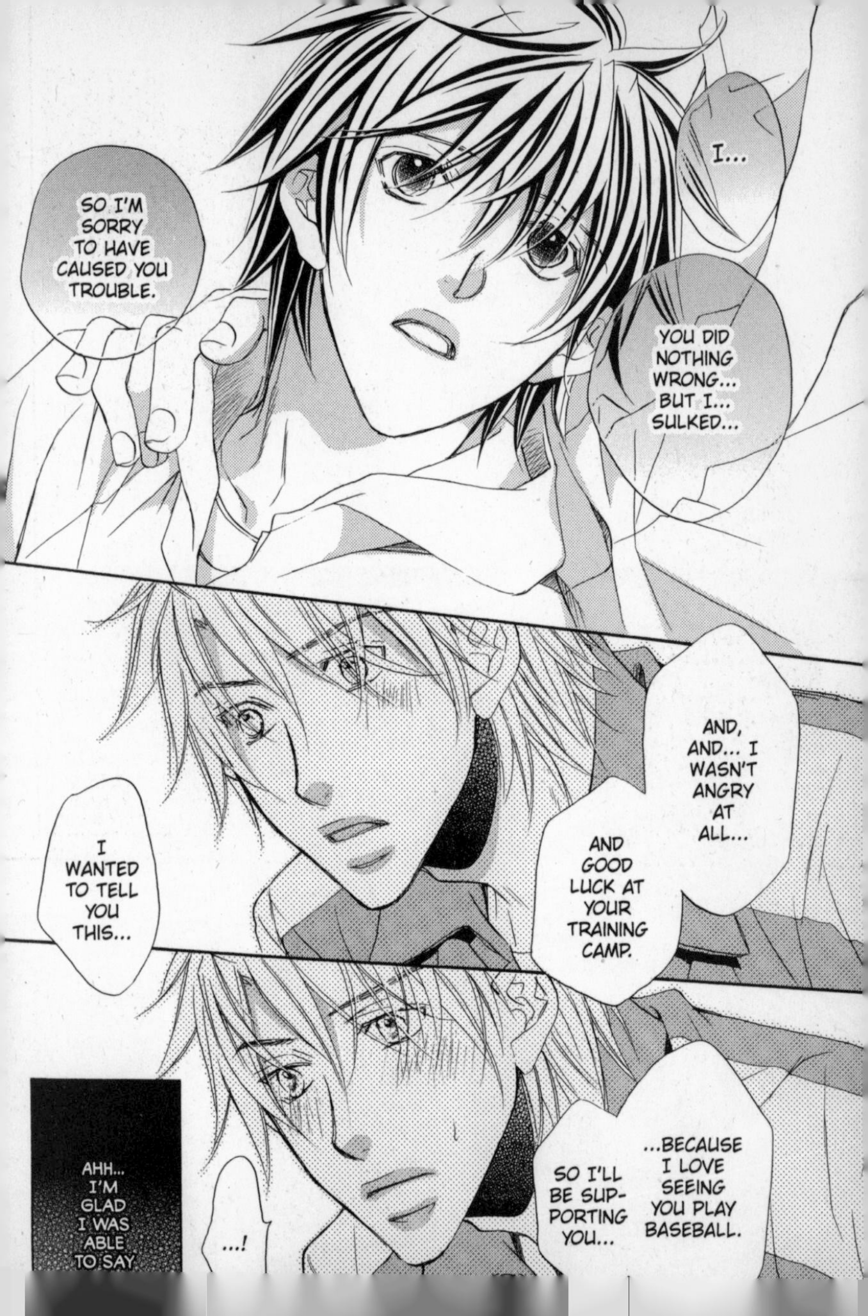
I...
YOU DID NOTHING WRONG... BUT I... SULKED...
SO I'M SORRY TO HAVE CAUSED YOU TROUBLE.
AND, AND... I WASN'T ANGRY AT ALL...
AND GOOD LUCK AT YOUR TRAINING CAMP.
I WANTED TO TELL YOU THIS...
...BECAUSE I LOVE SEEING YOU PLAY BASEBALL.
SO I'LL BE SUP-PORTING YOU...
...!
AHH... I'M GLAD I WAS ABLE TO SAY

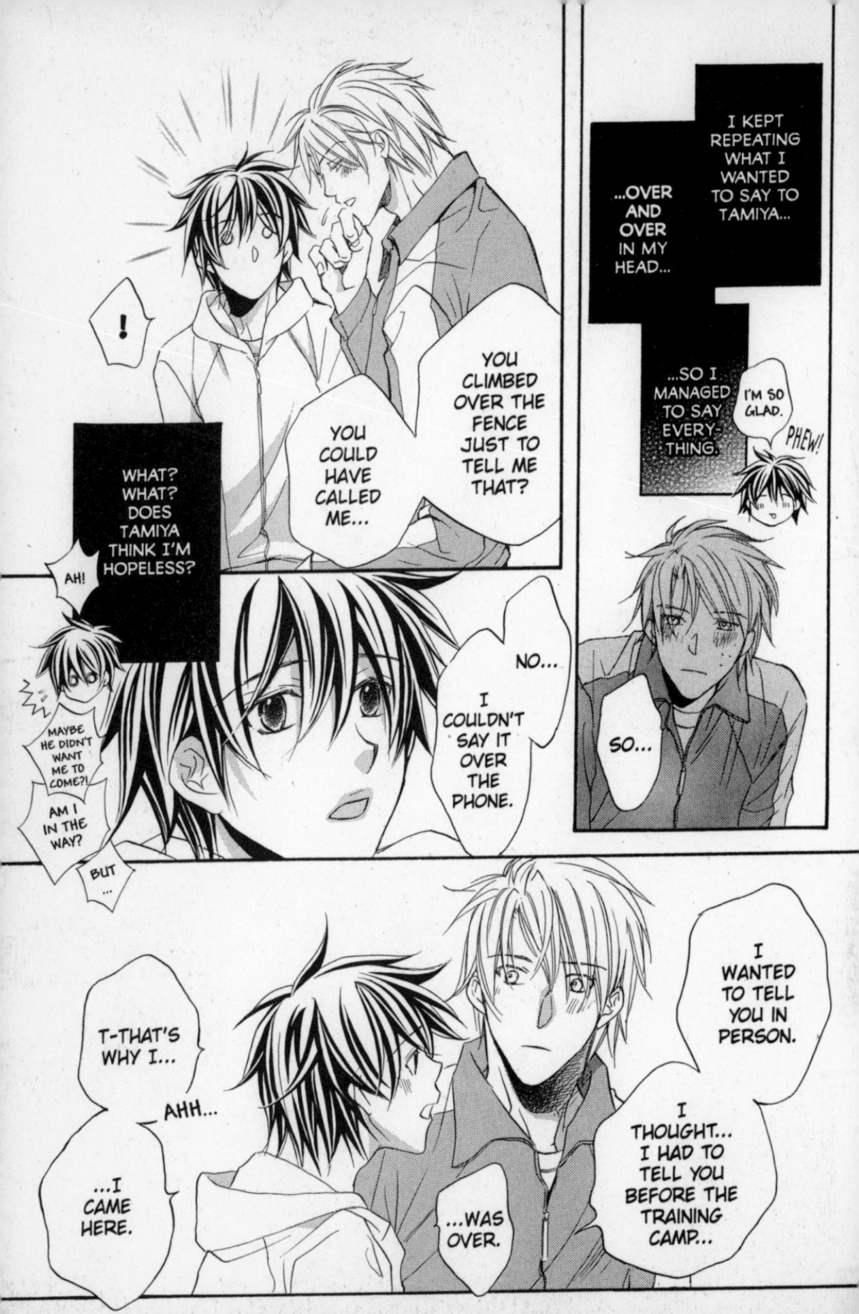
I KEPT REPEATING WHAT I WANTED TO SAY TO TAMIYA...
...OVER AND OVER IN MY HEAD...
...SO I MANAGED TO SAY EVERY-THING.
I'M SO GLAD.
PHEW!
SO...
YOU CLIMBED OVER THE FENCE JUST TO TELL ME THAT?
YOU COULD HAVE CALLED ME...
!
WHAT? WHAT? DOES TAMIYA THINK I'M HOPELESS?
AH!
NO...
I COULDN'T SAY IT OVER THE PHONE.
MAYBE HE DIDN'T WANT ME TO COME?!
AM I IN THE WAY?
BUT...
I WANTED TO TELL YOU IN PERSON.
I THOUGHT... I HAD TO TELL YOU BEFORE THE TRAINING CAMP...
...WAS OVER.
T-THAT'S WHY I...
AHH...
...I CAME HERE.

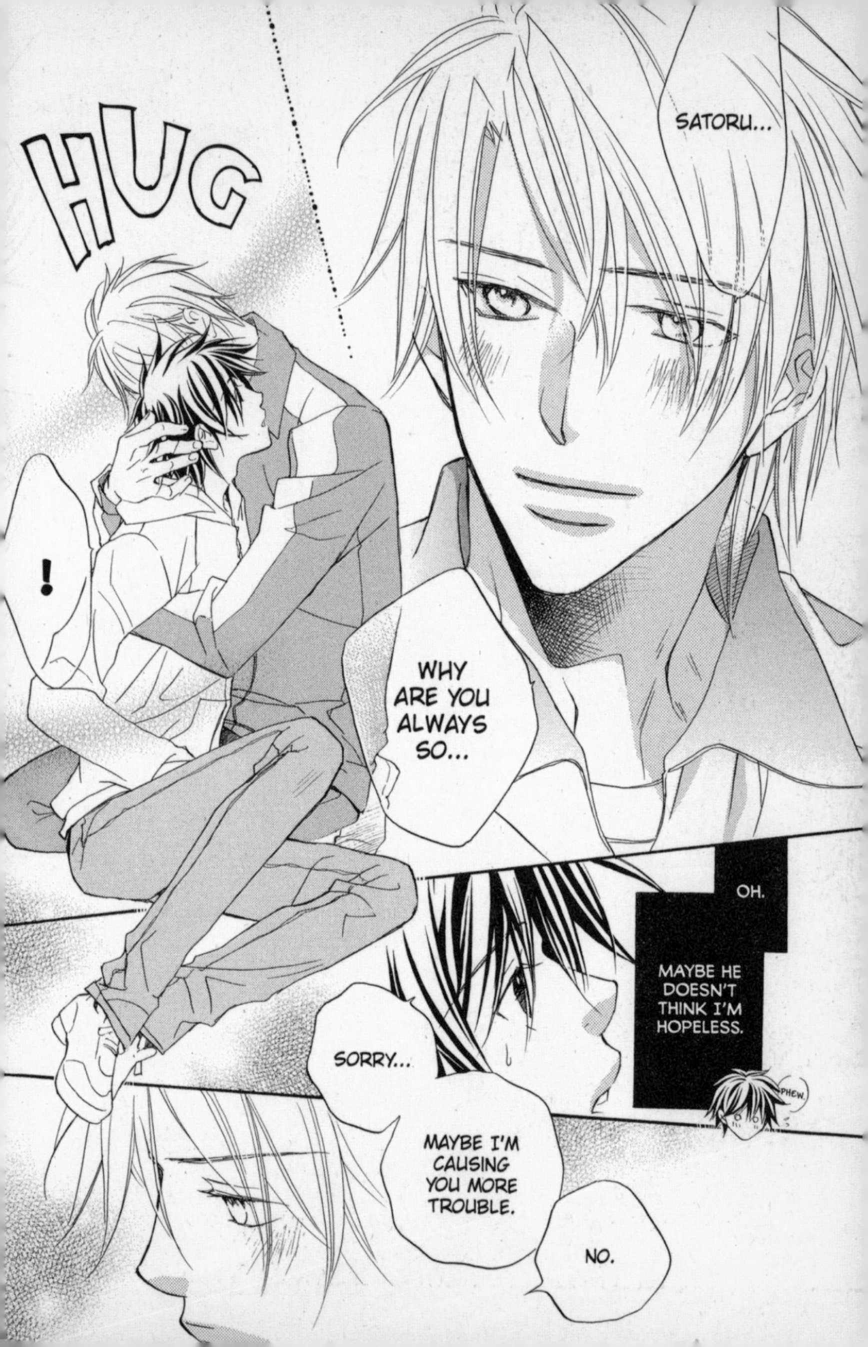
SATORU...
WHY ARE YOU ALWAYS SO...
HUG
!
OH.
MAYBE HE DOESN'T THINK I'M HOPELESS.
PHEW.
SORRY...
MAYBE I'M CAUSING YOU MORE TROUBLE.
NO.

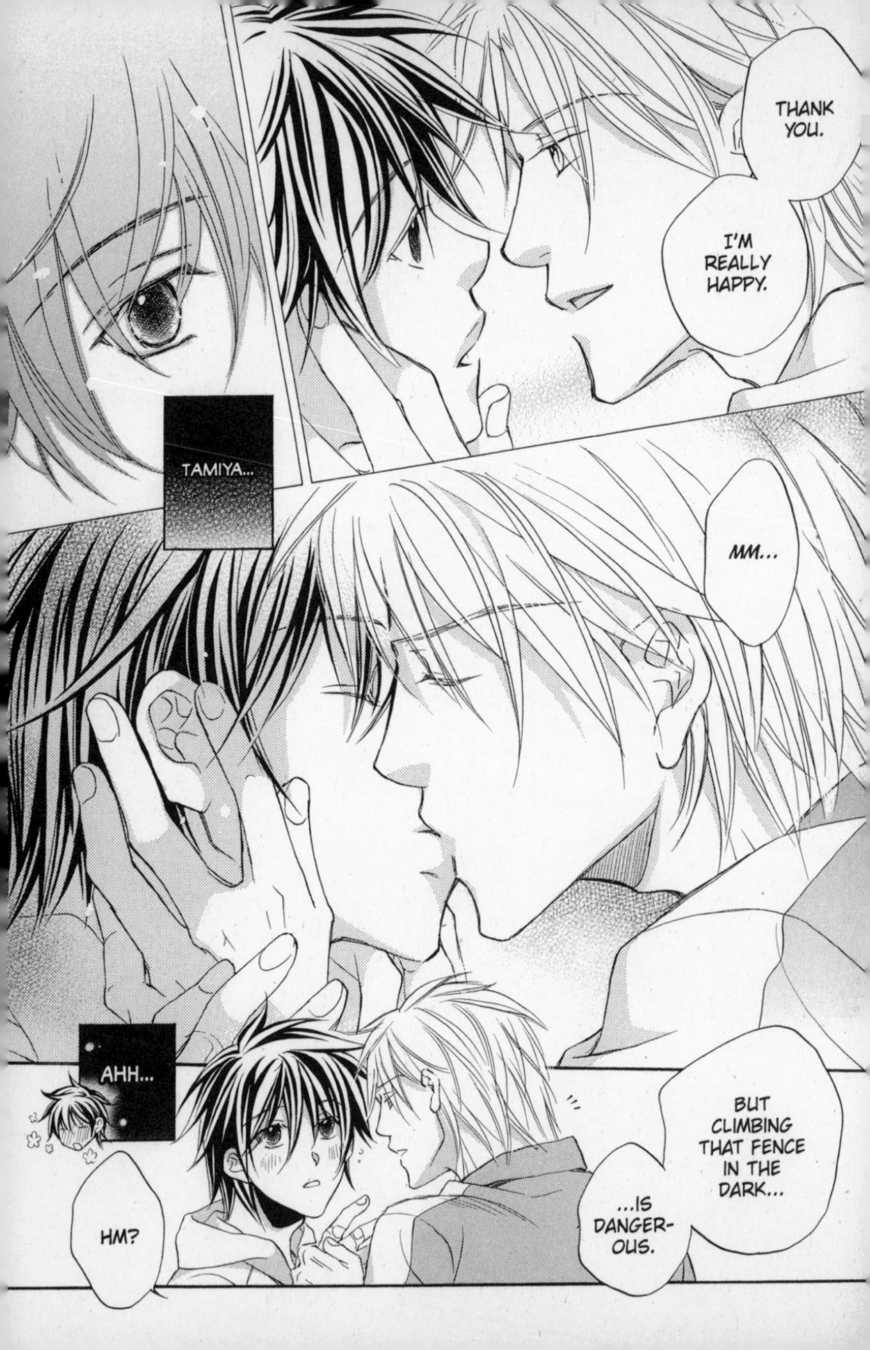
THANK YOU.
I'M REALLY HAPPY.
TAMIYA...
MM...
AHH...
BUT CLIMBING THAT FENCE IN THE DARK...
...IS DANGER-OUS.
HM?

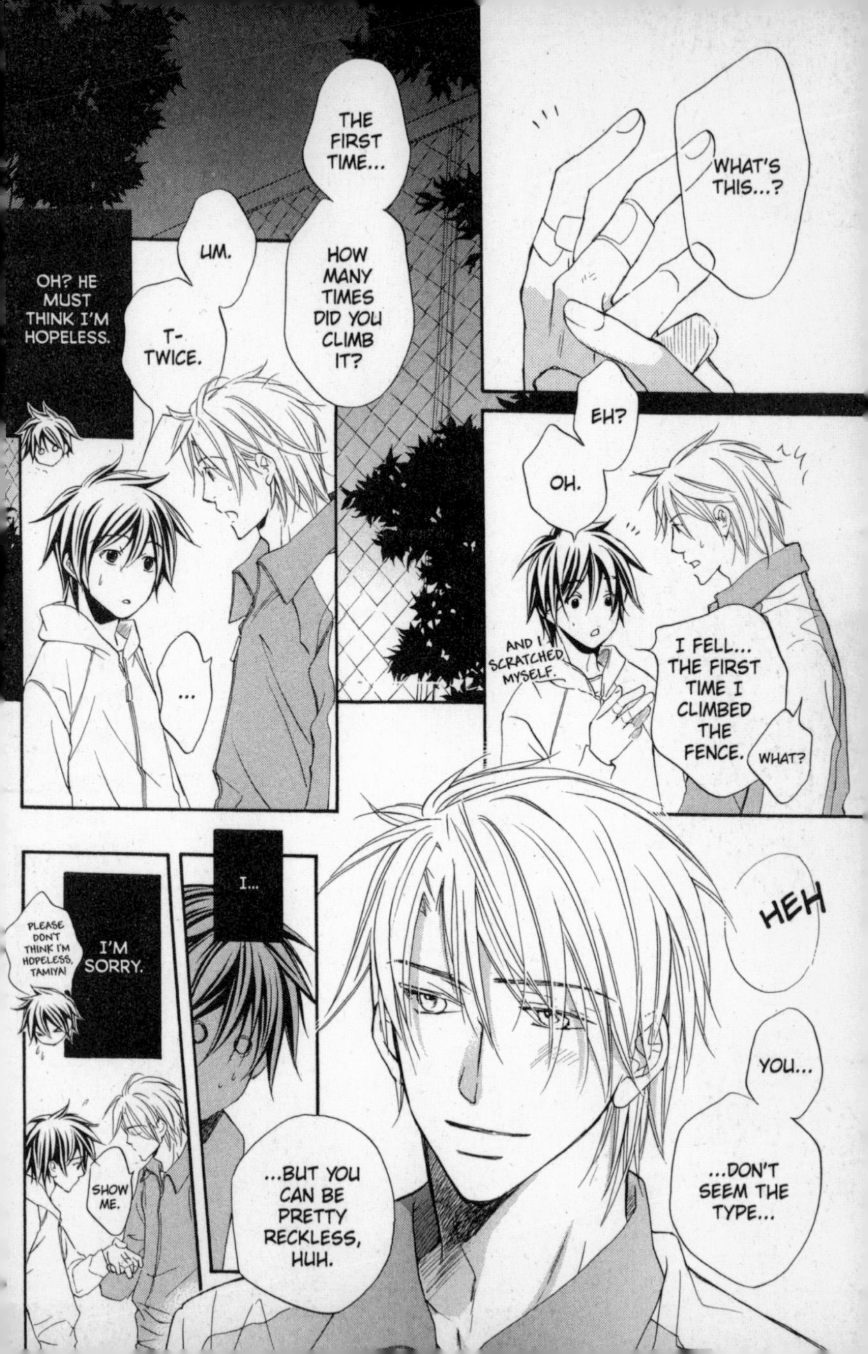
WHAT'S THIS...?
EH?
OH.
I FELL... THE FIRST TIME I CLIMBED THE FENCE.
WHAT?
AND I SCRATCHED MYSELF.
THE FIRST TIME...
HOW MANY TIMES DID YOU CLIMB IT?
UM.
T-TWICE.
OH? HE MUST THINK I'M HOPELESS.
...
HEH
YOU...
...DON'T SEEM THE TYPE...
...BUT YOU CAN BE PRETTY RECKLESS, HUH.
I...
I'M SORRY.
PLEASE DON'T THINK I'M HOPELESS, TAMIYA!
SHOW ME.

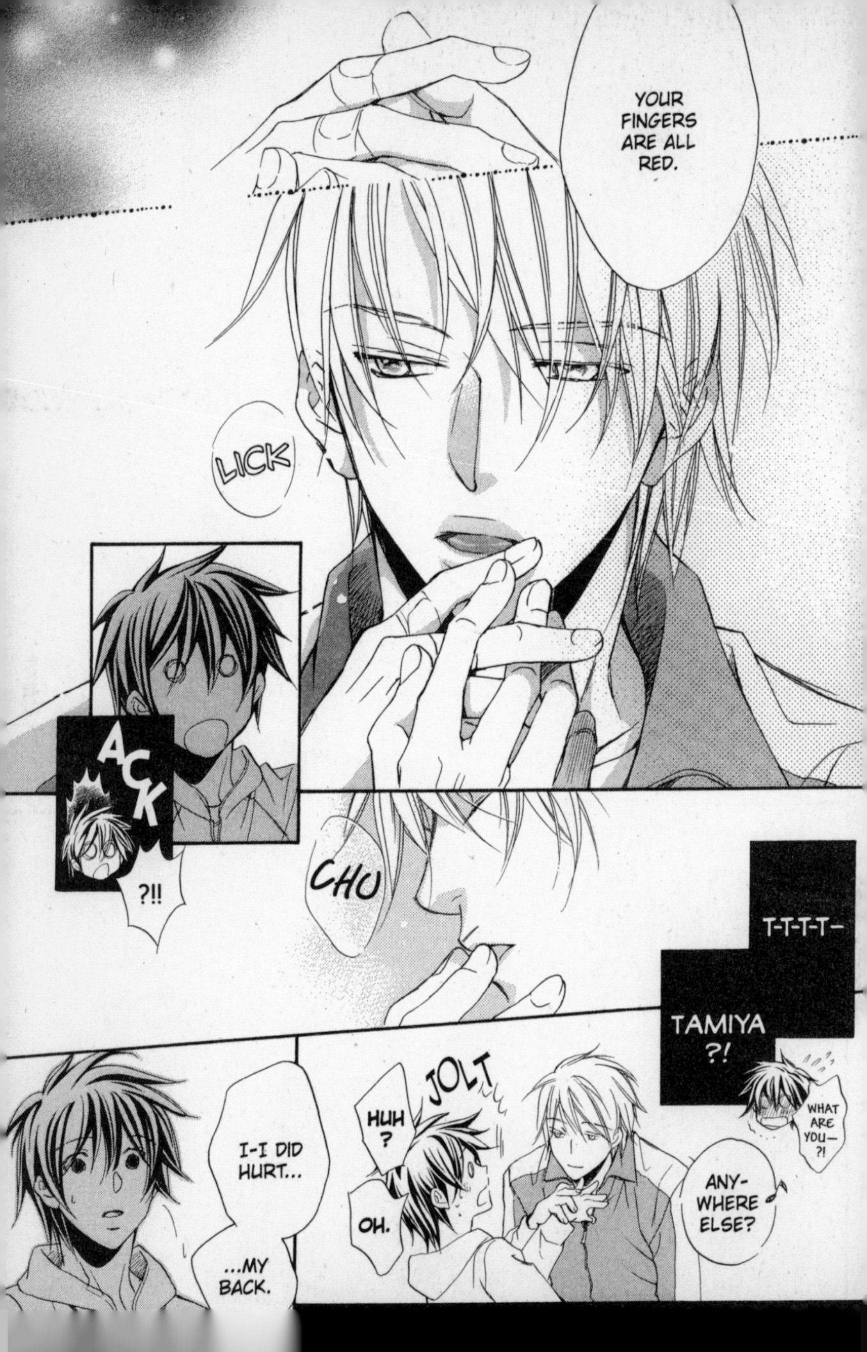
YOUR FINGERS ARE ALL RED.
LICK
ACK
?!!
CHU
T-T-T-T-
TAMIYA ?!
WHAT ARE YOU—?!
ANY-WHERE ELSE?
JOLT
HUH?
OH.
I-I DID HURT...
...MY BACK.

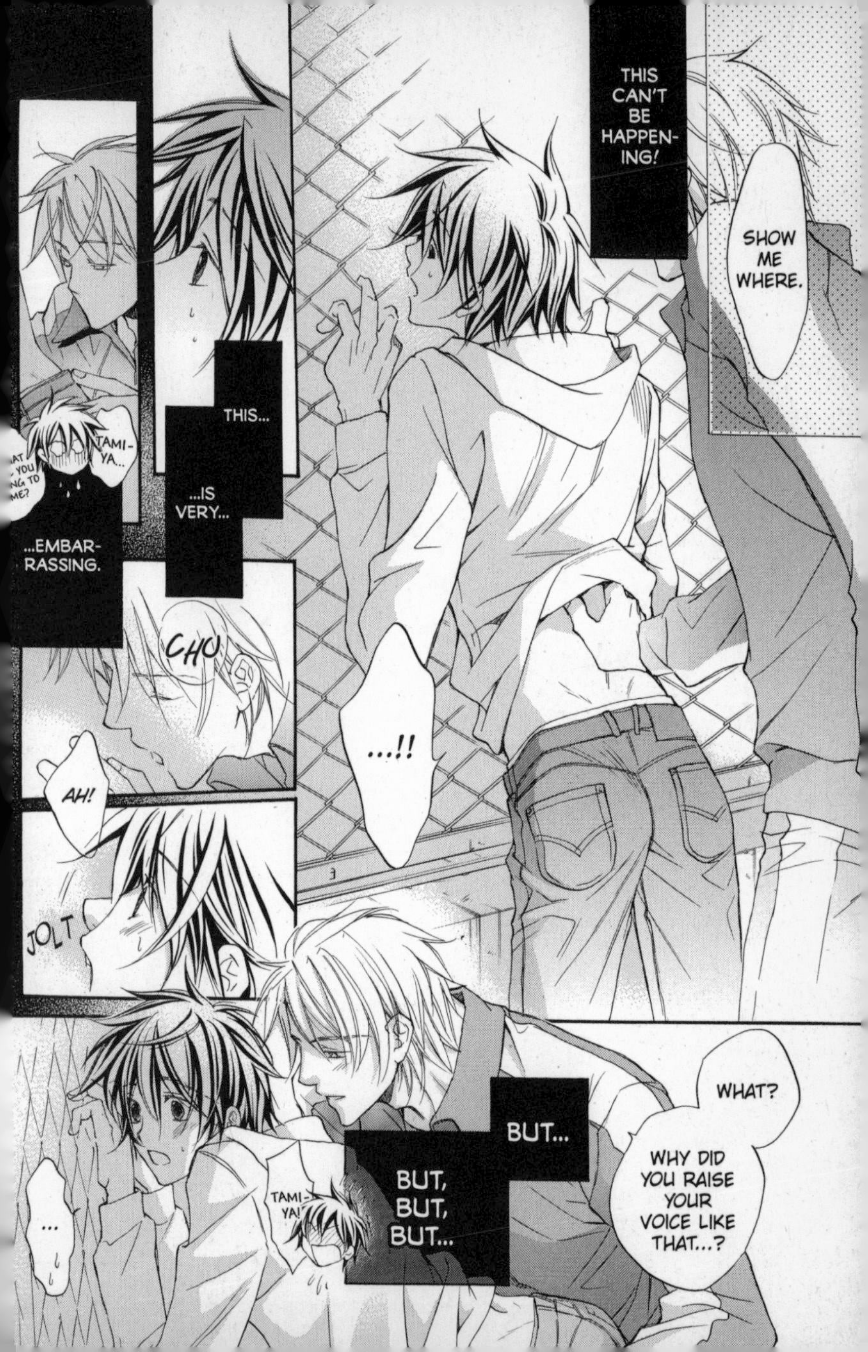
THIS CAN'T BE HAPPENING!
SHOW ME WHERE.
...!!
THIS...
TAMI-YA...
...IS VERY...
...EMBARRASSING.
CHU
AH!
JOLT
WHAT?
WHY DID YOU RAISE YOUR VOICE LIKE THAT...?
BUT...
BUT, BUT, BUT...
TAMI-YA!
...

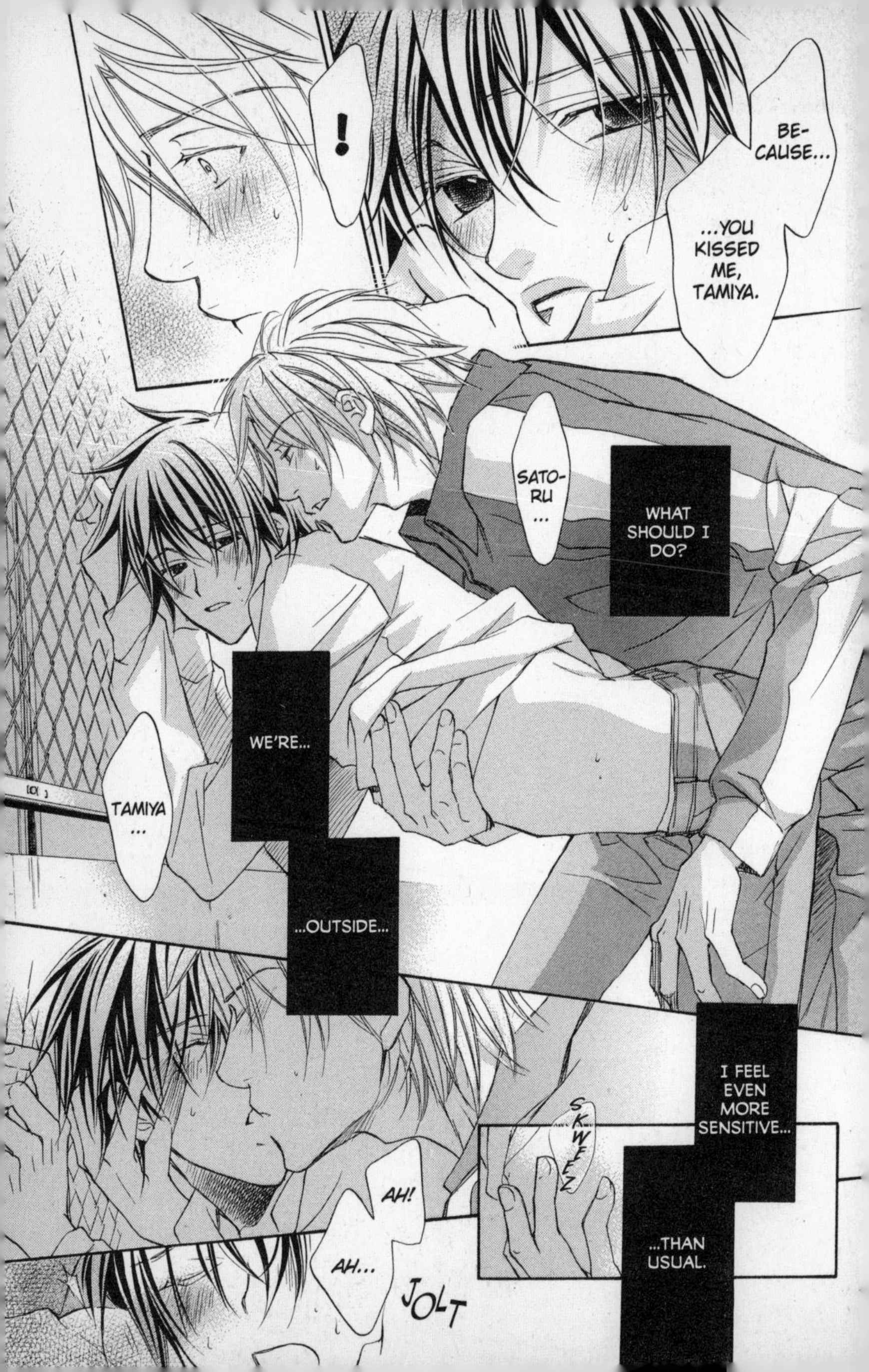
BE-CAUSE...
...YOU KISSED ME, TAMIYA.
!
SATO-RU...
WHAT SHOULD I DO?
WE'RE...
...OUTSIDE...
TAMIYA...
I FEEL EVEN MORE SENSITIVE...
SKWEEZ
...THAN USUAL.
AH!
AH...
JOLT

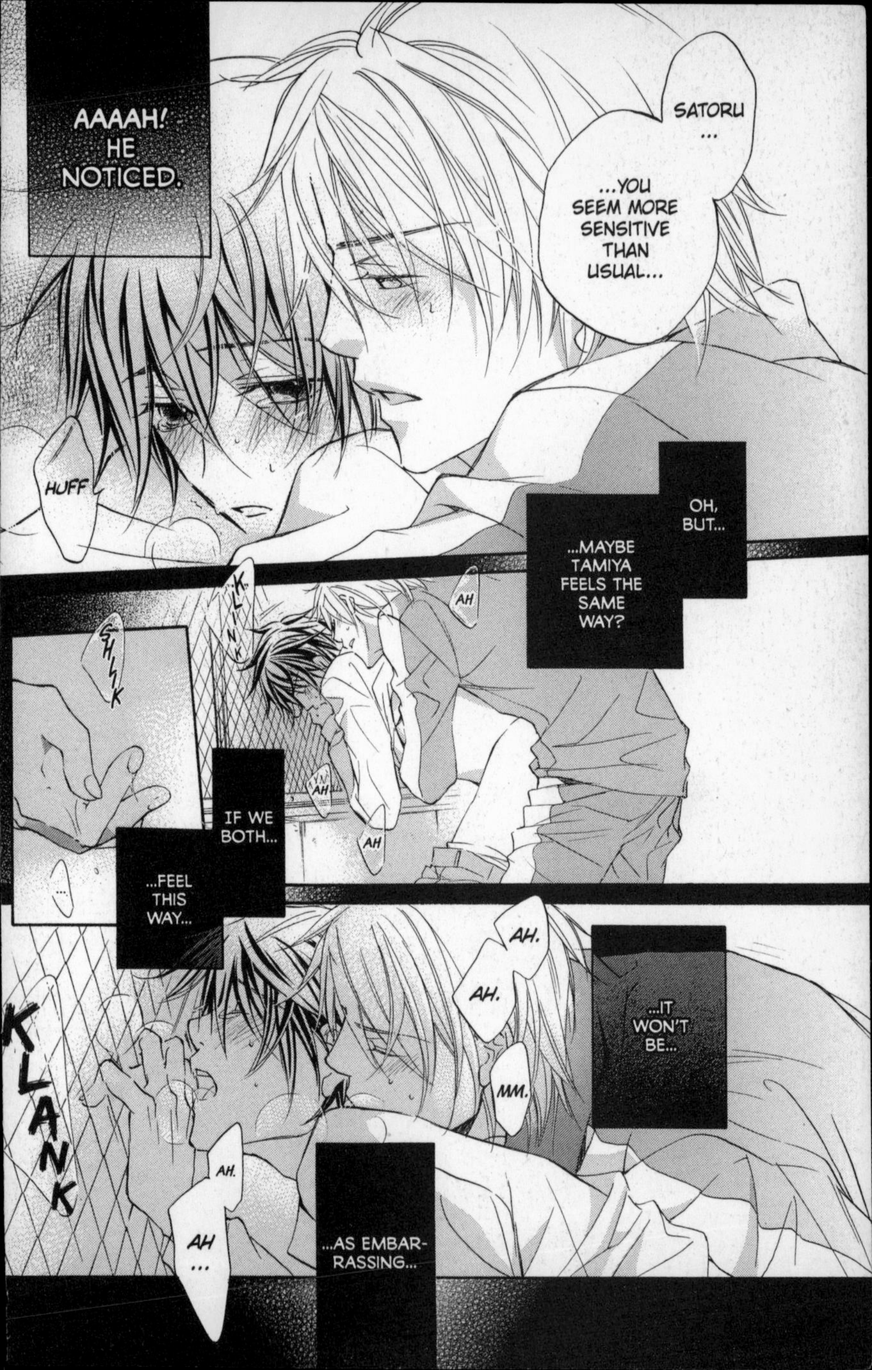
SATORU ...
...YOU SEEM MORE SENSITIVE THAN USUAL...
AAAAH! HE NOTICED.
HUFF
OH, BUT...
...MAYBE TAMIYA FEELS THE SAME WAY?
AH
KLINK
AH
SHINK
IF WE BOTH...
...FEEL THIS WAY...
...IT WON'T BE...
AH.
AH.
MM.
AH.
AH ...
KLANK
...AS EMBARRASSING...

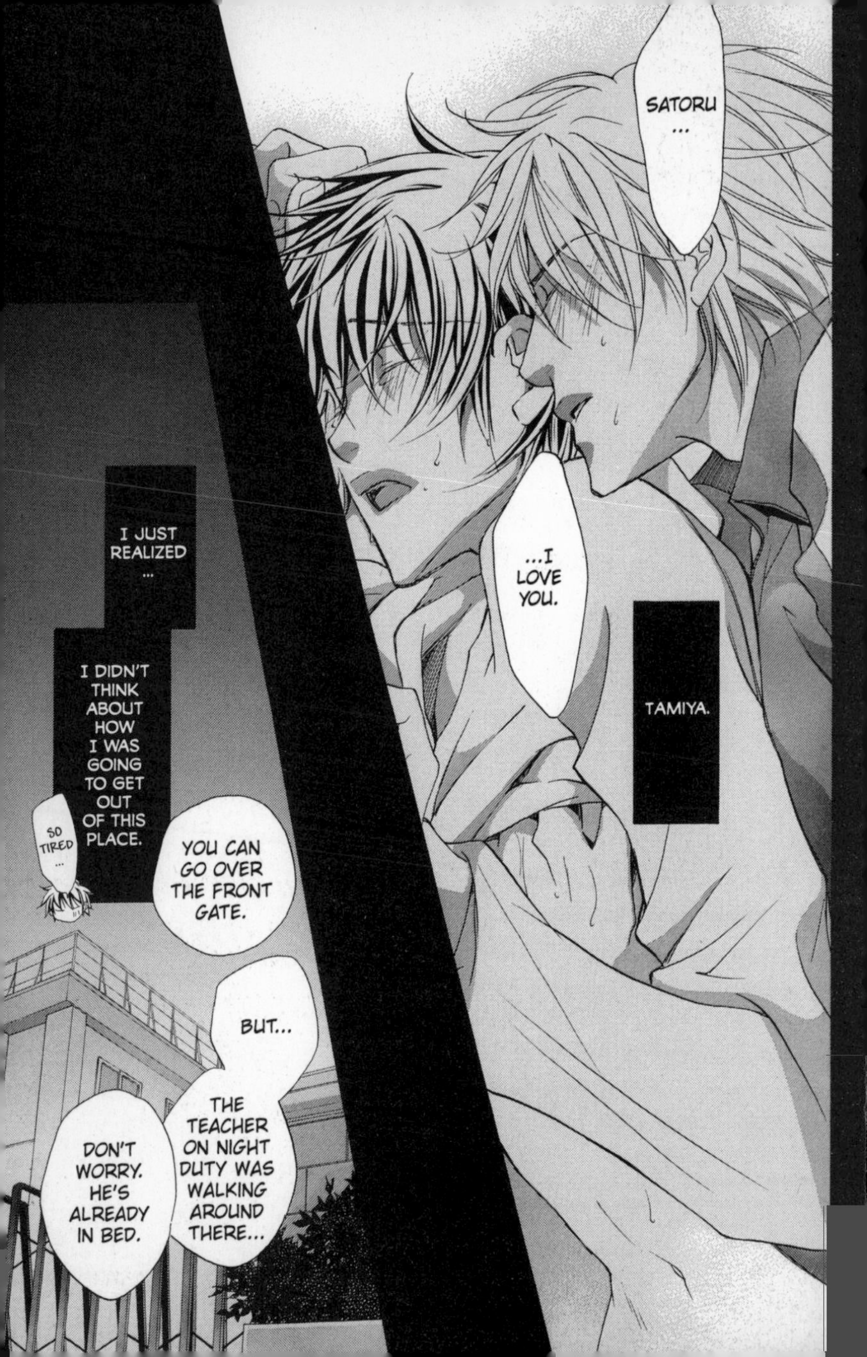
SATORU ...
...I LOVE YOU.
TAMIYA.
I JUST REALIZED ...
I DIDN'T THINK ABOUT HOW I WAS GOING TO GET OUT OF THIS PLACE.
YOU CAN GO OVER THE FRONT GATE.
SO TIRED ...
BUT...
THE TEACHER ON NIGHT DUTY WAS WALKING AROUND THERE...
DON'T WORRY. HE'S ALREADY IN BED.

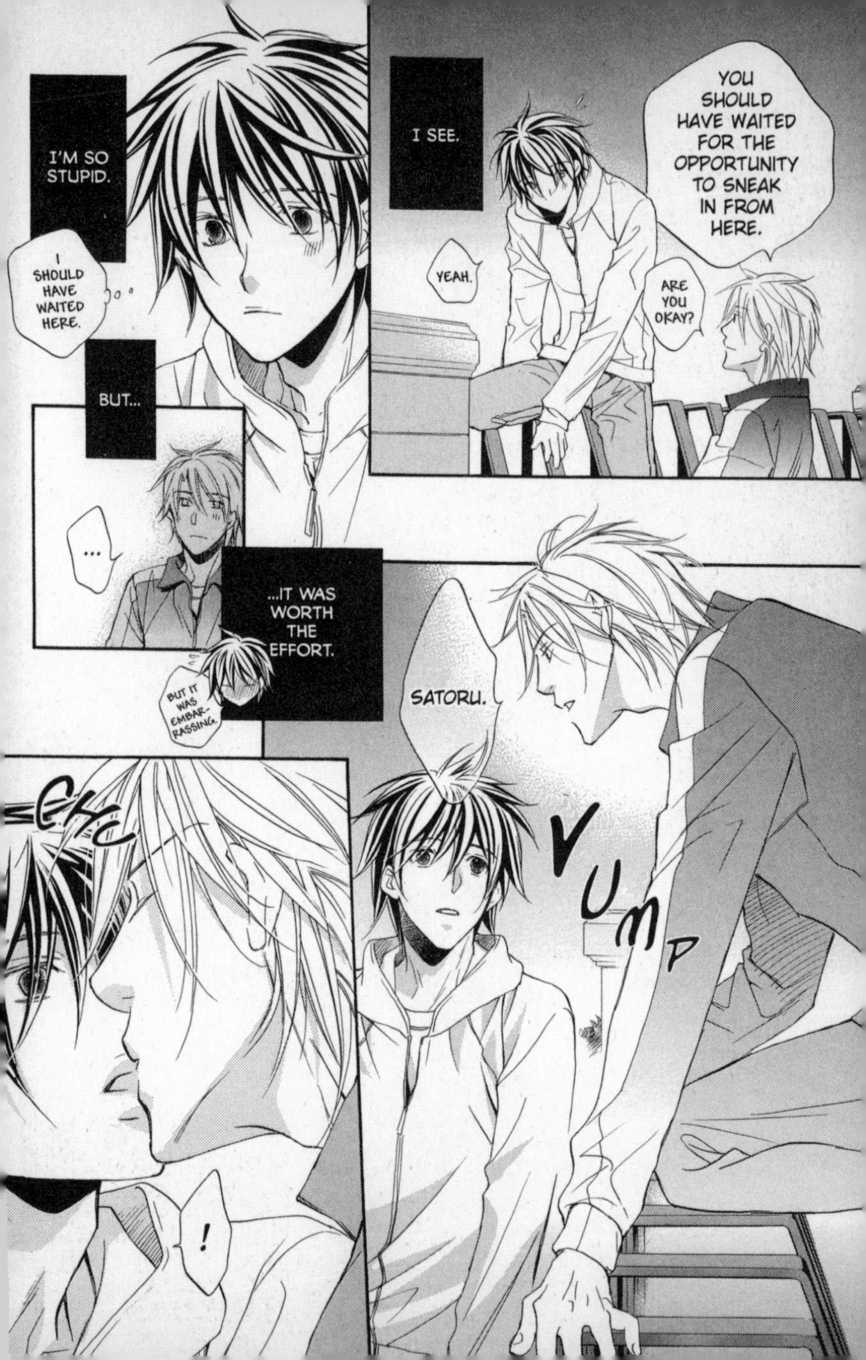

YOU SHOULD HAVE WAITED FOR THE OPPORTUNITY TO SNEAK IN FROM HERE.
ARE YOU OKAY?
YEAH.
I SEE.
I'M SO STUPID.
I SHOULD HAVE WAITED HERE.
BUT...
...IT WAS WORTH THE EFFORT.
...
BUT IT WAS EMBAR-RASSING.
SATORU.
VUMP
EHC
!

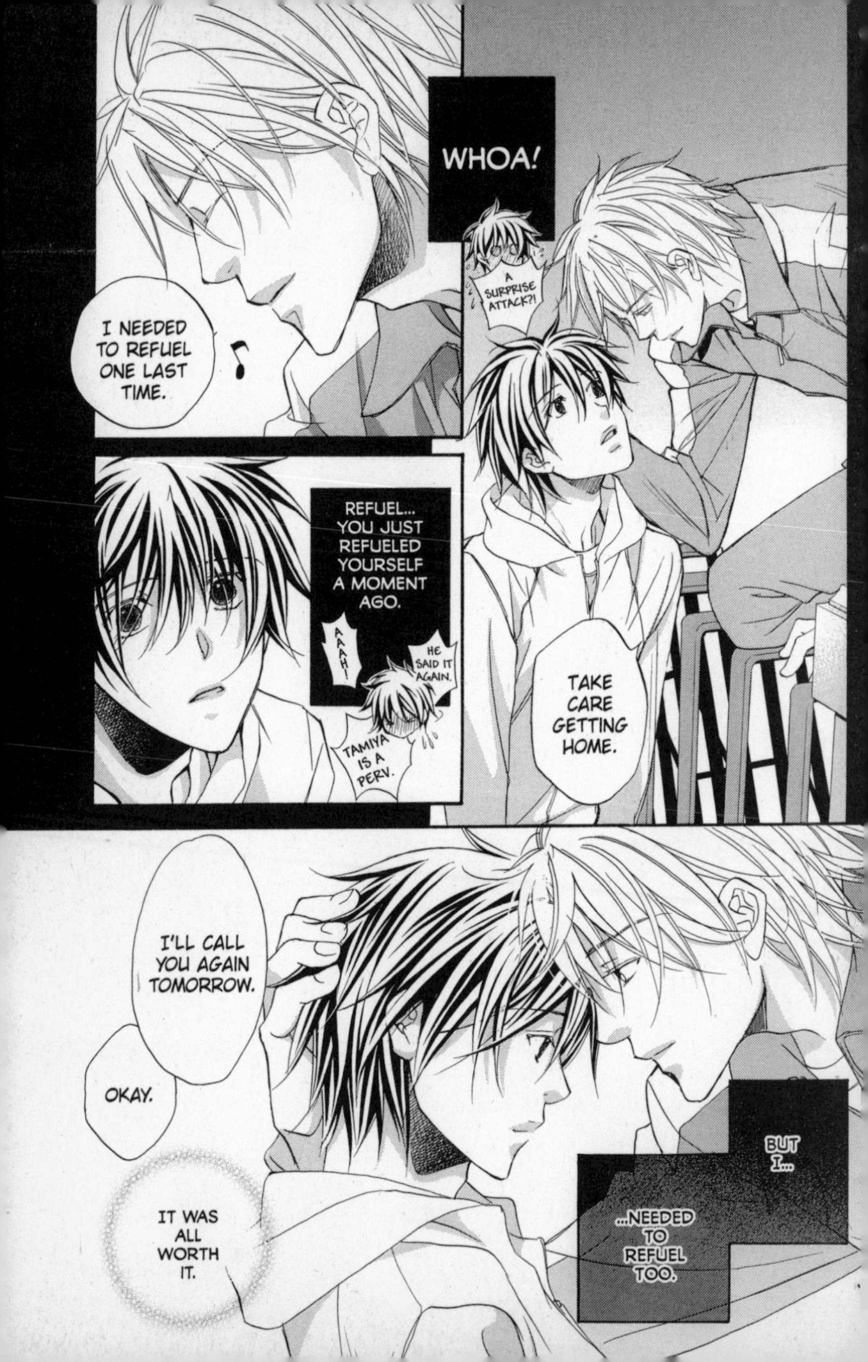
WHOA!
A SURPRISE ATTACK?!
TAKE CARE GETTING HOME.
I NEEDED TO REFUEL ONE LAST TIME.
REFUEL... YOU JUST REFUELED YOURSELF A MOMENT AGO.
HE SAID IT AGAIN.
AAAH!
TAMIYA IS A PERV.
I'LL CALL YOU AGAIN TOMORROW.
OKAY.
IT WAS ALL WORTH IT.
BUT I...
...NEEDED TO REFUEL TOO.

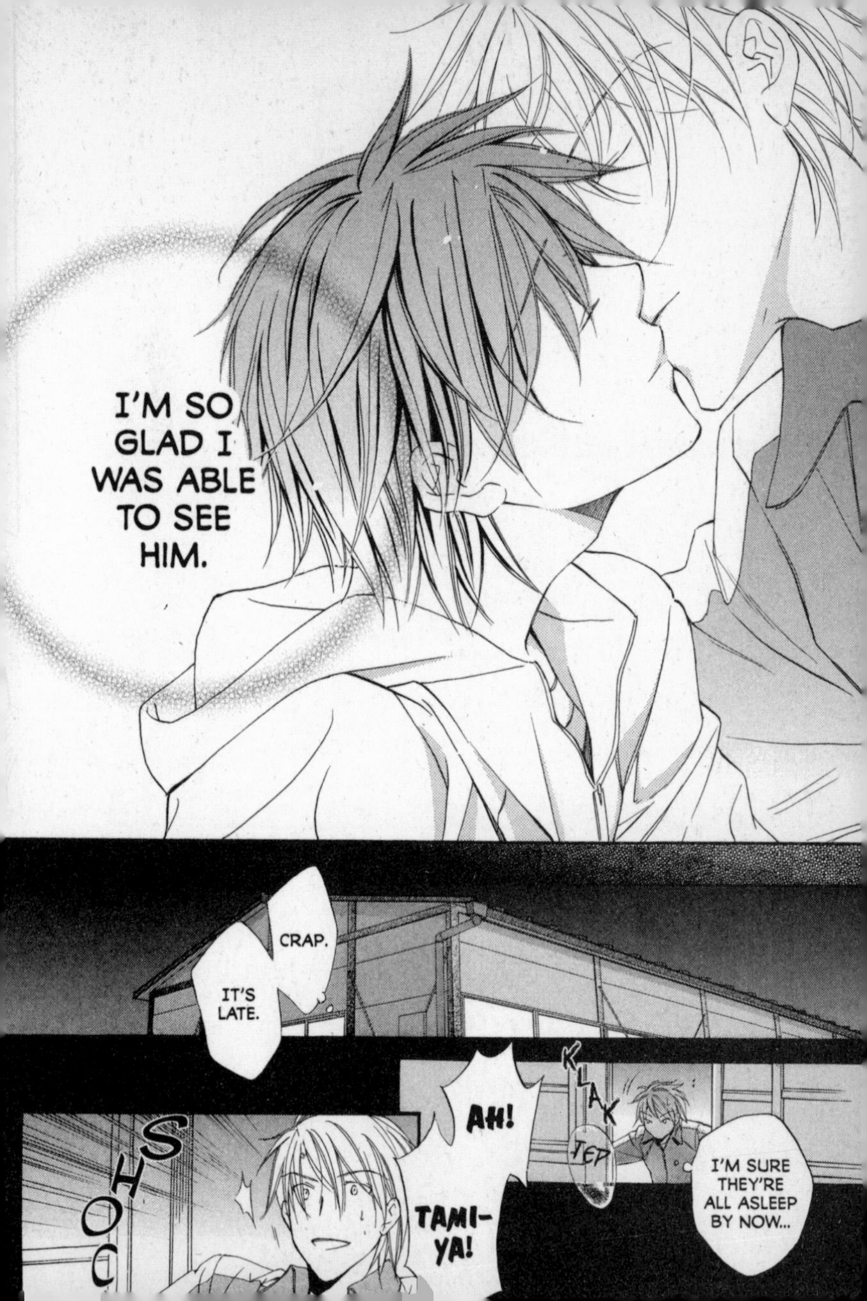
I'M SO GLAD I WAS ABLE TO SEE HIM.
CRAP.
IT'S LATE.
KLAK
I'M SURE THEY'RE ALL ASLEEP BY NOW...
SHOC
AH!
TAMI-YA!

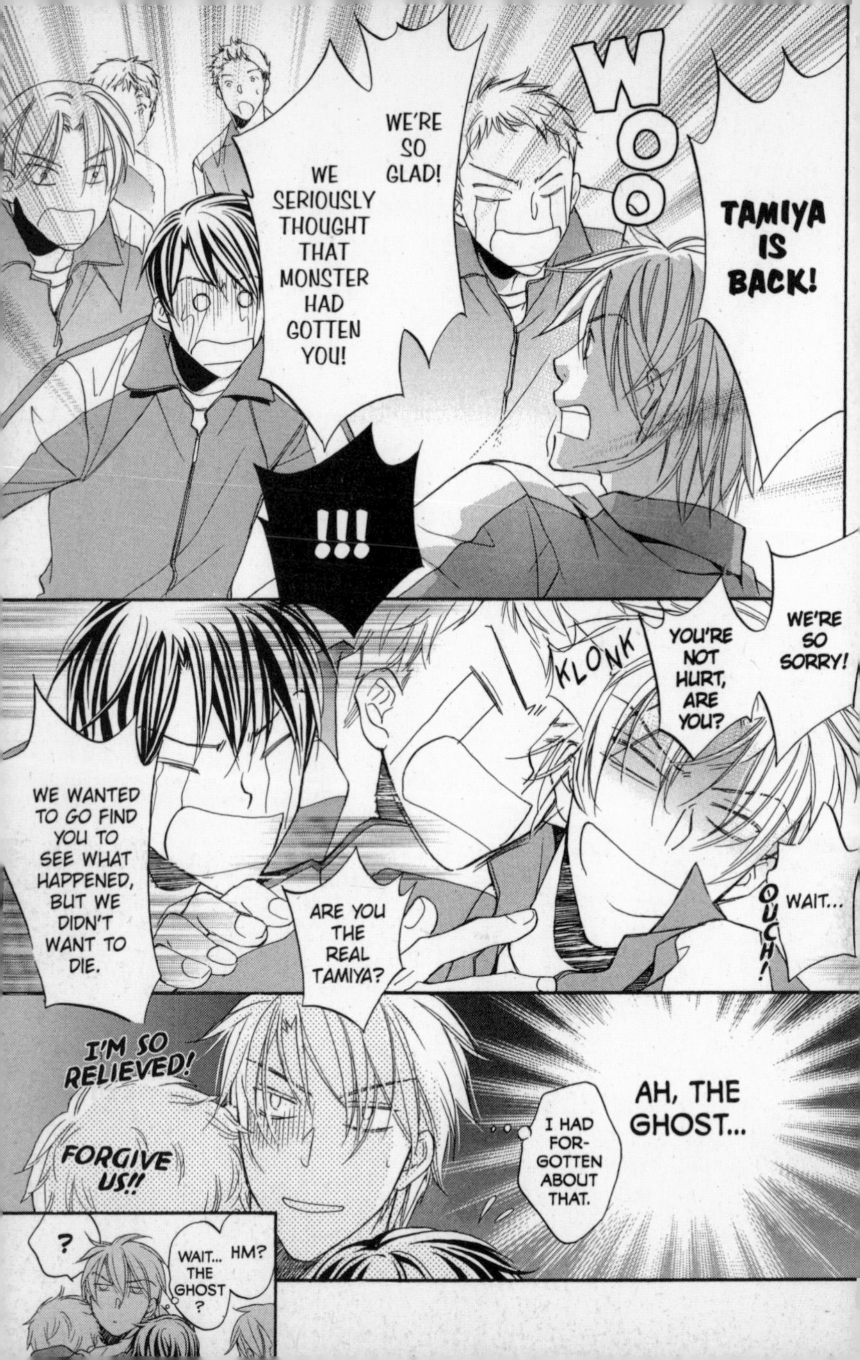
WOO
TAMIYA IS BACK!
WE'RE SO GLAD!
WE SERIOUSLY THOUGHT THAT MONSTER HAD GOTTEN YOU!
!!!
WE'RE SO SORRY!
YOU'RE NOT HURT, ARE YOU?
KLONK
WAIT...
OUCH!
ARE YOU THE REAL TAMIYA?
WE WANTED TO GO FIND YOU TO SEE WHAT HAPPENED, BUT WE DIDN'T WANT TO DIE.
AH, THE GHOST...
I HAD FOR-GOTTEN ABOUT THAT.
I'M SO RELIEVED!
FORGIVE US!!
HM?
WAIT... THE GHOST?
?

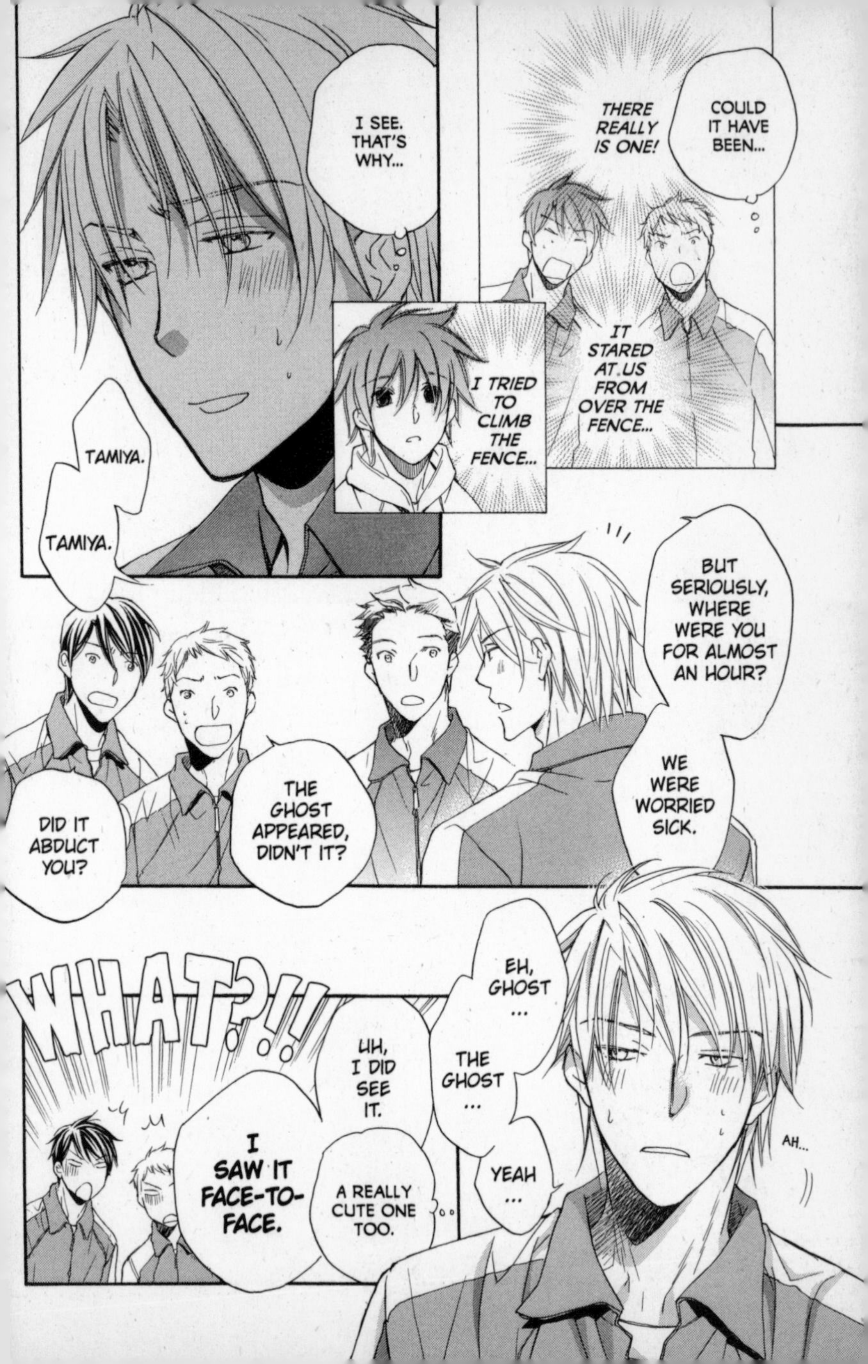
COULD IT HAVE BEEN...
THERE REALLY IS ONE!
IT STARED AT US FROM OVER THE FENCE...
I TRIED TO CLIMB THE FENCE...
I SEE. THAT'S WHY...
TAMIYA.
TAMIYA.
BUT SERIOUSLY, WHERE WERE YOU FOR ALMOST AN HOUR?
WE WERE WORRIED SICK.
THE GHOST APPEARED, DIDN'T IT?
DID IT ABDUCT YOU?
AH...
EH, GHOST ...
THE GHOST ...
YEAH ...
UH, I DID SEE IT.
A REALLY CUTE ONE TOO.
WHAT?!!
I SAW IT FACE-TO-FACE.

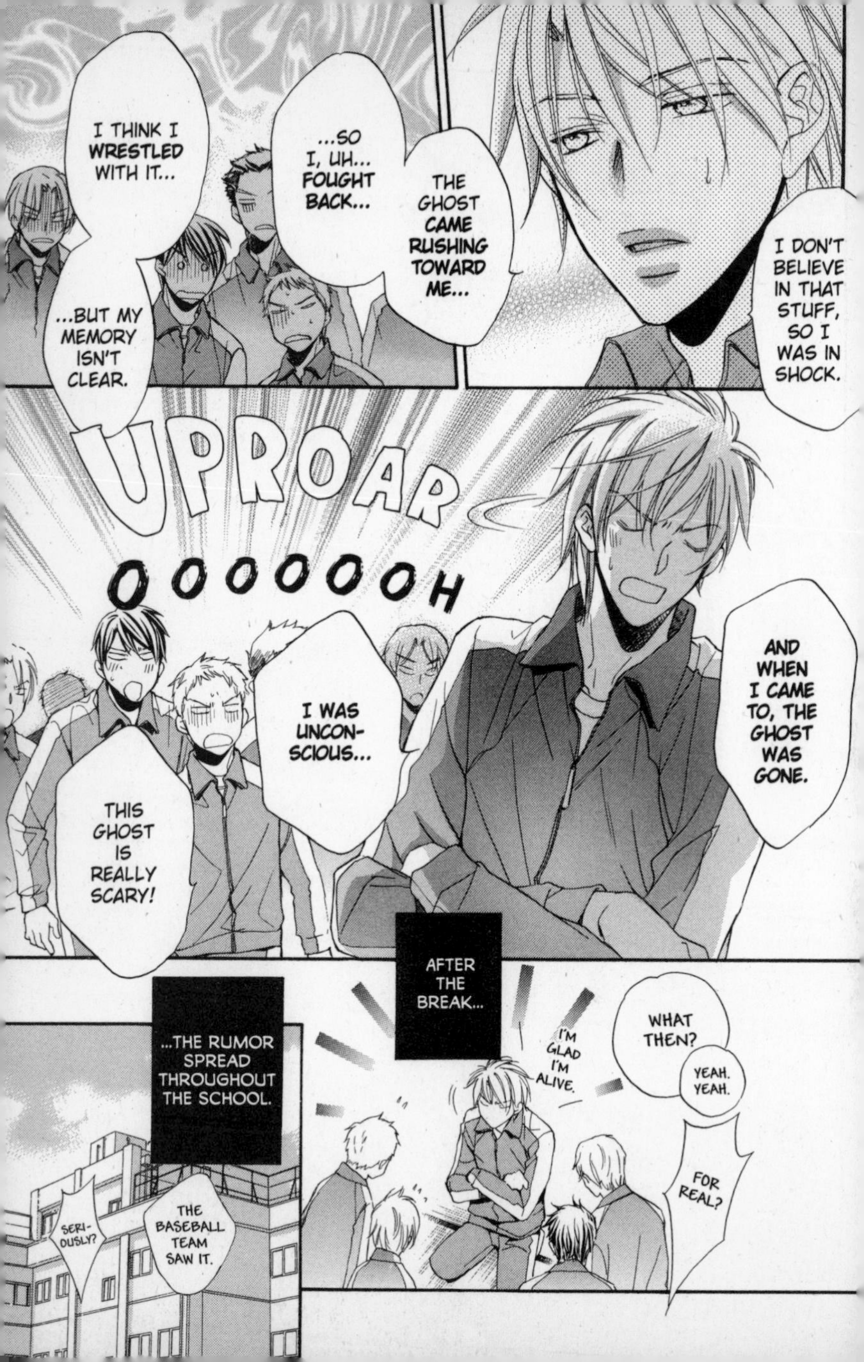
I DON'T BELIEVE IN THAT STUFF, SO I WAS IN SHOCK.
THE GHOST CAME RUSHING TOWARD ME...
...SO I, UH... FOUGHT BACK...
I THINK I WRESTLED WITH IT...
...BUT MY MEMORY ISN'T CLEAR.
AND WHEN I CAME TO, THE GHOST WAS GONE.
UPROAR
OOOOOOH
I WAS UNCON-SCIOUS...
THIS GHOST IS REALLY SCARY!
AFTER THE BREAK...
WHAT THEN?
YEAH. YEAH.
I'M GLAD I'M ALIVE.
FOR REAL?
...THE RUMOR SPREAD THROUGHOUT THE SCHOOL.
THE BASEBALL TEAM SAW IT.
SERI-OUSLY?

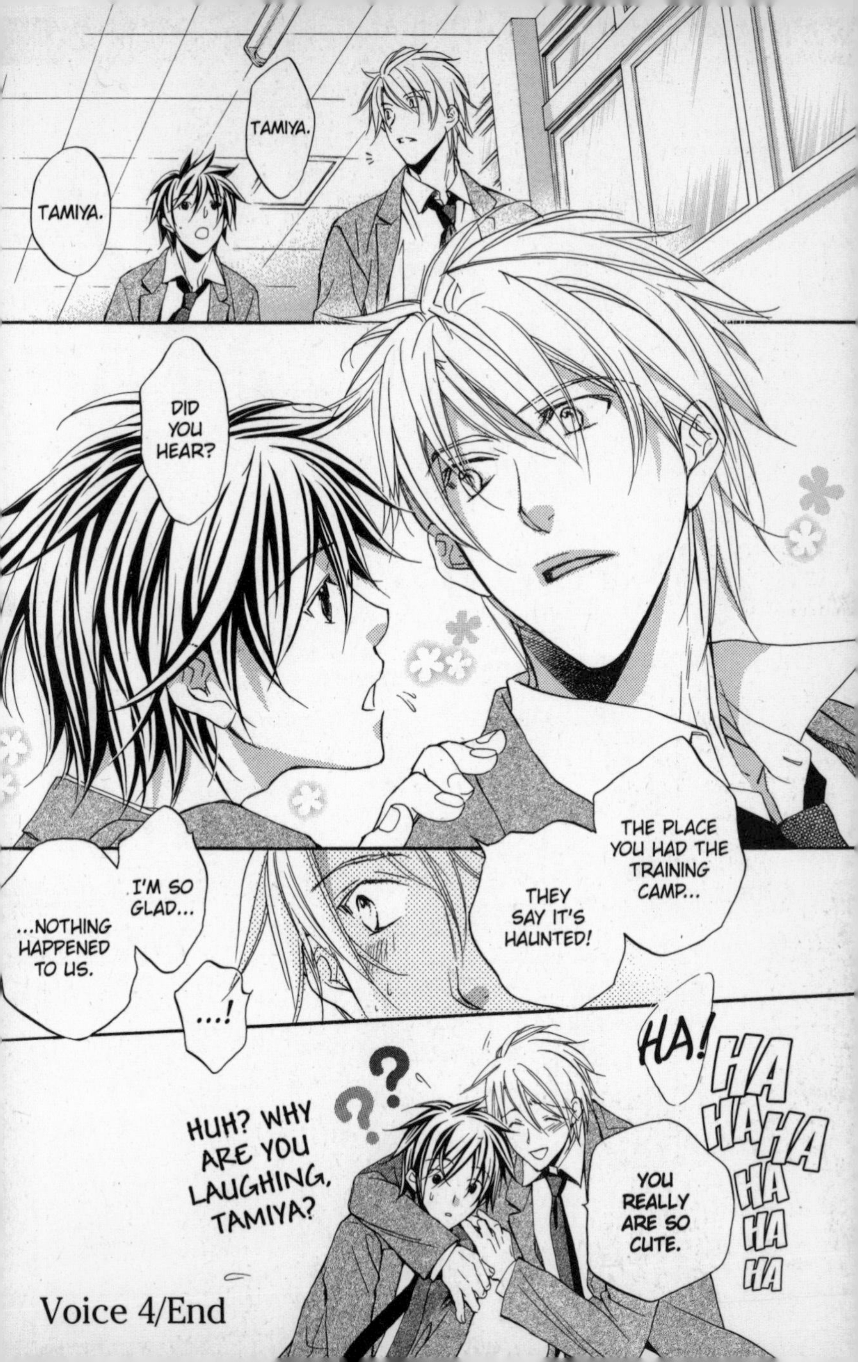
TAMIYA.
TAMIYA.
DID YOU HEAR?
THE PLACE YOU HAD THE TRAINING CAMP...
THEY SAY IT'S HAUNTED!
...!
I'M SO GLAD...
...NOTHING HAPPENED TO US.
HA! HA HA HA HA HA HA
YOU REALLY ARE SO CUTE.
HUH? WHY ARE YOU LAUGHING, TAMIYA?

Voice 4/End

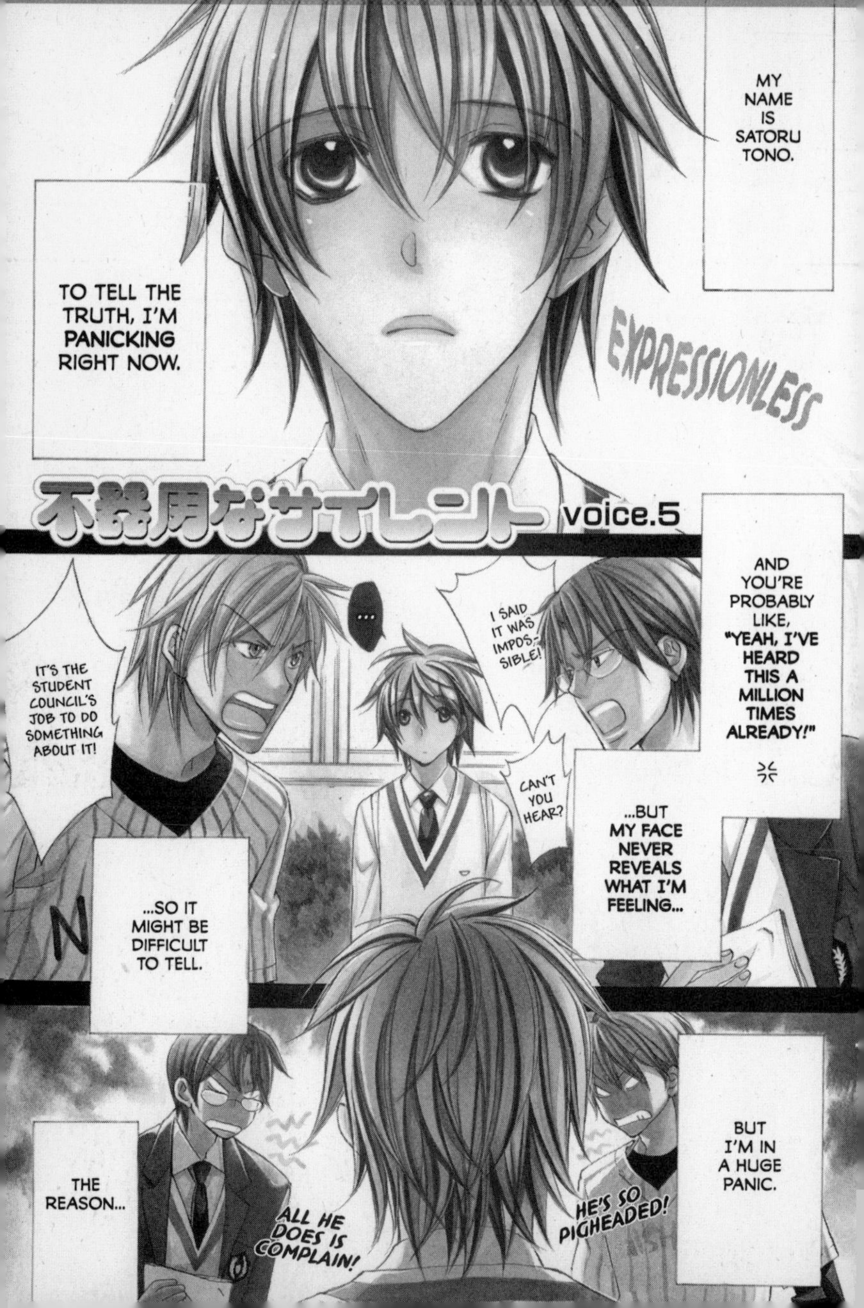
MY NAME IS SATORU TONO.
EXPRESSIONLESS
TO TELL THE TRUTH, I'M PANICKING RIGHT NOW.
不器用なサイレント voice.5
AND YOU'RE PROBABLY LIKE, "YEAH, I'VE HEARD THIS A MILLION TIMES ALREADY!"
...BUT MY FACE NEVER REVEALS WHAT I'M FEELING...
I SAID IT WAS IMPOS-SIBLE!
CAN'T YOU HEAR?
...
IT'S THE STUDENT COUNCIL'S JOB TO DO SOMETHING ABOUT IT!
...SO IT MIGHT BE DIFFICULT TO TELL.
BUT I'M IN A HUGE PANIC.
HE'S SO PIGHEADED!
ALL HE DOES IS COMPLAIN!
THE REASON...

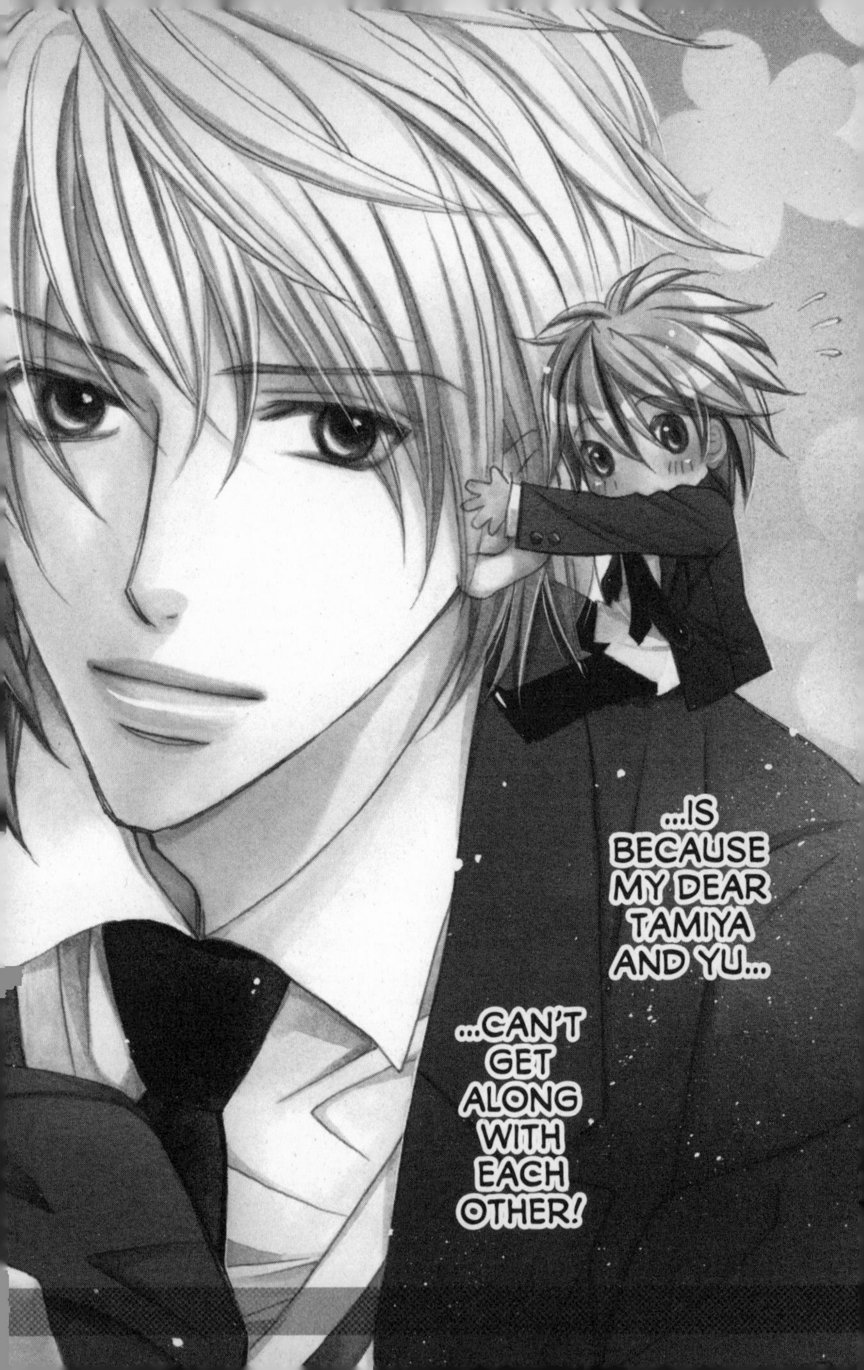
...IS BECAUSE MY DEAR TAMIYA AND YU...
...CAN'T GET ALONG WITH EACH OTHER!

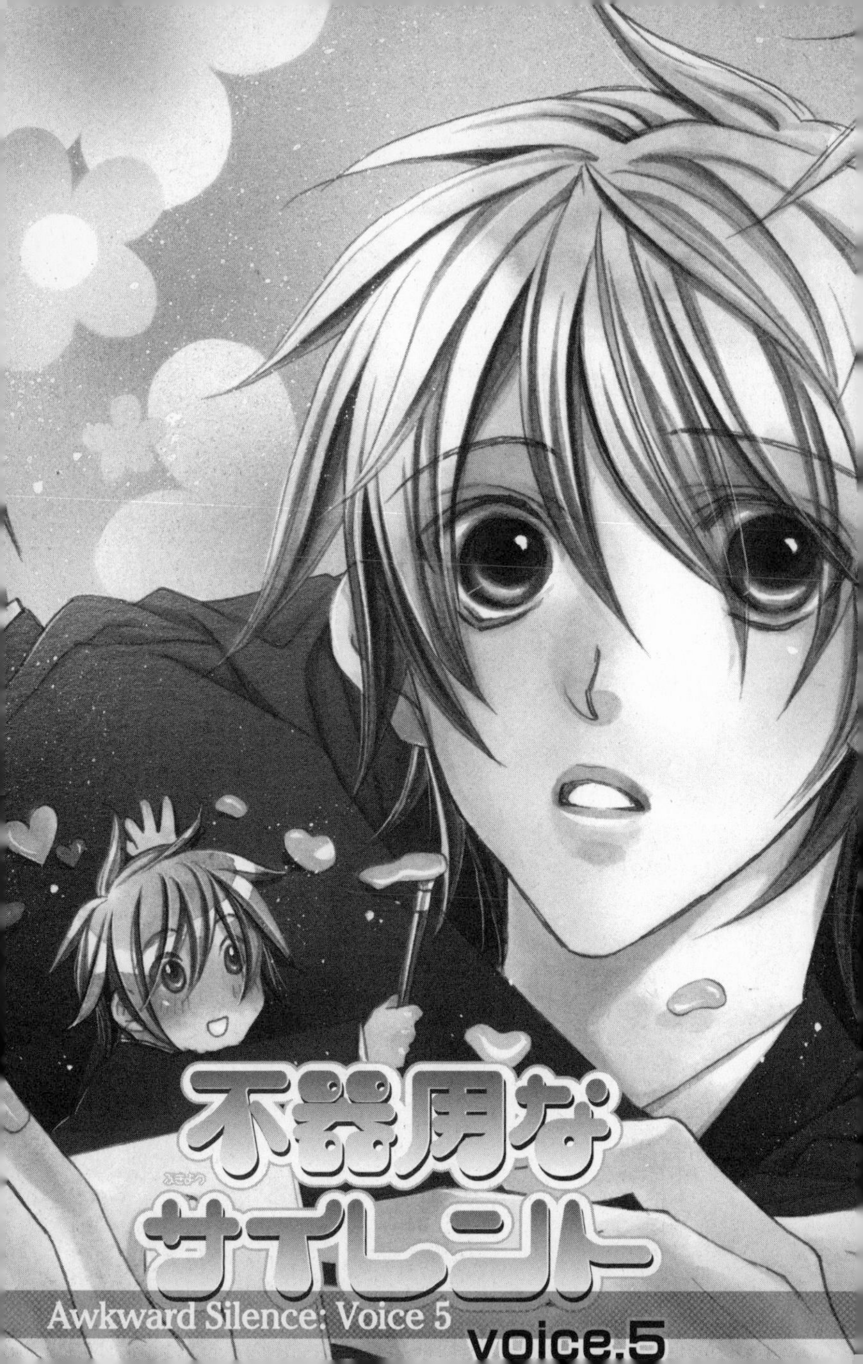
不器用なサイレント
ぶきよう
Awkward Silence: Voice 5
voice.5

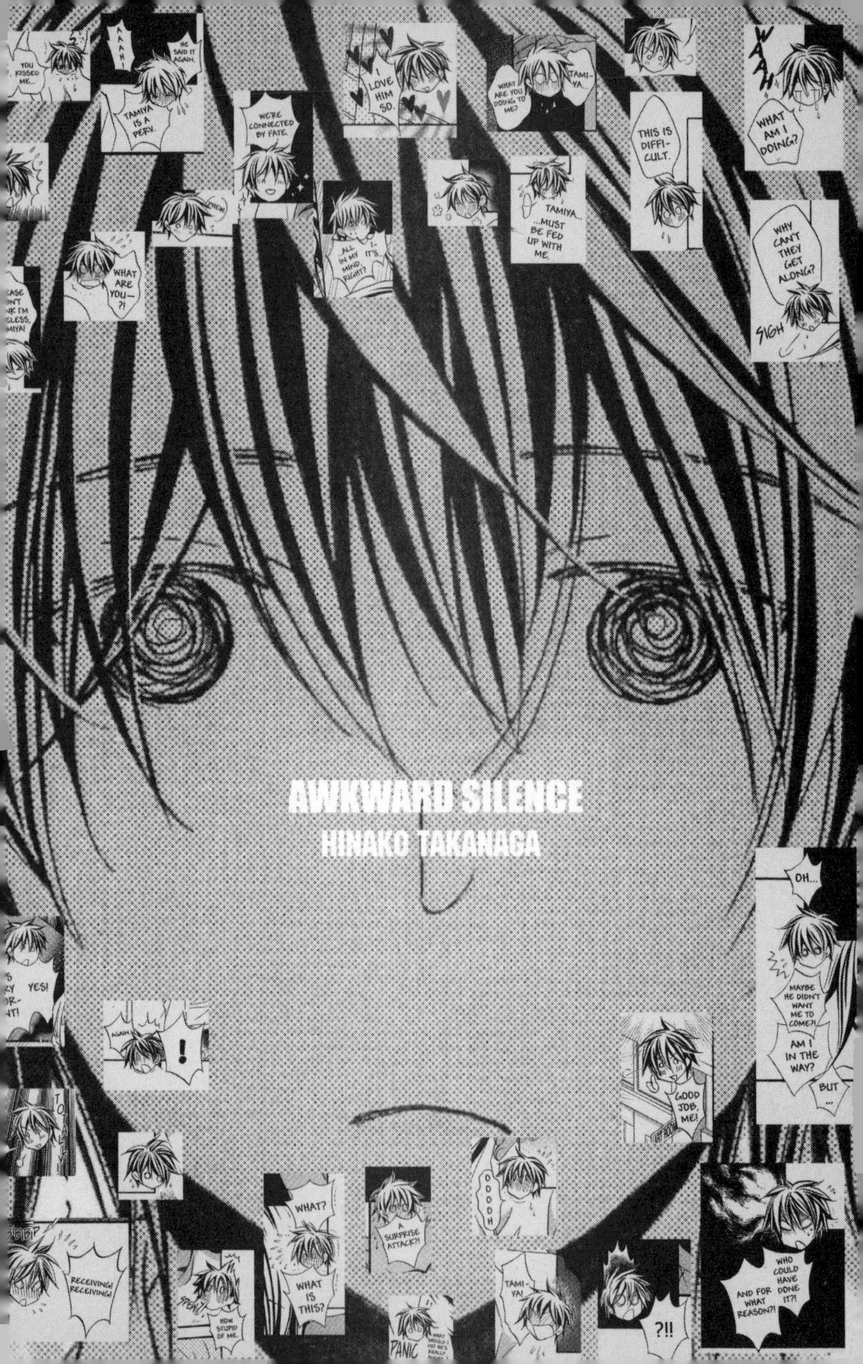
WAAAH
WHAT AM I DOING?
THIS IS DIFFI-CULT.
TAMI-YA...
WHAT ARE YOU DOING TO ME?
I LOVE HIM SO.
HE SAID IT AGAIN.
AAAH!
TAMIYA IS A PERV.
KISSED ME...
WHY CAN'T THEY GET ALONG?
SIGH
TAMIYA...
...MUST BE FED UP WITH ME.
WE'RE CONNECTED BY FATE.
I-IT'S ALL IN MY MIND, RIGHT?
PHEW
WHAT ARE YOU—?!
AWKWARD SILENCE
HINAKO TAKANAGA
OH...
MAYBE HE DIDN'T WANT ME TO COME?!
AM I IN THE WAY?
BUT...
GOOD JOB, ME!
YES!
!
WHO COULD HAVE DONE IT?!
AND FOR WHAT REASON?!
?!!
TAMI-YA!
OOOOH
A SURPRISE ATTACK?!
WHAT?
WHAT IS THIS?
HOW STUPID OF ME.
RECEIVING! RECEIVING!
PANIC

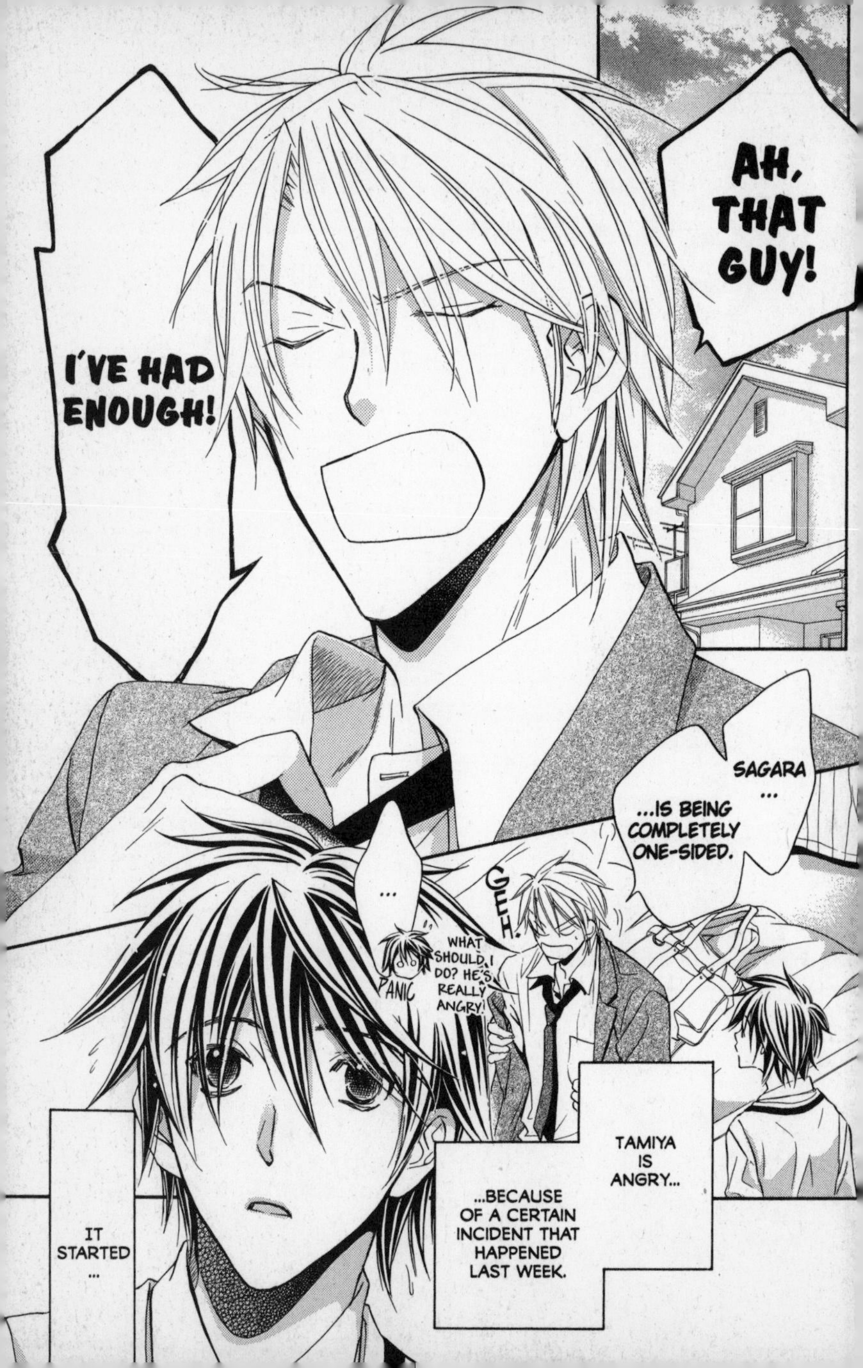
AH, THAT GUY!
I'VE HAD ENOUGH!
SAGARA ...
...IS BEING COMPLETELY ONE-SIDED.
GEH.
...
WHAT SHOULD I DO? HE'S REALLY ANGRY!
PANIC
TAMIYA IS ANGRY...
...BECAUSE OF A CERTAIN INCIDENT THAT HAPPENED LAST WEEK.
IT STARTED ...

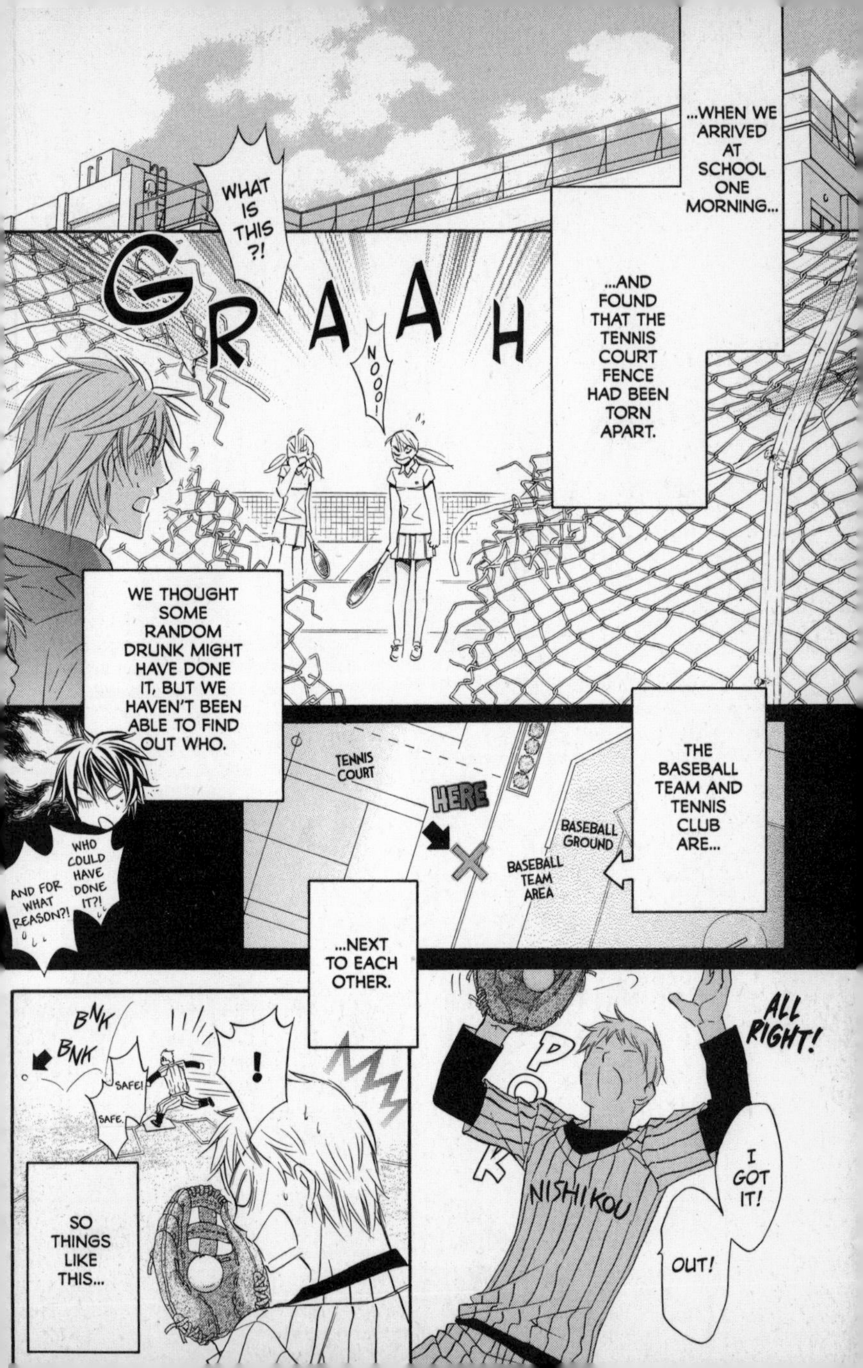
...WHEN WE ARRIVED AT SCHOOL ONE MORNING...
...AND FOUND THAT THE TENNIS COURT FENCE HAD BEEN TORN APART.
WHAT IS THIS ?!
GRAAH
NOOOO!
WE THOUGHT SOME RANDOM DRUNK MIGHT HAVE DONE IT, BUT WE HAVEN'T BEEN ABLE TO FIND OUT WHO.
THE BASEBALL TEAM AND TENNIS CLUB ARE...
BASEBALL GROUND
BASEBALL TEAM AREA
HERE
TENNIS COURT
...NEXT TO EACH OTHER.
WHO COULD HAVE DONE IT?!
AND FOR WHAT REASON?!
ALL RIGHT!
POK
I GOT IT!
OUT!
NISHIKOU
!
SAFE!
SAFE.
BNK
BNK
SO THINGS LIKE THIS...

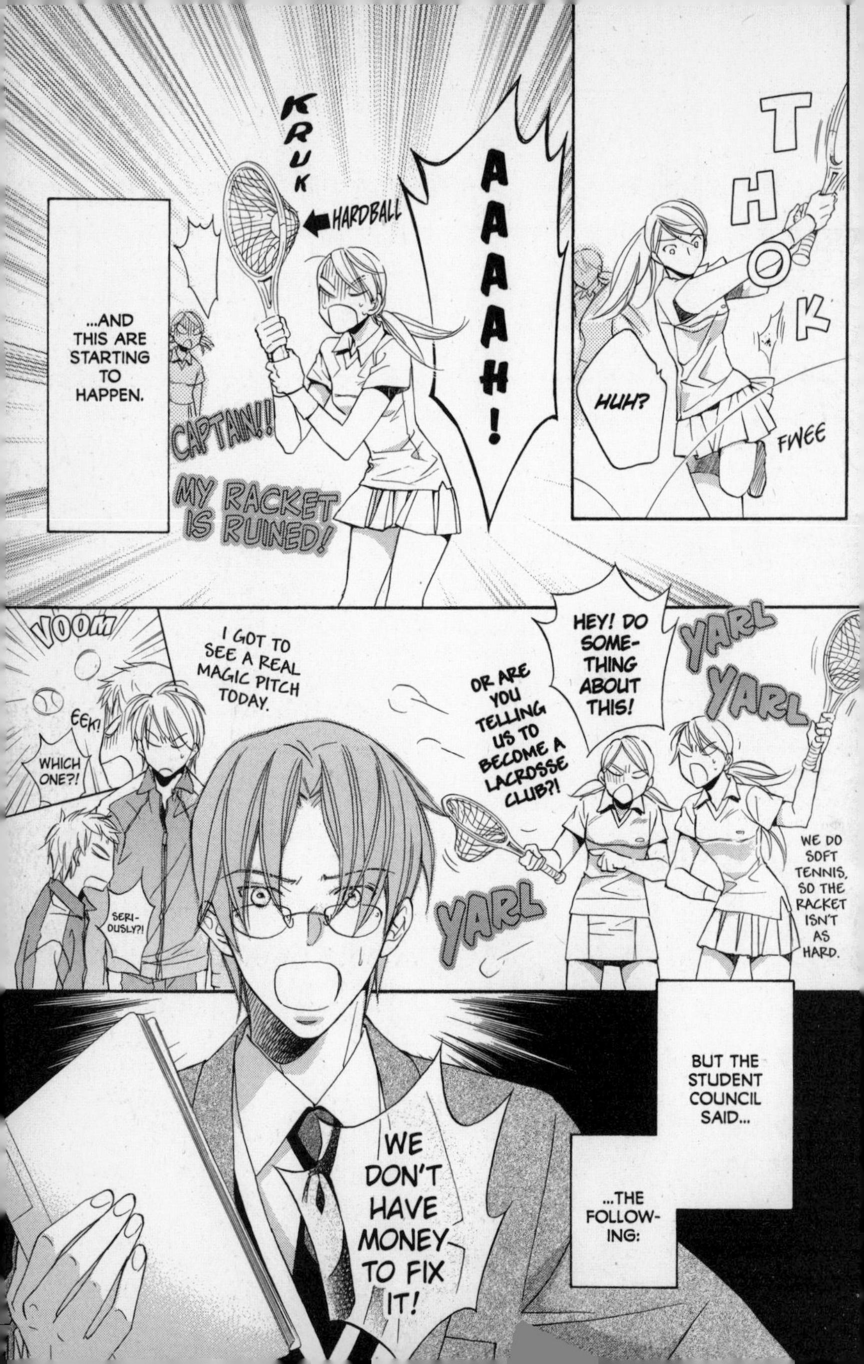
THOK
HUH?
FWEE
KRUK
HARDBALL
AAAAH!
CAPTAIN!!
MY RACKET IS RUINED!
...AND THIS ARE STARTING TO HAPPEN.
WE DO SOFT TENNIS, SO THE RACKET ISN'T AS HARD.
YARL YARL
HEY! DO SOME-THING ABOUT THIS!
OR ARE YOU TELLING US TO BECOME A LACROSSE CLUB?!
YARL
I GOT TO SEE A REAL MAGIC PITCH TODAY.
VOOM
EEK!
WHICH ONE?!
SERI-OUSLY?!
BUT THE STUDENT COUNCIL SAID...
...THE FOLLOW-ING:
WE DON'T HAVE MONEY TO FIX IT!

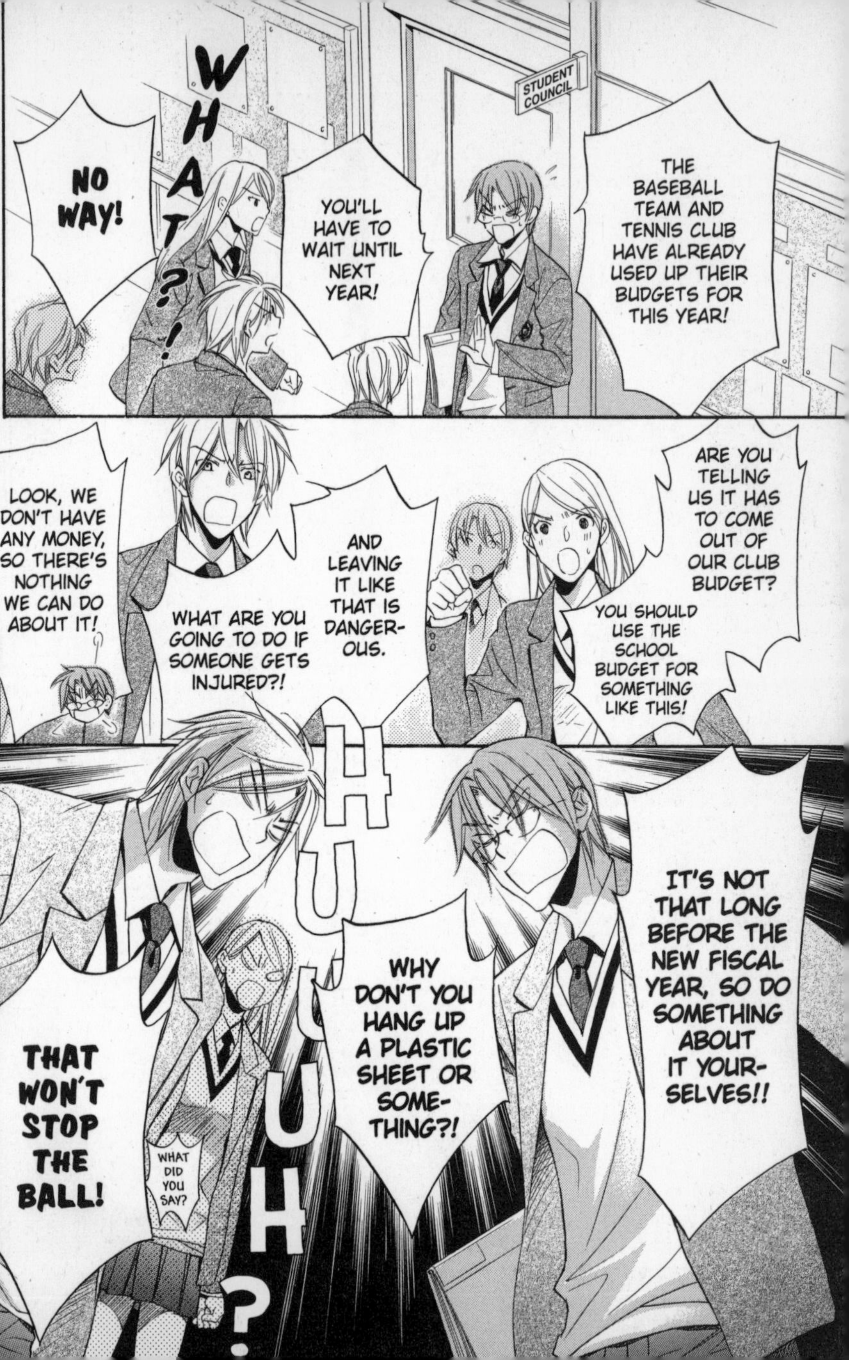
STUDENT COUNCIL
THE BASEBALL TEAM AND TENNIS CLUB HAVE ALREADY USED UP THEIR BUDGETS FOR THIS YEAR!
YOU'LL HAVE TO WAIT UNTIL NEXT YEAR!
WHAT?!
NO WAY!
ARE YOU TELLING US IT HAS TO COME OUT OF OUR CLUB BUDGET?
YOU SHOULD USE THE SCHOOL BUDGET FOR SOMETHING LIKE THIS!
AND LEAVING IT LIKE THAT IS DANGER-OUS.
WHAT ARE YOU GOING TO DO IF SOMEONE GETS INJURED?!
LOOK, WE DON'T HAVE ANY MONEY, SO THERE'S NOTHING WE CAN DO ABOUT IT!
IT'S NOT THAT LONG BEFORE THE NEW FISCAL YEAR, SO DO SOMETHING ABOUT IT YOUR-SELVES!!
HUUUH?
WHY DON'T YOU HANG UP A PLASTIC SHEET OR SOME-THING?!
WHAT DID YOU SAY?
THAT WON'T STOP THE BALL!

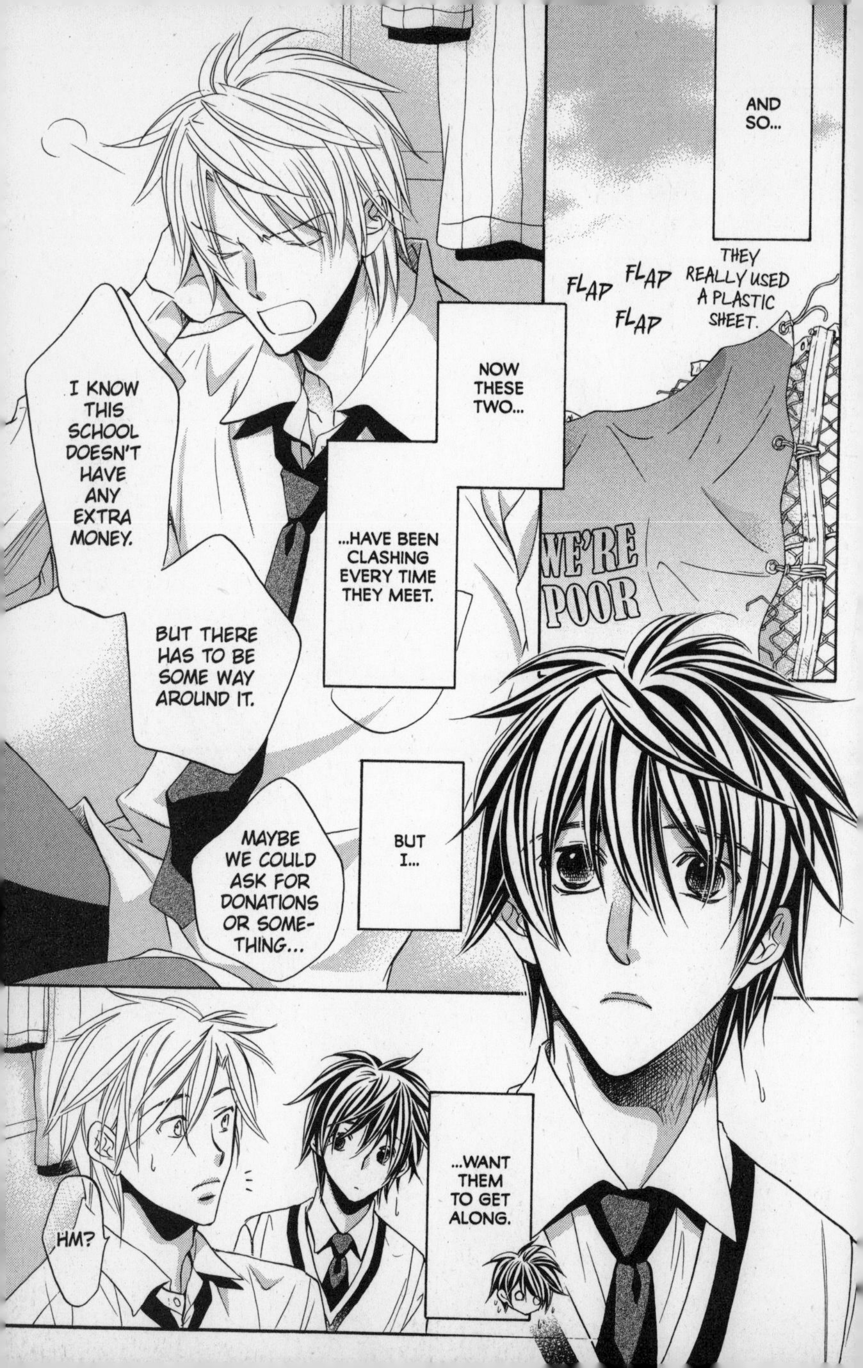
AND SO...
THEY REALLY USED A PLASTIC SHEET.
FLAP FLAP FLAP
WE'RE POOR
NOW THESE TWO...
...HAVE BEEN CLASHING EVERY TIME THEY MEET.
I KNOW THIS SCHOOL DOESN'T HAVE ANY EXTRA MONEY.
BUT THERE HAS TO BE SOME WAY AROUND IT.
BUT I...
MAYBE WE COULD ASK FOR DONATIONS OR SOME-THING...
...WANT THEM TO GET ALONG.
HM?

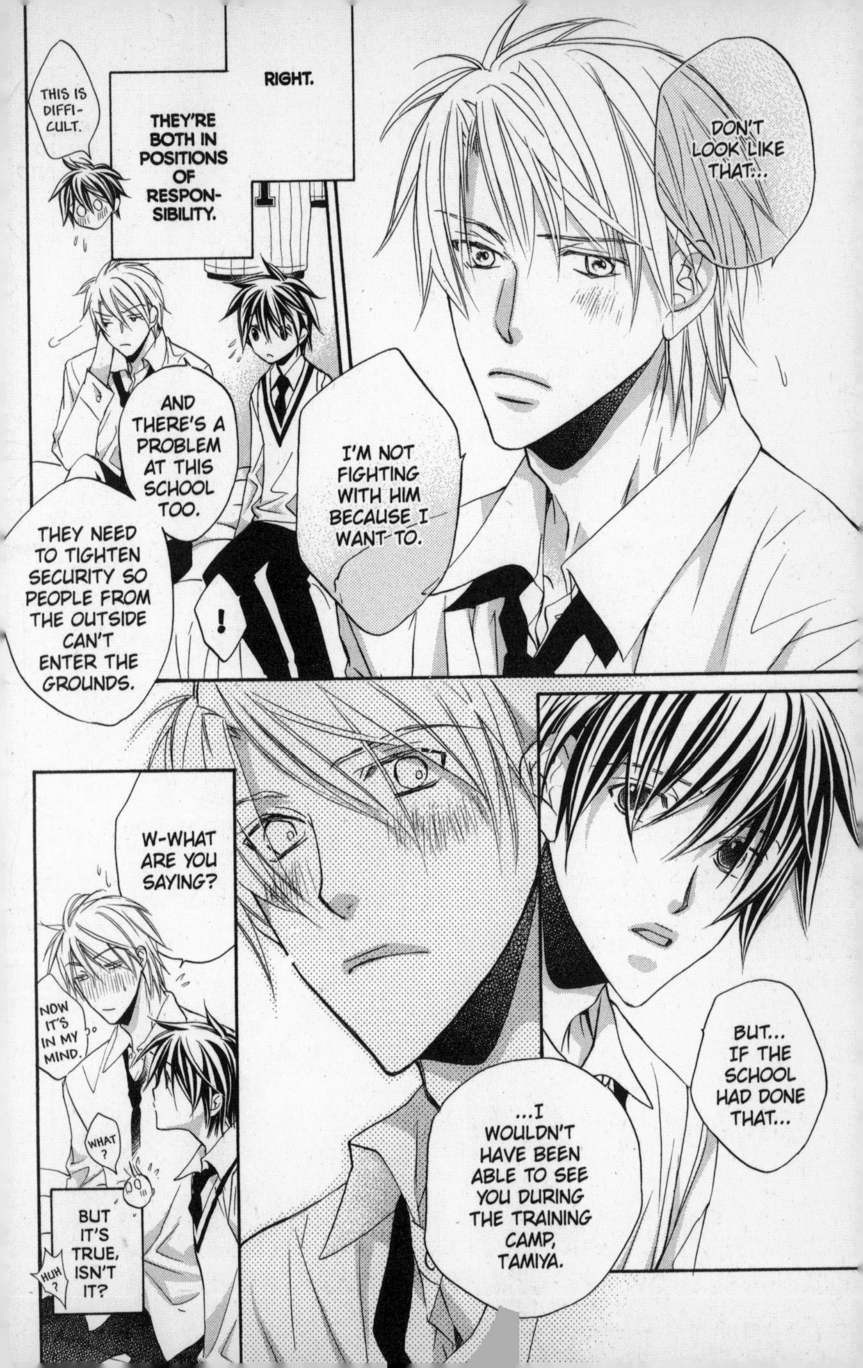

DON'T LOOK LIKE THAT...
I'M NOT FIGHTING WITH HIM BECAUSE I WANT TO.
RIGHT.
THEY'RE BOTH IN POSITIONS OF RESPONSIBILITY.
THIS IS DIFFICULT.
AND THERE'S A PROBLEM AT THIS SCHOOL TOO.
THEY NEED TO TIGHTEN SECURITY SO PEOPLE FROM THE OUTSIDE CAN'T ENTER THE GROUNDS.
!
BUT... IF THE SCHOOL HAD DONE THAT...
...I WOULDN'T HAVE BEEN ABLE TO SEE YOU DURING THE TRAINING CAMP, TAMIYA.
W-WHAT ARE YOU SAYING?
NOW IT'S IN MY MIND.
WHAT?
BUT IT'S TRUE, ISN'T IT?
HUH?

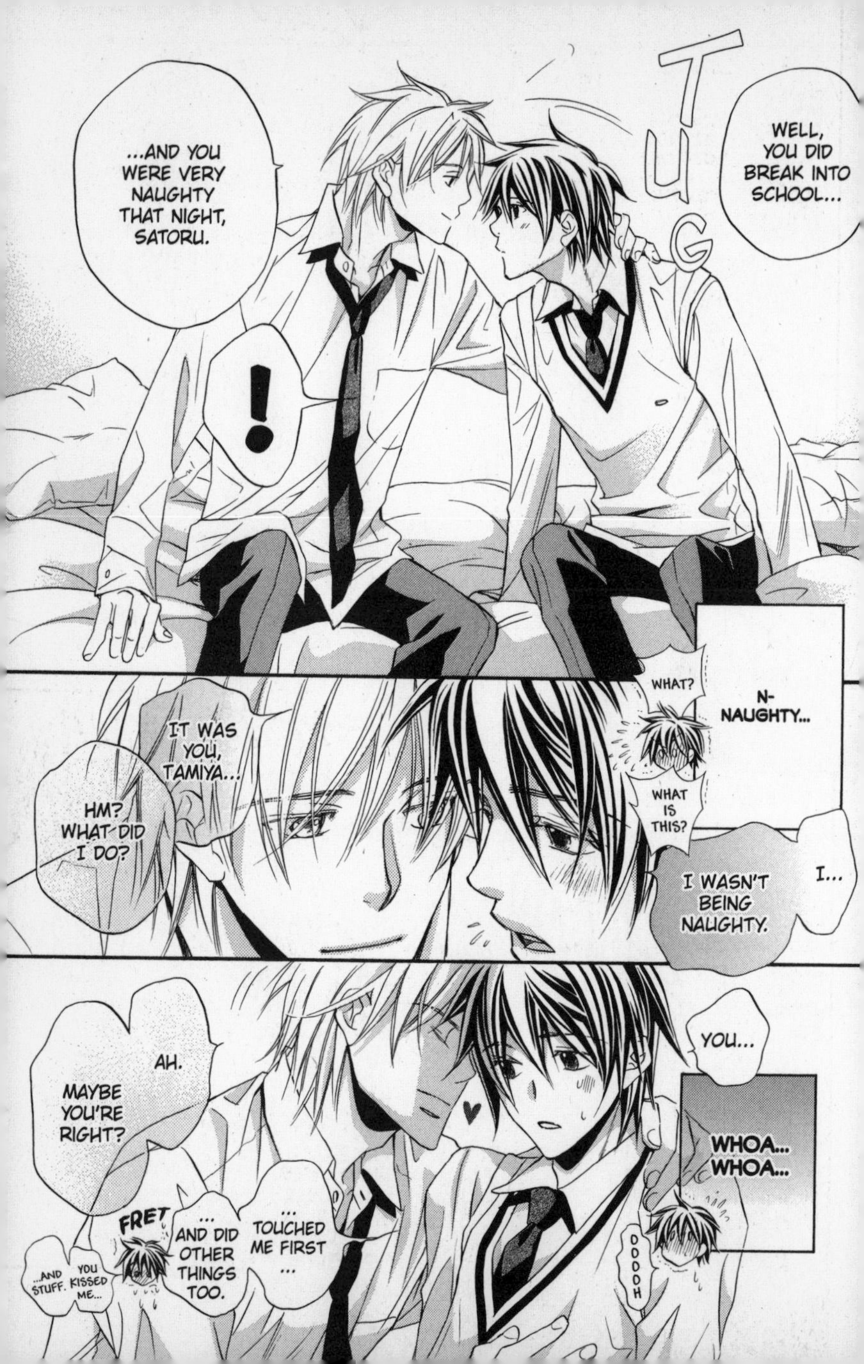
WELL, YOU DID BREAK INTO SCHOOL...
TUG
...AND YOU WERE VERY NAUGHTY THAT NIGHT, SATORU.
!
N-NAUGHTY...
WHAT?
WHAT IS THIS?
I...
I WASN'T BEING NAUGHTY.
IT WAS YOU, TAMIYA...
HM? WHAT DID I DO?
YOU...
WHOA... WHOA...
DDDDDH
AH.
MAYBE YOU'RE RIGHT?
...TOUCHED ME FIRST...
...AND DID OTHER THINGS TOO.
FRET
YOU KISSED ME...
...AND STUFF.

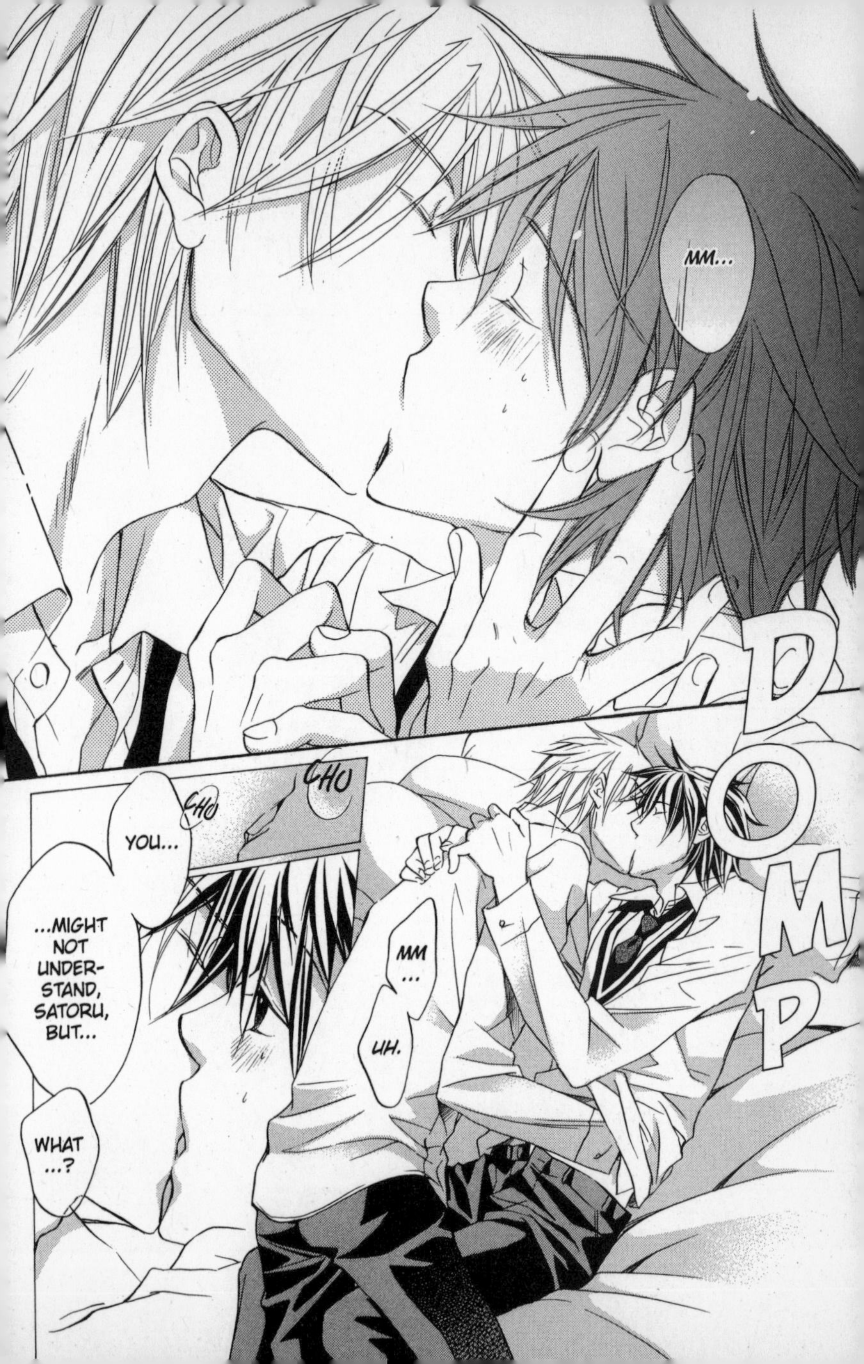
MM...
DOMP
CHU
CHU
YOU...
MM...
UH.
...MIGHT NOT UNDERSTAND, SATORU, BUT...
WHAT...?

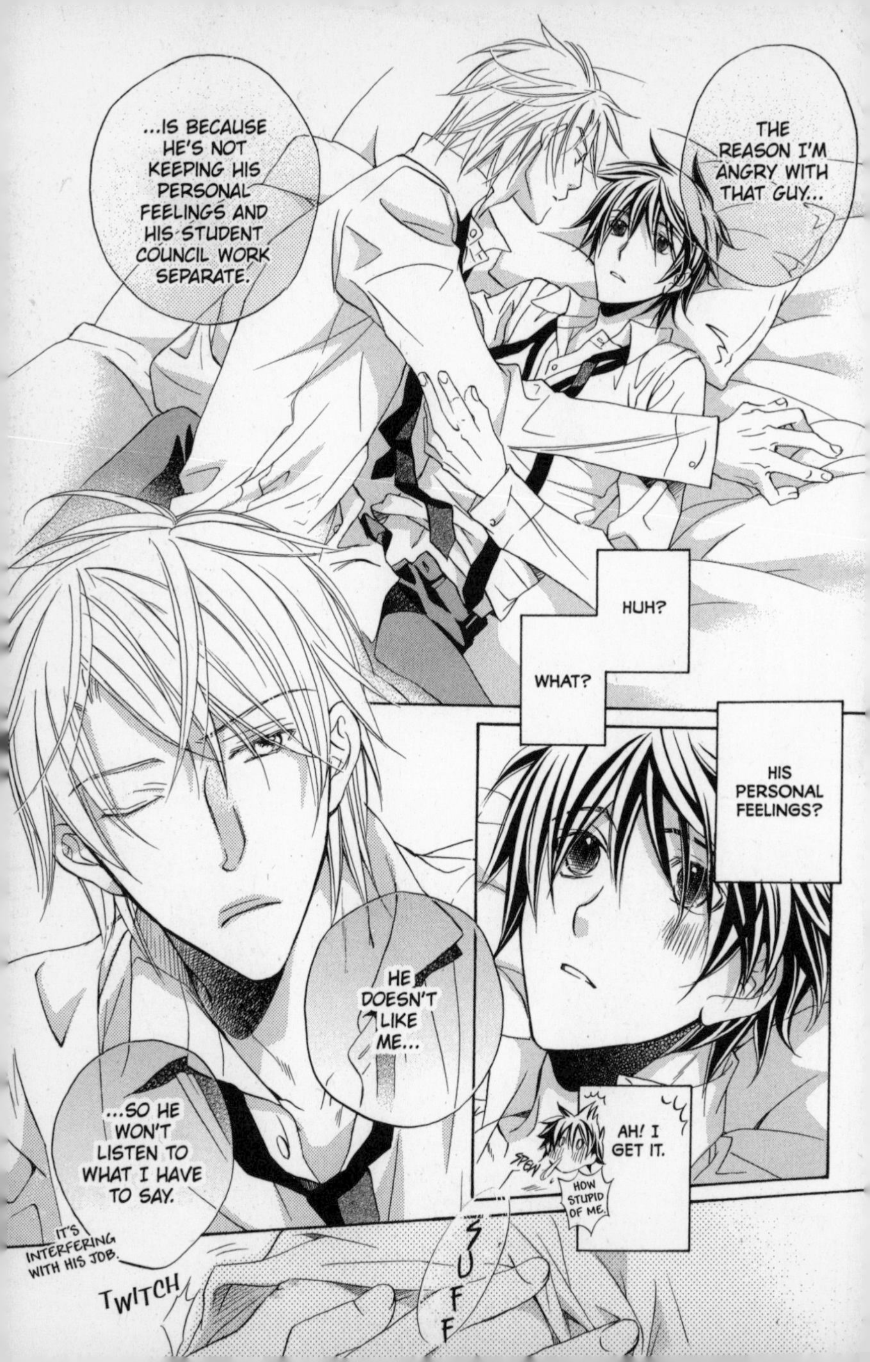
THE REASON I'M ANGRY WITH THAT GUY...
...IS BECAUSE HE'S NOT KEEPING HIS PERSONAL FEELINGS AND HIS STUDENT COUNCIL WORK SEPARATE.
HUH?
WHAT?
HIS PERSONAL FEELINGS?
AH! I GET IT.
SPEW
HOW STUPID OF ME.
HE DOESN'T LIKE ME...
...SO HE WON'T LISTEN TO WHAT I HAVE TO SAY.
IT'S INTERFERING WITH HIS JOB.
TWITCH
SUFF

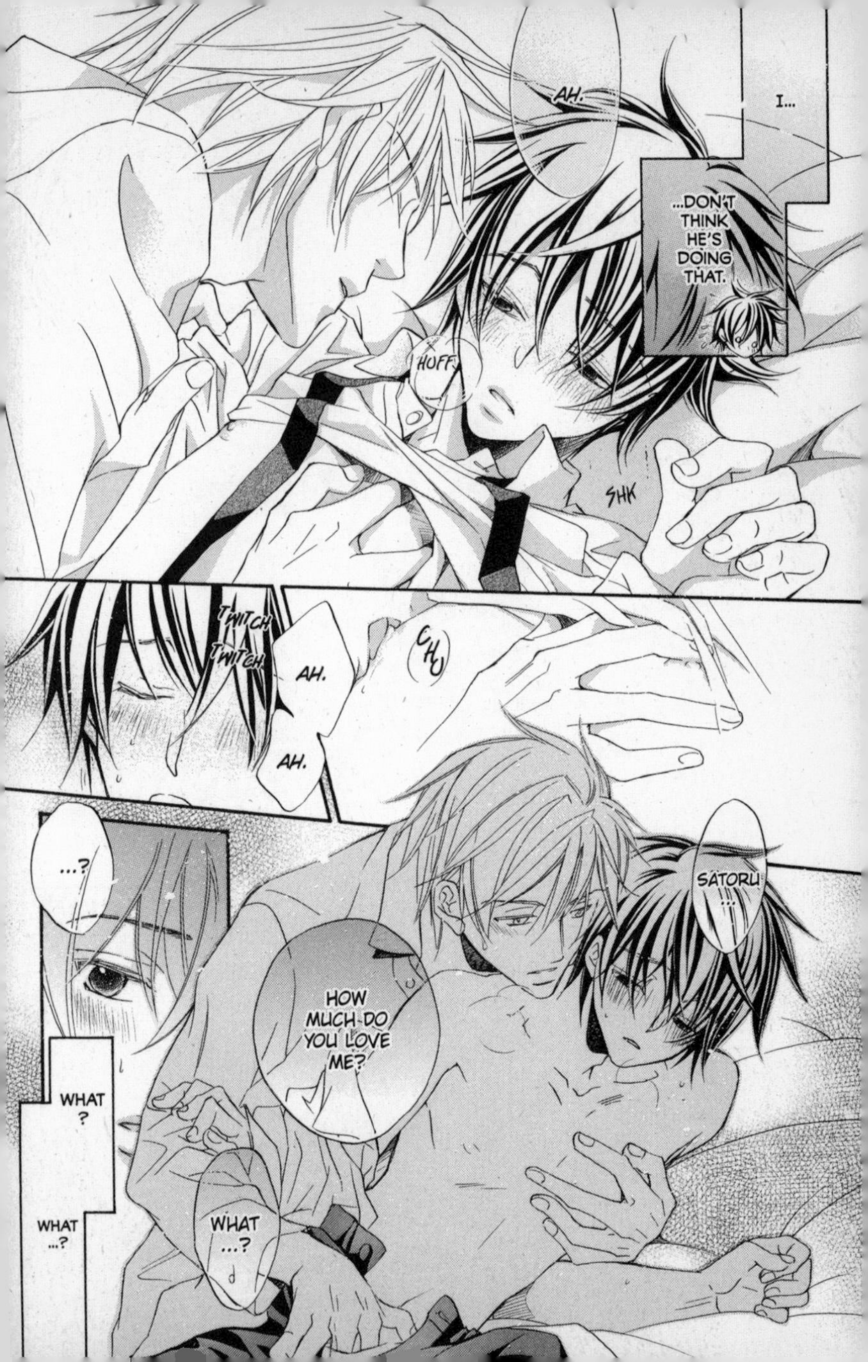
I...
...DON'T THINK HE'S DOING THAT.
AH.
SHK
HUFF
CHU
TWITCH
TWITCH
AH.
AH.
SATORU ...
HOW MUCH DO YOU LOVE ME?
WHAT ...?
...?
WHAT ?
WHAT ...?

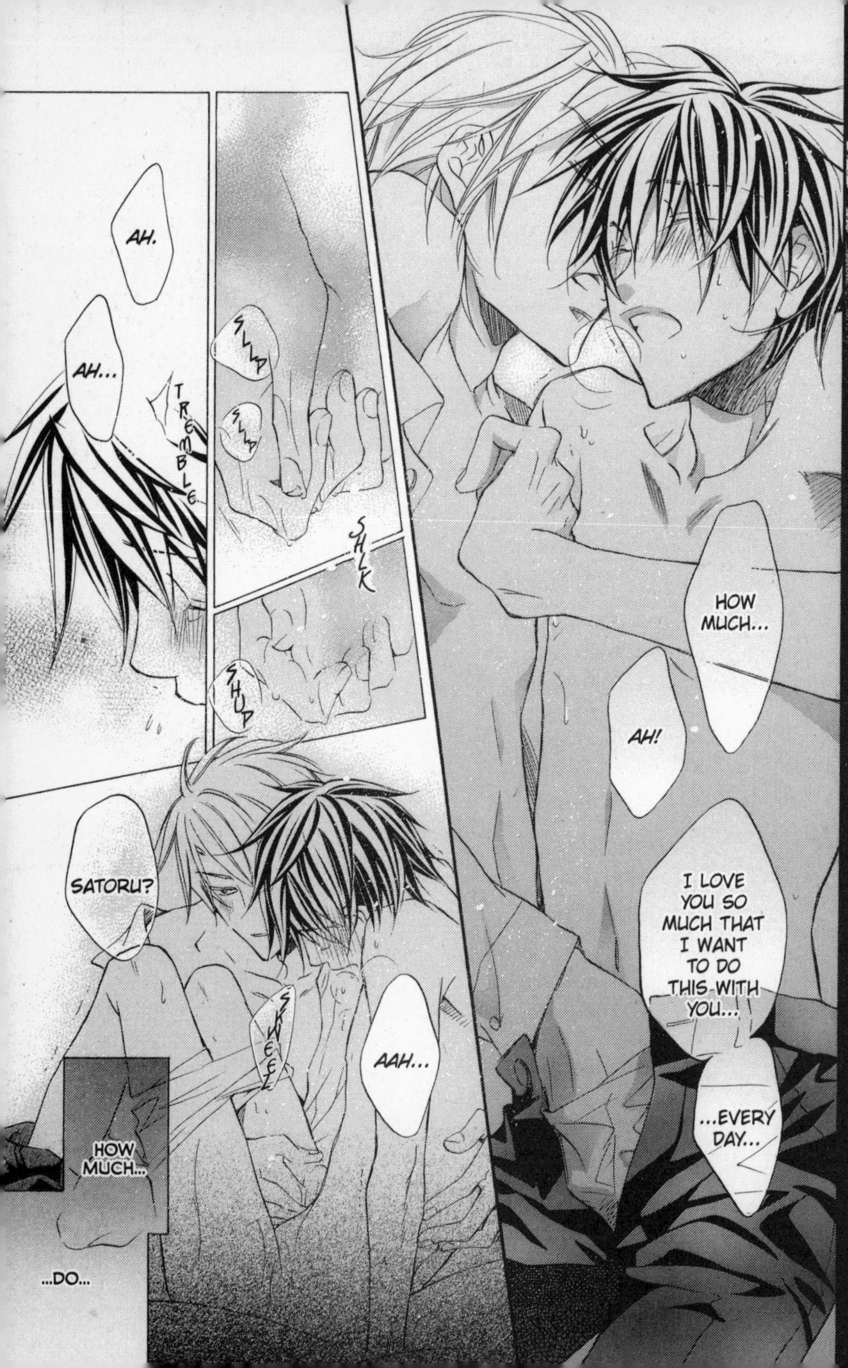
HOW MUCH...
AH!
I LOVE YOU SO MUCH THAT I WANT TO DO THIS WITH YOU...
...EVERY DAY...
SLLP
SLLP
SHLK
SHLP
AH.
AH...
TREMBLE
SATORU?
SKWEEZ
AAH...
HOW MUCH...
...DO...

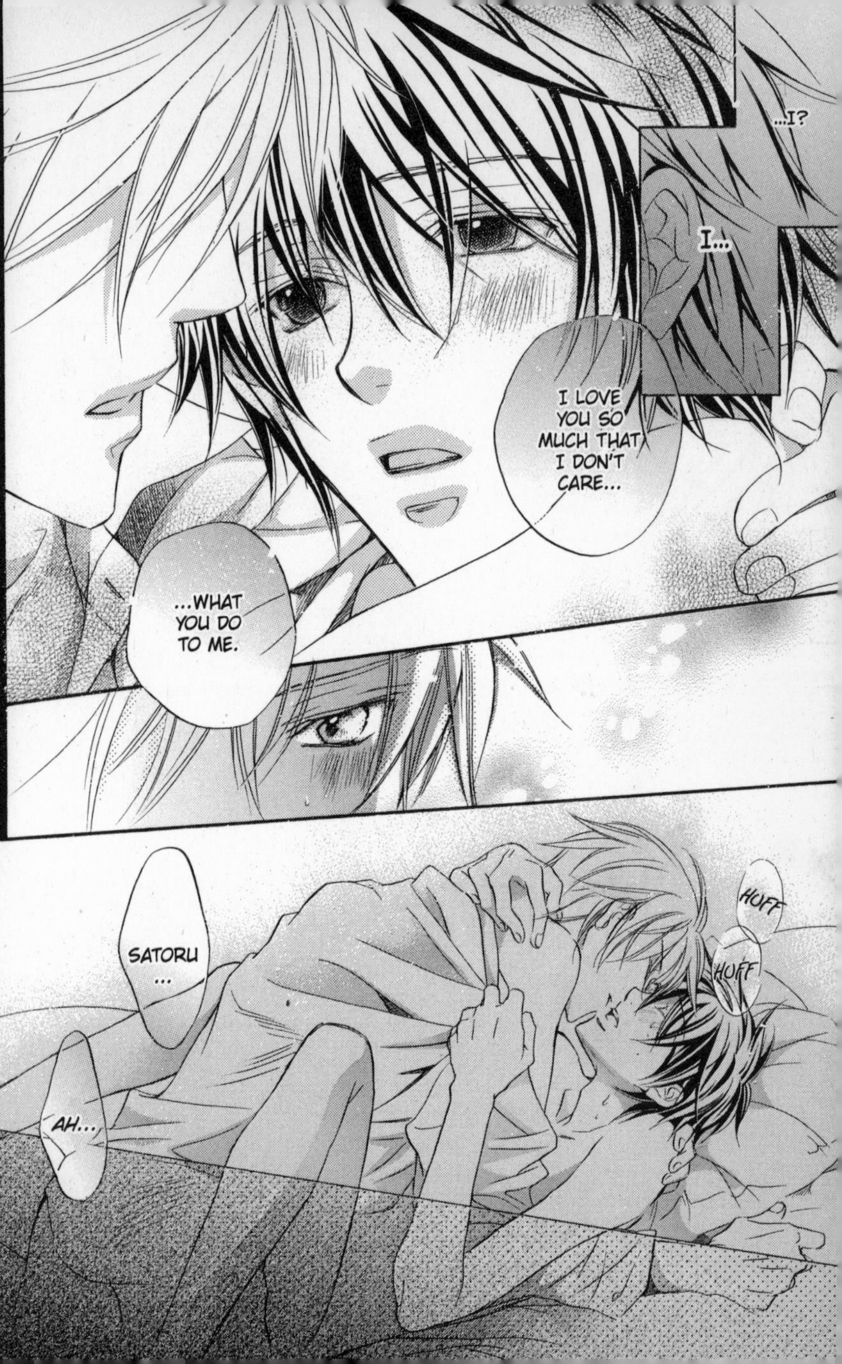
...I?
I...
I LOVE YOU SO MUCH THAT I DON'T CARE...
...WHAT YOU DO TO ME.
HUFF
HUFF
SATORU ...
AH...

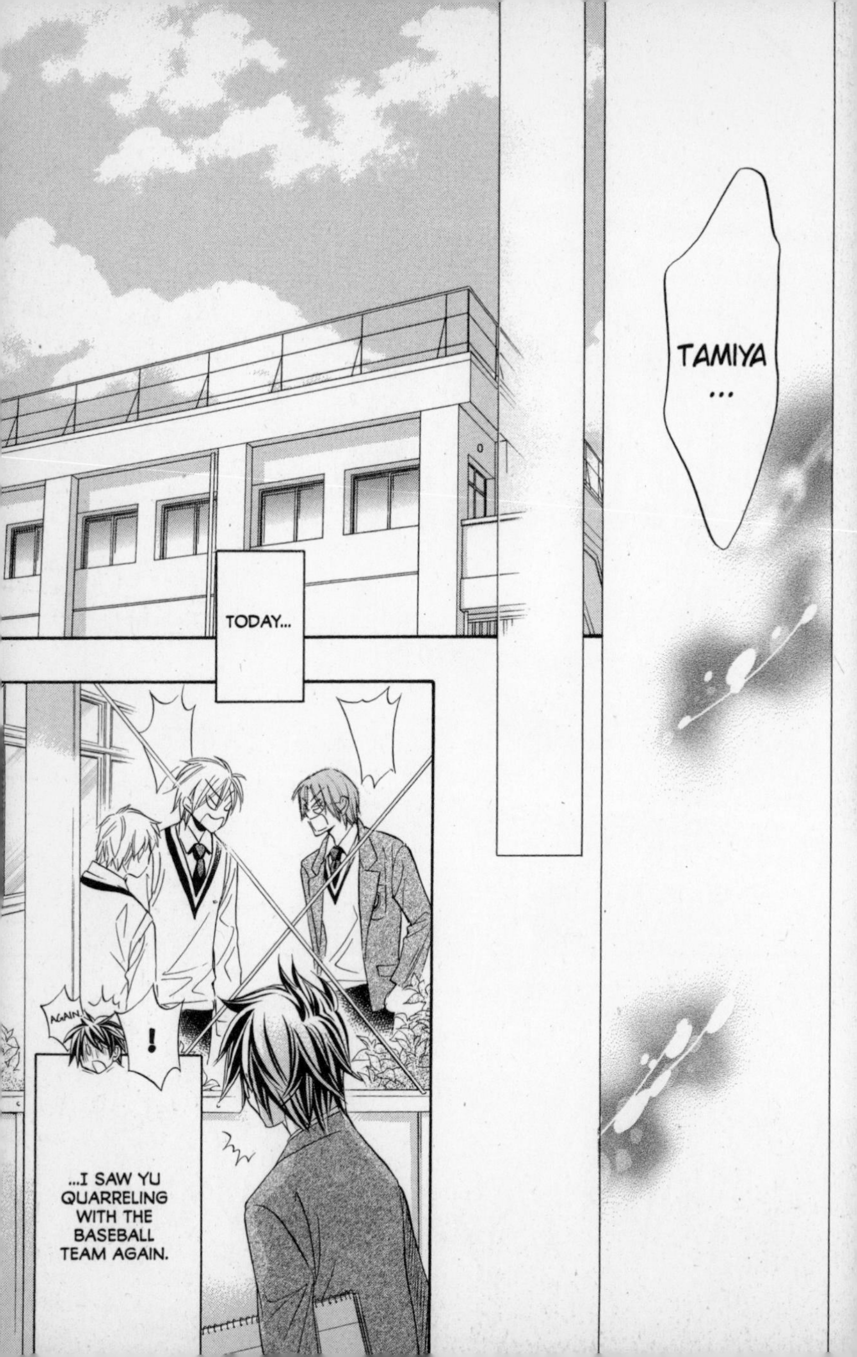
TAMIYA ...
TODAY...
AGAIN.
!
...I SAW YU QUARRELING WITH THE BASEBALL TEAM AGAIN.

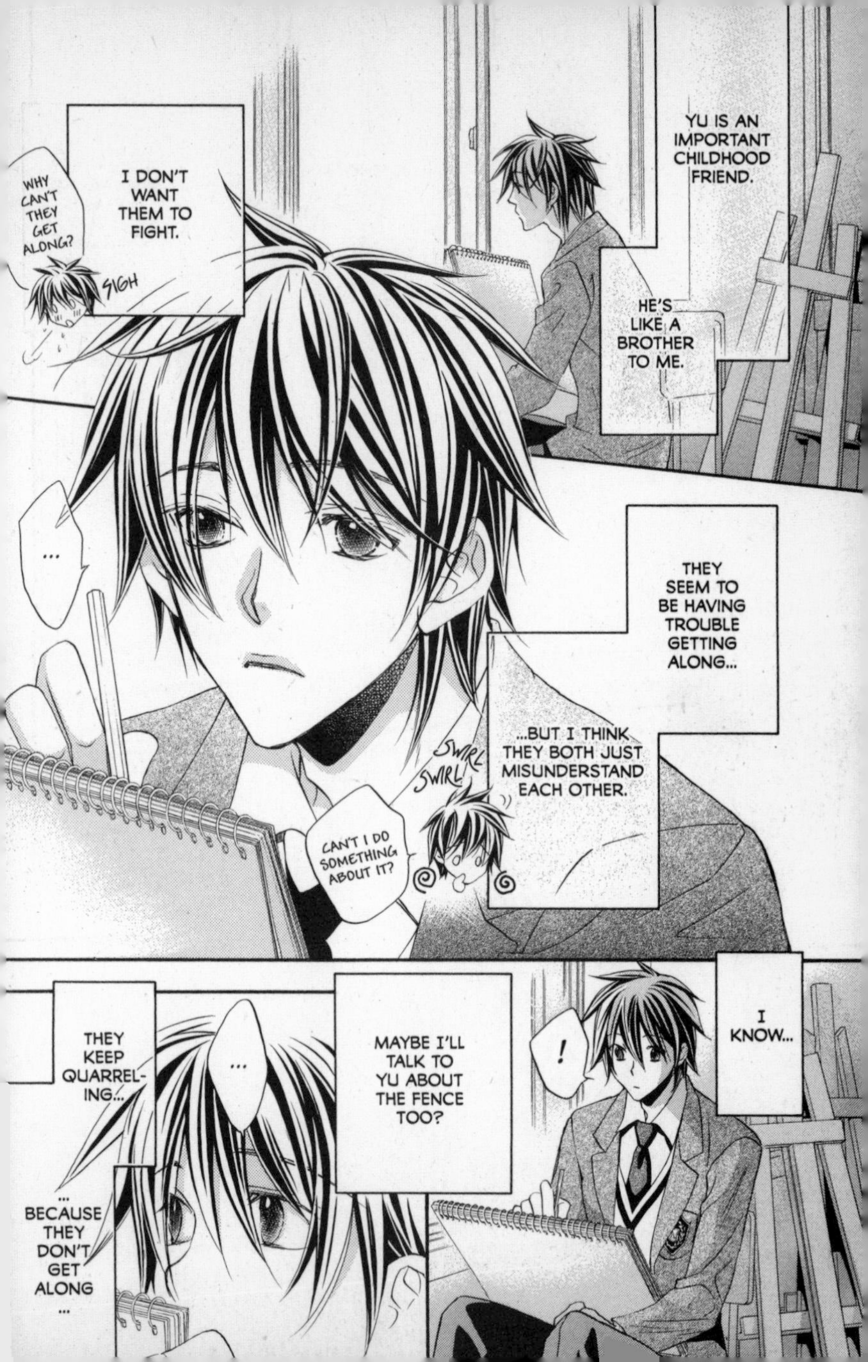
YU IS AN IMPORTANT CHILDHOOD FRIEND.
HE'S LIKE A BROTHER TO ME.
I DON'T WANT THEM TO FIGHT.
WHY CAN'T THEY GET ALONG?
SIGH
THEY SEEM TO BE HAVING TROUBLE GETTING ALONG...
...BUT I THINK THEY BOTH JUST MISUNDERSTAND EACH OTHER.
SWIRL SWIRL
CAN'T I DO SOMETHING ABOUT IT?
...
I KNOW...
!
MAYBE I'LL TALK TO YU ABOUT THE FENCE TOO?
...
THEY KEEP QUARREL-ING...
...BECAUSE THEY DON'T GET ALONG...

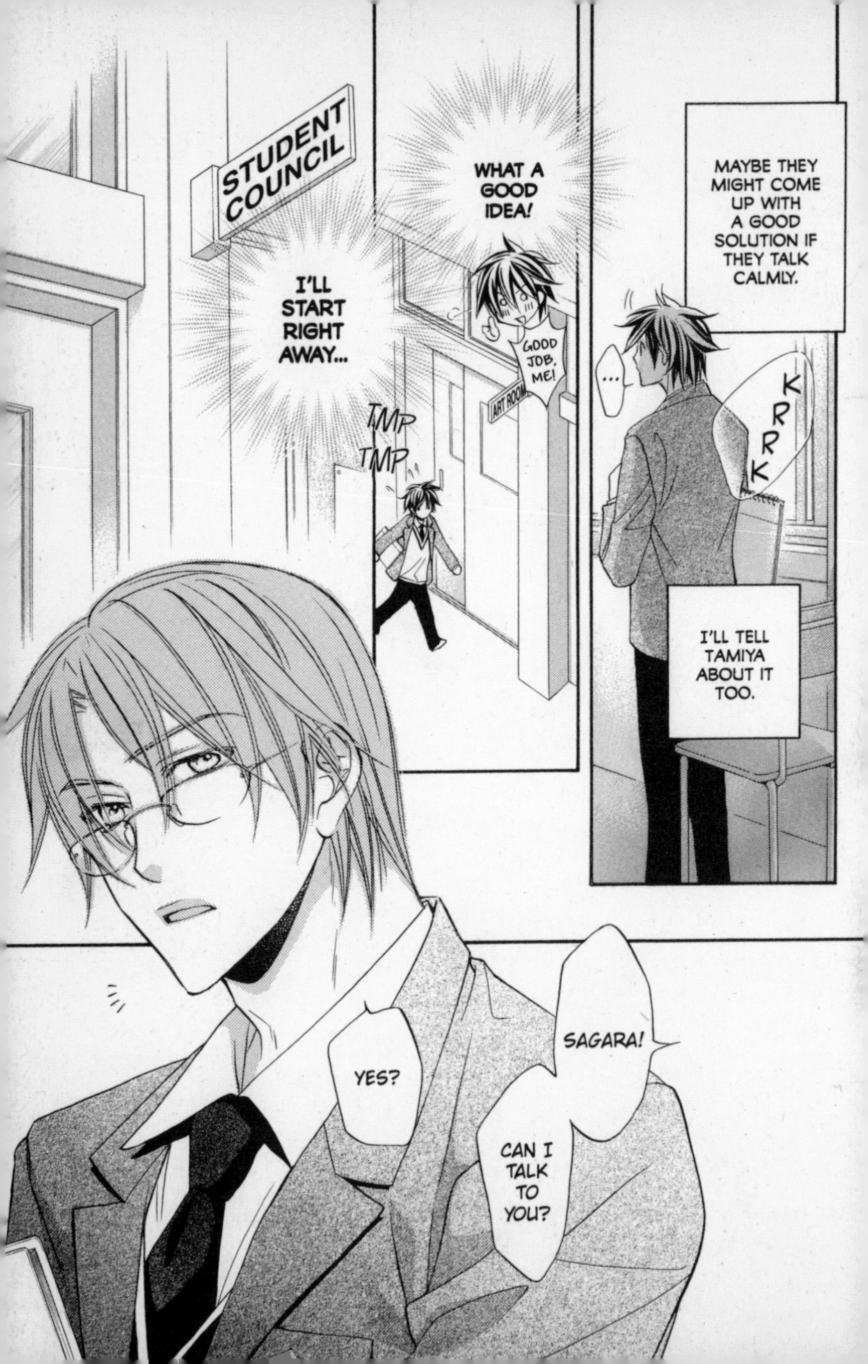
MAYBE THEY MIGHT COME UP WITH A GOOD SOLUTION IF THEY TALK CALMLY.
...
KRRK
I'LL TELL TAMIYA ABOUT IT TOO.
WHAT A GOOD IDEA!
GOOD JOB, ME!
ART ROOM
TMP TMP
STUDENT COUNCIL
I'LL START RIGHT AWAY...
SAGARA!
YES?
CAN I TALK TO YOU?

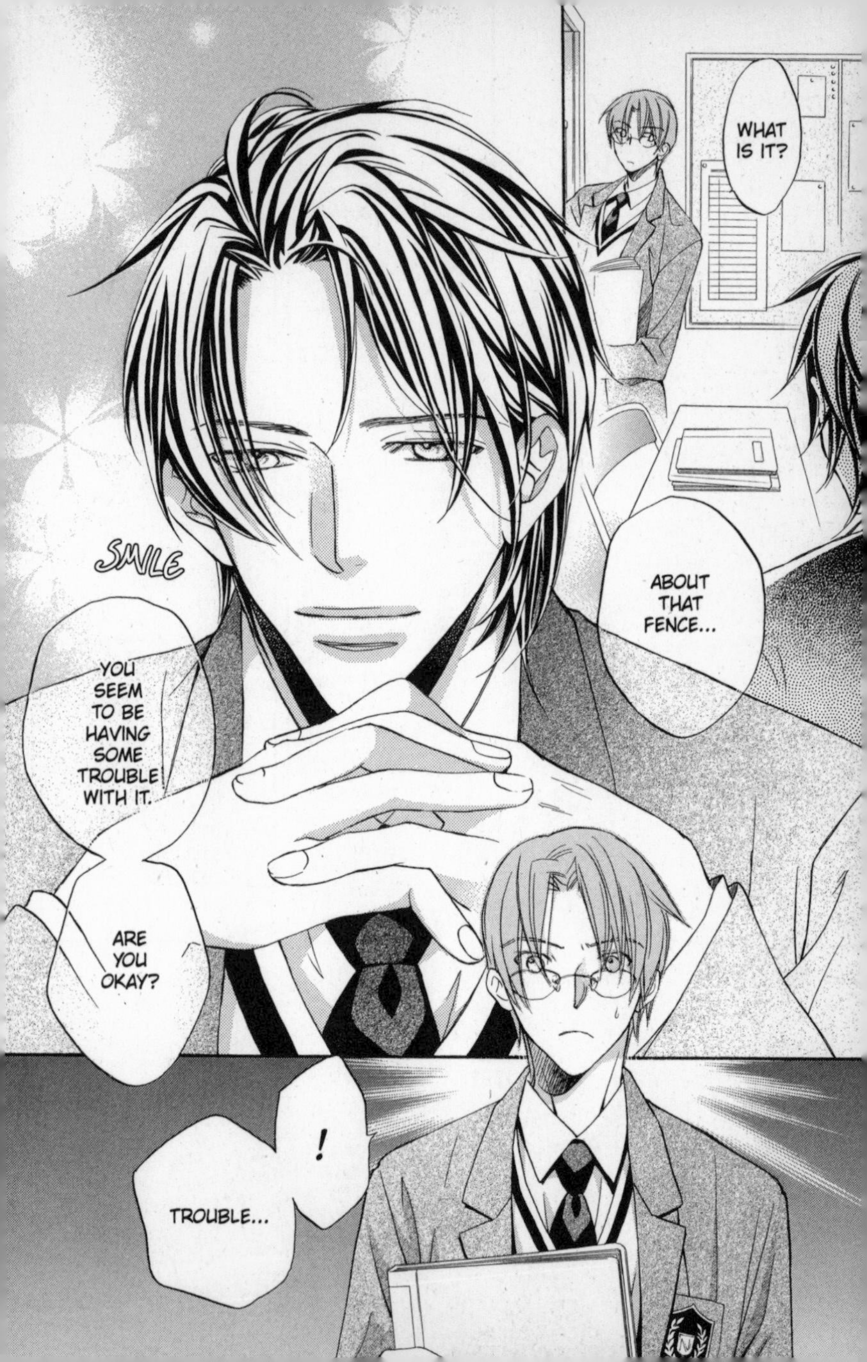
WHAT IS IT?
ABOUT THAT FENCE...
SMILE
YOU SEEM TO BE HAVING SOME TROUBLE WITH IT.
ARE YOU OKAY?
!
TROUBLE...

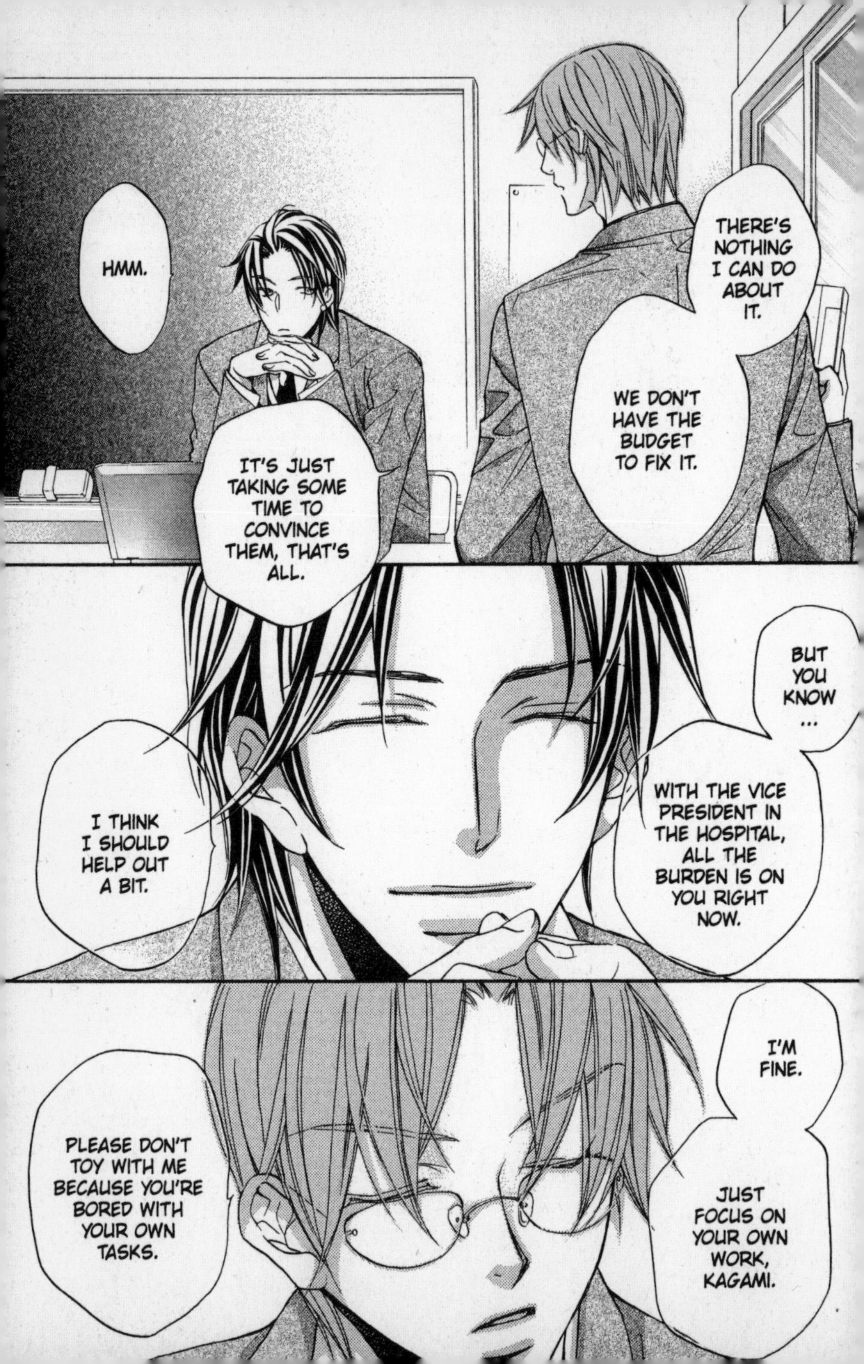
THERE'S NOTHING I CAN DO ABOUT IT.
WE DON'T HAVE THE BUDGET TO FIX IT.
HMM.
IT'S JUST TAKING SOME TIME TO CONVINCE THEM, THAT'S ALL.
BUT YOU KNOW ...
WITH THE VICE PRESIDENT IN THE HOSPITAL, ALL THE BURDEN IS ON YOU RIGHT NOW.
I THINK I SHOULD HELP OUT A BIT.
I'M FINE.
JUST FOCUS ON YOUR OWN WORK, KAGAMI.
PLEASE DON'T TOY WITH ME BECAUSE YOU'RE BORED WITH YOUR OWN TASKS.

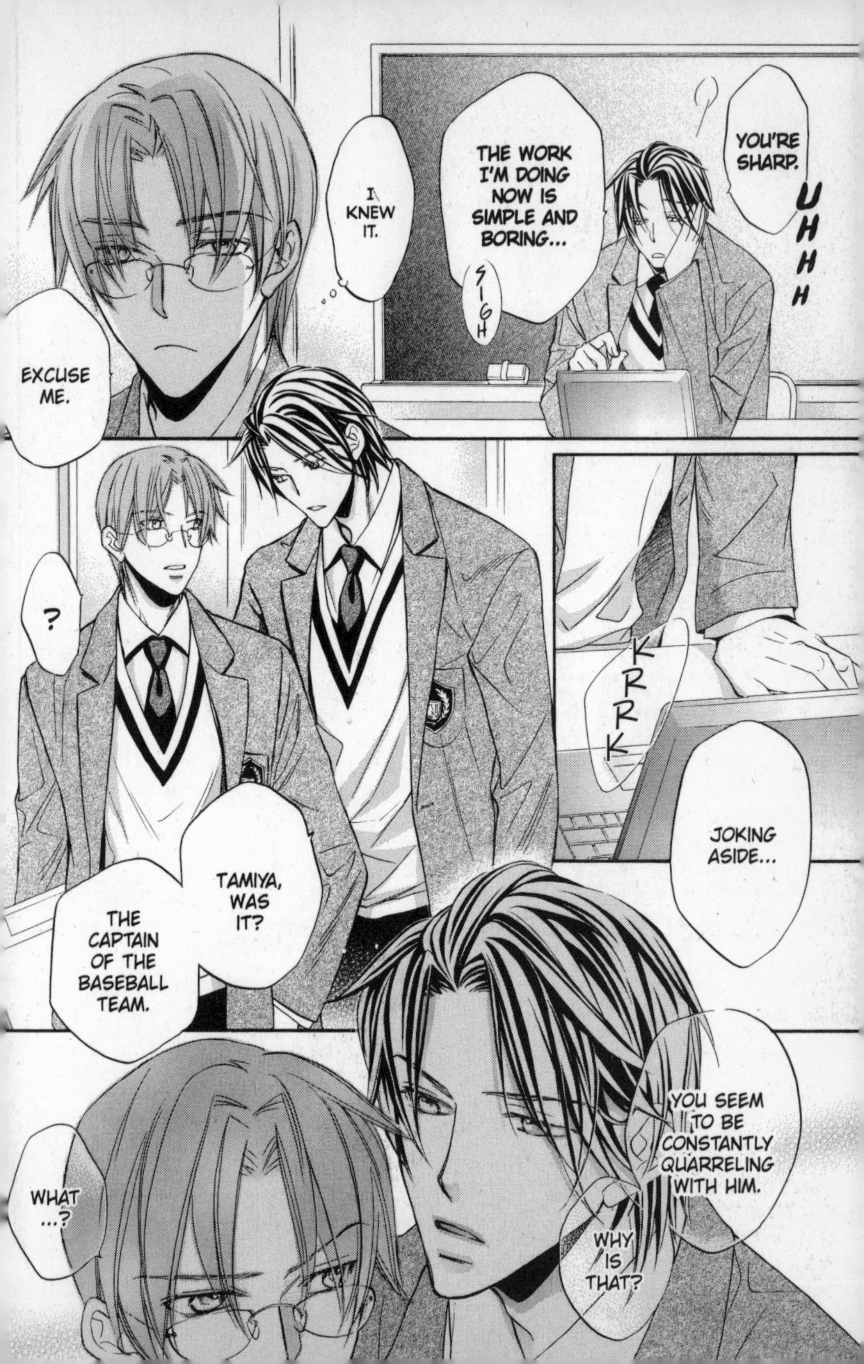
YOU'RE SHARP.
UHHHH
THE WORK I'M DOING NOW IS SIMPLE AND BORING...
SIGH
I KNEW IT.
EXCUSE ME.
KRRRK
JOKING ASIDE...
?
TAMIYA, WAS IT?
THE CAPTAIN OF THE BASEBALL TEAM.
YOU SEEM TO BE CONSTANTLY QUARRELING WITH HIM.
WHY IS THAT?
WHAT ...?

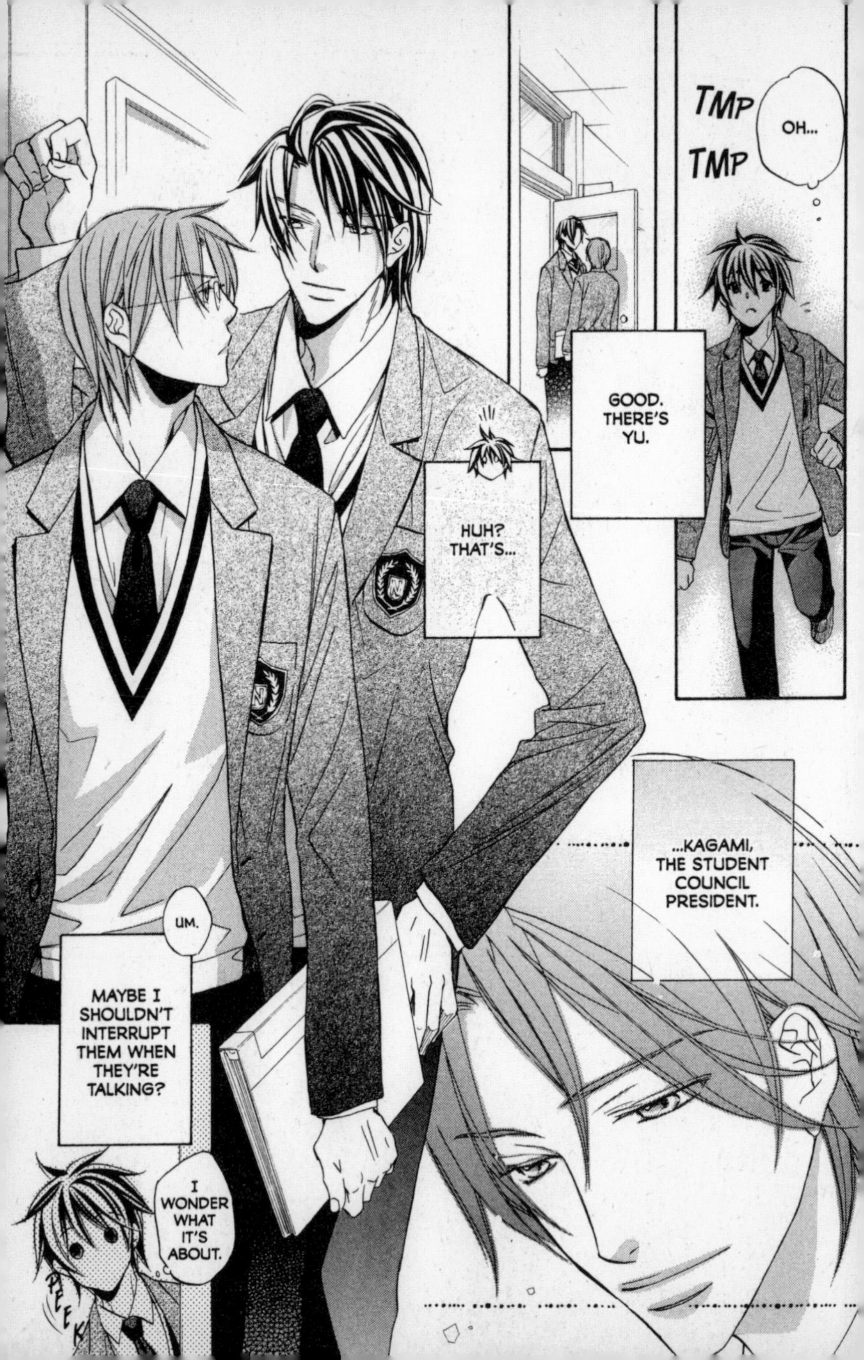
TMP
TMP
OH...
GOOD. THERE'S YU.
HUH? THAT'S...
...KAGAMI, THE STUDENT COUNCIL PRESIDENT.
UM.
MAYBE I SHOULDN'T INTERRUPT THEM WHEN THEY'RE TALKING?
I WONDER WHAT IT'S ABOUT.
PEEK

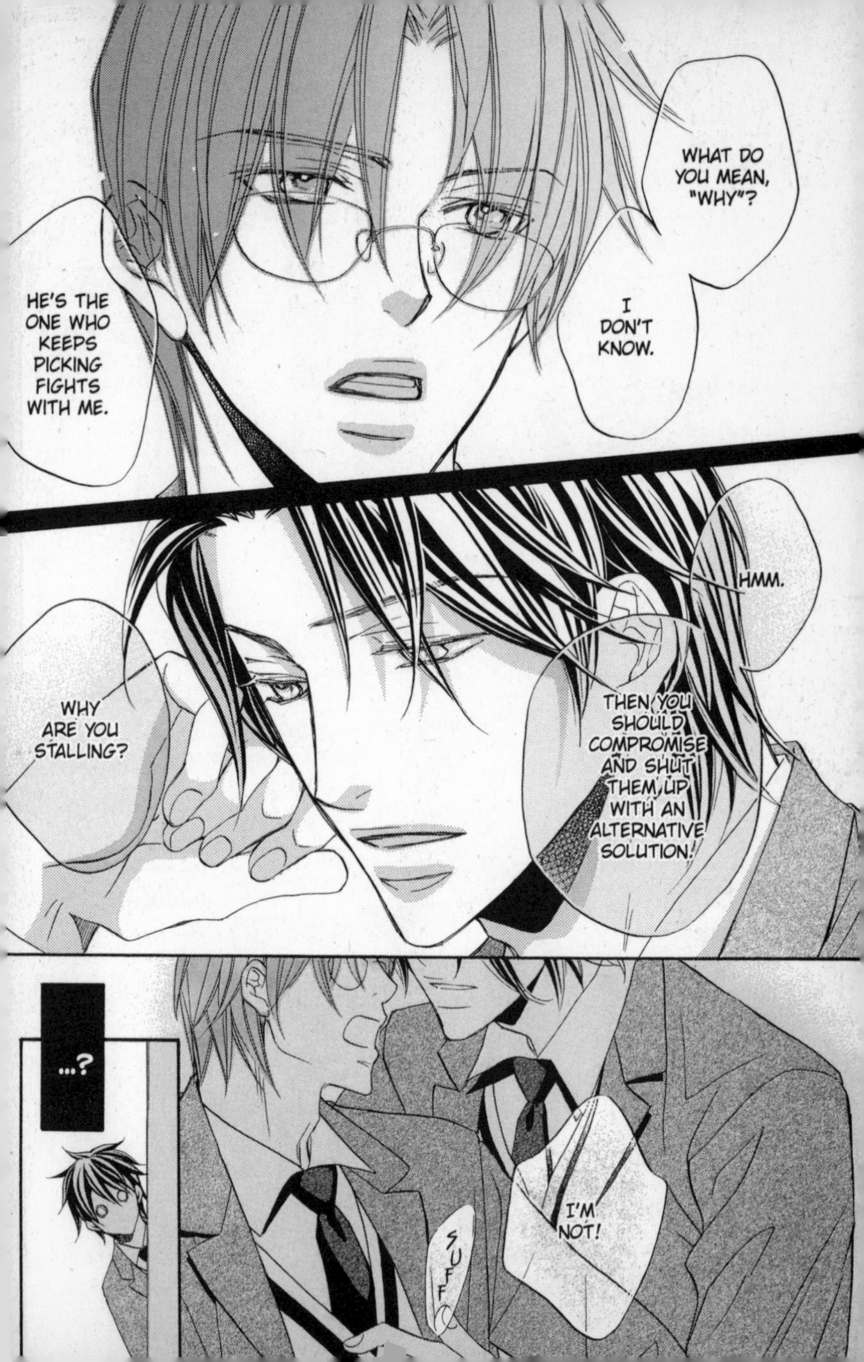
WHAT DO YOU MEAN, "WHY"?
I DON'T KNOW.
HE'S THE ONE WHO KEEPS PICKING FIGHTS WITH ME.
HMM.
THEN YOU SHOULD COMPROMISE AND SHUT THEM UP WITH AN ALTERNATIVE SOLUTION!
WHY ARE YOU STALLING?
I'M NOT!
SUFF
...?

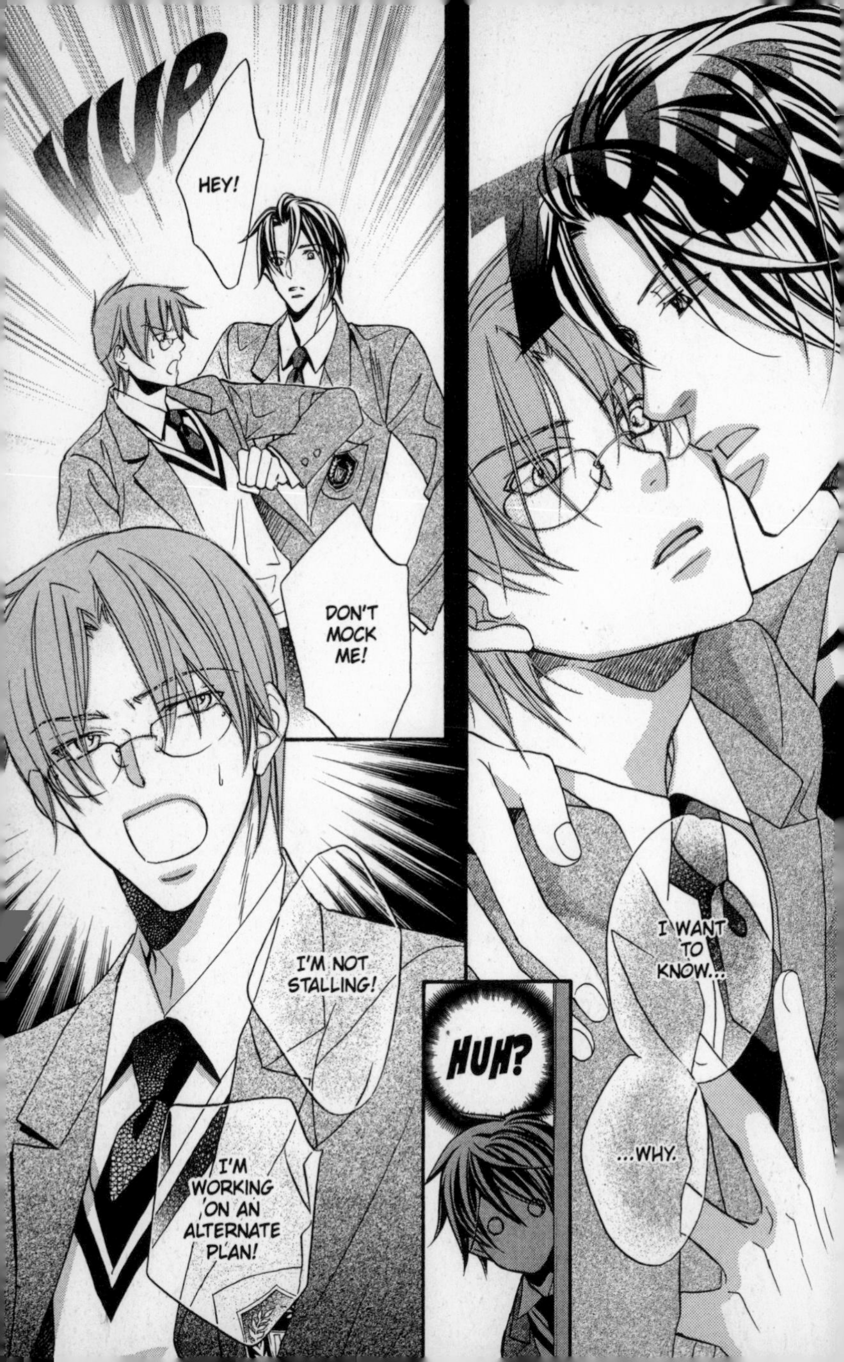
I WANT TO KNOW...
...WHY.
HUH?
WUP
HEY!
DON'T MOCK ME!
I'M NOT STALLING!
I'M WORKING ON AN ALTERNATE PLAN!

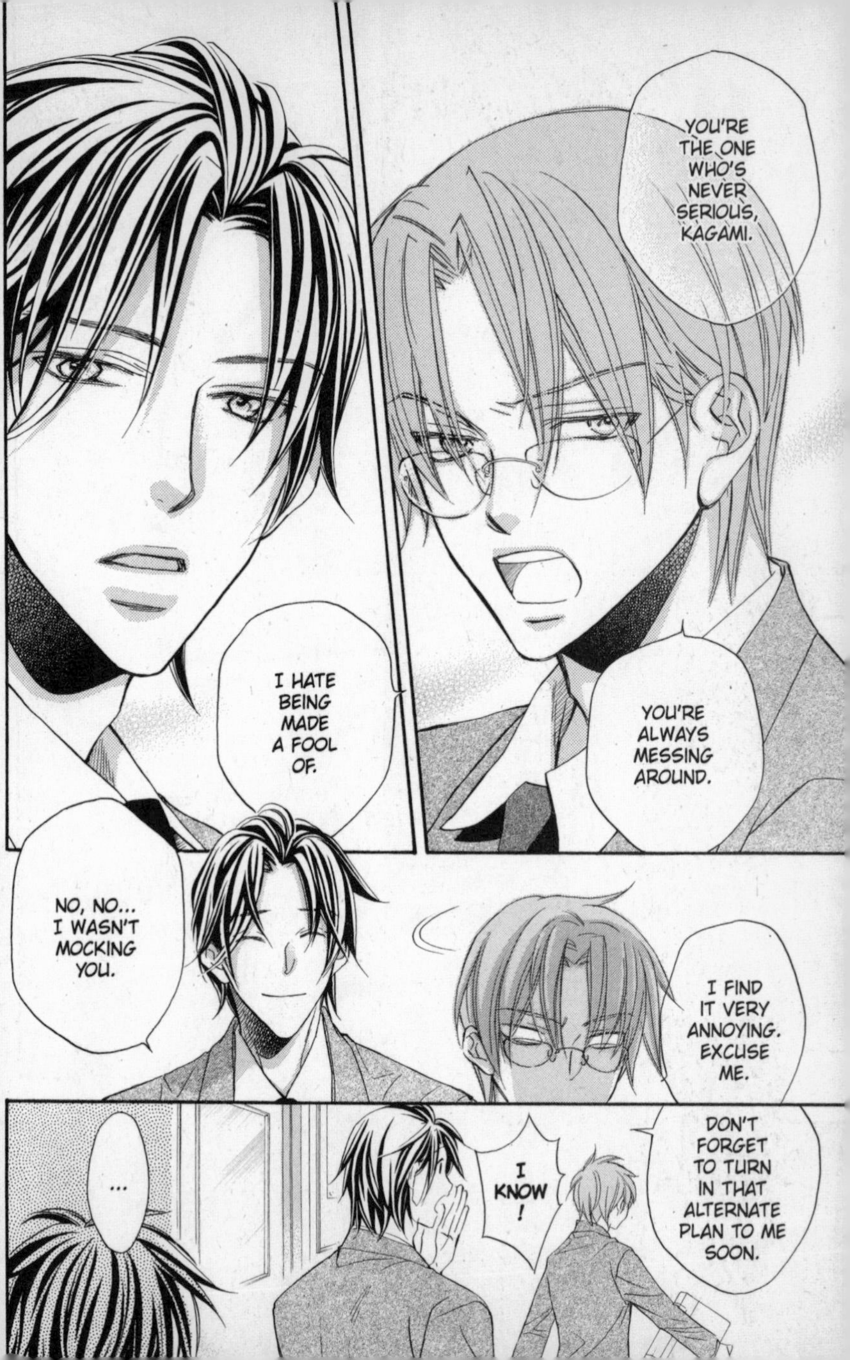
YOU'RE THE ONE WHO'S NEVER SERIOUS, KAGAMI.
YOU'RE ALWAYS MESSING AROUND.
I HATE BEING MADE A FOOL OF.
NO, NO... I WASN'T MOCKING YOU.
I FIND IT VERY ANNOYING. EXCUSE ME.
DON'T FORGET TO TURN IN THAT ALTERNATE PLAN TO ME SOON.
I KNOW!
...

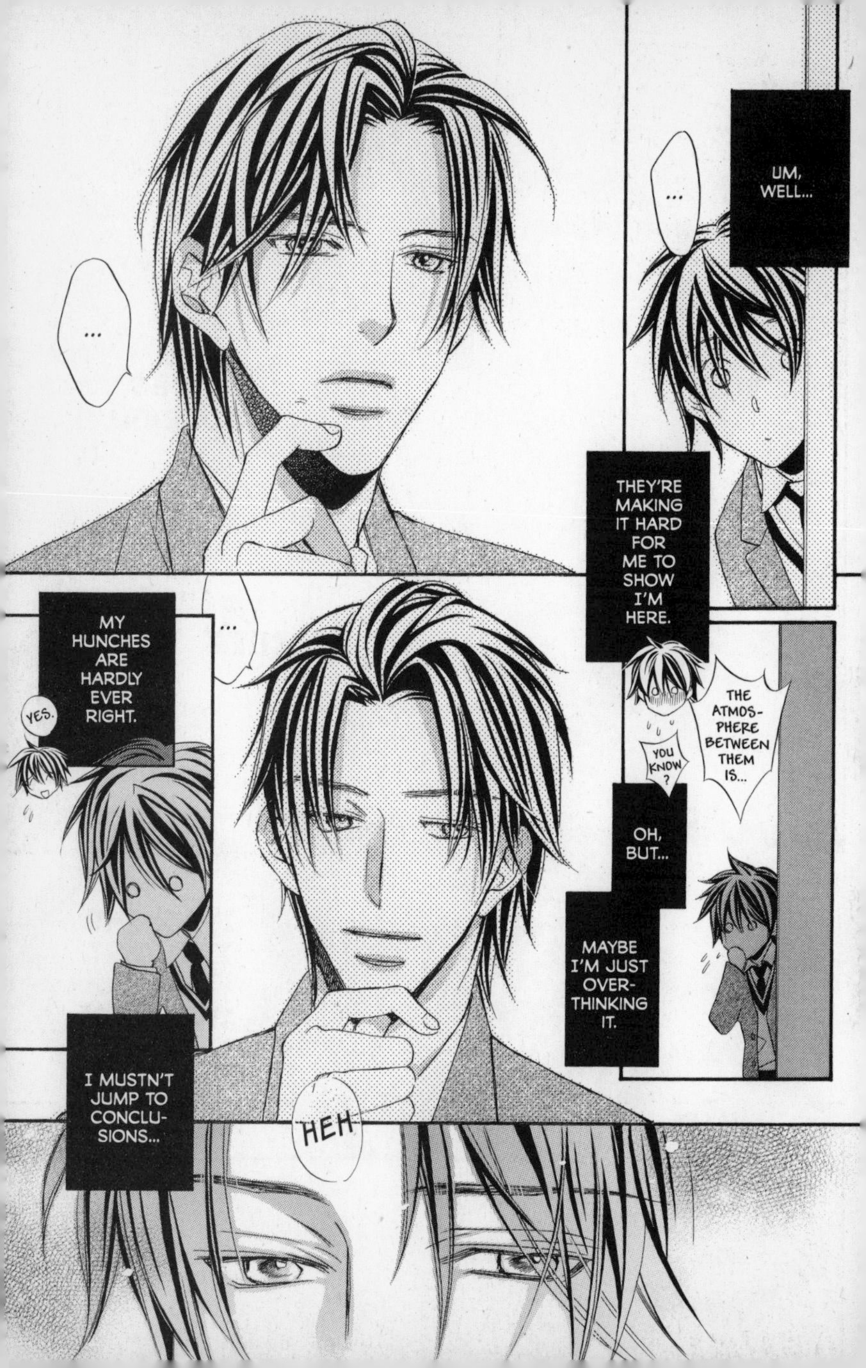
UM, WELL...
...
THEY'RE MAKING IT HARD FOR ME TO SHOW I'M HERE.
...
THE ATMOS-PHERE BETWEEN THEM IS...
YOU KNOW?
OH, BUT...
MAYBE I'M JUST OVER-THINKING IT.
...
MY HUNCHES ARE HARDLY EVER RIGHT.
YES.
HEH
I MUSTN'T JUMP TO CONCLU-SIONS...

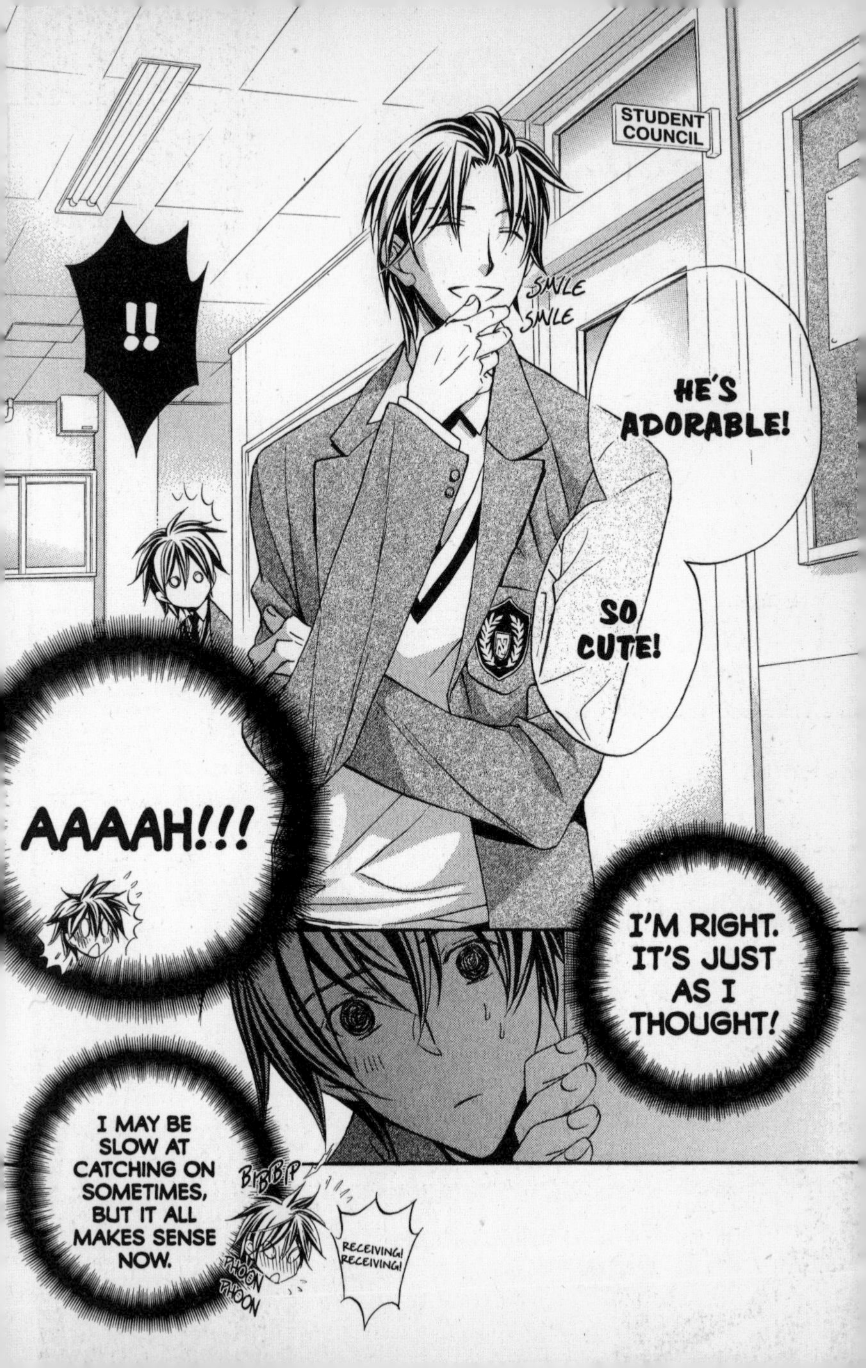
STUDENT COUNCIL
HE'S ADORABLE!
SMILE SMILE
SO CUTE!
!!
AAAAH!!!
I'M RIGHT. IT'S JUST AS I THOUGHT!
RECEIVING! RECEIVING!
BIBBIP
PHOON PHOON
I MAY BE SLOW AT CATCHING ON SOMETIMES, BUT IT ALL MAKES SENSE NOW.

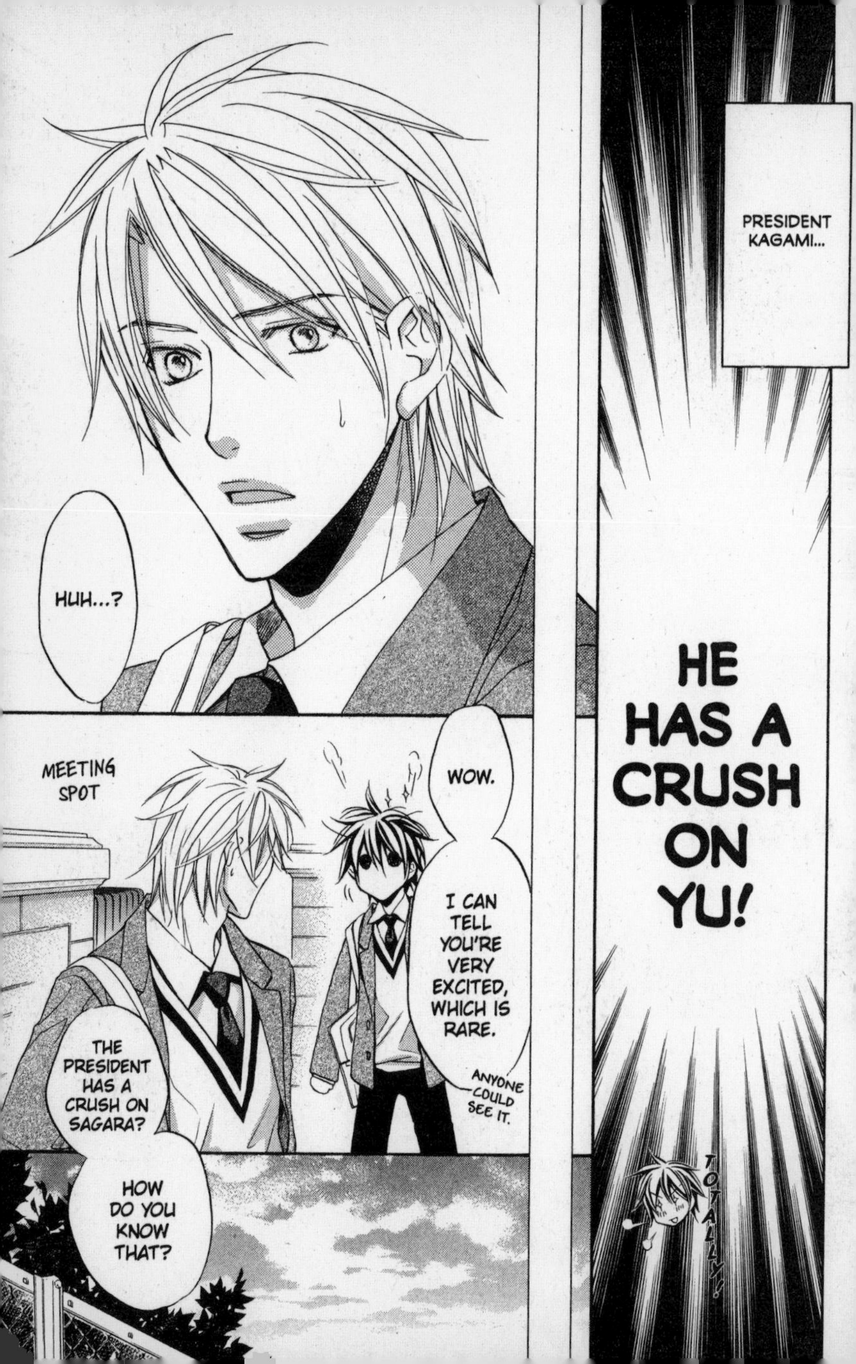
PRESIDENT KAGAMI...
HE HAS A CRUSH ON YU!
TOTALLY!
HUH...?
WOW.
I CAN TELL YOU'RE VERY EXCITED, WHICH IS RARE.
ANYONE COULD SEE IT.
MEETING SPOT
THE PRESIDENT HAS A CRUSH ON SAGARA?
HOW DO YOU KNOW THAT?

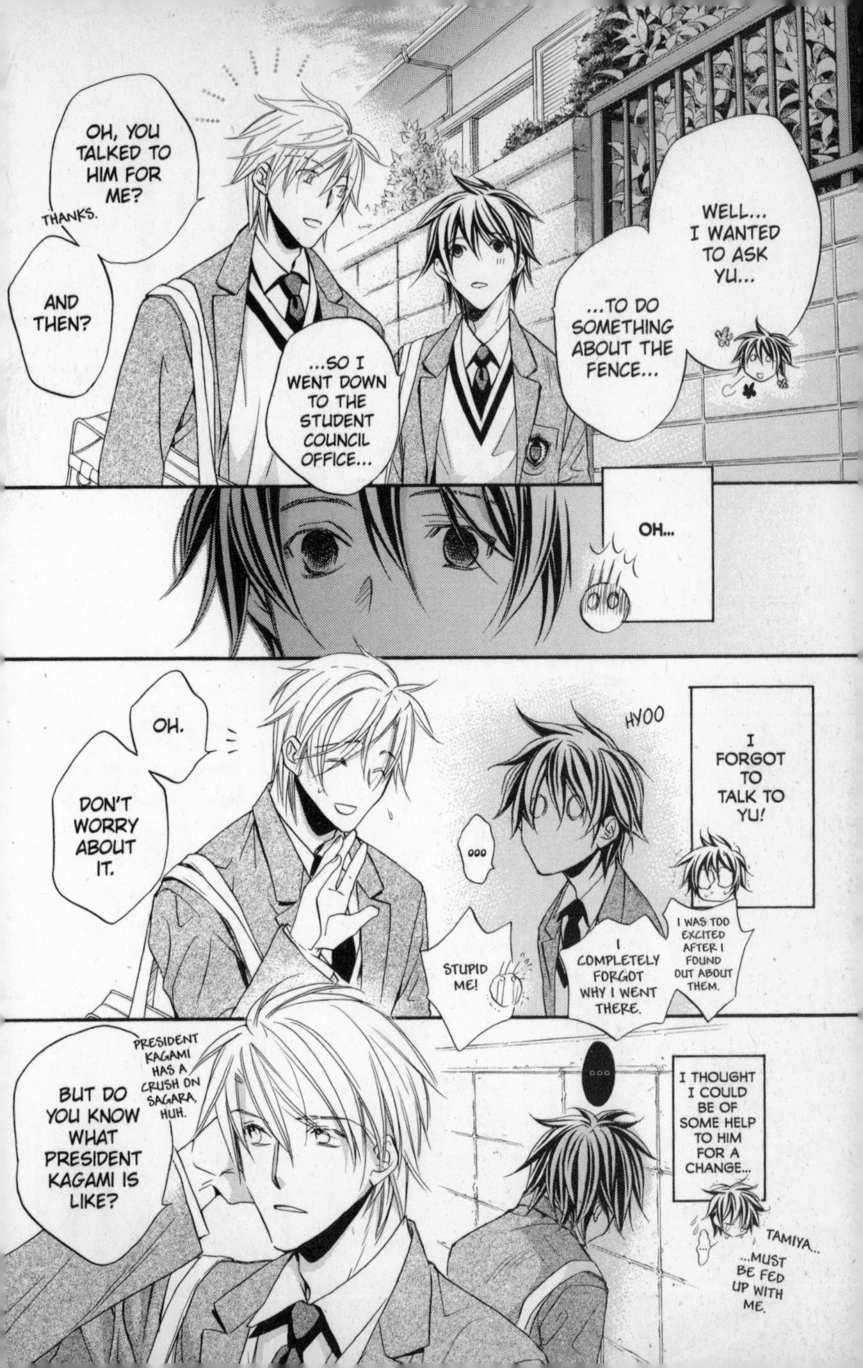
WELL... I WANTED TO ASK YU...
...TO DO SOMETHING ABOUT THE FENCE...
...SO I WENT DOWN TO THE STUDENT COUNCIL OFFICE...
OH, YOU TALKED TO HIM FOR ME?
THANKS.
AND THEN?
OH...
I FORGOT TO TALK TO YU!
I WAS TOO EXCITED AFTER I FOUND OUT ABOUT THEM.
I COMPLETELY FORGOT WHY I WENT THERE.
STUPID ME!
HYOO
...
OH.
DON'T WORRY ABOUT IT.
I THOUGHT I COULD BE OF SOME HELP TO HIM FOR A CHANGE...
TAMIYA...
...MUST BE FED UP WITH ME.
...
PRESIDENT KAGAMI HAS A CRUSH ON SAGARA, HUH.
BUT DO YOU KNOW WHAT PRESIDENT KAGAMI IS LIKE?

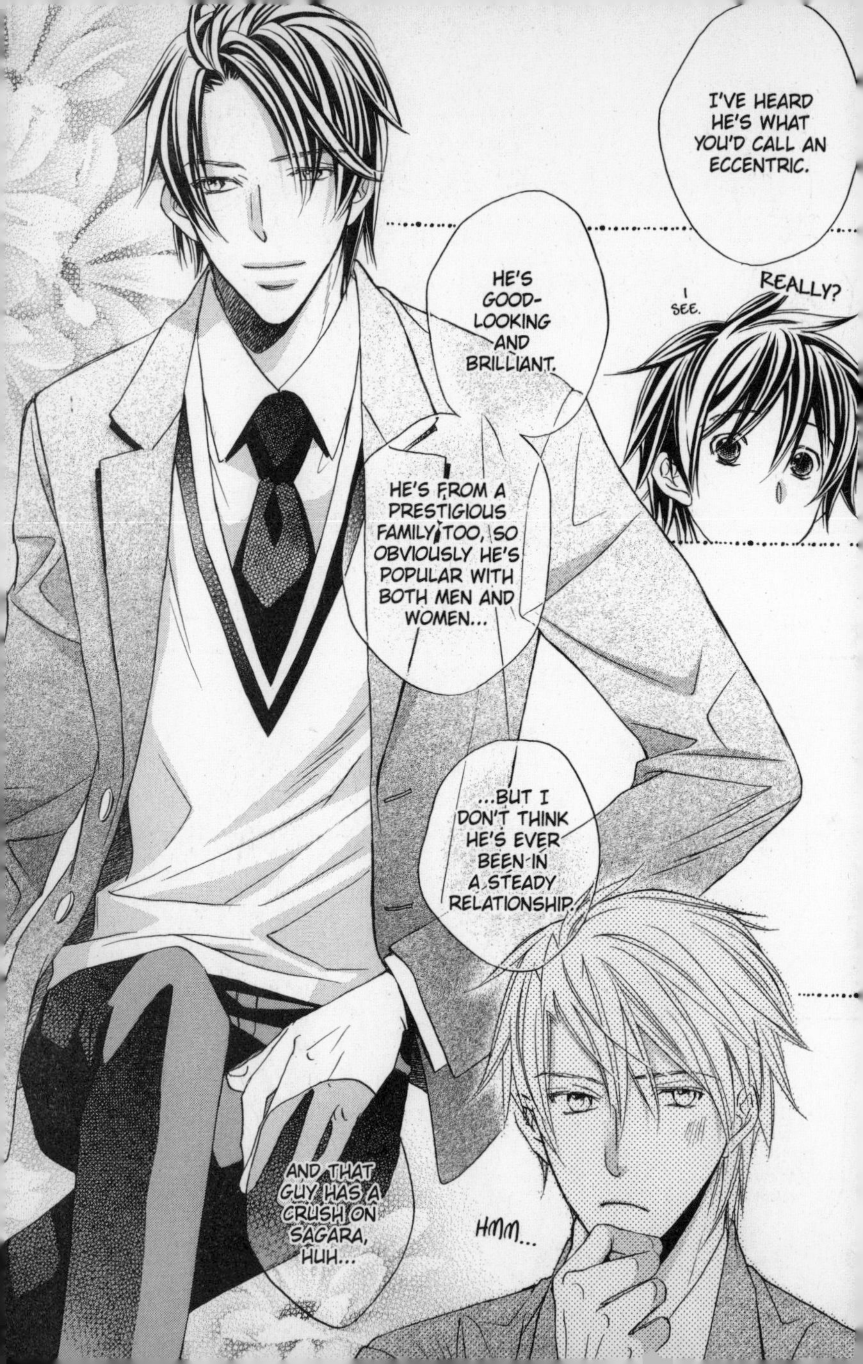
I'VE HEARD HE'S WHAT YOU'D CALL AN ECCENTRIC.
REALLY?
I SEE.
HE'S GOOD-LOOKING AND BRILLIANT.
HE'S FROM A PRESTIGIOUS FAMILY TOO, SO OBVIOUSLY HE'S POPULAR WITH BOTH MEN AND WOMEN...
...BUT I DON'T THINK HE'S EVER BEEN IN A STEADY RELATIONSHIP.
HMM...
AND THAT GUY HAS A CRUSH ON SAGARA, HUH...

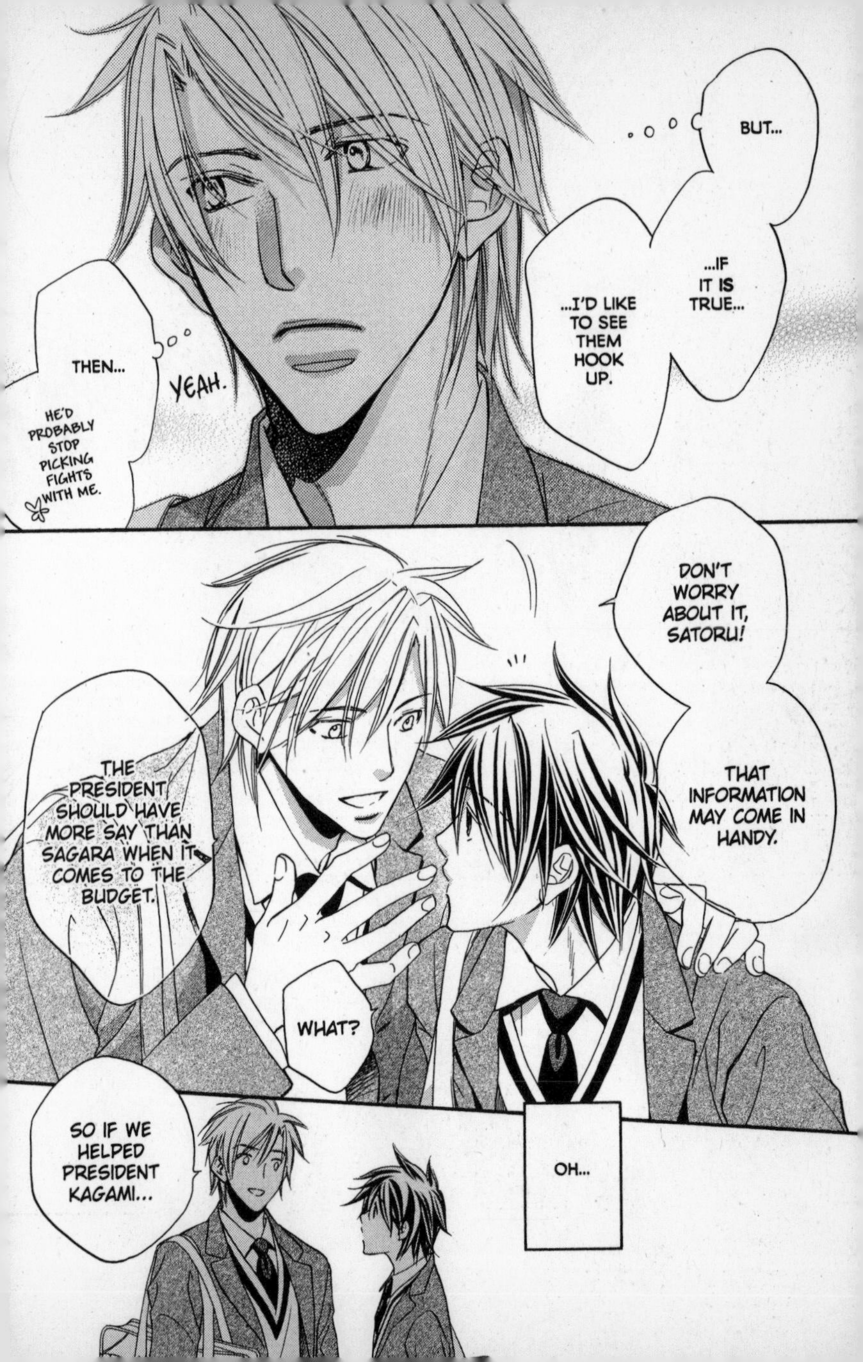
BUT...
...IF IT IS TRUE...
...I'D LIKE TO SEE THEM HOOK UP.
YEAH.
THEN...
HE'D PROBABLY STOP PICKING FIGHTS WITH ME.
DON'T WORRY ABOUT IT, SATORU!
THAT INFORMATION MAY COME IN HANDY.
THE PRESIDENT SHOULD HAVE MORE SAY THAN SAGARA WHEN IT COMES TO THE BUDGET.
WHAT?
OH...
SO IF WE HELPED PRESIDENT KAGAMI...

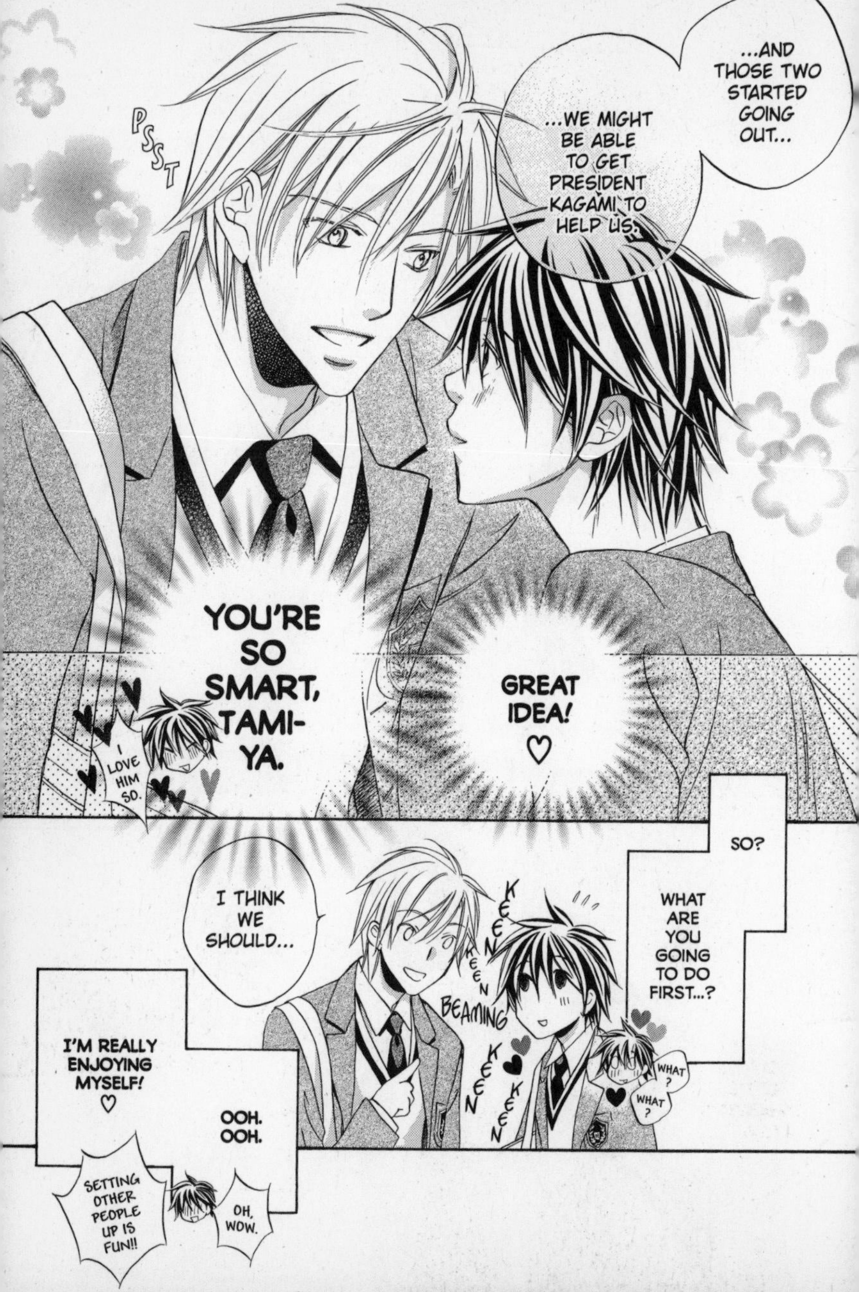
...AND THOSE TWO STARTED GOING OUT...
...WE MIGHT BE ABLE TO GET PRESIDENT KAGAMI TO HELP US.
PSST
GREAT IDEA! ♡
YOU'RE SO SMART, TAMI-YA.
I LOVE HIM SO.
SO?
WHAT ARE YOU GOING TO DO FIRST...?
I THINK WE SHOULD...
KEEN KEEN
BEAMING
KEEN KEEN
WHAT? WHAT?
I'M REALLY ENJOYING MYSELF! ♡
OOH. OOH.
OH, WOW.
SETTING OTHER PEOPLE UP IS FUN!!

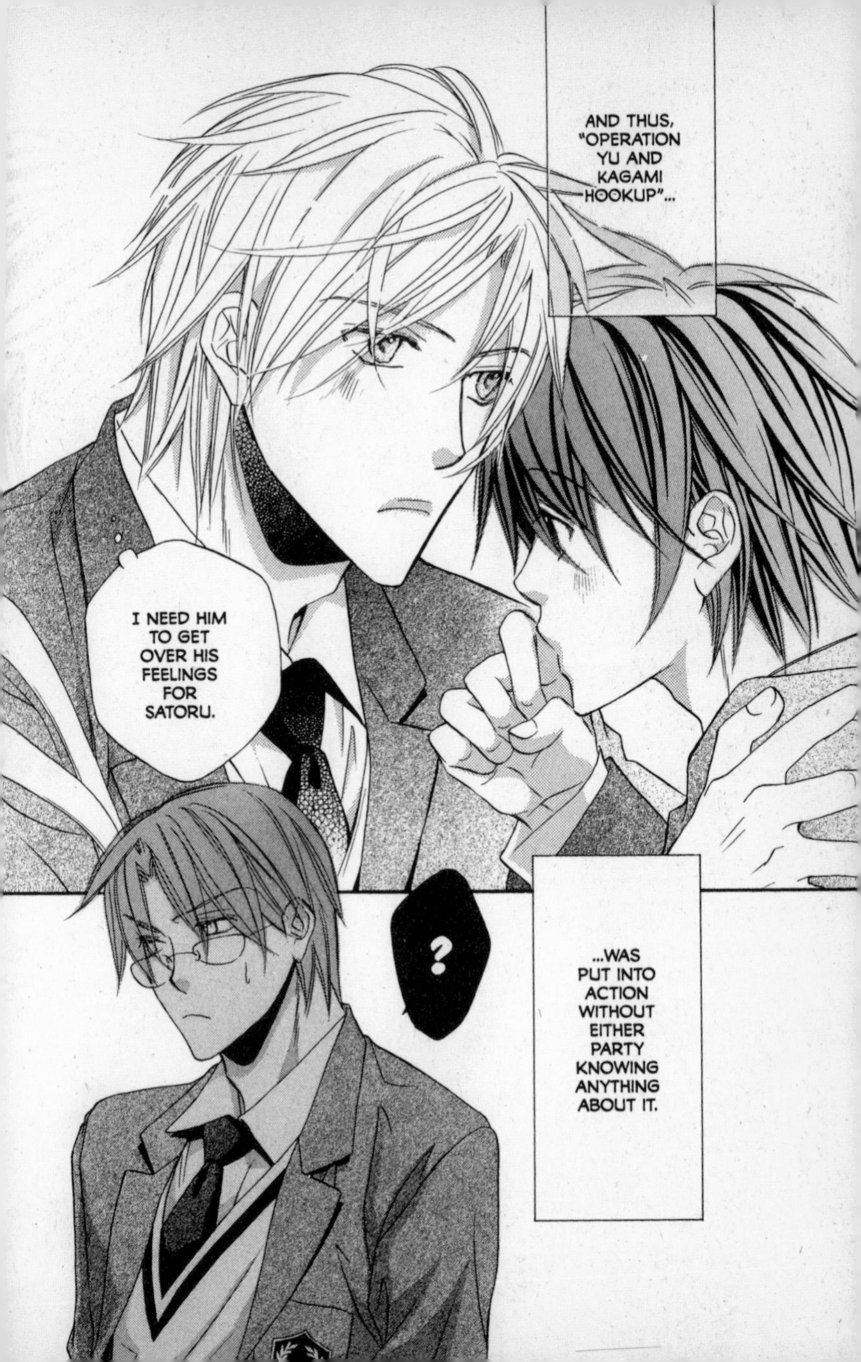
AND THUS, "OPERATION YU AND KAGAMI HOOKUP"...
I NEED HIM TO GET OVER HIS FEELINGS FOR SATORU.
...WAS PUT INTO ACTION WITHOUT EITHER PARTY KNOWING ANYTHING ABOUT IT.
?

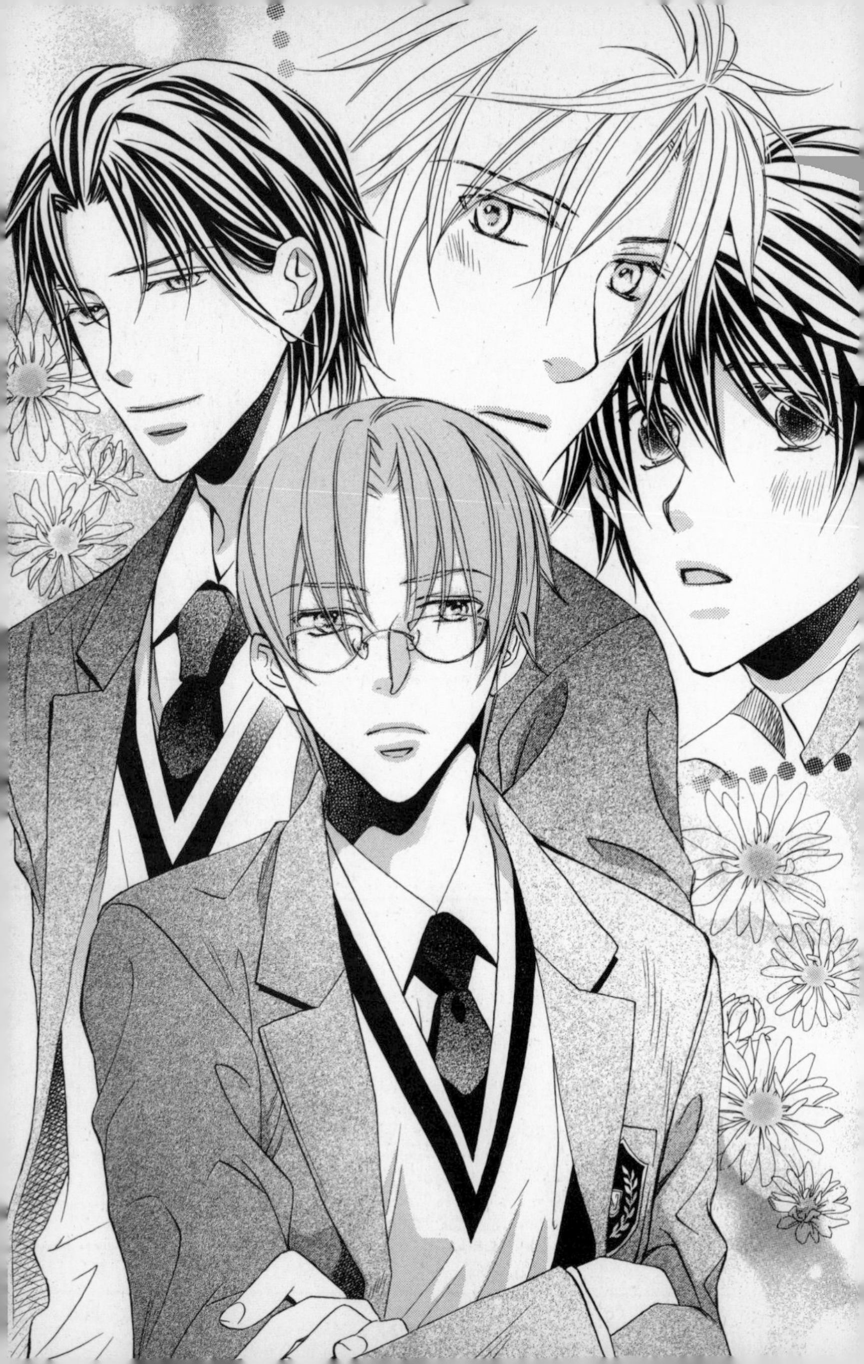

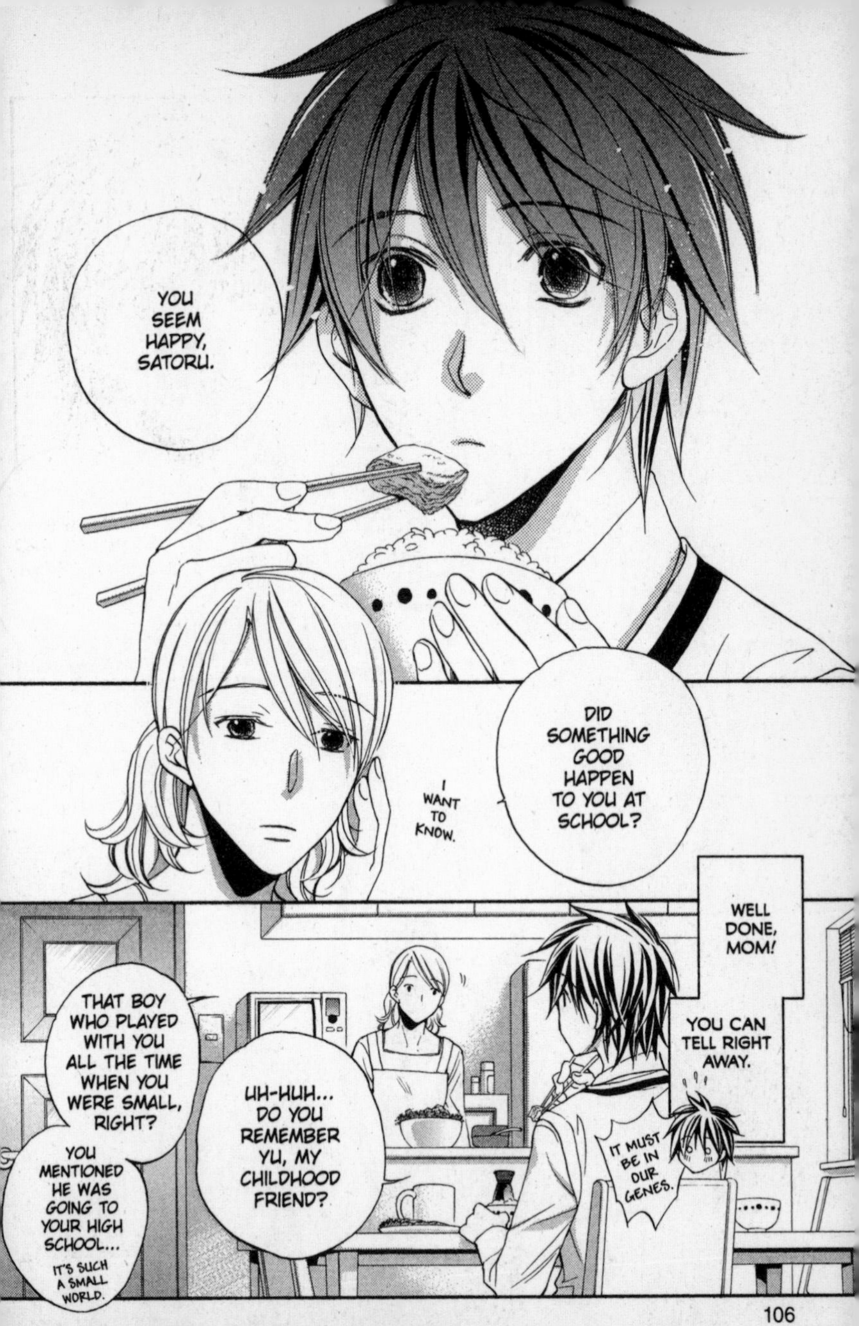

YOU SEEM HAPPY, SATORU.
DID SOMETHING GOOD HAPPEN TO YOU AT SCHOOL?
I WANT TO KNOW.
WELL DONE, MOM!
YOU CAN TELL RIGHT AWAY.
IT MUST BE IN OUR GENES.
UH-HUH... DO YOU REMEMBER YU, MY CHILDHOOD FRIEND?
THAT BOY WHO PLAYED WITH YOU ALL THE TIME WHEN YOU WERE SMALL, RIGHT?
YOU MENTIONED HE WAS GOING TO YOUR HIGH SCHOOL...
IT'S SUCH A SMALL WORLD.

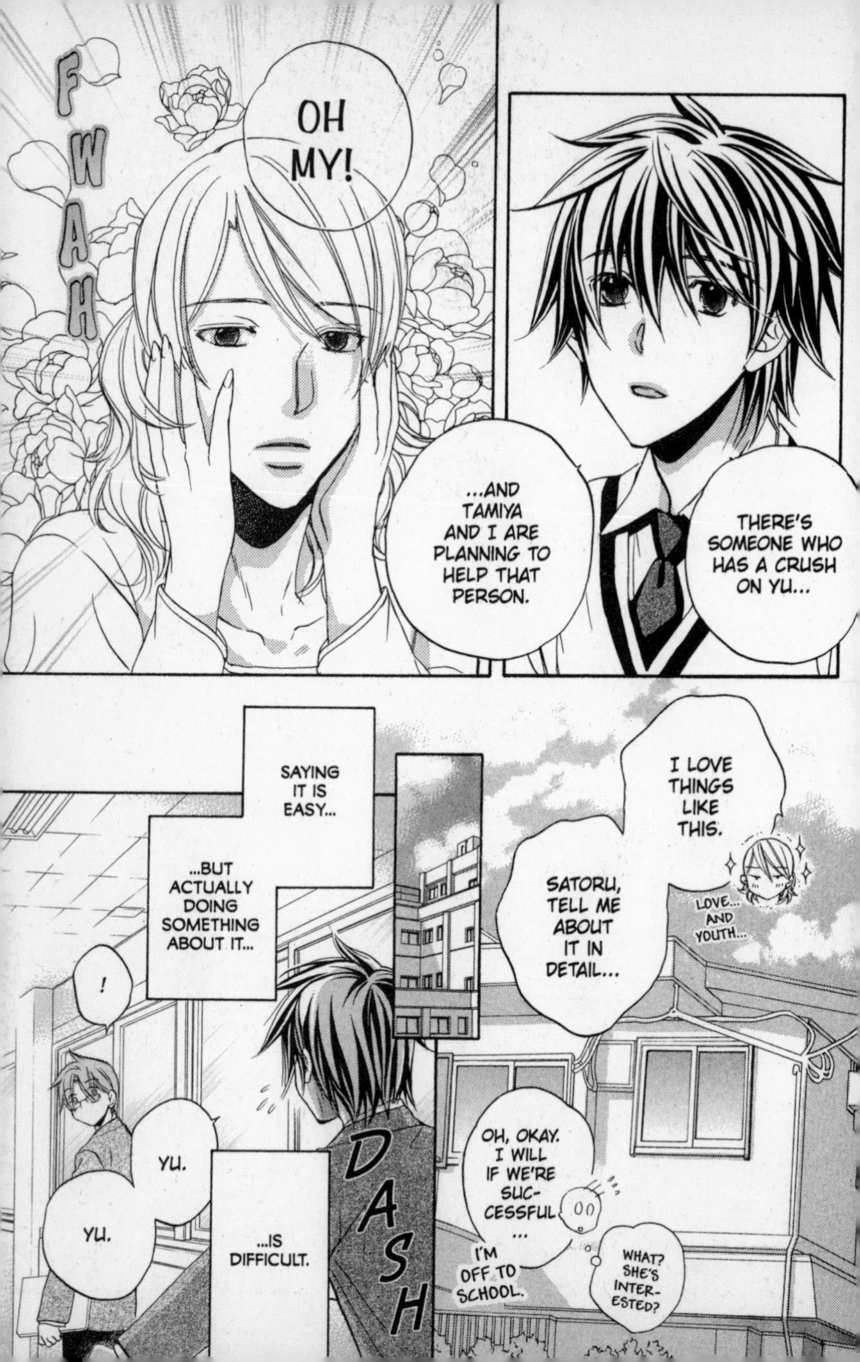
THERE'S SOMEONE WHO HAS A CRUSH ON YU...
...AND TAMIYA AND I ARE PLANNING TO HELP THAT PERSON.
FWAH
OH MY!
I LOVE THINGS LIKE THIS.
LOVE... AND YOUTH...
SATORU, TELL ME ABOUT IT IN DETAIL...
OH, OKAY. I WILL IF WE'RE SUC-CESSFUL...
WHAT? SHE'S INTER-ESTED?
I'M OFF TO SCHOOL.
SAYING IT IS EASY...
...BUT ACTUALLY DOING SOMETHING ABOUT IT...
DASH
!
YU.
YU.
...IS DIFFICULT.

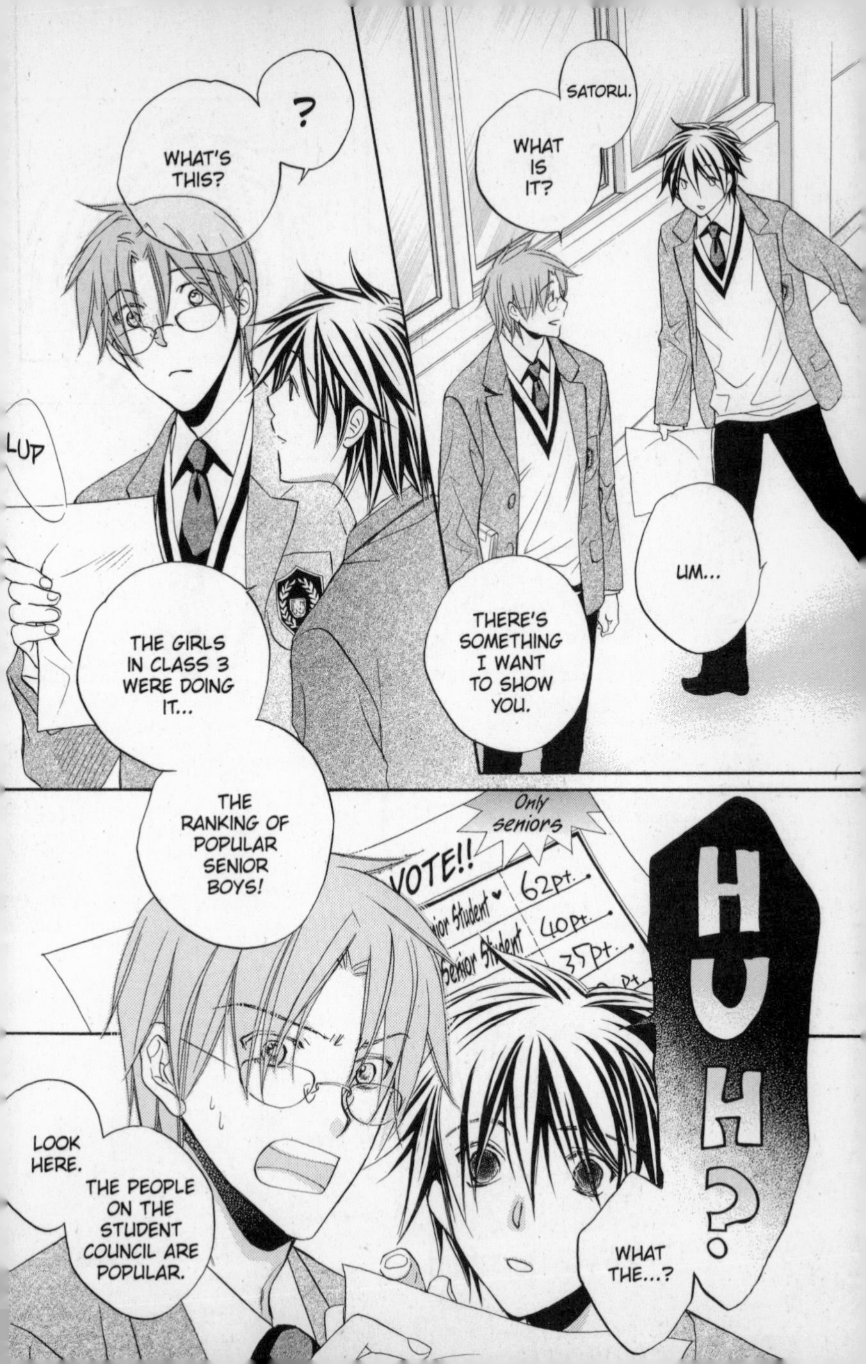
SATORU.
WHAT IS IT?
UM...
THERE'S SOMETHING I WANT TO SHOW YOU.
?
WHAT'S THIS?
LUP
THE GIRLS IN CLASS 3 WERE DOING IT...
THE RANKING OF POPULAR SENIOR BOYS!
HUH?
Only seniors
VOTE!!
62pt.
40pt.
35pt.
WHAT THE...?
LOOK HERE.
THE PEOPLE ON THE STUDENT COUNCIL ARE POPULAR.

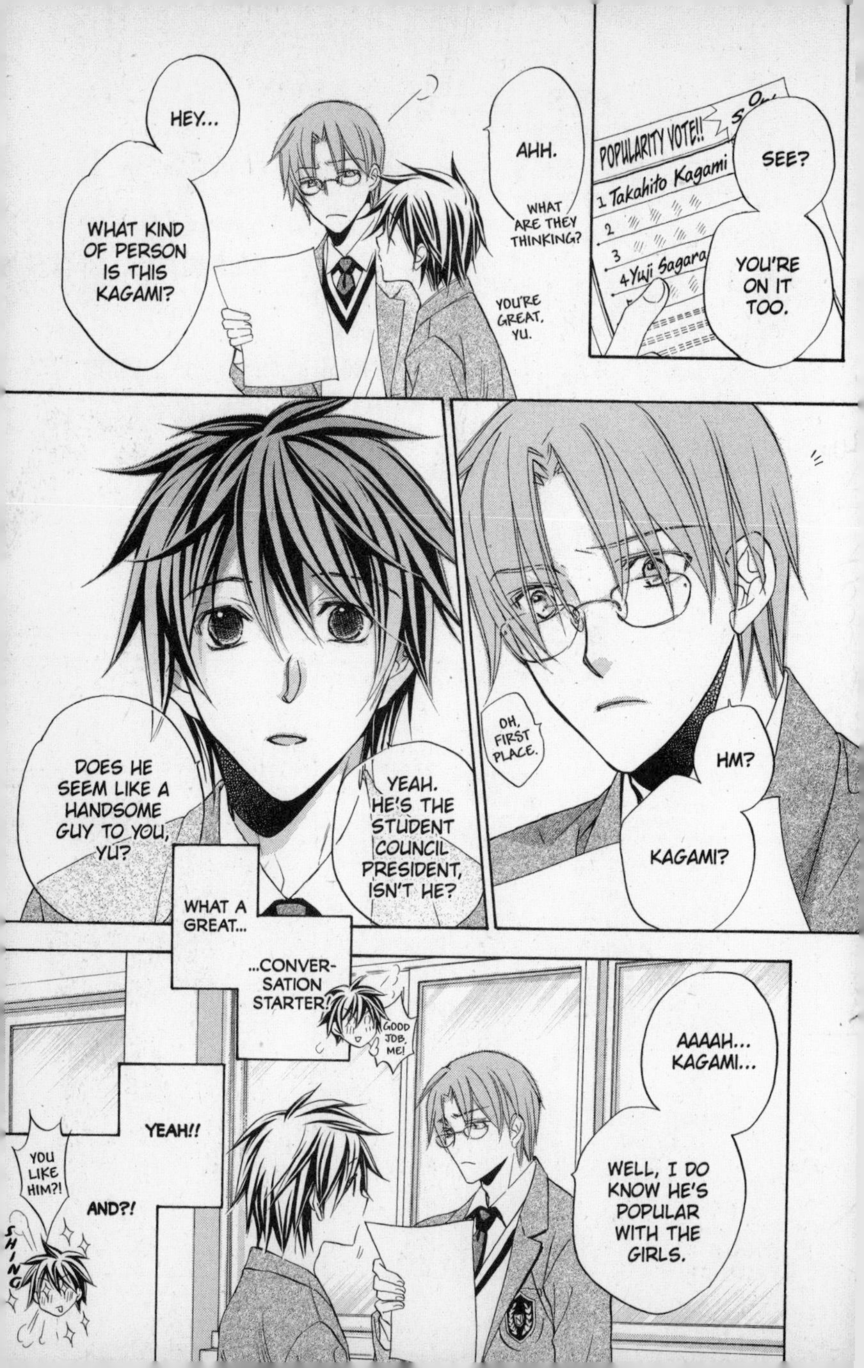
POPULARITY VOTE!!
1 Takahito Kagami
2
3
4 Yuji Sagara
SEE?
YOU'RE ON IT TOO.
AHH.
WHAT ARE THEY THINKING?
YOU'RE GREAT, YU.
HEY...
WHAT KIND OF PERSON IS THIS KAGAMI?
OH, FIRST PLACE.
HM?
KAGAMI?
YEAH. HE'S THE STUDENT COUNCIL PRESIDENT, ISN'T HE?
DOES HE SEEM LIKE A HANDSOME GUY TO YOU, YU?
WHAT A GREAT...
...CONVER-SATION STARTER!
GOOD JOB, ME!
AAAAH... KAGAMI...
WELL, I DO KNOW HE'S POPULAR WITH THE GIRLS.
YEAH!!
AND?!
YOU LIKE HIM?!
SHING

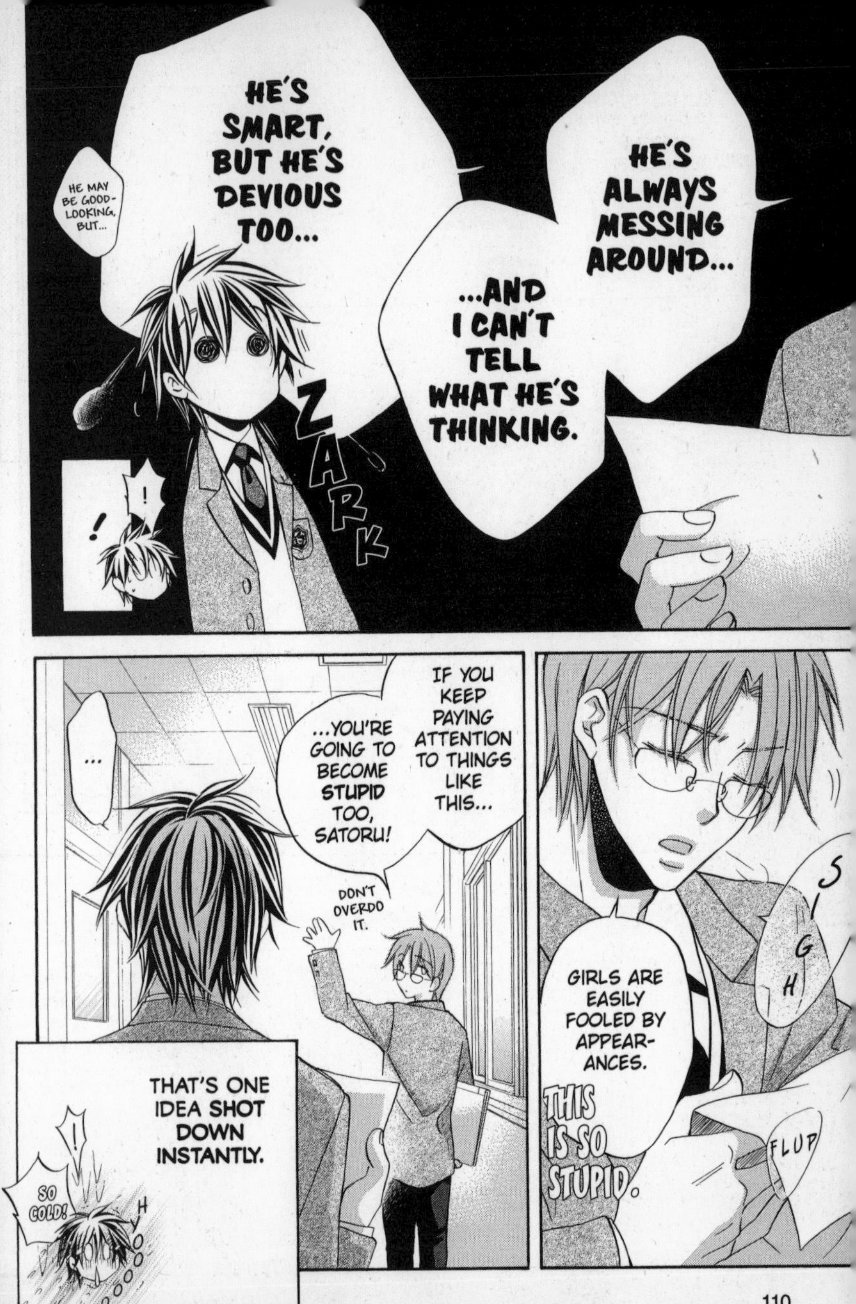
HE'S ALWAYS MESSING AROUND...
...AND I CAN'T TELL WHAT HE'S THINKING.
HE'S SMART, BUT HE'S DEVIOUS TOO...
HE MAY BE GOOD-LOOKING, BUT...
ZARK
!
!
SIGH
GIRLS ARE EASILY FOOLED BY APPEAR-ANCES.
THIS IS SO STUPID.
FLUP
IF YOU KEEP PAYING ATTENTION TO THINGS LIKE THIS...
...YOU'RE GOING TO BECOME STUPID TOO, SATORU!
...
DON'T OVERDO IT.
THAT'S ONE IDEA SHOT DOWN INSTANTLY.
!
SO COLD!
HYOOOO

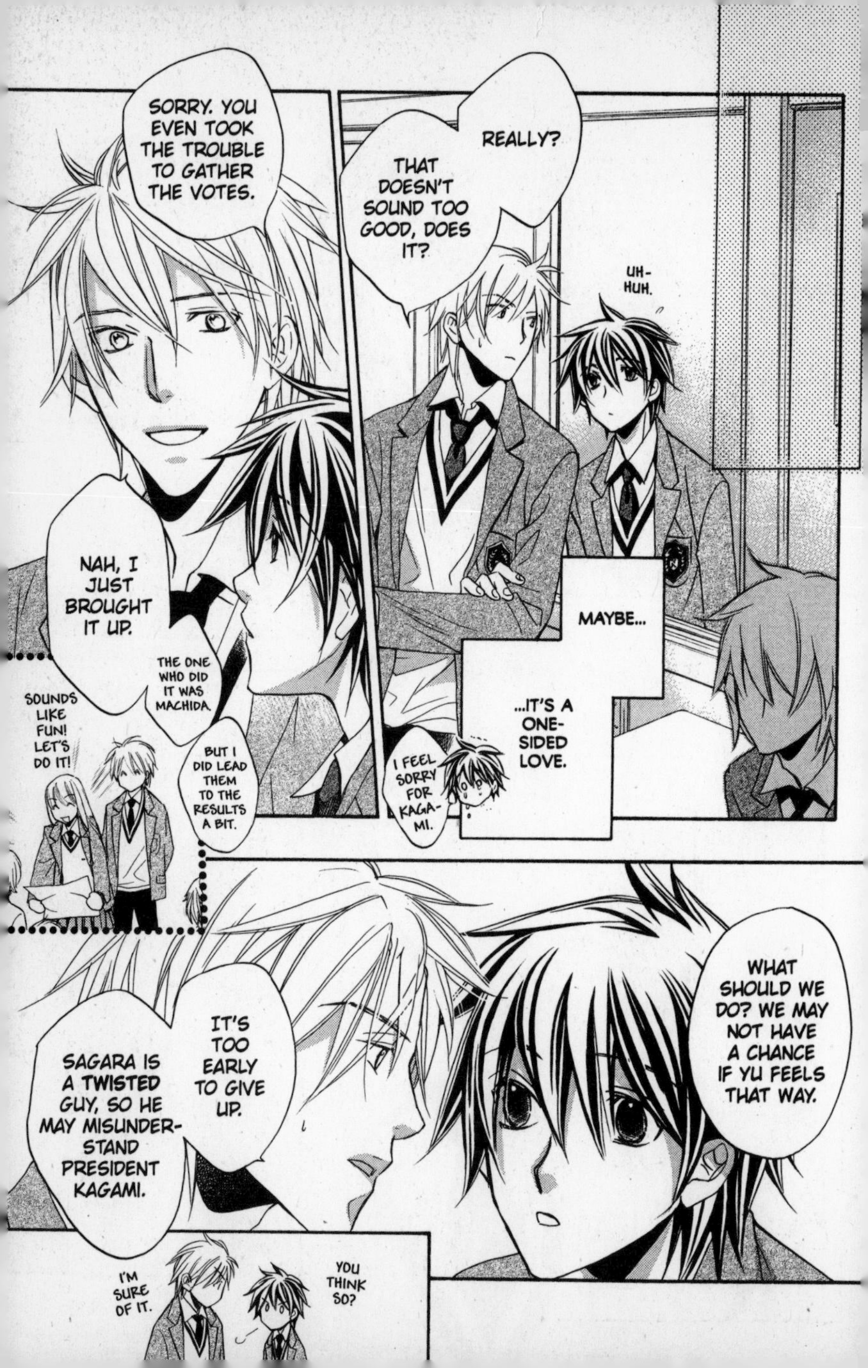
REALLY?
THAT DOESN'T SOUND TOO GOOD, DOES IT?
UH-HUH.
MAYBE...
...IT'S A ONE-SIDED LOVE.
I FEEL SORRY FOR KAGA-MI.
SORRY. YOU EVEN TOOK THE TROUBLE TO GATHER THE VOTES.
NAH, I JUST BROUGHT IT UP.
THE ONE WHO DID IT WAS MACHIDA.
BUT I DID LEAD THEM TO THE RESULTS A BIT.
SOUNDS LIKE FUN! LET'S DO IT!
WHAT SHOULD WE DO? WE MAY NOT HAVE A CHANCE IF YU FEELS THAT WAY.
IT'S TOO EARLY TO GIVE UP.
SAGARA IS A TWISTED GUY, SO HE MAY MISUNDER-STAND PRESIDENT KAGAMI.
YOU THINK SO?
I'M SURE OF IT.

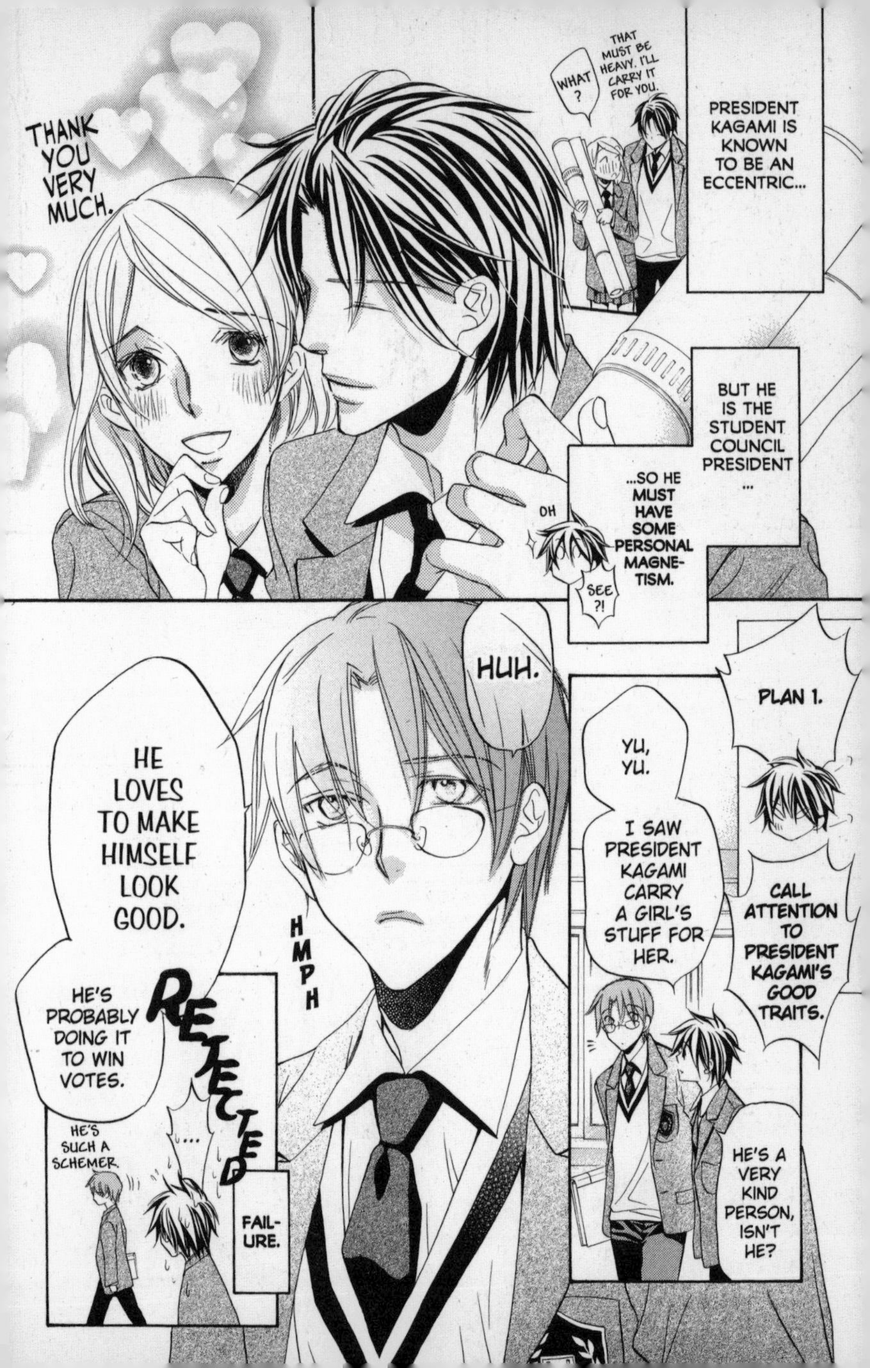
PRESIDENT KAGAMI IS KNOWN TO BE AN ECCENTRIC...
THAT MUST BE HEAVY. I'LL CARRY IT FOR YOU.
WHAT?
BUT HE IS THE STUDENT COUNCIL PRESIDENT ...
...SO HE MUST HAVE SOME PERSONAL MAGNETISM.
OH
SEE?!
THANK YOU VERY MUCH.
PLAN 1.
CALL ATTENTION TO PRESIDENT KAGAMI'S GOOD TRAITS.
YU, YU.
I SAW PRESIDENT KAGAMI CARRY A GIRL'S STUFF FOR HER.
HE'S A VERY KIND PERSON, ISN'T HE?
HUH.
HE LOVES TO MAKE HIMSELF LOOK GOOD.
HMPH
HE'S PROBABLY DOING IT TO WIN VOTES.
REJECTED
...
FAIL-URE.
HE'S SUCH A SCHEMER.

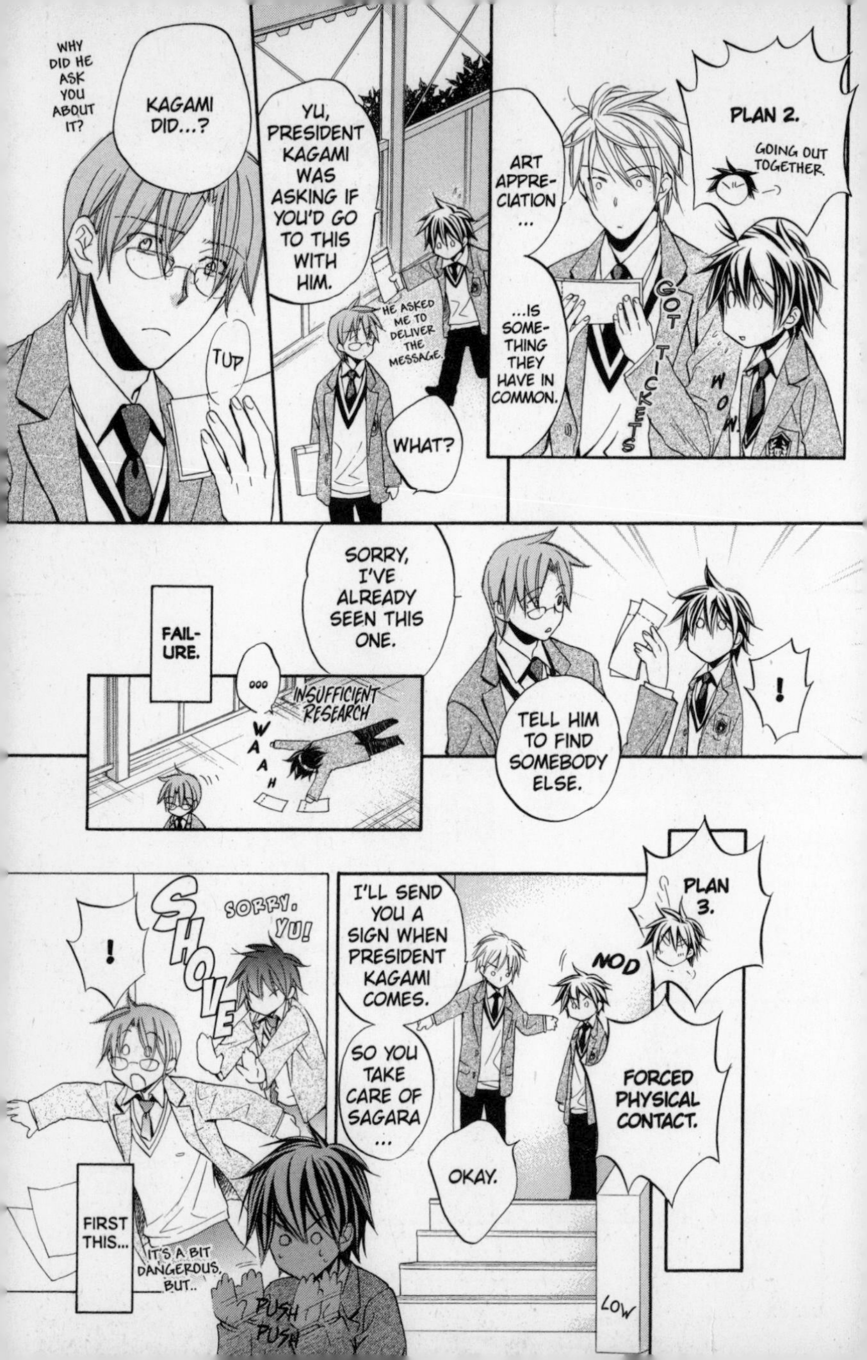
PLAN 2.
GOING OUT TOGETHER.
ART APPRE-CIATION ...
...IS SOME-THING THEY HAVE IN COMMON.
GOT TICKETS
WOW
YU, PRESIDENT KAGAMI WAS ASKING IF YOU'D GO TO THIS WITH HIM.
HE ASKED ME TO DELIVER THE MESSAGE.
WHAT?
KAGAMI DID...?
WHY DID HE ASK YOU ABOUT IT?
TUP
!
SORRY, I'VE ALREADY SEEN THIS ONE.
TELL HIM TO FIND SOMEBODY ELSE.
FAIL-URE.
...
INSUFFICIENT RESEARCH
WAAH
PLAN 3.
FORCED PHYSICAL CONTACT.
NOD
I'LL SEND YOU A SIGN WHEN PRESIDENT KAGAMI COMES.
SO YOU TAKE CARE OF SAGARA ...
OKAY.
LOW
SORRY. YU!
SHOVE
!
FIRST THIS...
IT'S A BIT DANGEROUS, BUT..
PUSH PUSH

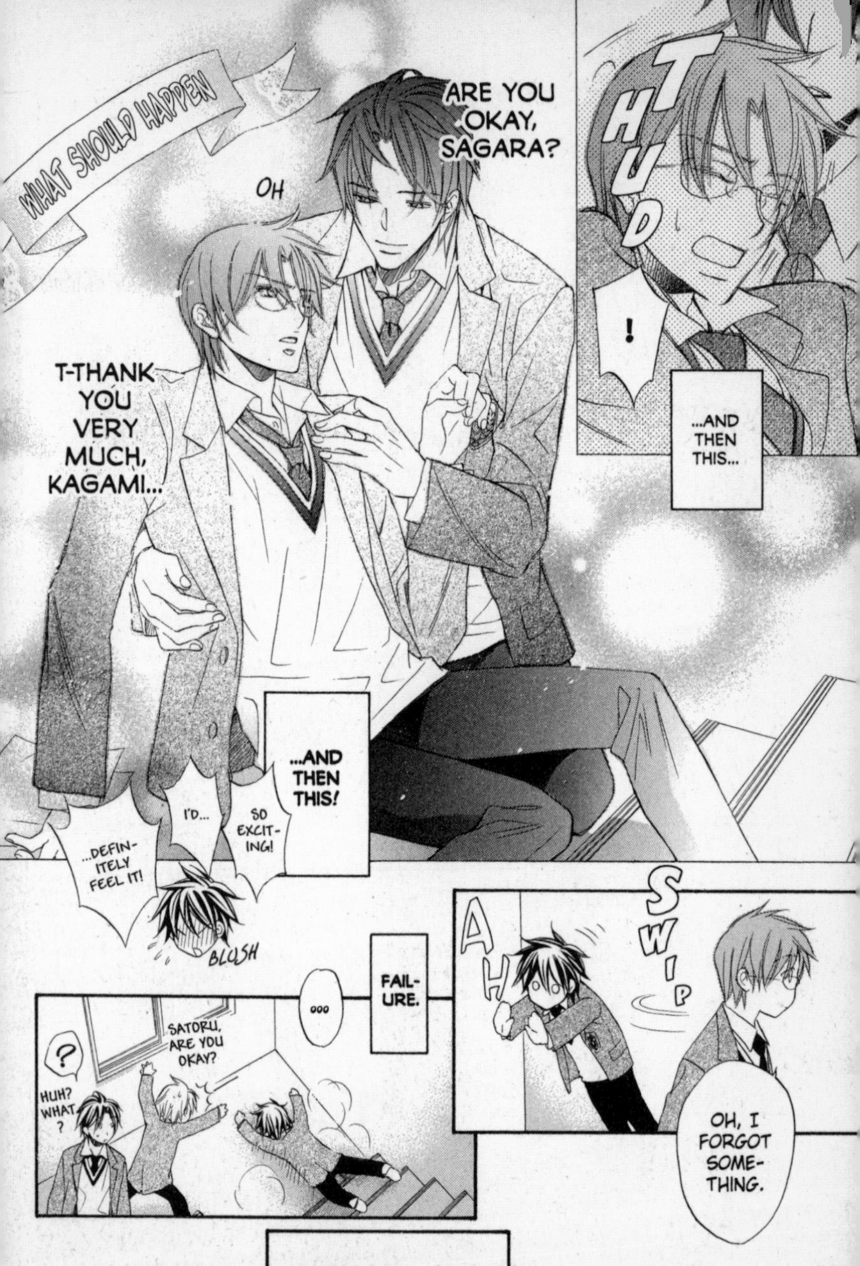
THUD
!
...AND THEN THIS...
WHAT SHOULD HAPPEN
ARE YOU OKAY, SAGARA?
OH
T-THANK YOU VERY MUCH, KAGAMI...
...AND THEN THIS!
SO EXCIT-ING!
I'D...
...DEFIN-ITELY FEEL IT!
BLUSH
SWIP
AH
OH, I FORGOT SOME-THING.
FAIL-URE.
...
SATORU, ARE YOU OKAY?
?
HUH? WHAT?

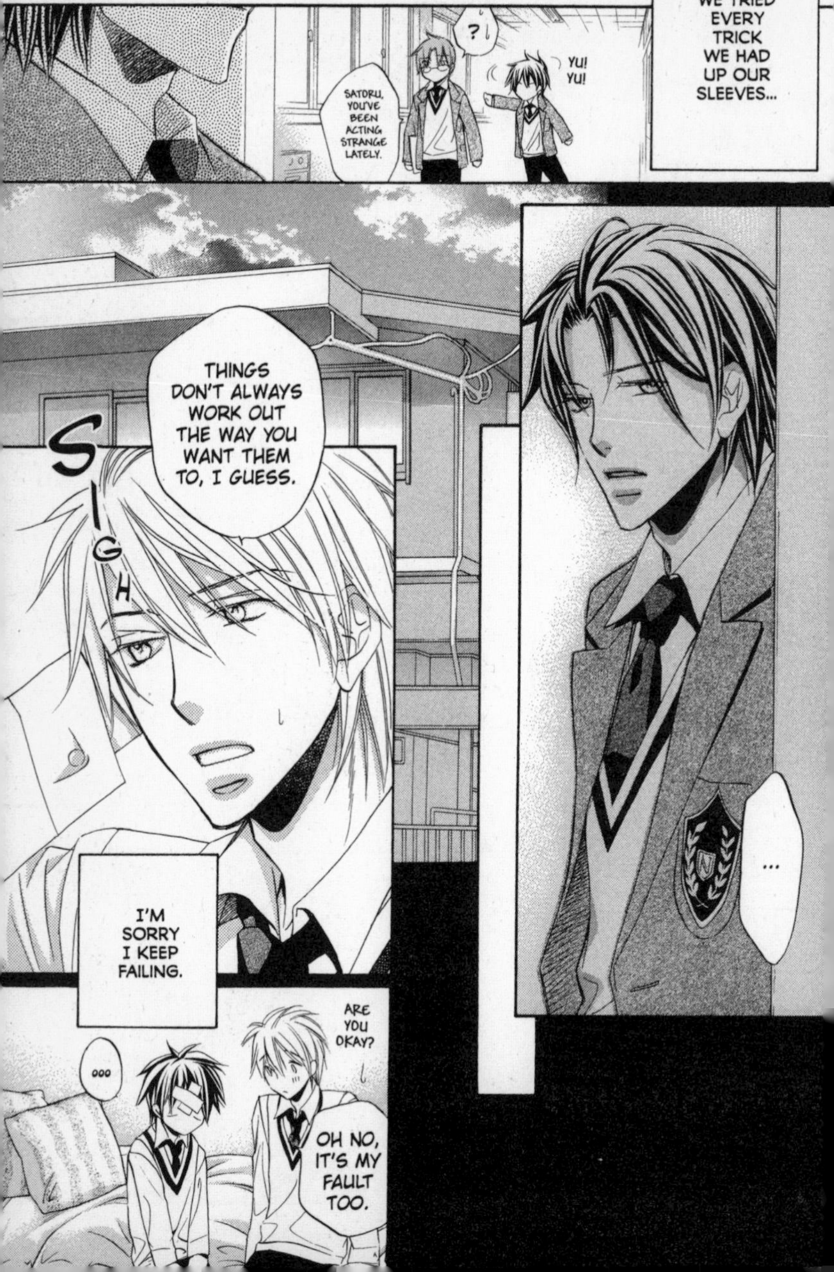
WE TRIED EVERY TRICK WE HAD UP OUR SLEEVES...
?!
YU! YU!
SATORU, YOU'VE BEEN ACTING STRANGE LATELY.
...
THINGS DON'T ALWAYS WORK OUT THE WAY YOU WANT THEM TO, I GUESS.
SIGH
I'M SORRY I KEEP FAILING.
ARE YOU OKAY?
...
OH NO, IT'S MY FAULT TOO.

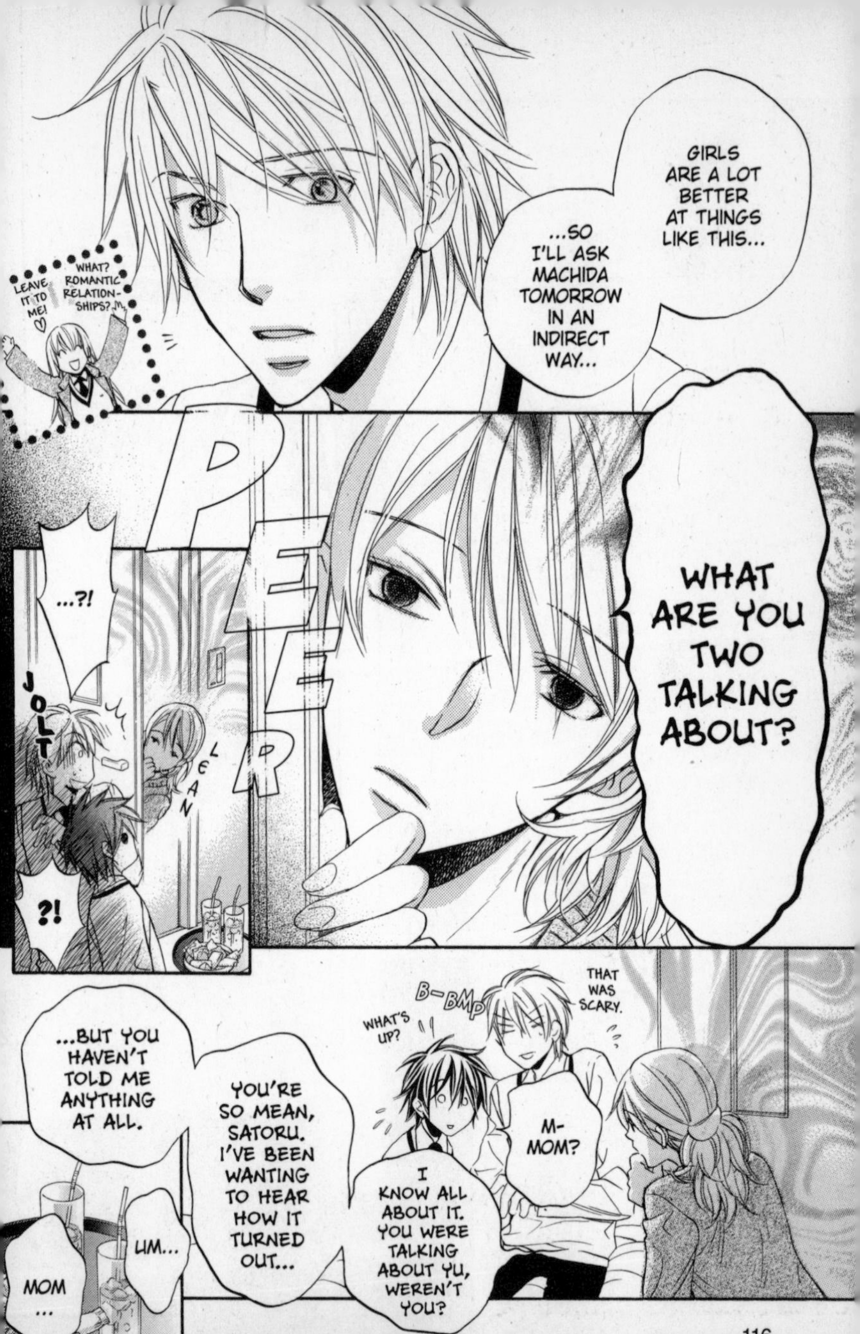
GIRLS ARE A LOT BETTER AT THINGS LIKE THIS...
...SO I'LL ASK MACHIDA TOMORROW IN AN INDIRECT WAY...
WHAT? ROMANTIC RELATION-SHIPS?
LEAVE IT TO ME!
PEER
WHAT ARE YOU TWO TALKING ABOUT?
...?!
JOLT
LEAN
?!
THAT WAS SCARY.
B-BMP
WHAT'S UP?
M-MOM?
I KNOW ALL ABOUT IT. YOU WERE TALKING ABOUT YU, WEREN'T YOU?
YOU'RE SO MEAN, SATORU. I'VE BEEN WANTING TO HEAR HOW IT TURNED OUT...
...BUT YOU HAVEN'T TOLD ME ANYTHING AT ALL.
UM...
MOM...

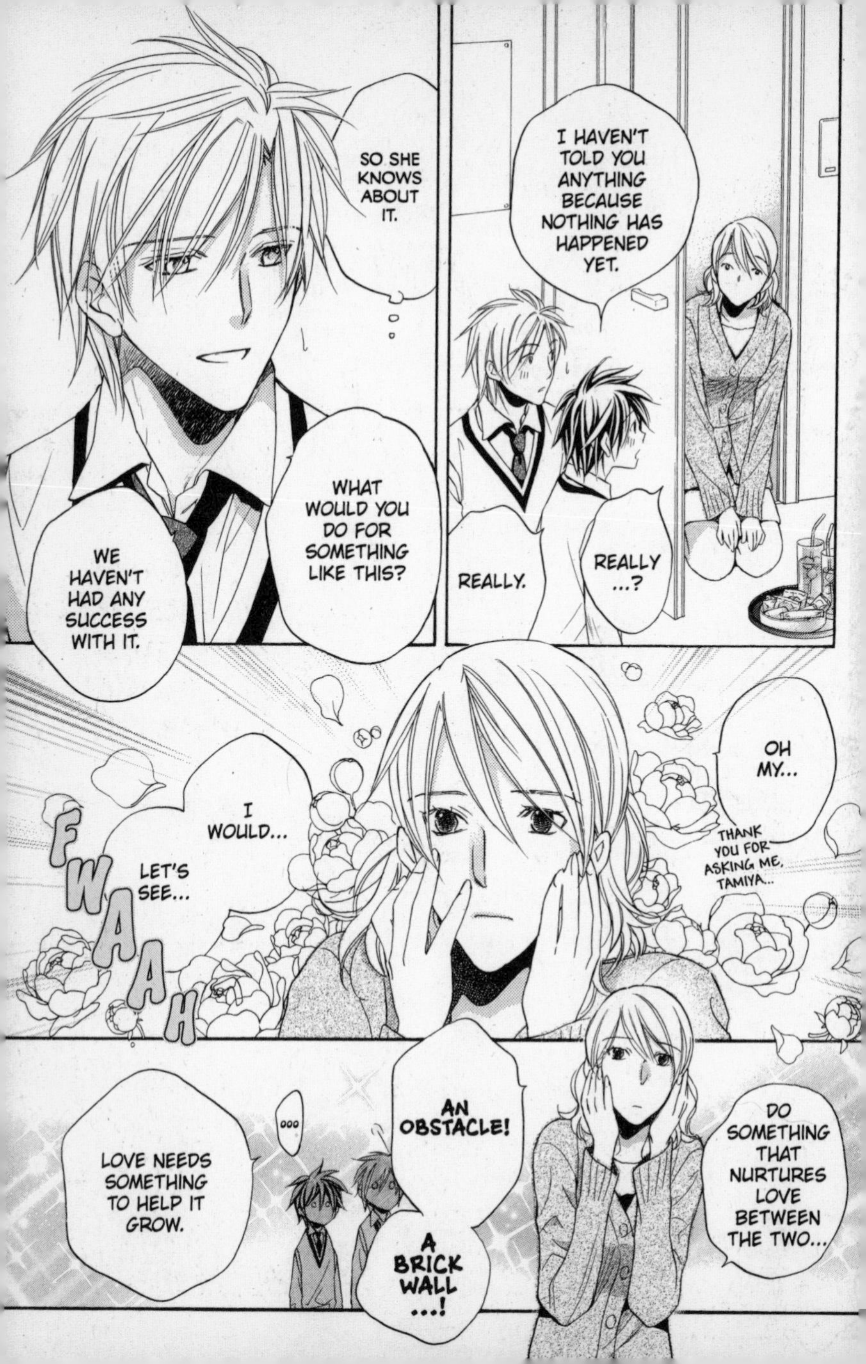
I HAVEN'T TOLD YOU ANYTHING BECAUSE NOTHING HAS HAPPENED YET.
REALLY ...?
REALLY.
SO SHE KNOWS ABOUT IT.
WHAT WOULD YOU DO FOR SOMETHING LIKE THIS?
WE HAVEN'T HAD ANY SUCCESS WITH IT.
OH MY...
THANK YOU FOR ASKING ME, TAMIYA...
I WOULD...
LET'S SEE...
FWAAAH
DO SOMETHING THAT NURTURES LOVE BETWEEN THE TWO...
AN OBSTACLE!
A BRICK WALL ...!
...
LOVE NEEDS SOMETHING TO HELP IT GROW.

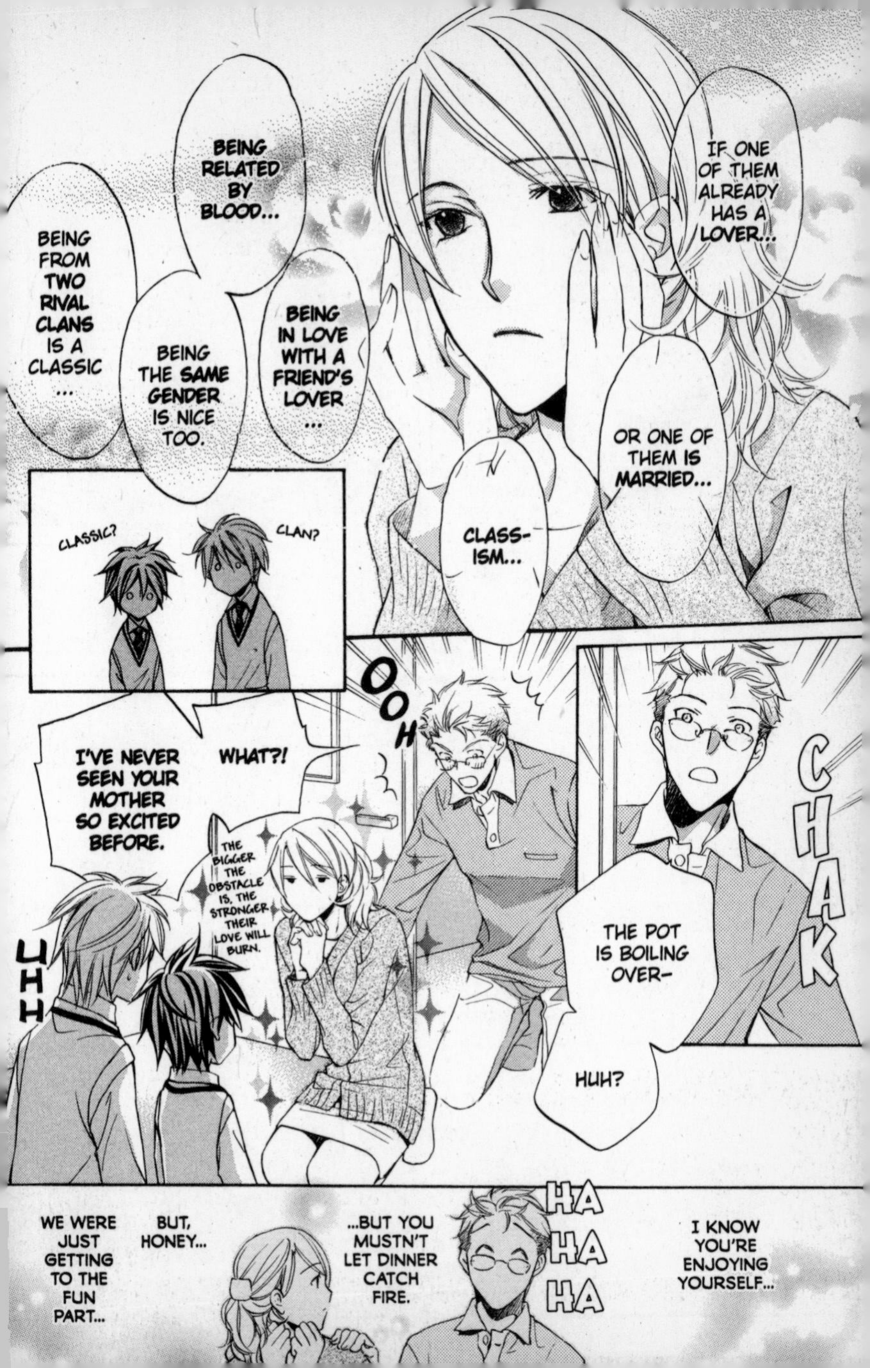
IF ONE OF THEM ALREADY HAS A LOVER...
OR ONE OF THEM IS MARRIED...
CLASS-ISM...
BEING RELATED BY BLOOD...
BEING IN LOVE WITH A FRIEND'S LOVER...
BEING FROM TWO RIVAL CLANS IS A CLASSIC...
BEING THE SAME GENDER IS NICE TOO.
CLAN?
CLASSIC?
CHAK
THE POT IS BOILING OVER-
OOH
HUH?
WHAT?!
I'VE NEVER SEEN YOUR MOTHER SO EXCITED BEFORE.
THE BIGGER THE OBSTACLE IS, THE STRONGER THEIR LOVE WILL BURN.
UHH
I KNOW YOU'RE ENJOYING YOURSELF...
HA HA HA
...BUT YOU MUSTN'T LET DINNER CATCH FIRE.
BUT, HONEY...
WE WERE JUST GETTING TO THE FUN PART...

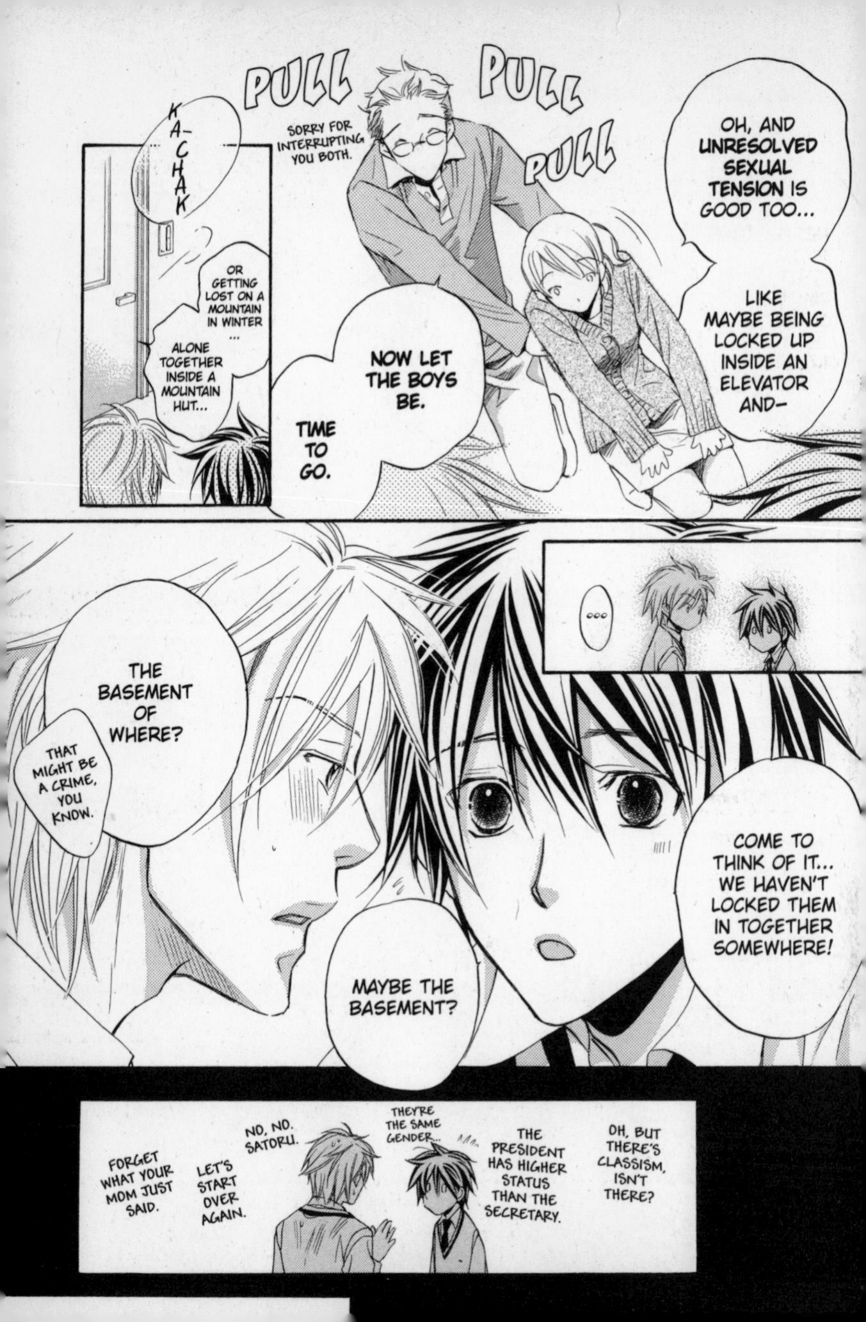
OH, AND UNRESOLVED SEXUAL TENSION IS GOOD TOO...
LIKE MAYBE BEING LOCKED UP INSIDE AN ELEVATOR AND—
PULL
PULL
PULL
SORRY FOR INTERRUPTING YOU BOTH.
NOW LET THE BOYS BE.
TIME TO GO.
OR GETTING LOST ON A MOUNTAIN IN WINTER ...
ALONE TOGETHER INSIDE A MOUNTAIN HUT...
KA-CHAK
...
COME TO THINK OF IT... WE HAVEN'T LOCKED THEM IN TOGETHER SOMEWHERE!
MAYBE THE BASEMENT?
THE BASEMENT OF WHERE?
THAT MIGHT BE A CRIME, YOU KNOW.
OH, BUT THERE'S CLASSISM, ISN'T THERE?
THE PRESIDENT HAS HIGHER STATUS THAN THE SECRETARY.
THEY'RE THE SAME GENDER...
NO, NO. SATORU.
LET'S START OVER AGAIN.
FORGET WHAT YOUR MOM JUST SAID.

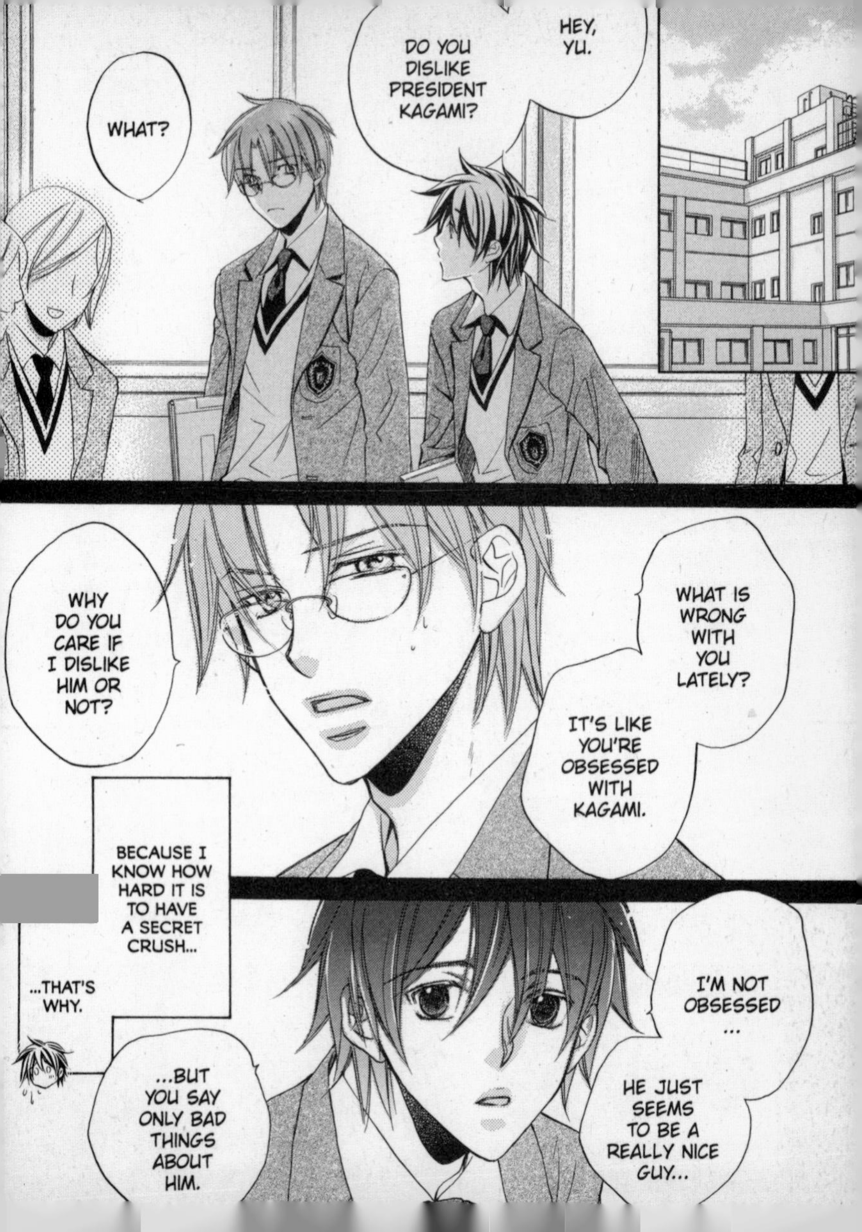
HEY, YU.
DO YOU DISLIKE PRESIDENT KAGAMI?
WHAT?
WHAT IS WRONG WITH YOU LATELY?
IT'S LIKE YOU'RE OBSESSED WITH KAGAMI.
WHY DO YOU CARE IF I DISLIKE HIM OR NOT?
I'M NOT OBSESSED ...
HE JUST SEEMS TO BE A REALLY NICE GUY...
...BUT YOU SAY ONLY BAD THINGS ABOUT HIM.
BECAUSE I KNOW HOW HARD IT IS TO HAVE A SECRET CRUSH...
...THAT'S WHY.

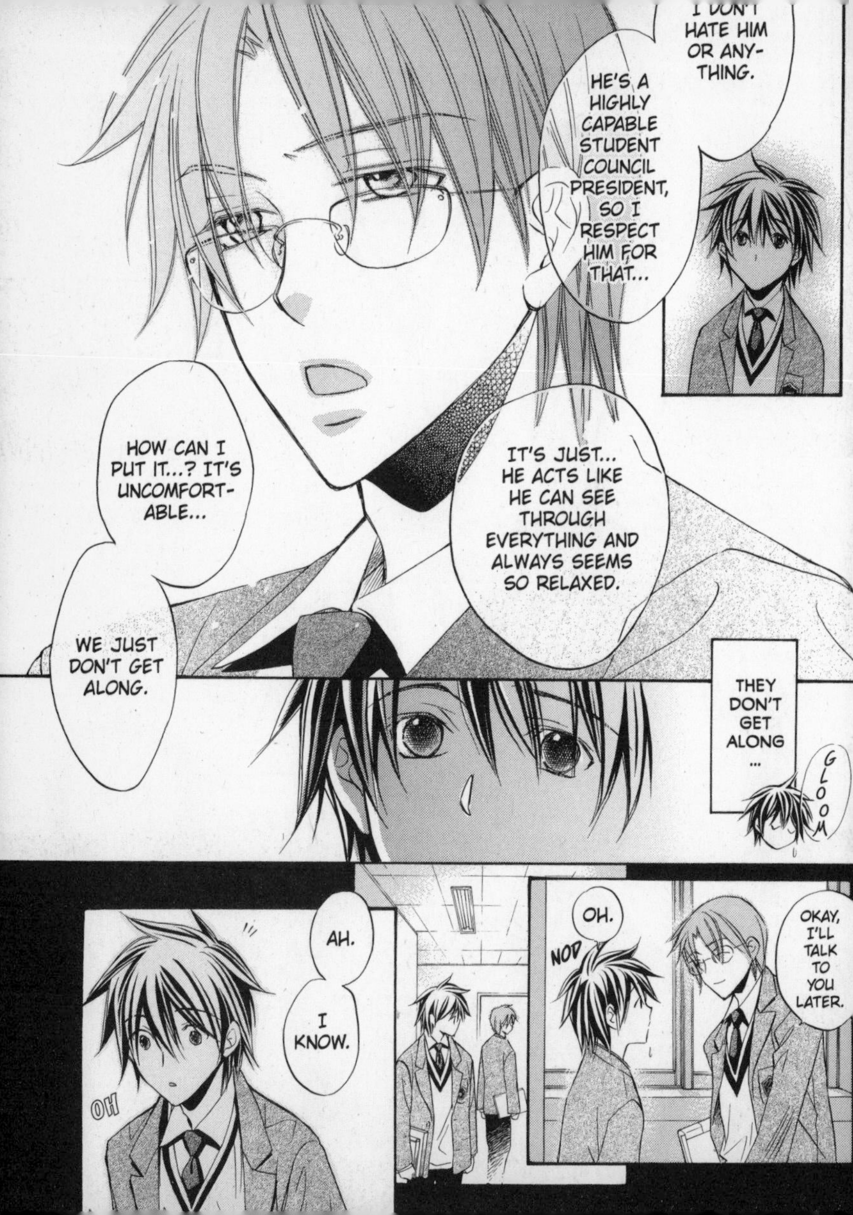
I DON'T HATE HIM OR ANY-THING.
HE'S A HIGHLY CAPABLE STUDENT COUNCIL PRESIDENT, SO I RESPECT HIM FOR THAT...
IT'S JUST... HE ACTS LIKE HE CAN SEE THROUGH EVERYTHING AND ALWAYS SEEMS SO RELAXED.
HOW CAN I PUT IT...? IT'S UNCOMFORT-ABLE...
WE JUST DON'T GET ALONG.
THEY DON'T GET ALONG ...
GLOOM
OKAY, I'LL TALK TO YOU LATER.
OH.
NOD
AH.
I KNOW.
OH

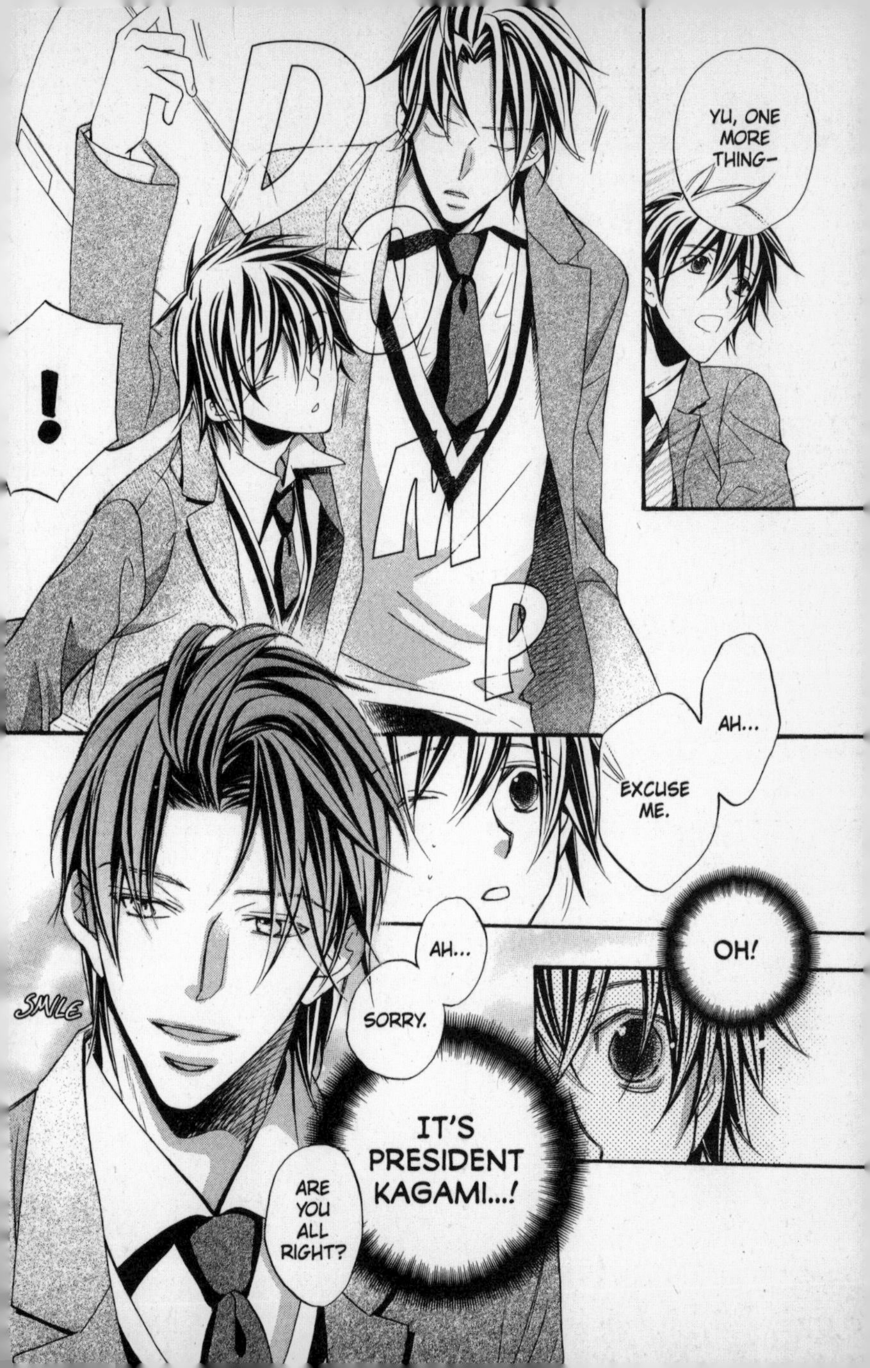
YU, ONE MORE THING—
DOMP
!
AH...
EXCUSE ME.
OH!
IT'S PRESIDENT KAGAMI...!
AH...
SORRY.
ARE YOU ALL RIGHT?
SMILE

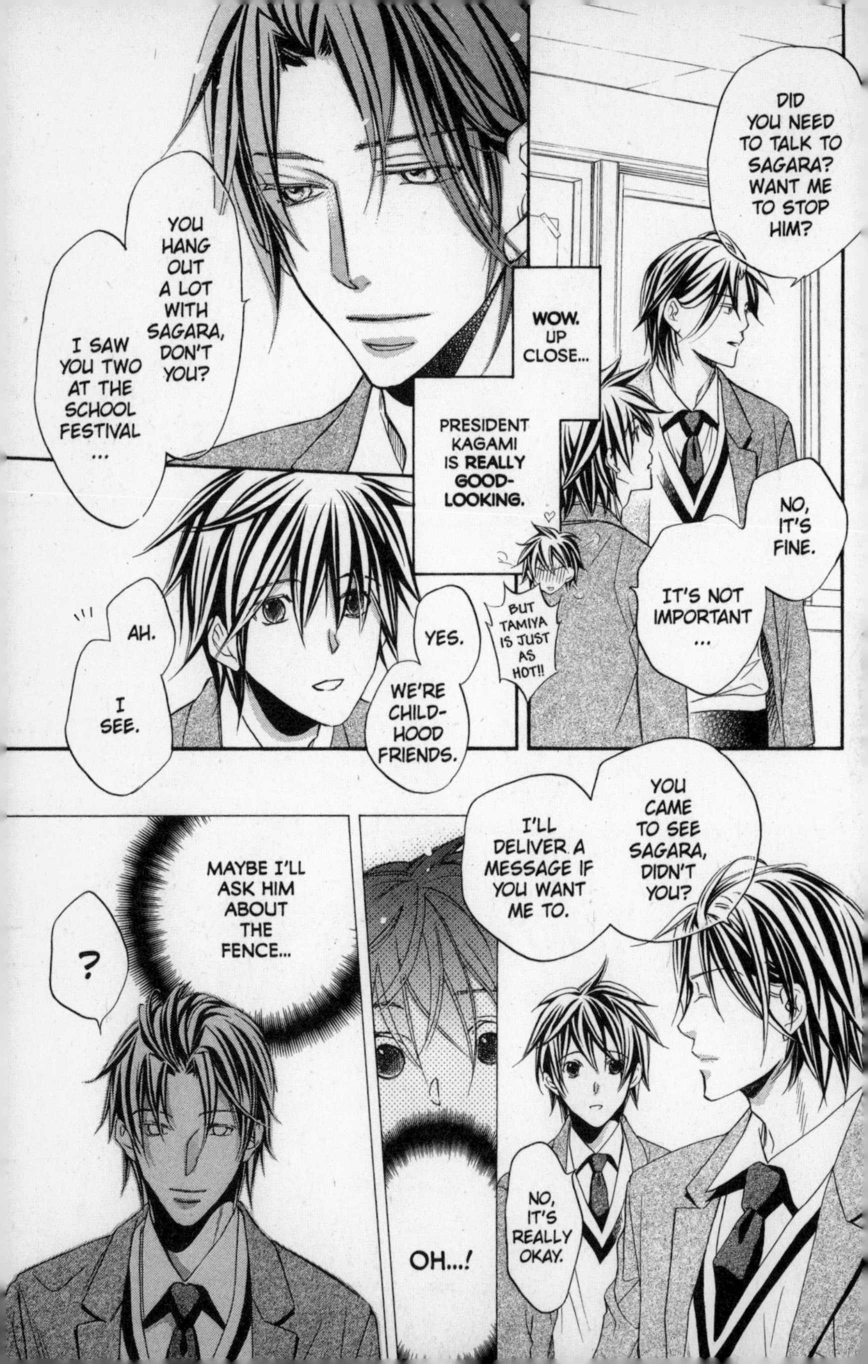
DID YOU NEED TO TALK TO SAGARA? WANT ME TO STOP HIM?
NO, IT'S FINE.
IT'S NOT IMPORTANT...
WOW. UP CLOSE...
PRESIDENT KAGAMI IS REALLY GOOD-LOOKING.
BUT TAMIYA IS JUST AS HOT!!
YOU HANG OUT A LOT WITH SAGARA, DON'T YOU?
I SAW YOU TWO AT THE SCHOOL FESTIVAL...
YES.
WE'RE CHILDHOOD FRIENDS.
AH.
I SEE.
YOU CAME TO SEE SAGARA, DIDN'T YOU?
I'LL DELIVER A MESSAGE IF YOU WANT ME TO.
NO, IT'S REALLY OKAY.
OH...!
MAYBE I'LL ASK HIM ABOUT THE FENCE...
?

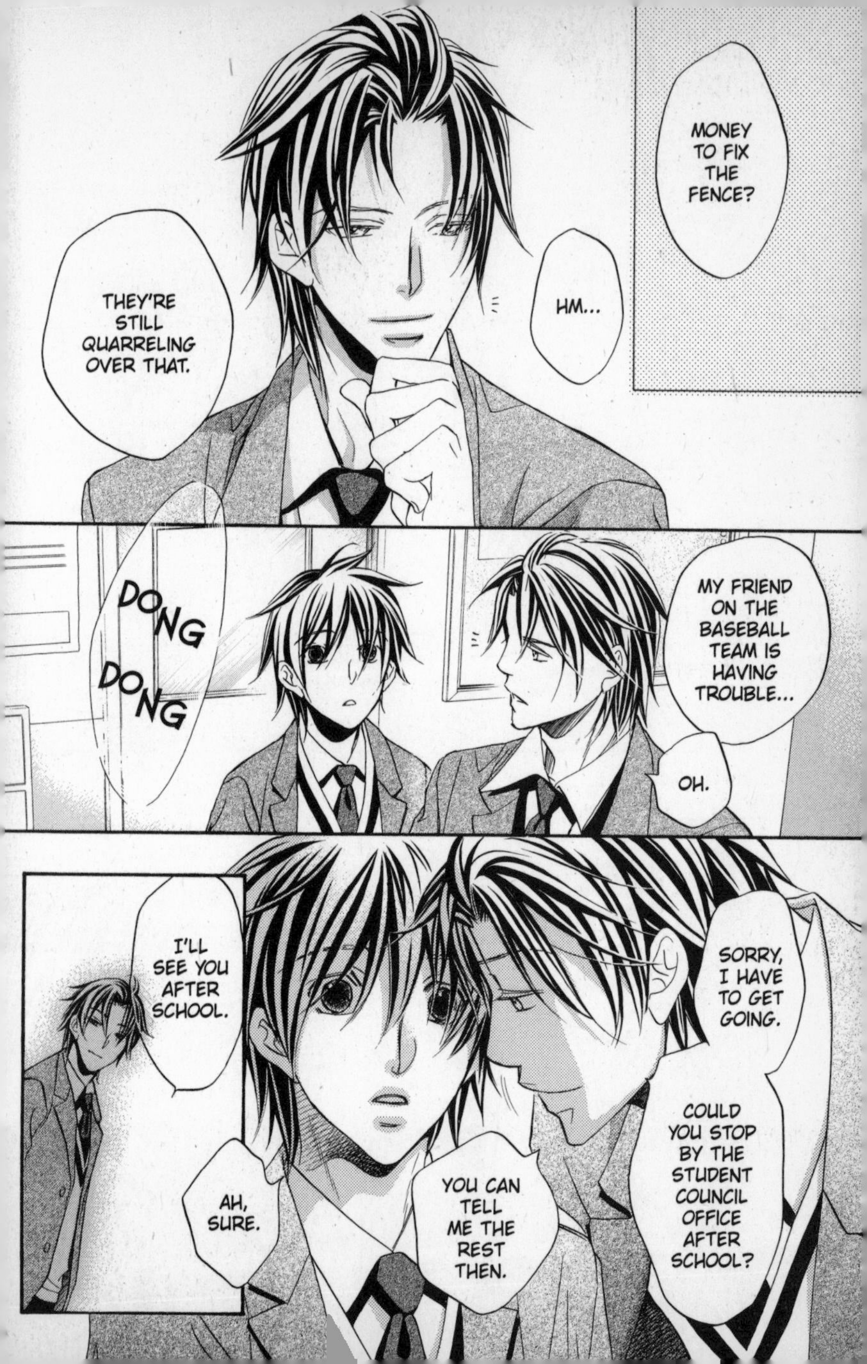
MONEY TO FIX THE FENCE?
HM...
THEY'RE STILL QUARRELING OVER THAT.
MY FRIEND ON THE BASEBALL TEAM IS HAVING TROUBLE...
OH.
DONG DONG
SORRY, I HAVE TO GET GOING.
COULD YOU STOP BY THE STUDENT COUNCIL OFFICE AFTER SCHOOL?
YOU CAN TELL ME THE REST THEN.
AH, SURE.
I'LL SEE YOU AFTER SCHOOL.

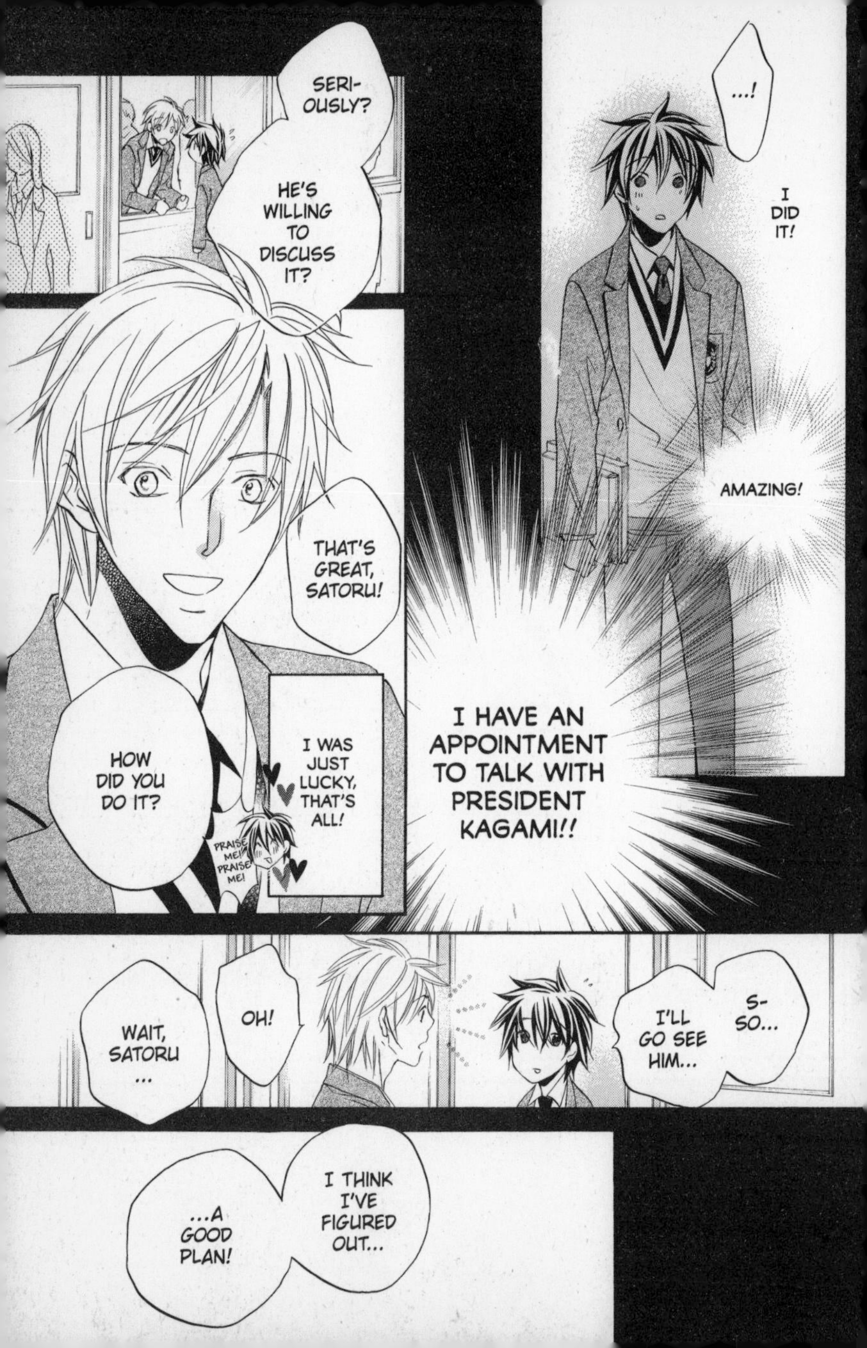
...!
I DID IT!
AMAZING!
I HAVE AN APPOINTMENT TO TALK WITH PRESIDENT KAGAMI!!
SERI-OUSLY?
HE'S WILLING TO DISCUSS IT?
THAT'S GREAT, SATORU!
HOW DID YOU DO IT?
I WAS JUST LUCKY, THAT'S ALL!
PRAISE ME! PRAISE ME!
S-SO...
I'LL GO SEE HIM...
OH!
WAIT, SATORU...
I THINK I'VE FIGURED OUT...
...A GOOD PLAN!

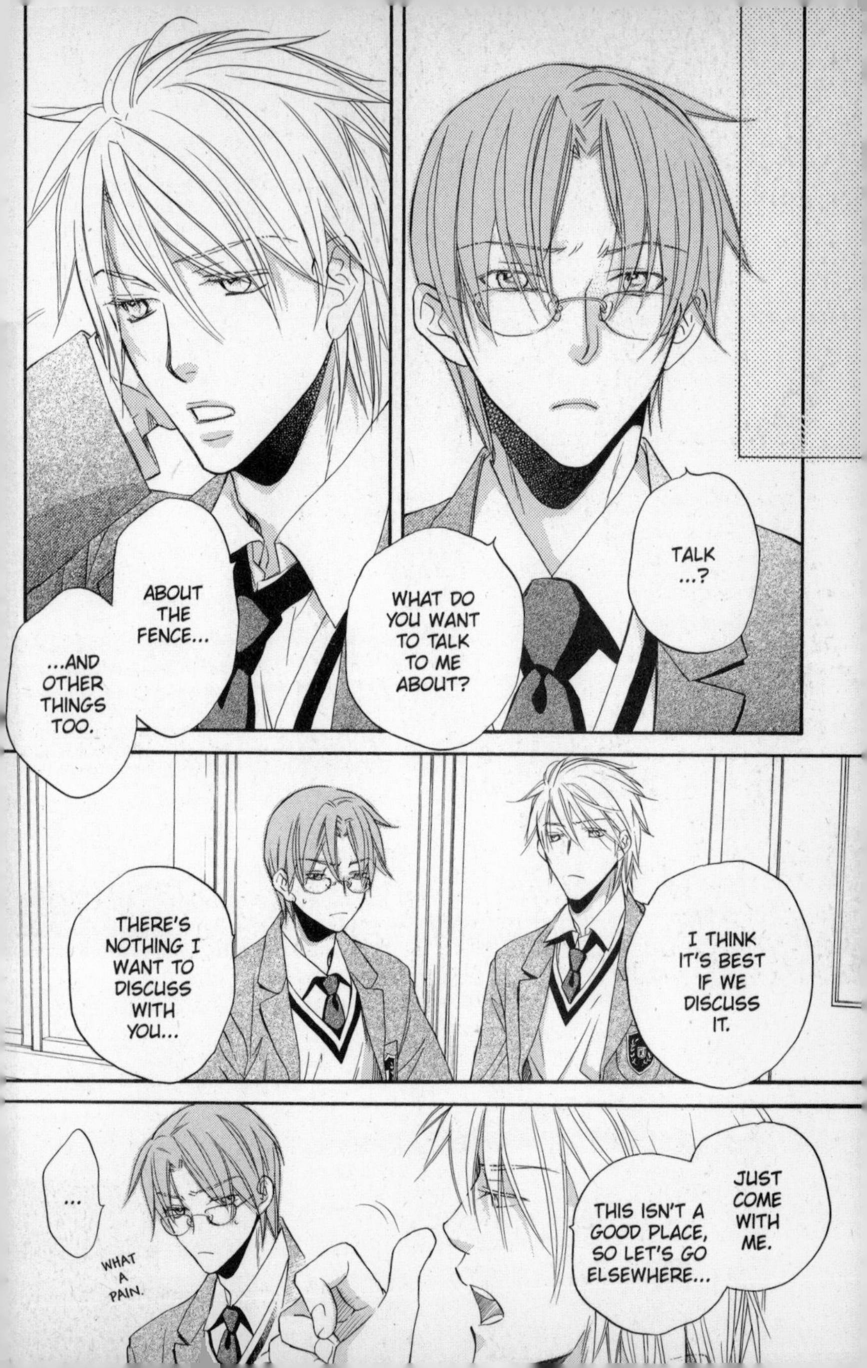
TALK ...?
WHAT DO YOU WANT TO TALK TO ME ABOUT?
ABOUT THE FENCE...
...AND OTHER THINGS TOO.
I THINK IT'S BEST IF WE DISCUSS IT.
THERE'S NOTHING I WANT TO DISCUSS WITH YOU...
JUST COME WITH ME.
THIS ISN'T A GOOD PLACE, SO LET'S GO ELSEWHERE...
...
WHAT A PAIN.

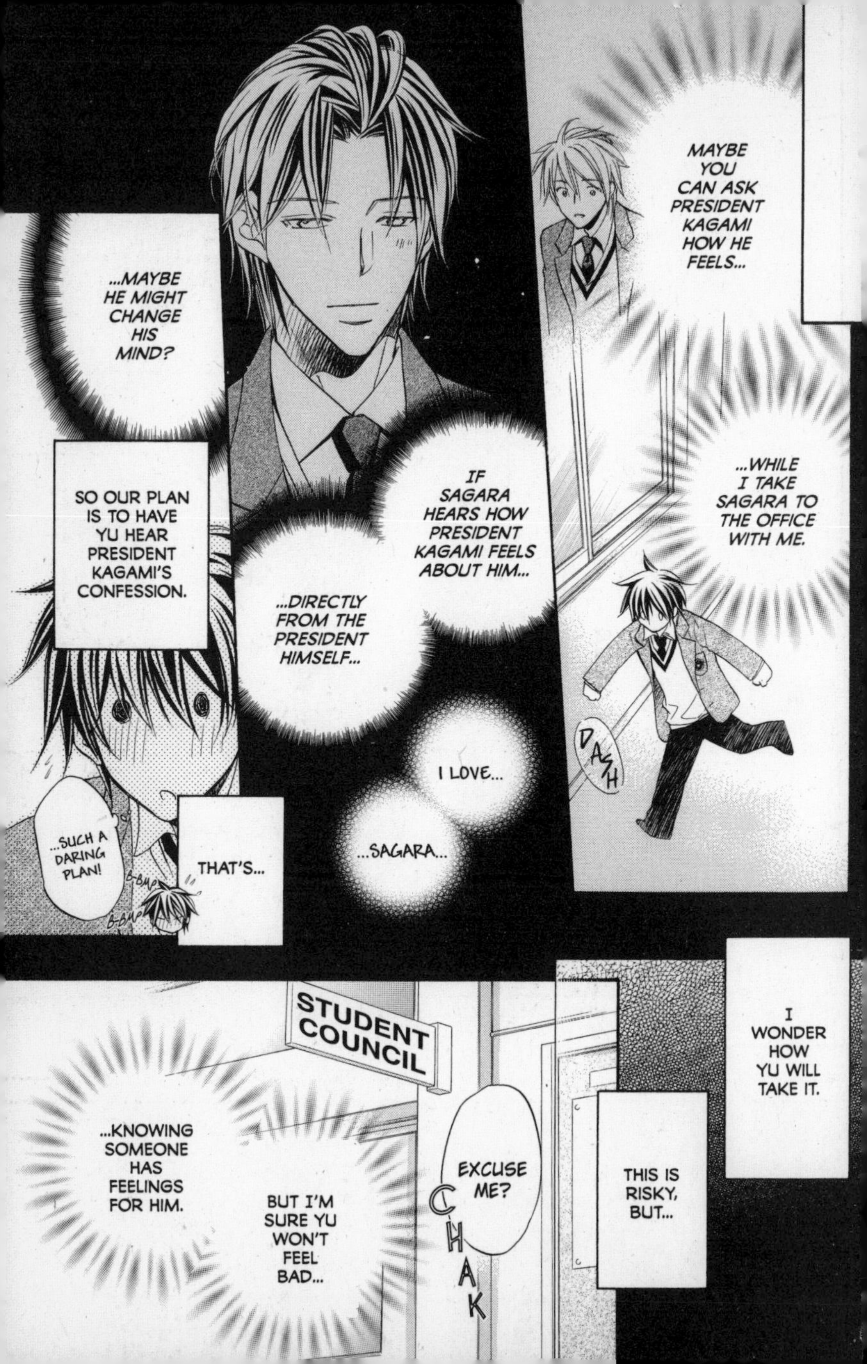
MAYBE YOU CAN ASK PRESIDENT KAGAMI HOW HE FEELS...
...WHILE I TAKE SAGARA TO THE OFFICE WITH ME.
DASH
...MAYBE HE MIGHT CHANGE HIS MIND?
IF SAGARA HEARS HOW PRESIDENT KAGAMI FEELS ABOUT HIM...
...DIRECTLY FROM THE PRESIDENT HIMSELF...
I LOVE...
...SAGARA...
SO OUR PLAN IS TO HAVE YU HEAR PRESIDENT KAGAMI'S CONFESSION.
THAT'S...
...SUCH A DARING PLAN!
B-BMP
B-BMP
I WONDER HOW YU WILL TAKE IT.
THIS IS RISKY, BUT...
EXCUSE ME?
CHAK
STUDENT COUNCIL
BUT I'M SURE YU WON'T FEEL BAD...
...KNOWING SOMEONE HAS FEELINGS FOR HIM.

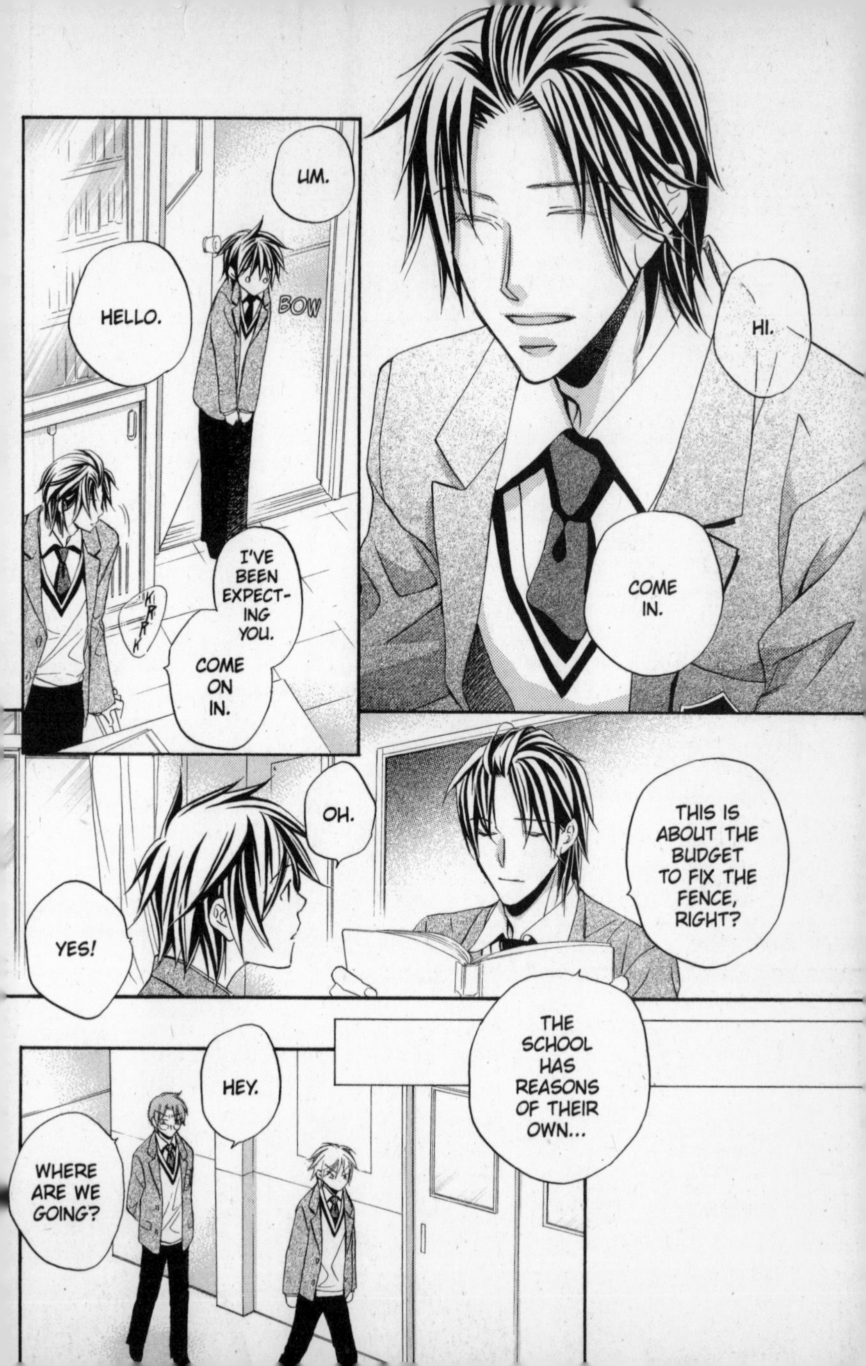
HI.
COME IN.
UM.
BOW
HELLO.
I'VE BEEN EXPECT-ING YOU.
COME ON IN.
KRRK
THIS IS ABOUT THE BUDGET TO FIX THE FENCE, RIGHT?
OH.
YES!
THE SCHOOL HAS REASONS OF THEIR OWN...
HEY.
WHERE ARE WE GOING?

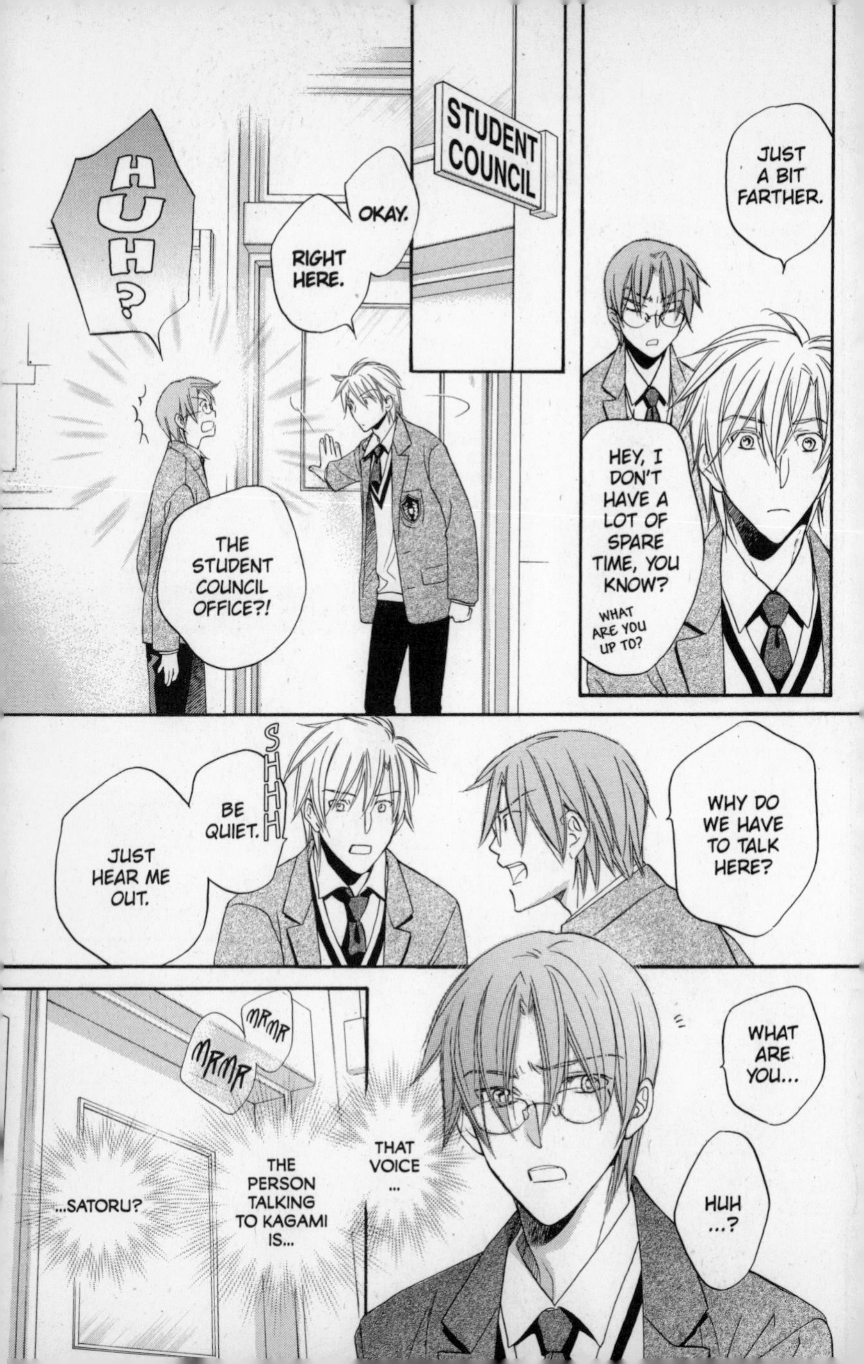
JUST A BIT FARTHER.
HEY, I DON'T HAVE A LOT OF SPARE TIME, YOU KNOW?
WHAT ARE YOU UP TO?
STUDENT COUNCIL
OKAY.
RIGHT HERE.
HUH?
THE STUDENT COUNCIL OFFICE?!
WHY DO WE HAVE TO TALK HERE?
SHHH
BE QUIET.
JUST HEAR ME OUT.
WHAT ARE YOU...
HUH ...?
MRMR
MRMR
THAT VOICE ...
THE PERSON TALKING TO KAGAMI IS...
...SATORU?

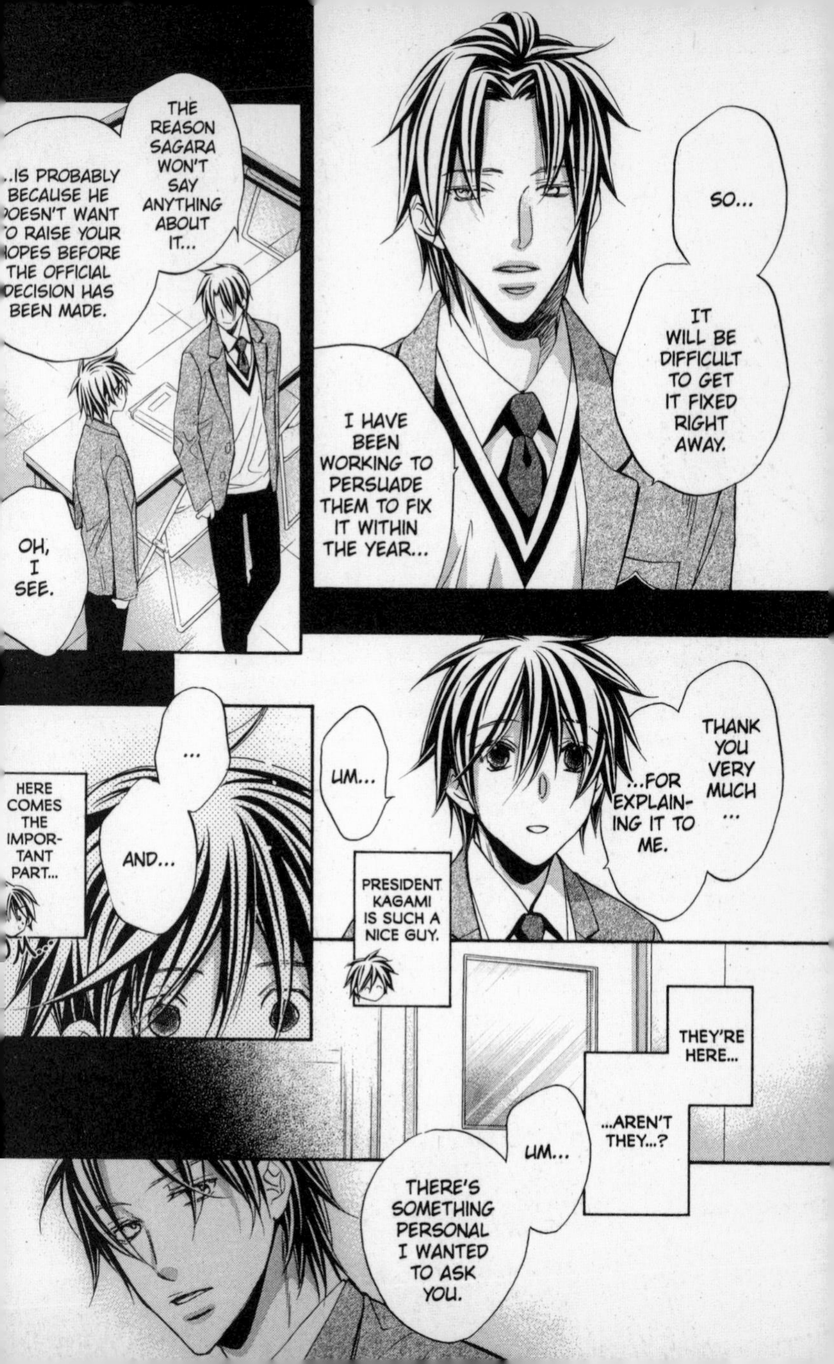
SO...
IT WILL BE DIFFICULT TO GET IT FIXED RIGHT AWAY.
I HAVE BEEN WORKING TO PERSUADE THEM TO FIX IT WITHIN THE YEAR...
THE REASON SAGARA WON'T SAY ANYTHING ABOUT IT...
..IS PROBABLY BECAUSE HE DOESN'T WANT TO RAISE YOUR HOPES BEFORE THE OFFICIAL DECISION HAS BEEN MADE.
OH, I SEE.
THANK YOU VERY MUCH...
...FOR EXPLAINING IT TO ME.
UM...
PRESIDENT KAGAMI IS SUCH A NICE GUY.
...
AND...
HERE COMES THE IMPORTANT PART...
THEY'RE HERE...
...AREN'T THEY...?
UM...
THERE'S SOMETHING PERSONAL I WANTED TO ASK YOU.

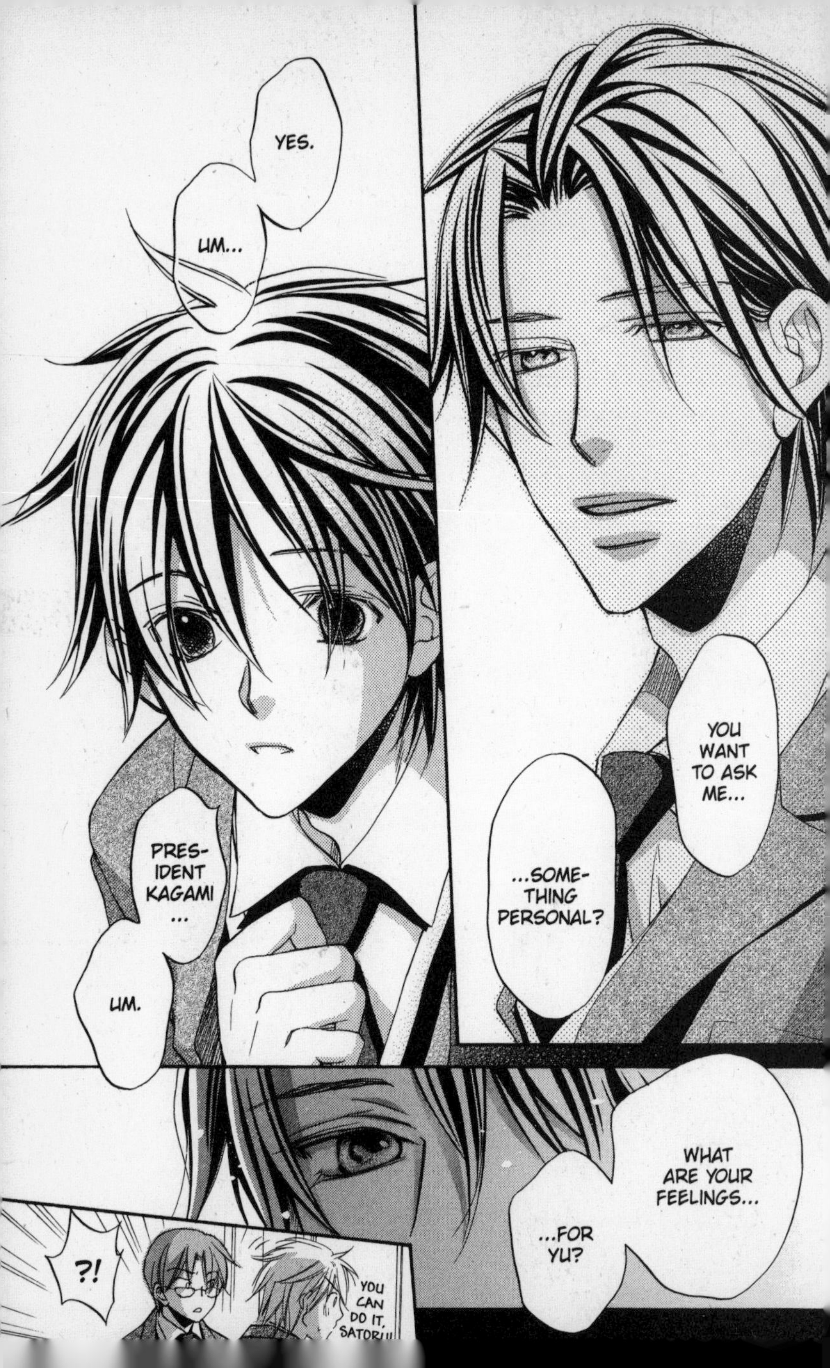
YOU WANT TO ASK ME...
...SOME-THING PERSONAL?
YES.
UM...
PRES-IDENT KAGAMI...
UM.
WHAT ARE YOUR FEELINGS...
...FOR YU?
?!
YOU CAN DO IT, SATORU!!

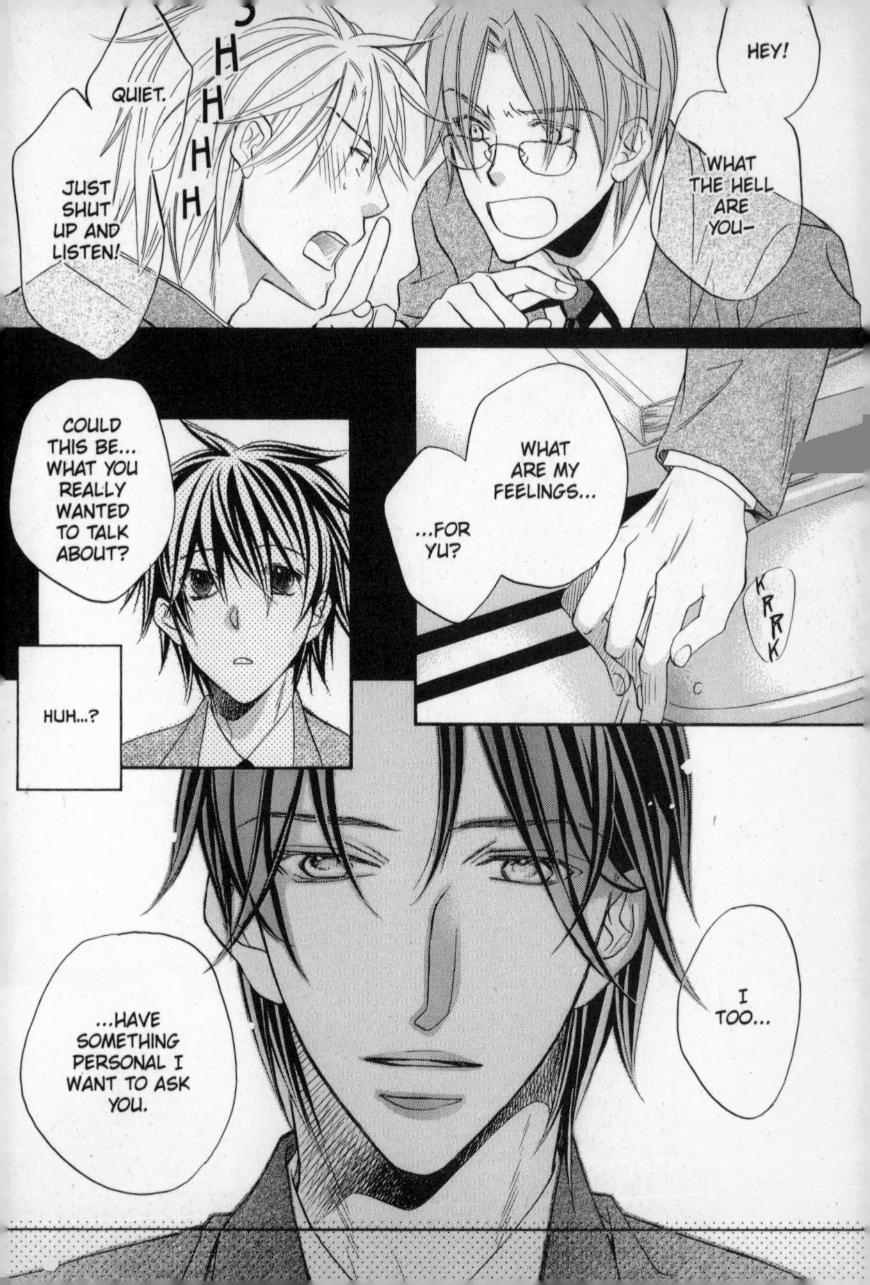
HEY!
WHAT THE HELL ARE YOU—
HHHH
QUIET.
JUST SHUT UP AND LISTEN!
WHAT ARE MY FEELINGS...
...FOR YU?
KRRK
COULD THIS BE... WHAT YOU REALLY WANTED TO TALK ABOUT?
HUH...?
I TOO...
...HAVE SOMETHING PERSONAL I WANT TO ASK YOU.

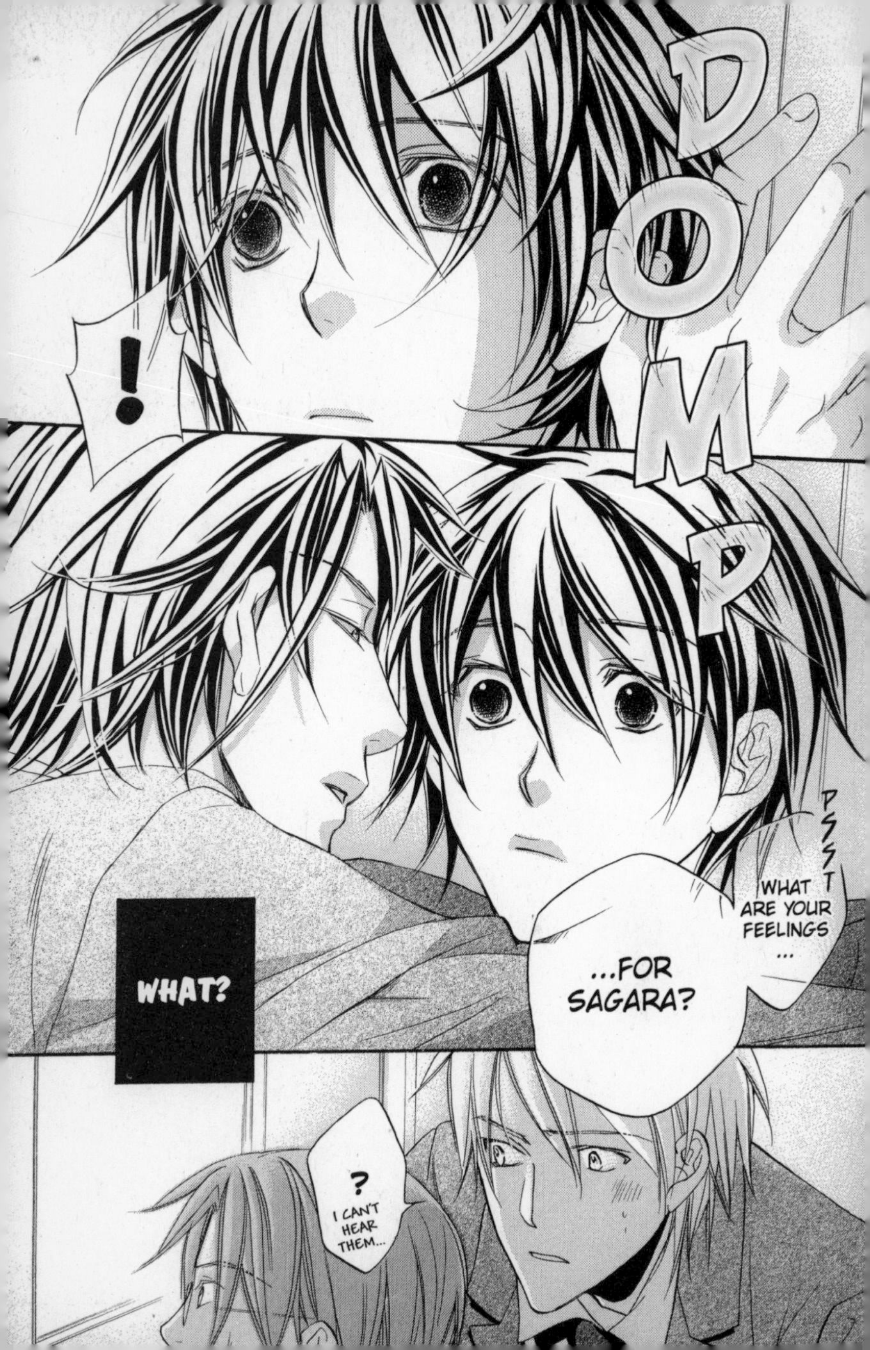
DOMP
!
PSST
WHAT ARE YOUR FEELINGS ...
...FOR SAGARA?
WHAT?
?
I CAN'T HEAR THEM...

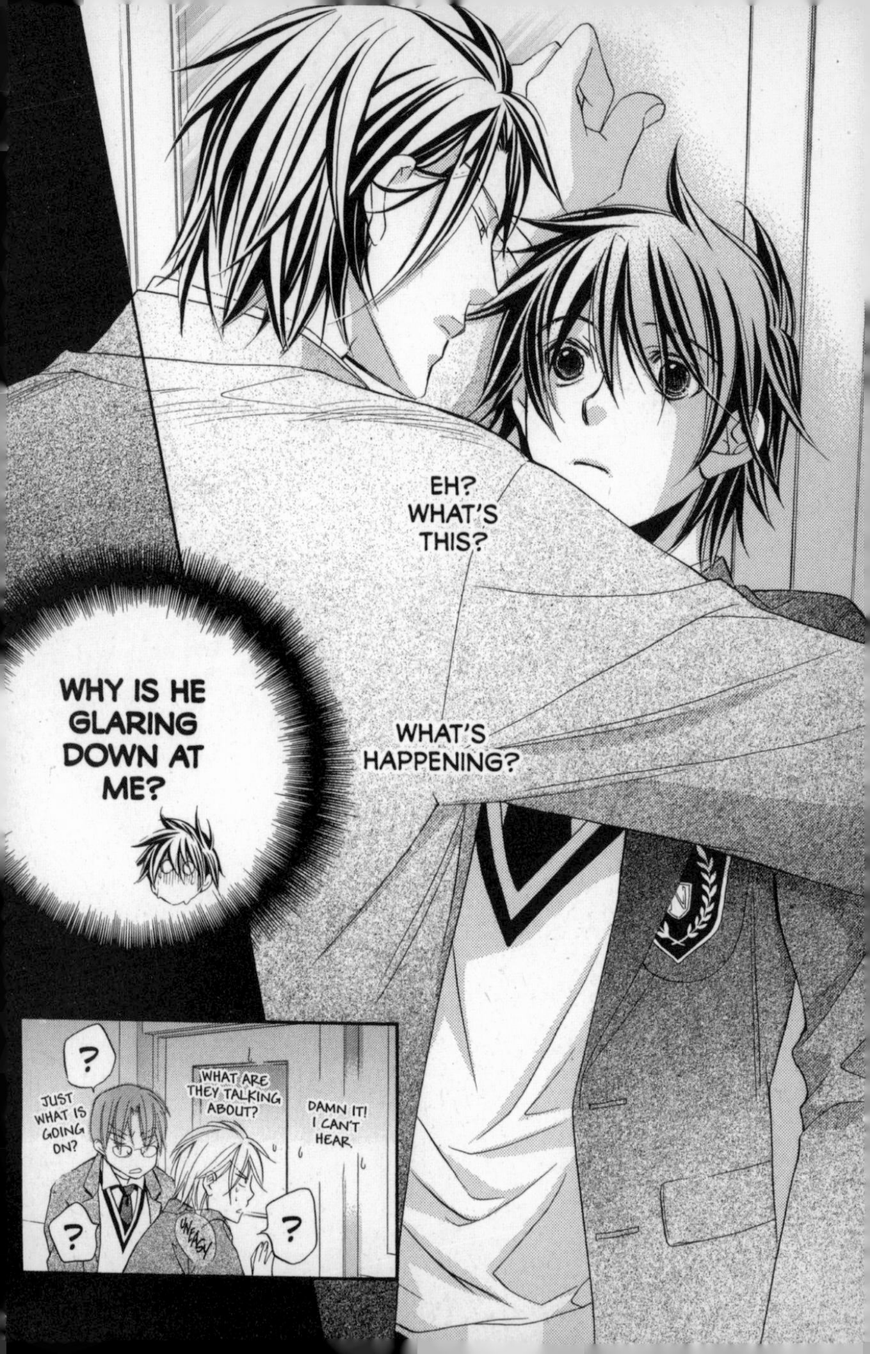
EH? WHAT'S THIS?
WHAT'S HAPPENING?
WHY IS HE GLARING DOWN AT ME?
DAMN IT! I CAN'T HEAR
WHAT ARE THEY TALKING ABOUT?
?
UNEASY
?
JUST WHAT IS GOING ON?
?

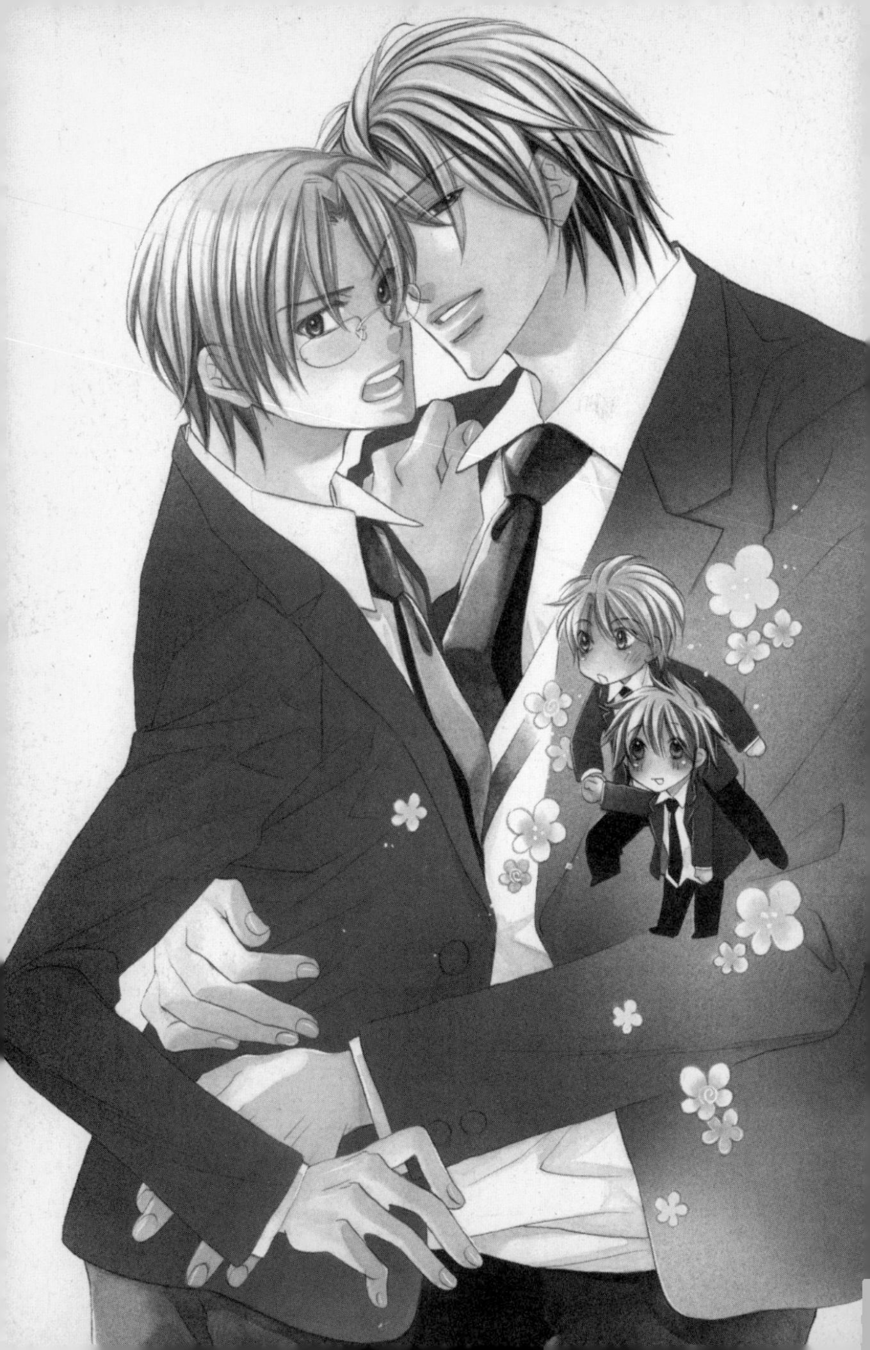

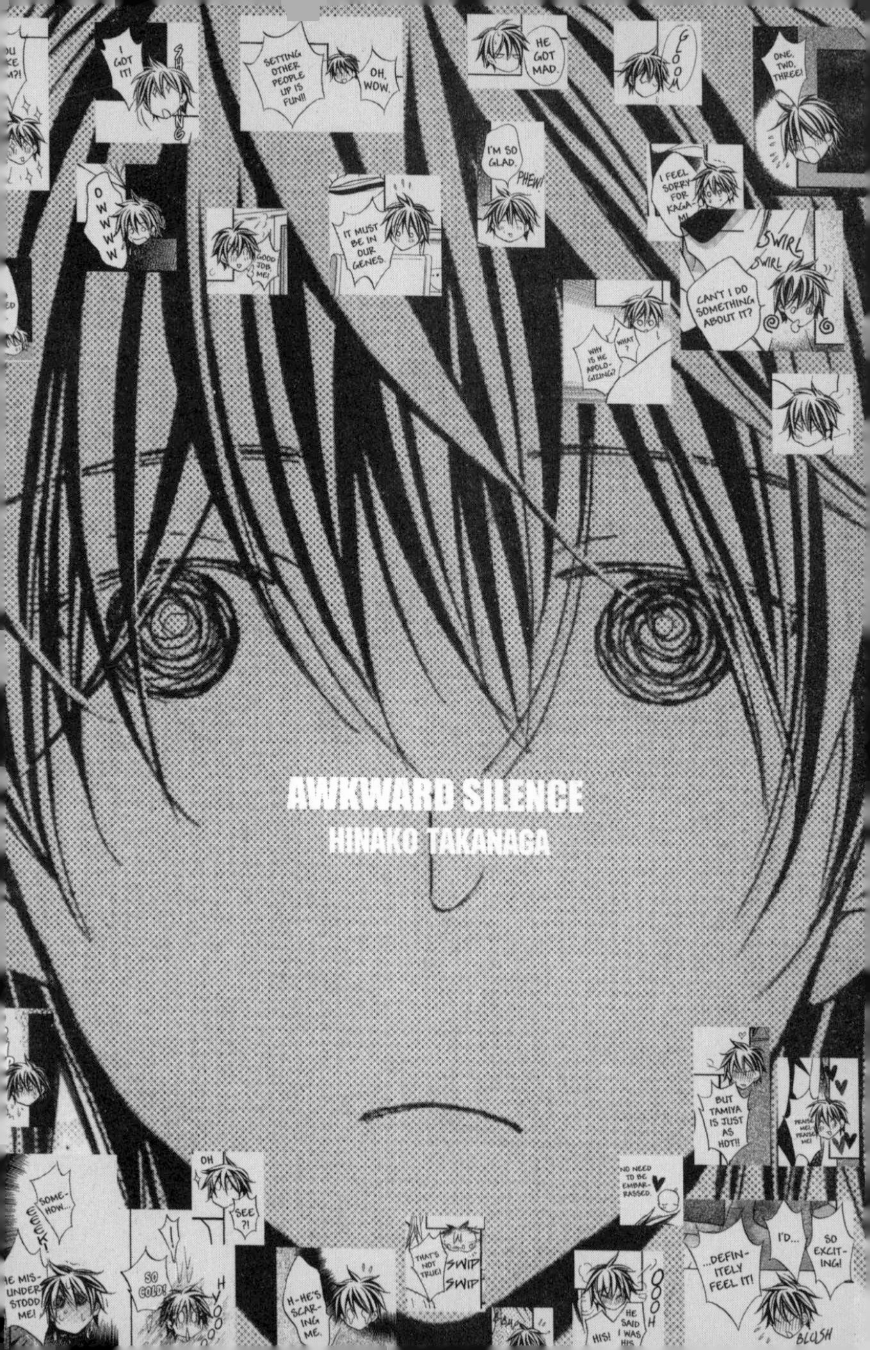
ONE, TWO, THREE!
GLOOM
HE GOT MAD.
OH, WOW.
SETTING OTHER PEOPLE UP IS FUN!!
I GOT IT!
SHING
I FEEL SORRY FOR KAGA-MI
I'M SO GLAD.
PHEW!
IT MUST BE IN OUR GENES.
GOOD JOB ME!
OWWWW
SWIRL SWIRL
CAN'T I DO SOMETHING ABOUT IT?
WHAT?
WHY IS HE APOLO-GIZING?
PRAISE ME! PRAISE ME!
BUT TAMIYA IS JUST AS HOT!!
SO EXCITING!
I'D...
...DEFIN-ITELY FEEL IT!
BLUSH
NO NEED TO BE EMBAR-RASSED.
OOOH
HE SAID I WAS HIS
HIS!
SWIP SWIP
THAT'S NOT TRUE!
H-HE'S SCAR-ING ME.
OH
SEE?!
HYOOO
SO COLD!
SOME-HOW...
EEEK!
HE MIS-UNDER-STOOD ME!

AWKWARD SILENCE

HINAKO TAKANAGA

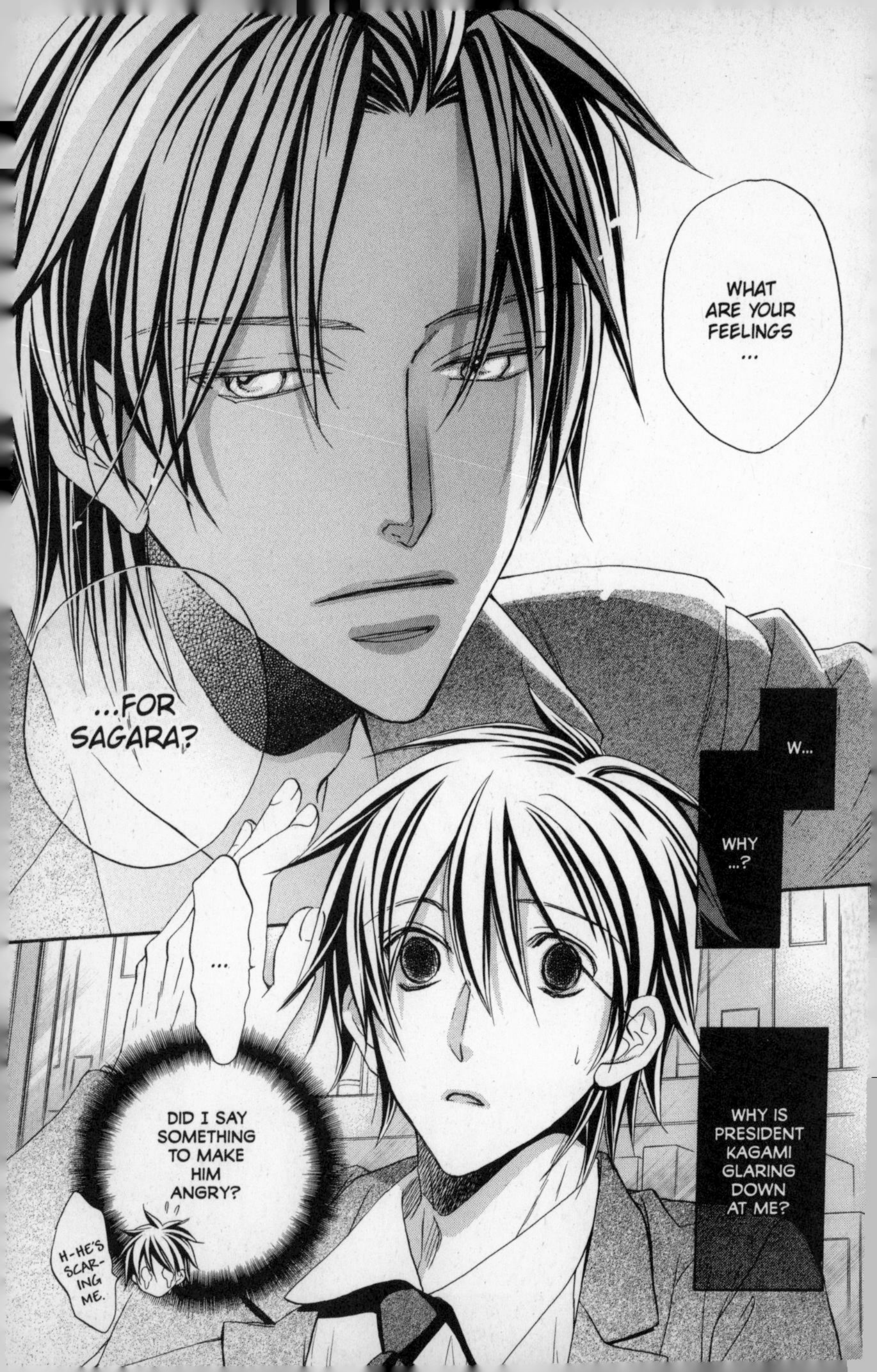
WHAT ARE YOUR FEELINGS ...
...FOR SAGARA?
W...
WHY ...?
...
WHY IS PRESIDENT KAGAMI GLARING DOWN AT ME?
DID I SAY SOMETHING TO MAKE HIM ANGRY?
H-HE'S SCAR-ING ME.

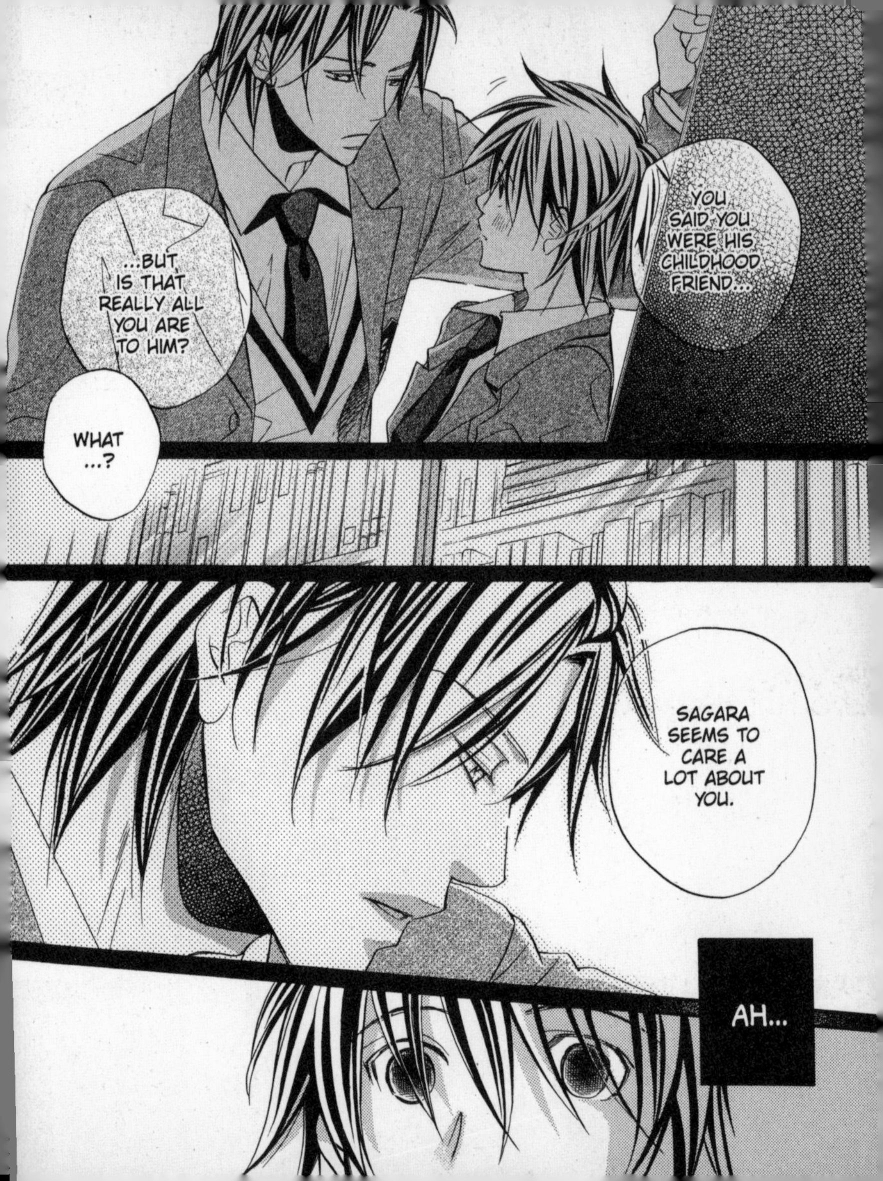

YOU SAID YOU WERE HIS CHILDHOOD FRIEND...
...BUT IS THAT REALLY ALL YOU ARE TO HIM?
WHAT ...?
SAGARA SEEMS TO CARE A LOT ABOUT YOU.
AH...

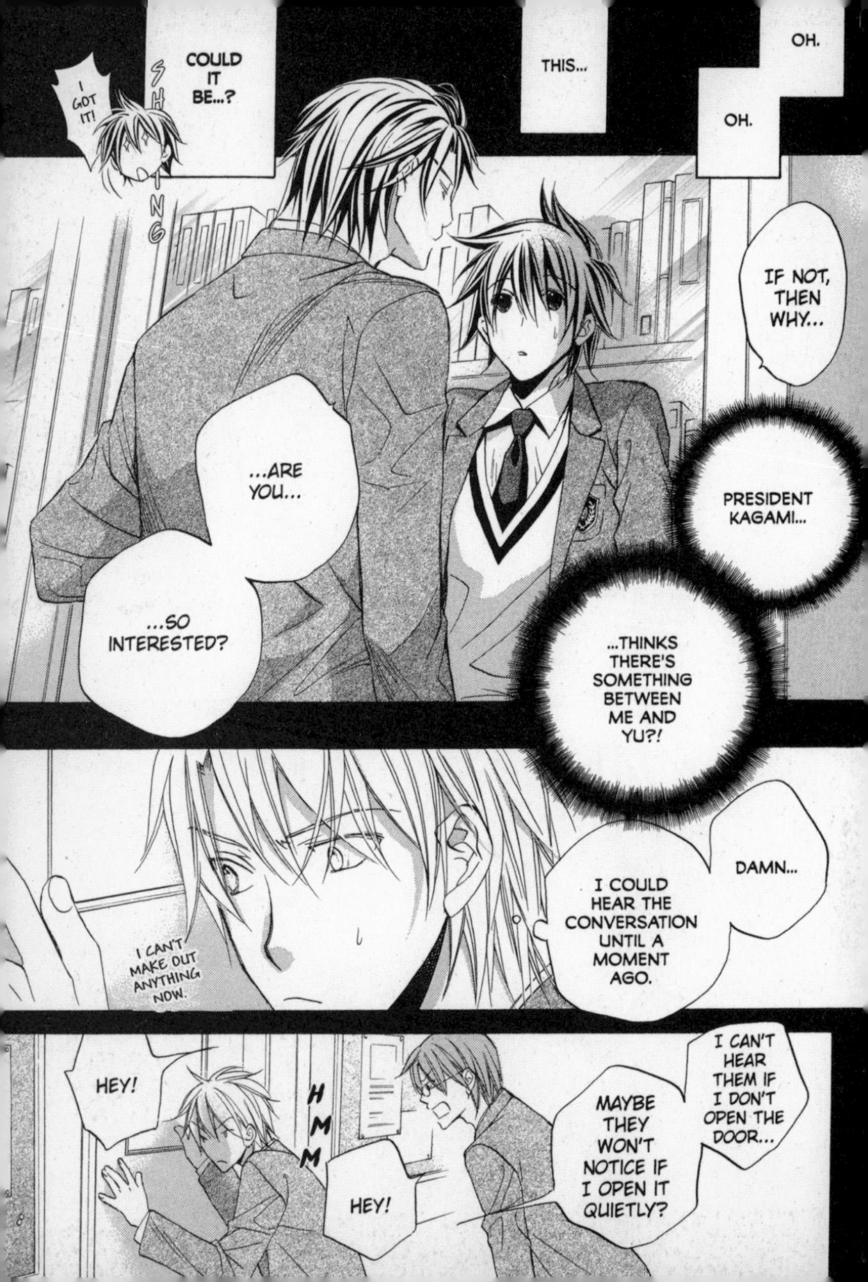
OH.
OH.
THIS...
COULD IT BE...?
SHING
I GOT IT!
IF NOT, THEN WHY...
...ARE YOU...
...SO INTERESTED?
PRESIDENT KAGAMI...
...THINKS THERE'S SOMETHING BETWEEN ME AND YU?!
DAMN...
I COULD HEAR THE CONVERSATION UNTIL A MOMENT AGO.
I CAN'T MAKE OUT ANYTHING NOW.
I CAN'T HEAR THEM IF I DON'T OPEN THE DOOR...
MAYBE THEY WON'T NOTICE IF I OPEN IT QUIETLY?
HMM
HEY!
HEY!

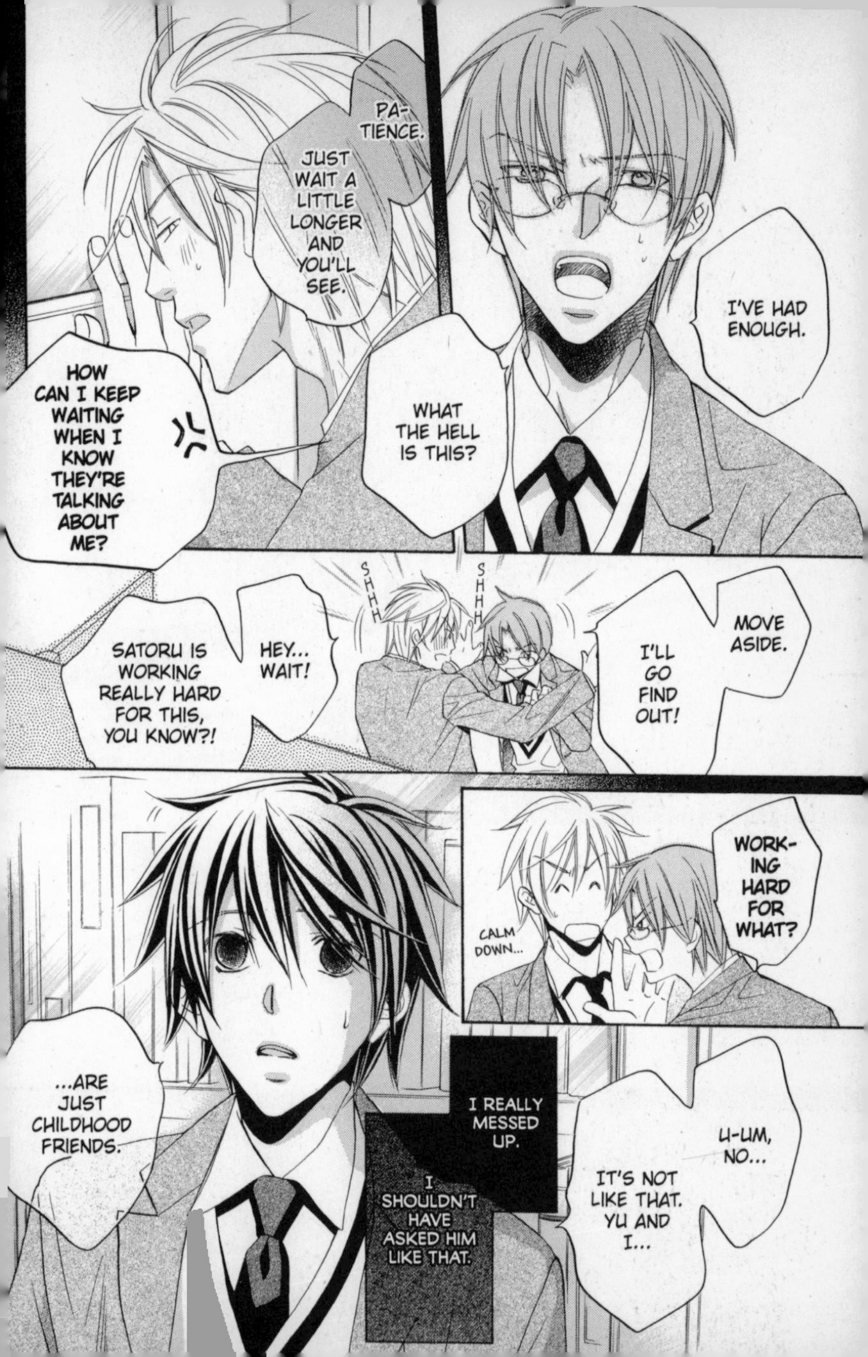
I'VE HAD ENOUGH.
WHAT THE HELL IS THIS?
PA-TIENCE.
JUST WAIT A LITTLE LONGER AND YOU'LL SEE.
HOW CAN I KEEP WAITING WHEN I KNOW THEY'RE TALKING ABOUT ME?
MOVE ASIDE.
I'LL GO FIND OUT!
SHHH
SHHH
HEY... WAIT!
SATORU IS WORKING REALLY HARD FOR THIS, YOU KNOW?!
WORK-ING HARD FOR WHAT?
CALM DOWN...
U-UM, NO...
IT'S NOT LIKE THAT. YU AND I...
I REALLY MESSED UP.
I SHOULDN'T HAVE ASKED HIM LIKE THAT.
...ARE JUST CHILDHOOD FRIENDS.

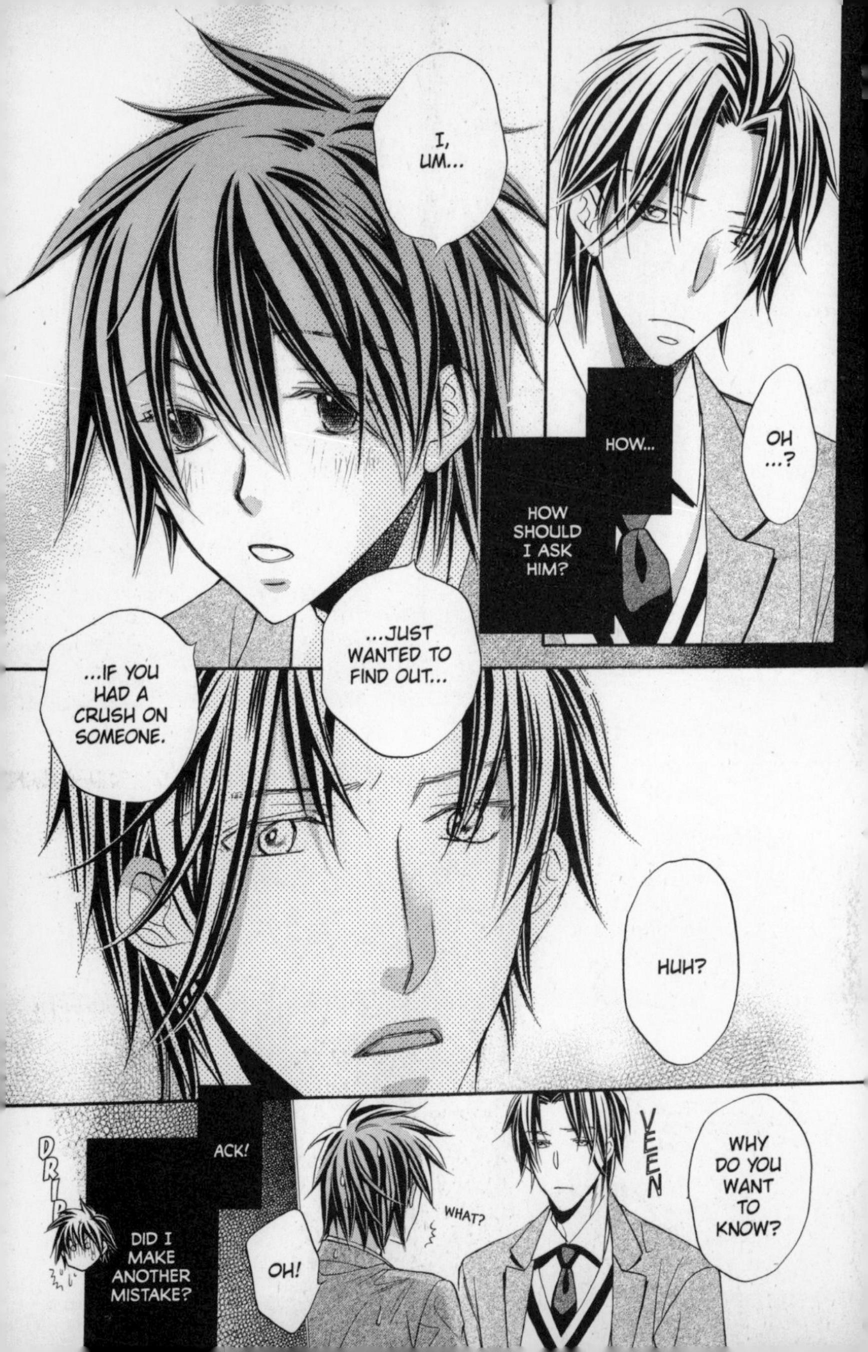
OH ...?
HOW...
HOW SHOULD I ASK HIM?
I, UM...
...JUST WANTED TO FIND OUT...
...IF YOU HAD A CRUSH ON SOMEONE.
HUH?
WHY DO YOU WANT TO KNOW?
VEEN
WHAT?
OH!
ACK!
DRIP
DID I MAKE ANOTHER MISTAKE?

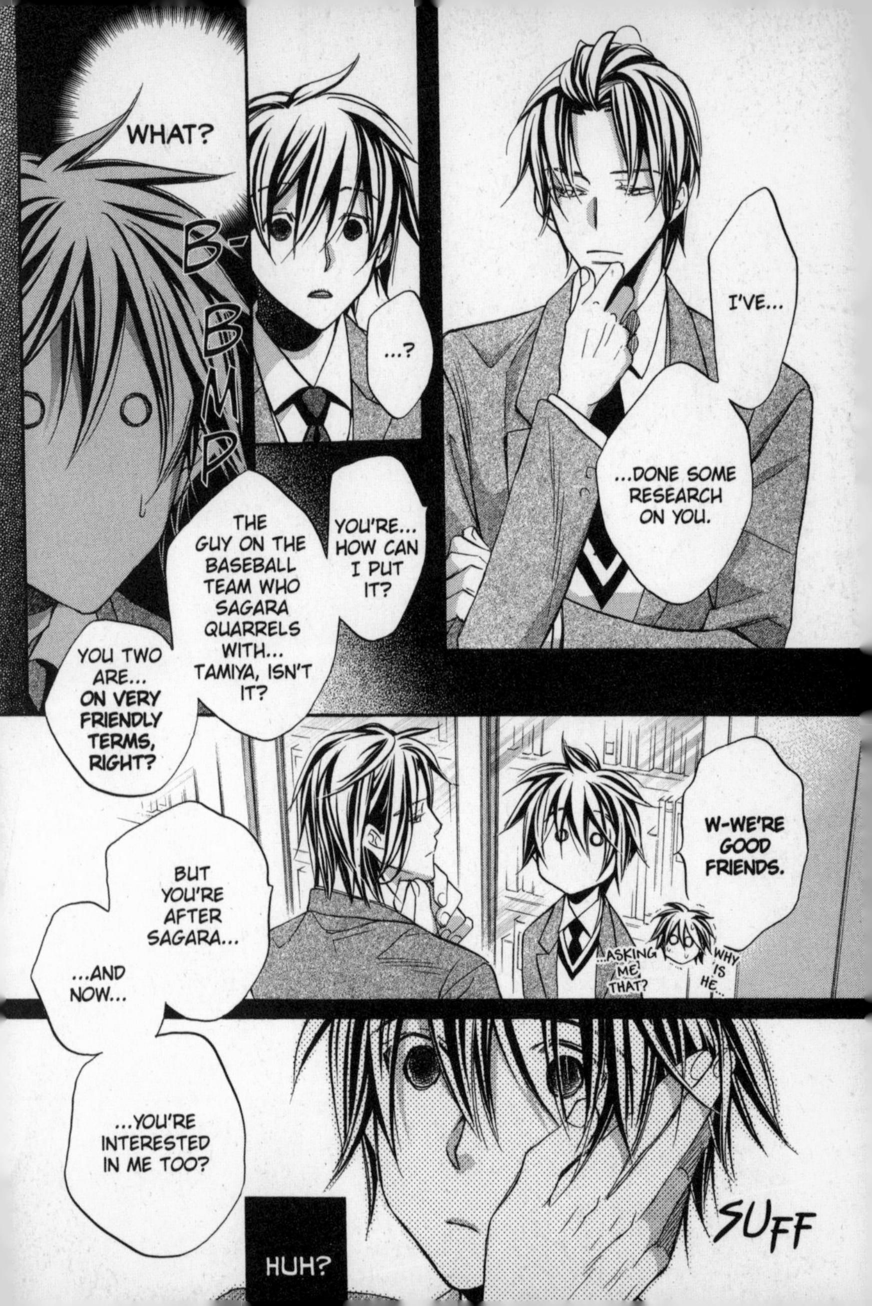
I'VE...
...DONE SOME RESEARCH ON YOU.
...?
WHAT?
B-BUMP
YOU'RE... HOW CAN I PUT IT?
THE GUY ON THE BASEBALL TEAM WHO SAGARA QUARRELS WITH... TAMIYA, ISN'T IT?
YOU TWO ARE... ON VERY FRIENDLY TERMS, RIGHT?
W-WE'RE GOOD FRIENDS.
WHY IS HE...
...ASKING ME THAT?
BUT YOU'RE AFTER SAGARA...
...AND NOW...
...YOU'RE INTERESTED IN ME TOO?
SUFF
HUH?

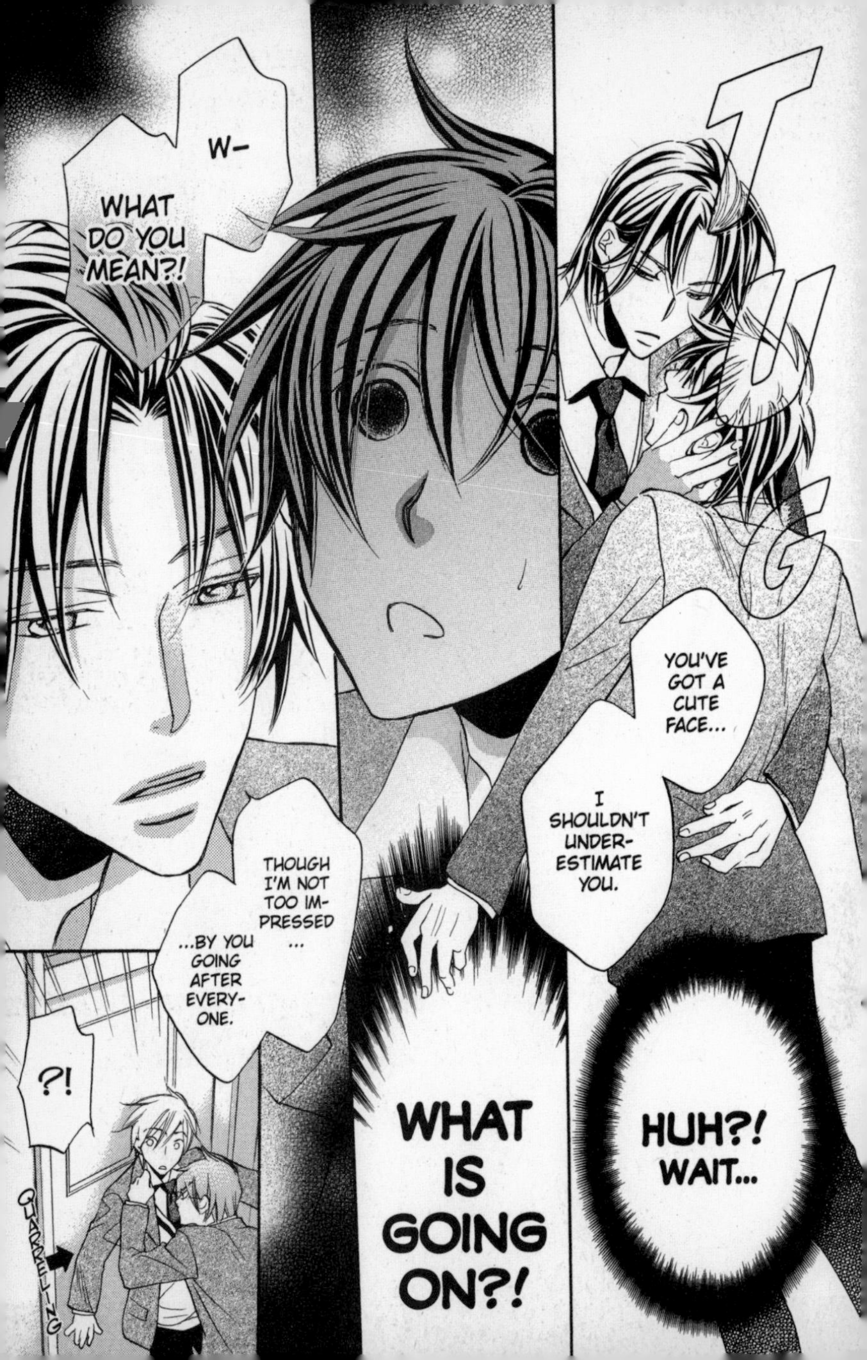
TUG
YOU'VE GOT A CUTE FACE...
I SHOULDN'T UNDER-ESTIMATE YOU.
HUH?! WAIT...
WHAT IS GOING ON?!
W-
WHAT DO YOU MEAN?!
THOUGH I'M NOT TOO IM-PRESSED ...
...BY YOU GOING AFTER EVERY-ONE.
?!
QUARRELING

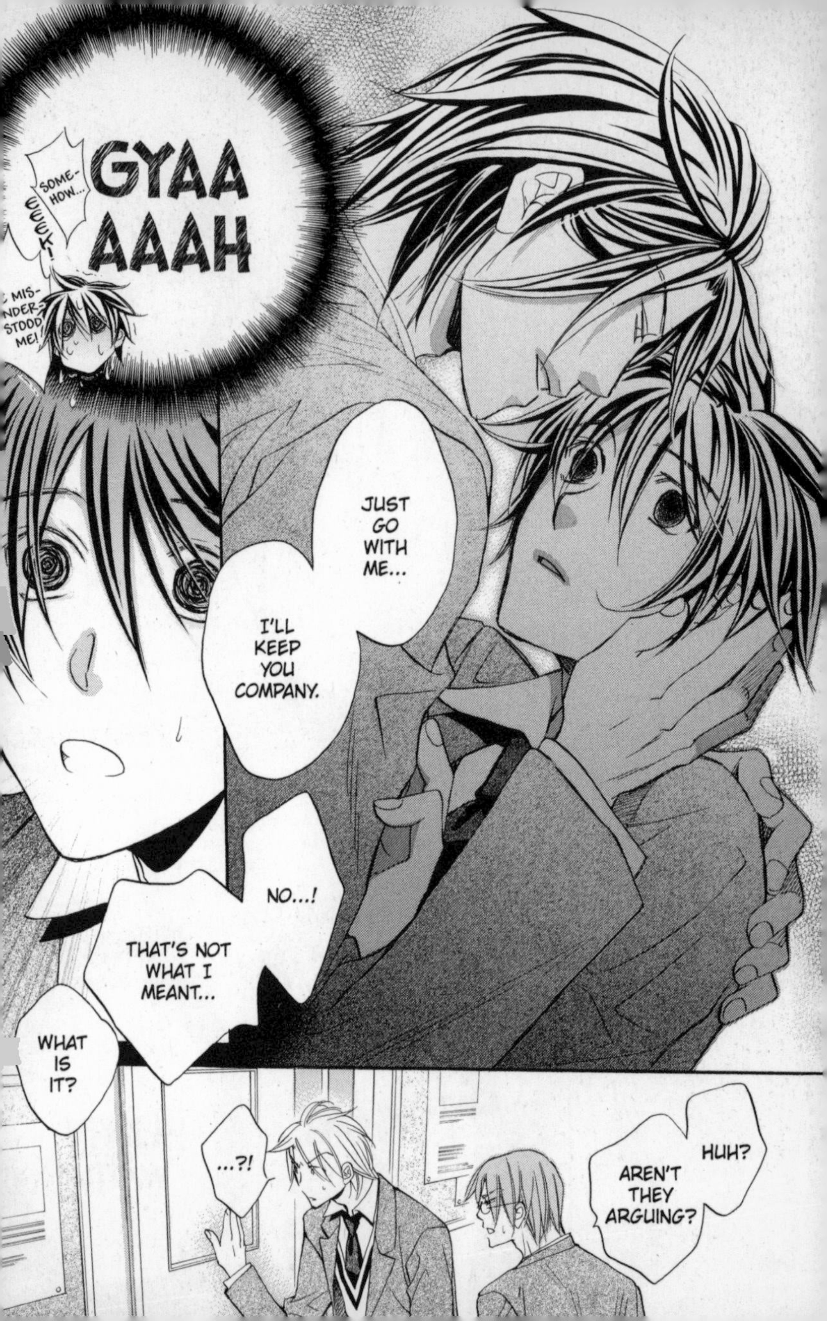
JUST GO WITH ME...
I'LL KEEP YOU COMPANY.
GYAA AAAH
SOME-HOW...
MIS-UNDER-STOOD ME!
EEEK!
NO...!
THAT'S NOT WHAT I MEANT...
WHAT IS IT?
HUH?
AREN'T THEY ARGUING?
...?!

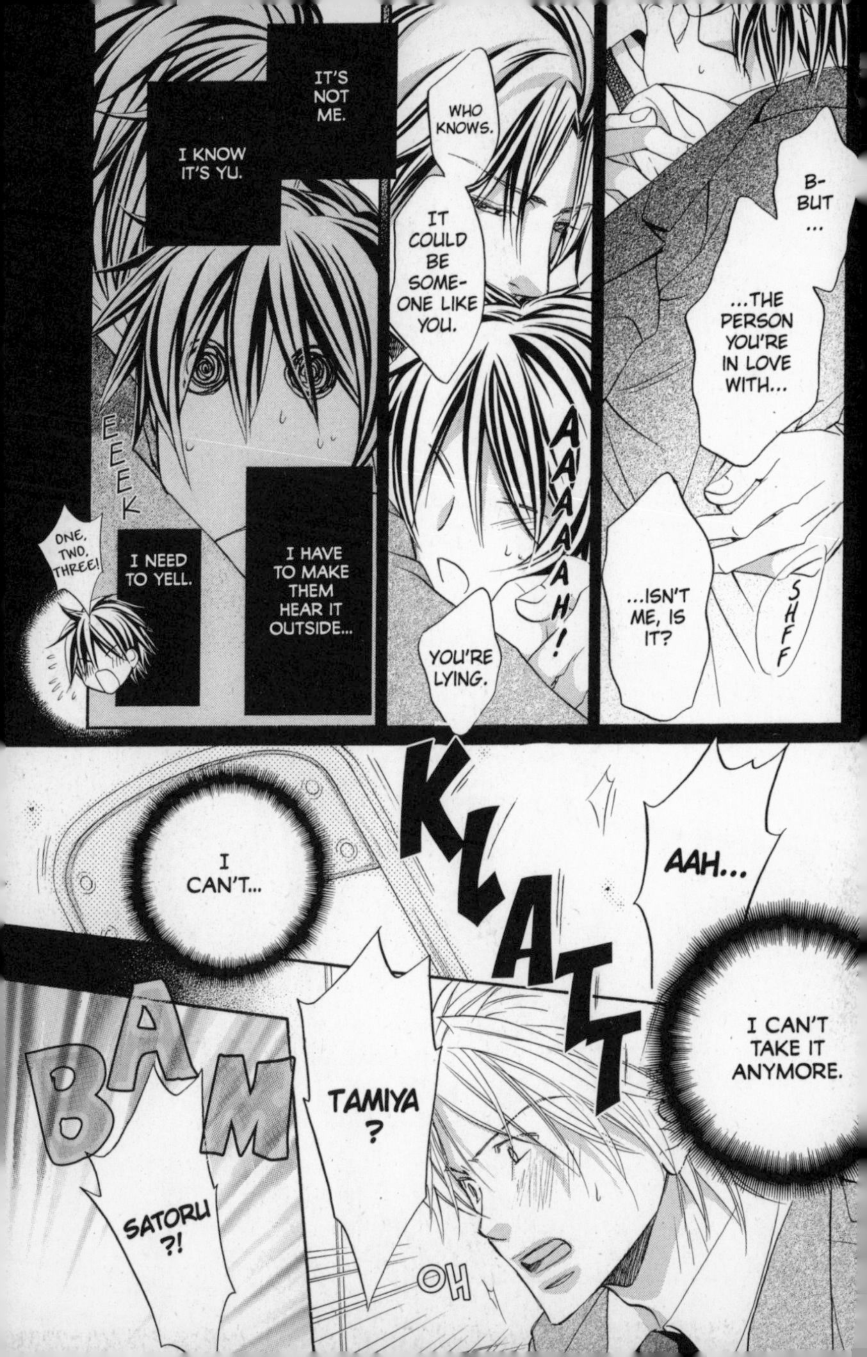
B-BUT...
...THE PERSON YOU'RE IN LOVE WITH...
...ISN'T ME, IS IT?
SHFF
WHO KNOWS.
IT COULD BE SOME-ONE LIKE YOU.
AAAAAAAH!
YOU'RE LYING.
IT'S NOT ME.
I KNOW IT'S YU.
EEEK
I HAVE TO MAKE THEM HEAR IT OUTSIDE...
I NEED TO YELL.
ONE, TWO, THREE!
AAH...
KLATT
I CAN'T...
I CAN'T TAKE IT ANYMORE.
TAMIYA?
BAM
SATORU?!
OH

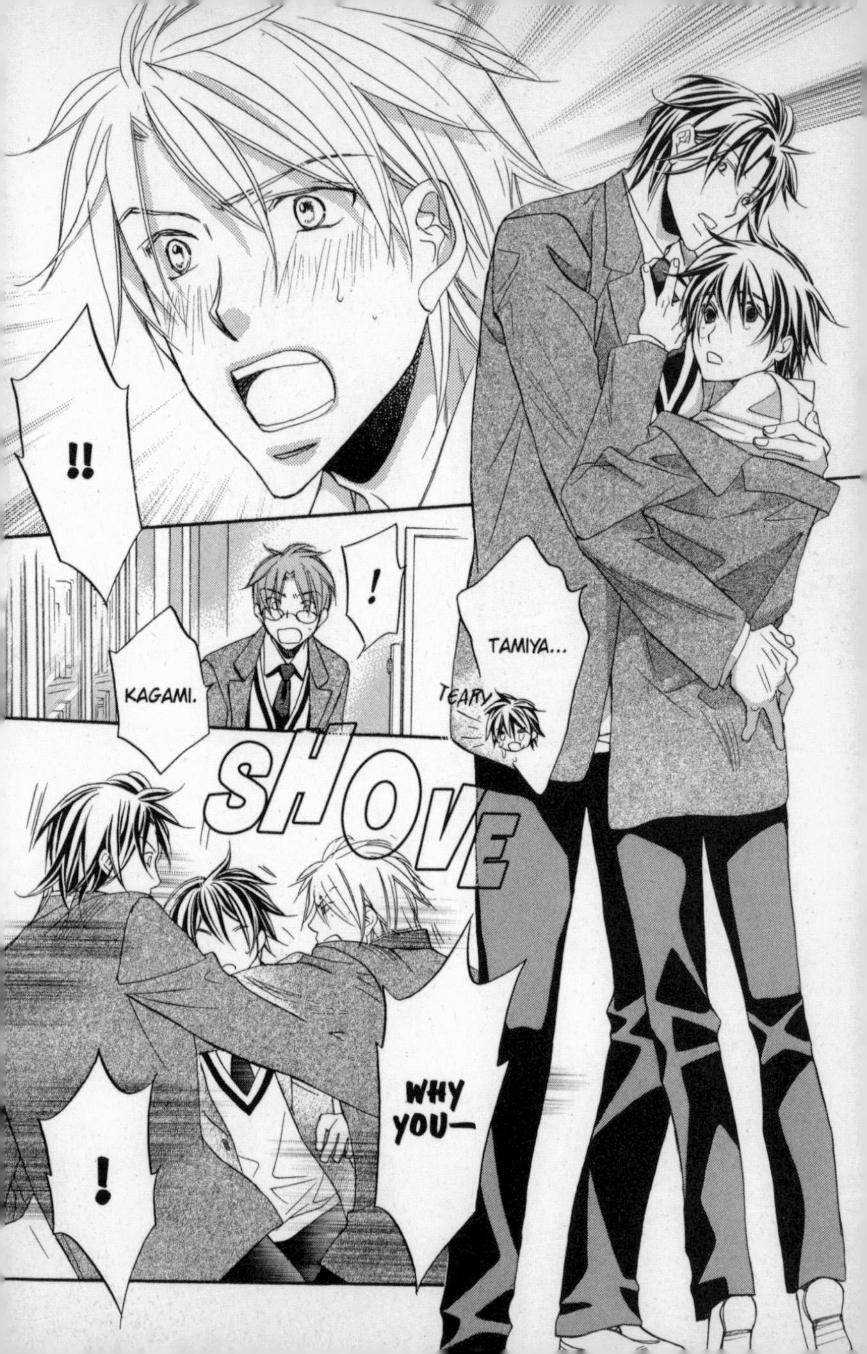
TAMIYA...
TEARY
!!
!
KAGAMI.
SHOVE
WHY YOU—
!

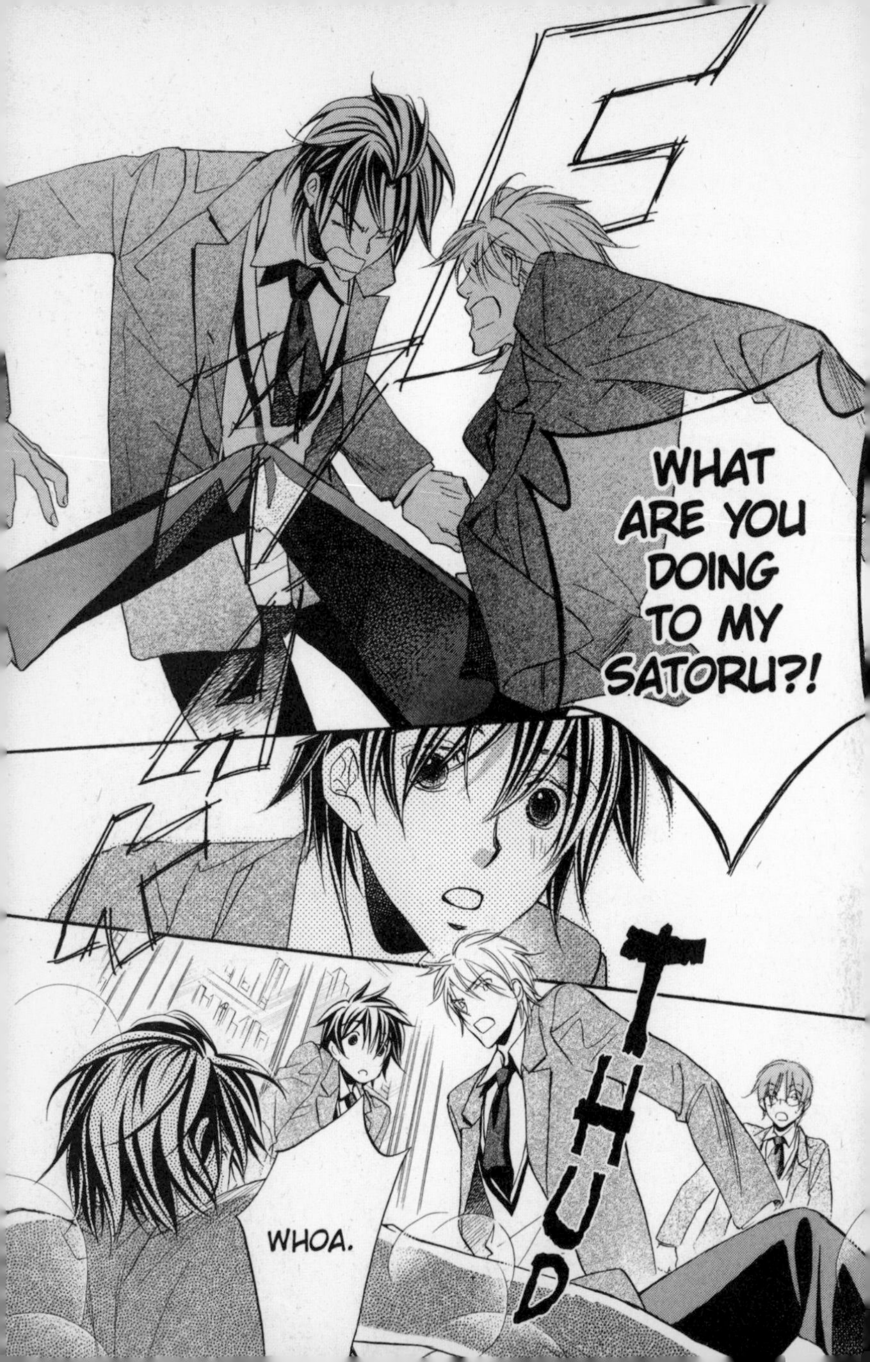
WHAT ARE YOU DOING TO MY SATORU?!
THUD
WHOA.

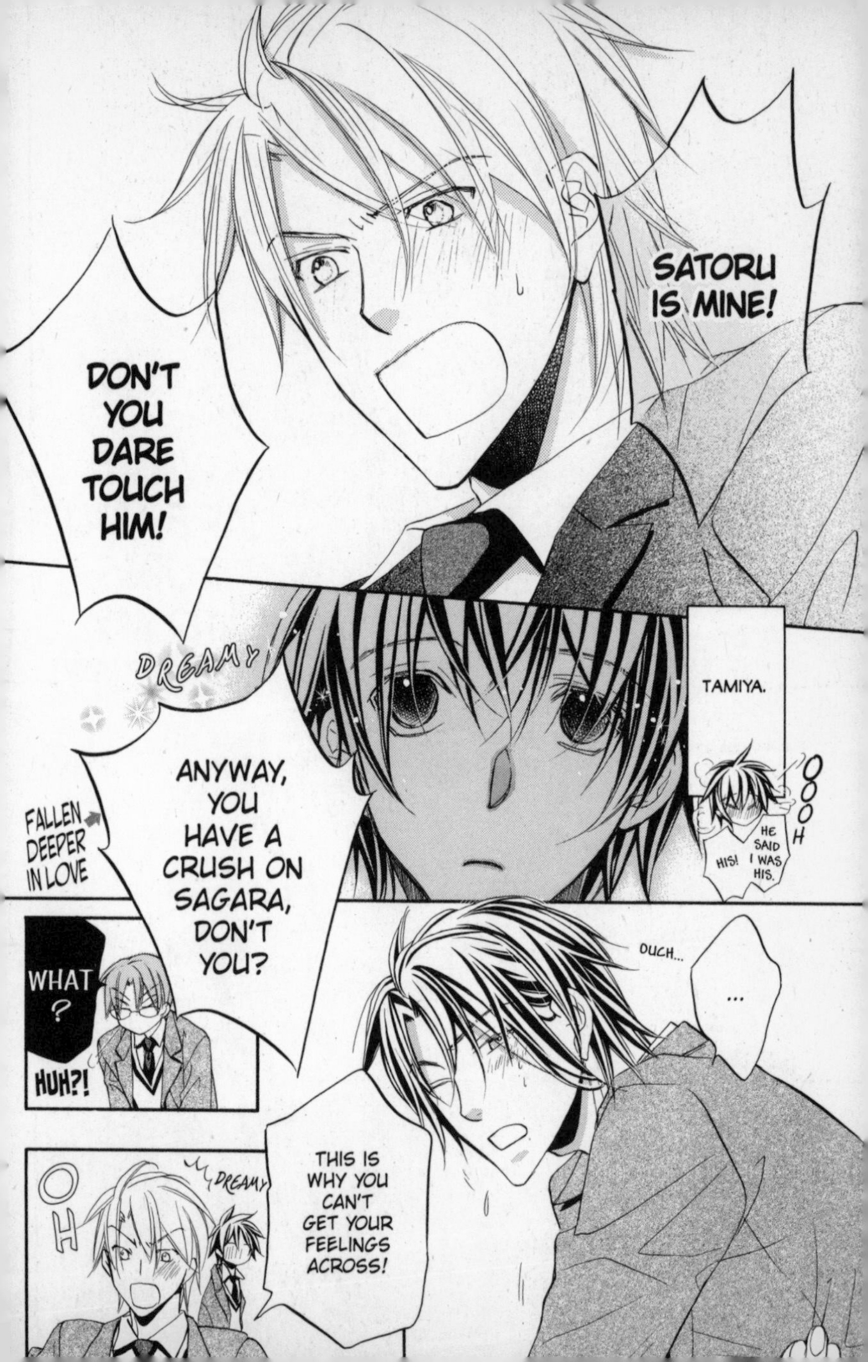
SATORU IS MINE!
DON'T YOU DARE TOUCH HIM!
TAMIYA.
OOOOH
HE SAID I WAS HIS.
HIS!
DREAMY
FALLEN DEEPER IN LOVE
OUCH...
...
ANYWAY, YOU HAVE A CRUSH ON SAGARA, DON'T YOU?
THIS IS WHY YOU CAN'T GET YOUR FEELINGS ACROSS!
WHAT?
HUH?!
OH
DREAMY

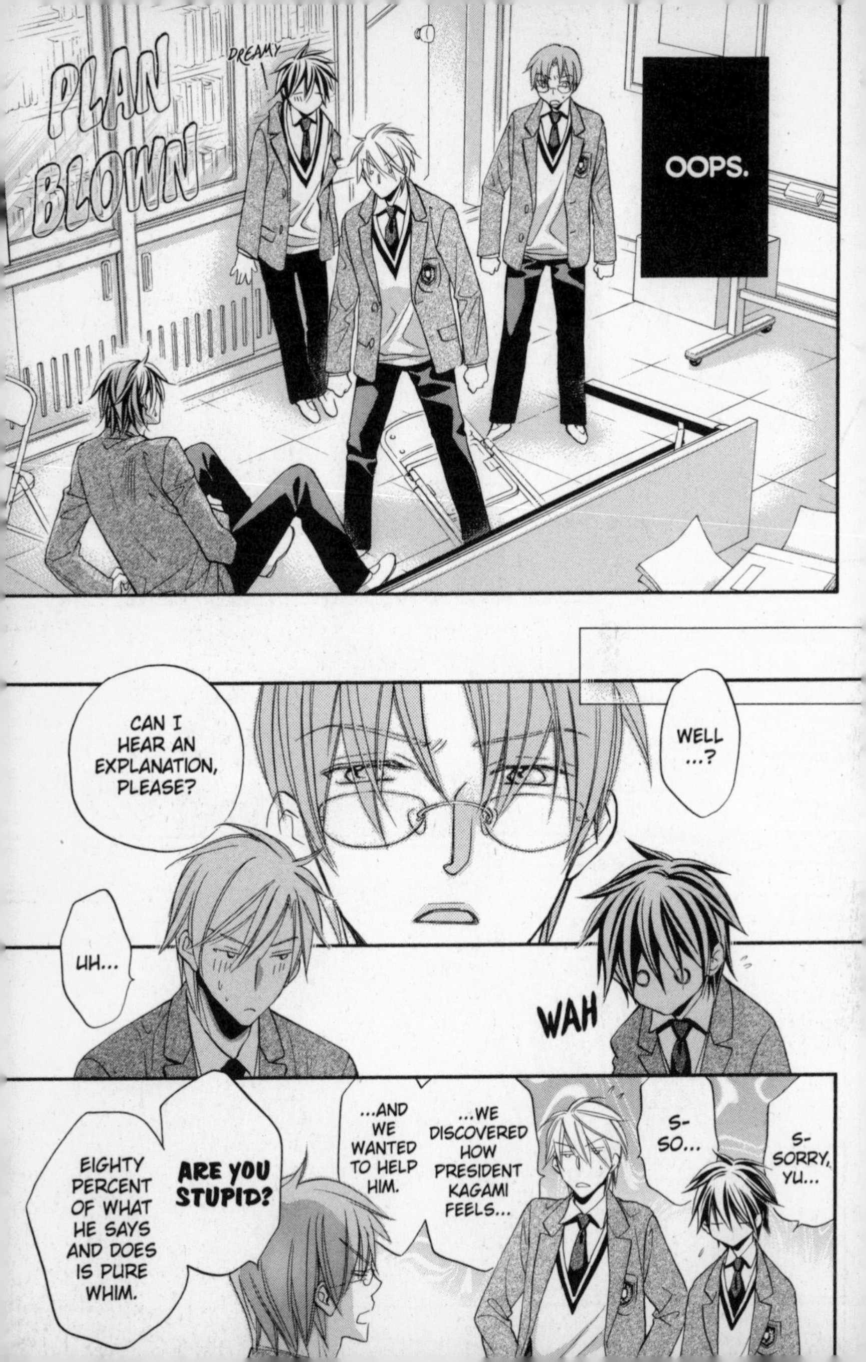
OOPS.
DREAMY
PLAN BLOWN
WELL ...?
CAN I HEAR AN EXPLANATION, PLEASE?
WAH
UH...
S-SORRY, YU...
S-SO...
...WE DISCOVERED HOW PRESIDENT KAGAMI FEELS...
...AND WE WANTED TO HELP HIM.
ARE YOU STUPID?
EIGHTY PERCENT OF WHAT HE SAYS AND DOES IS PURE WHIM.

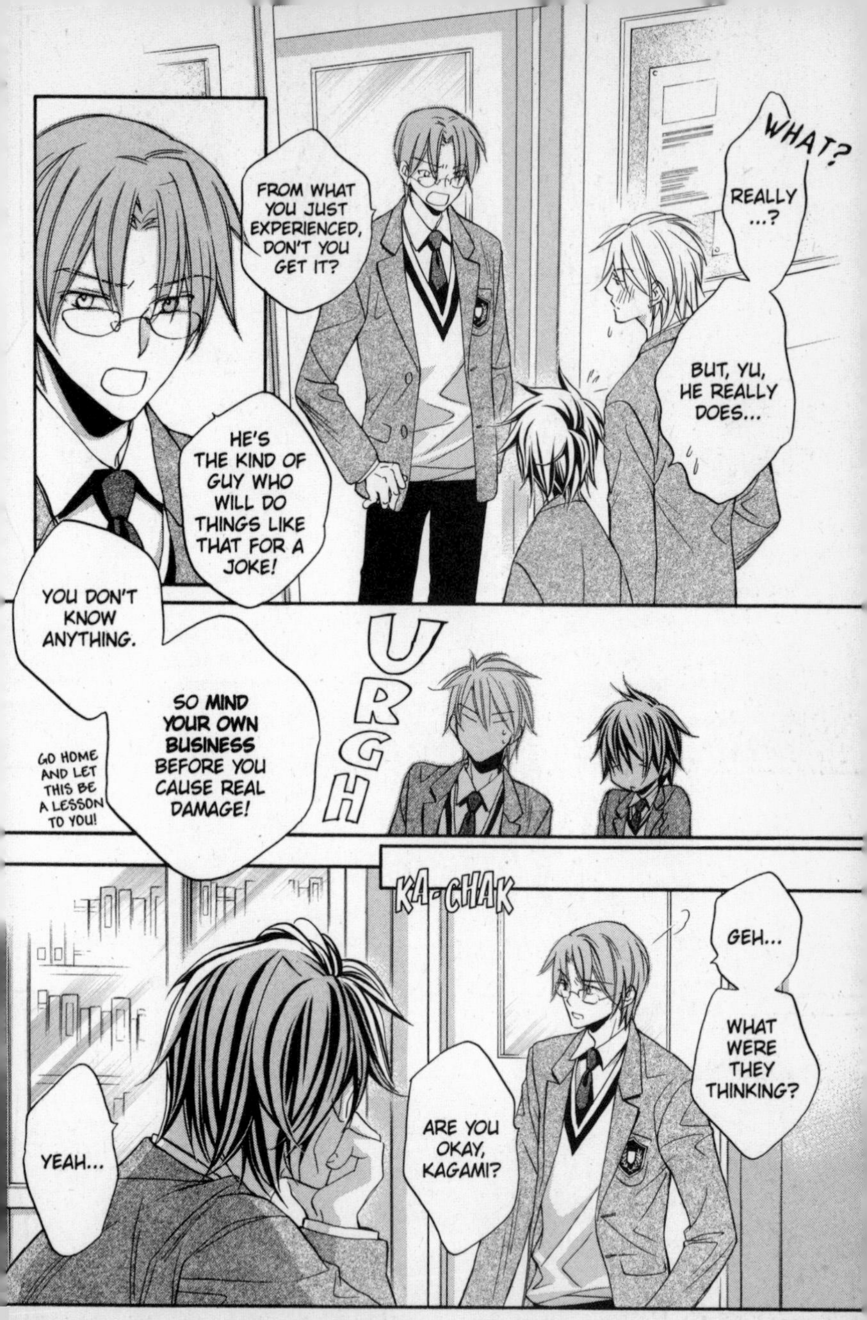
WHAT?
REALLY ...?
BUT, YU, HE REALLY DOES...
FROM WHAT YOU JUST EXPERIENCED, DON'T YOU GET IT?
HE'S THE KIND OF GUY WHO WILL DO THINGS LIKE THAT FOR A JOKE!
YOU DON'T KNOW ANYTHING.
URGH
SO MIND YOUR OWN BUSINESS BEFORE YOU CAUSE REAL DAMAGE!
GO HOME AND LET THIS BE A LESSON TO YOU!
KA-CHAK
GEH...
WHAT WERE THEY THINKING?
ARE YOU OKAY, KAGAMI?
YEAH...

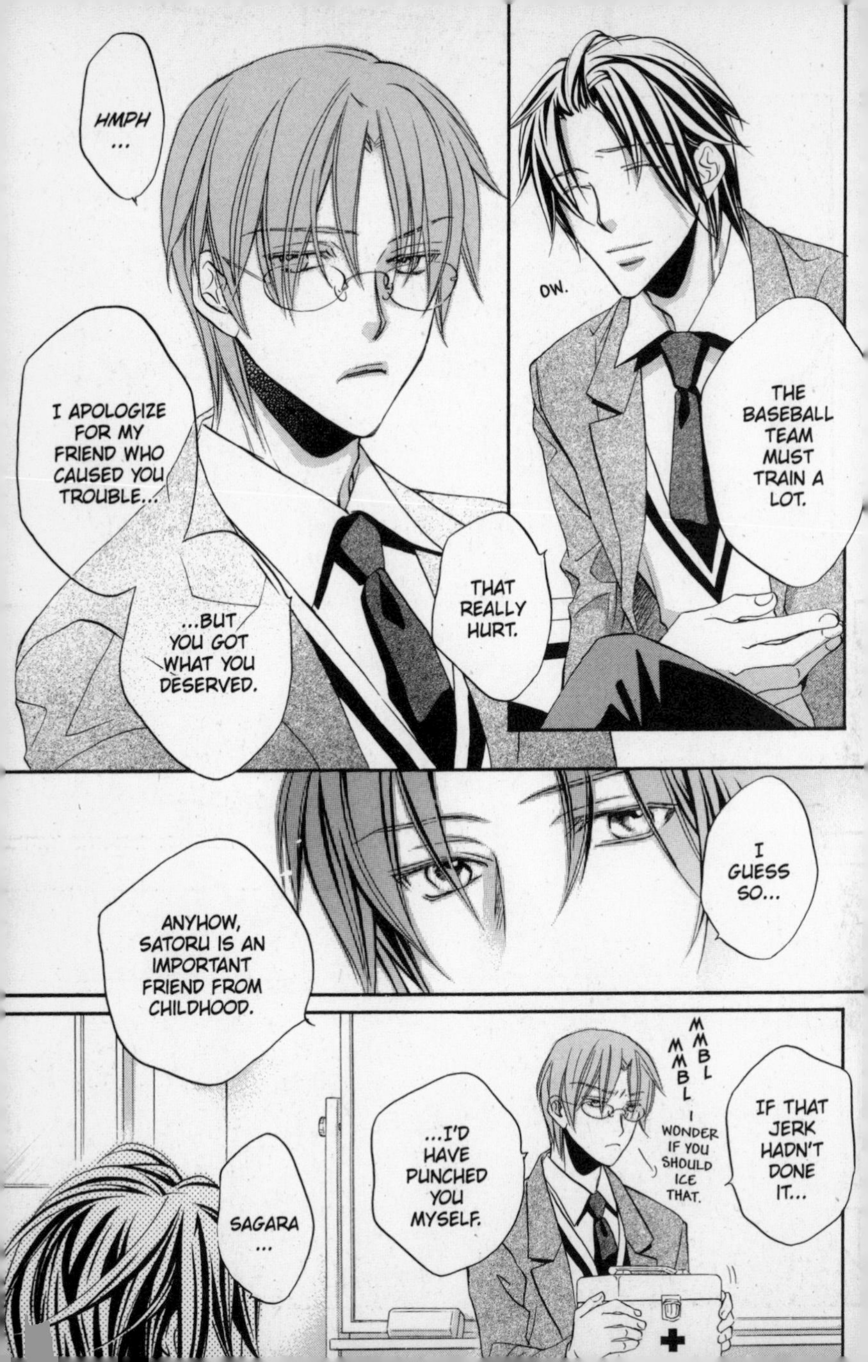
OW.
THE BASEBALL TEAM MUST TRAIN A LOT.
THAT REALLY HURT.
HMPH...
I APOLOGIZE FOR MY FRIEND WHO CAUSED YOU TROUBLE...
...BUT YOU GOT WHAT YOU DESERVED.
I GUESS SO...
ANYHOW, SATORU IS AN IMPORTANT FRIEND FROM CHILDHOOD.
IF THAT JERK HADN'T DONE IT...
MMBL MMBL
I WONDER IF YOU SHOULD ICE THAT.
...I'D HAVE PUNCHED YOU MYSELF.
SAGARA...

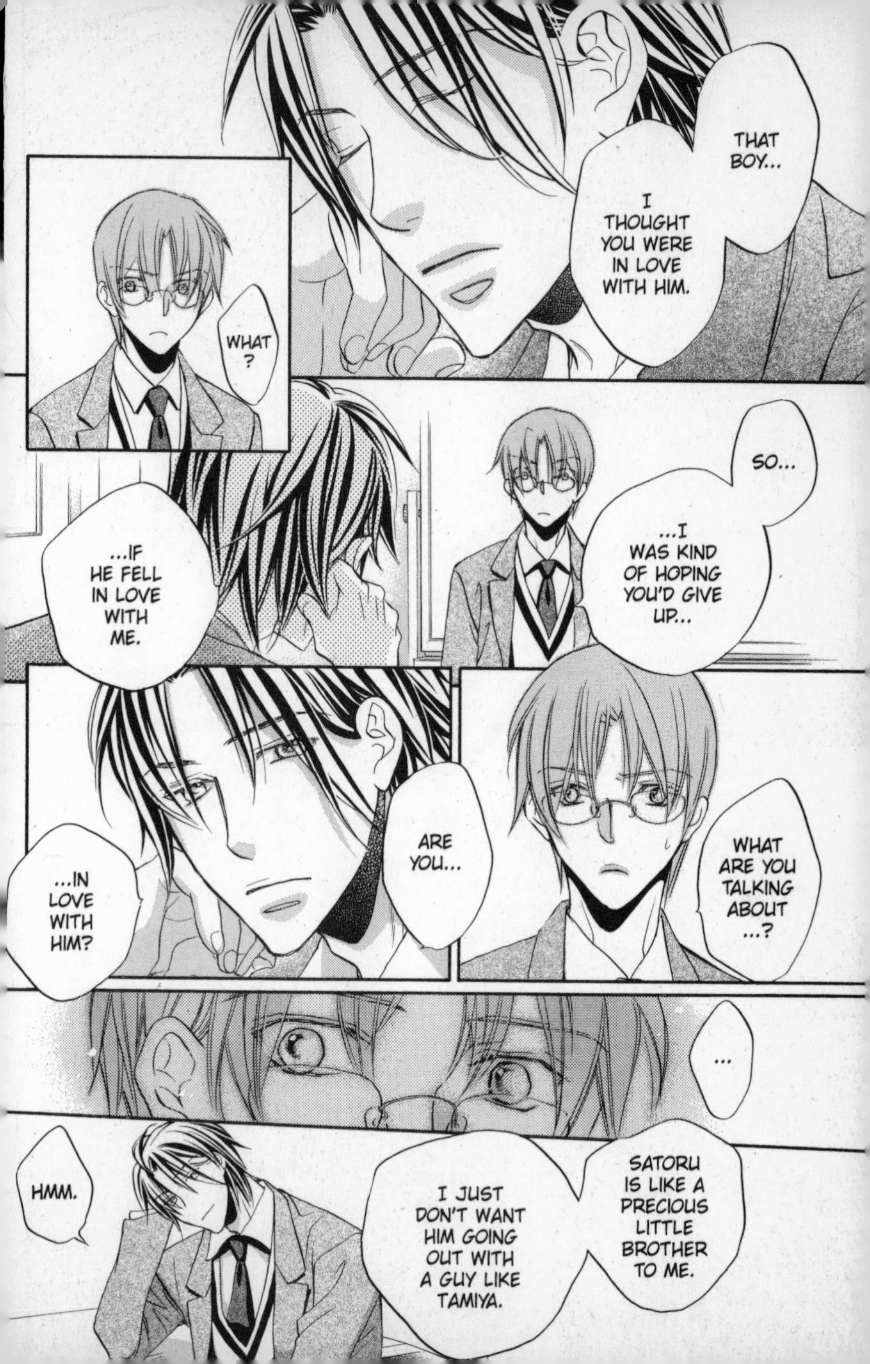
THAT BOY...
I THOUGHT YOU WERE IN LOVE WITH HIM.
WHAT?
SO...
...I WAS KIND OF HOPING YOU'D GIVE UP...
...IF HE FELL IN LOVE WITH ME.
WHAT ARE YOU TALKING ABOUT...?
ARE YOU...
...IN LOVE WITH HIM?
...
SATORU IS LIKE A PRECIOUS LITTLE BROTHER TO ME.
I JUST DON'T WANT HIM GOING OUT WITH A GUY LIKE TAMIYA.
HMM.

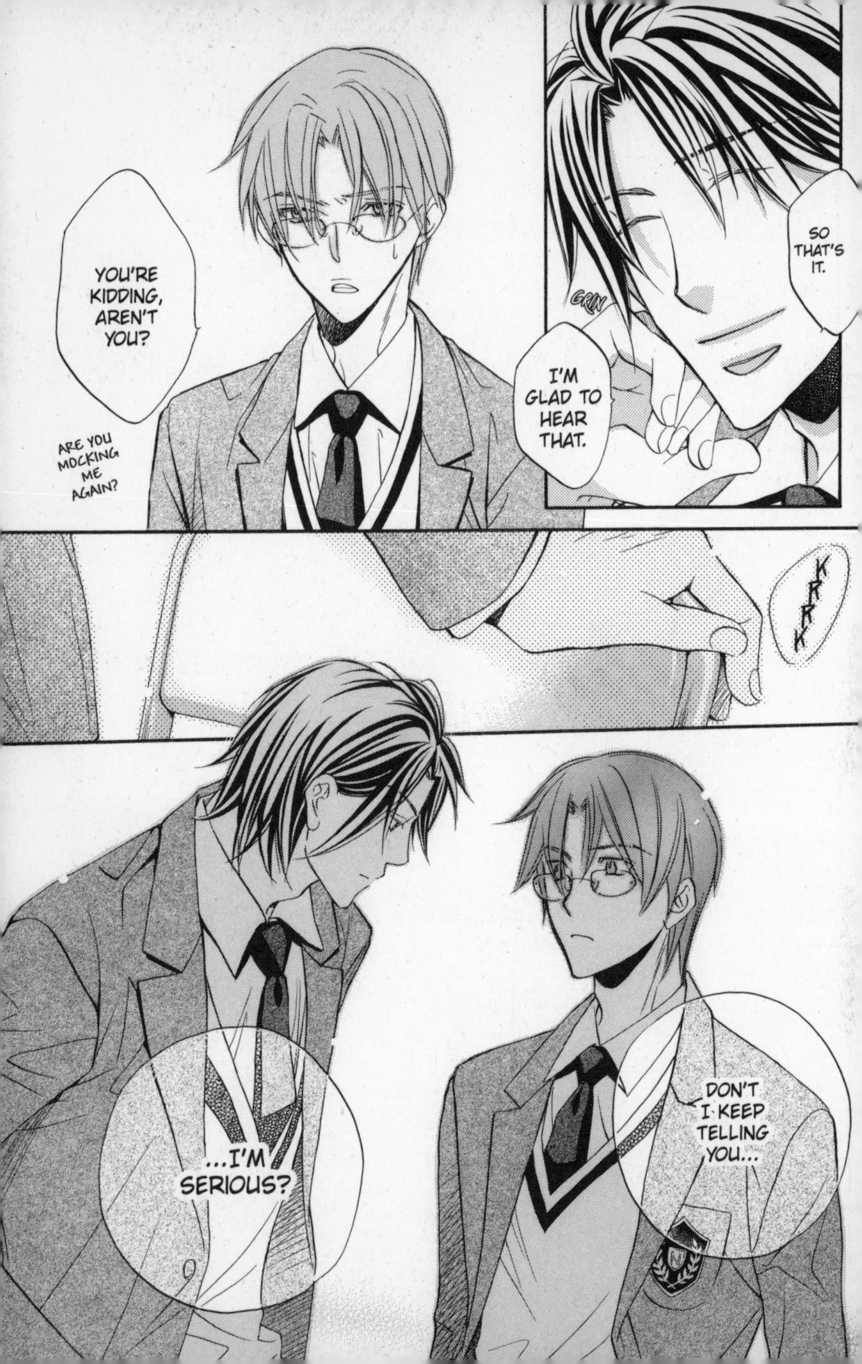
SO THAT'S IT.
GRIN
I'M GLAD TO HEAR THAT.
YOU'RE KIDDING, AREN'T YOU?
ARE YOU MOCKING ME AGAIN?
KRRK
DON'T I KEEP TELLING YOU...
...I'M SERIOUS?

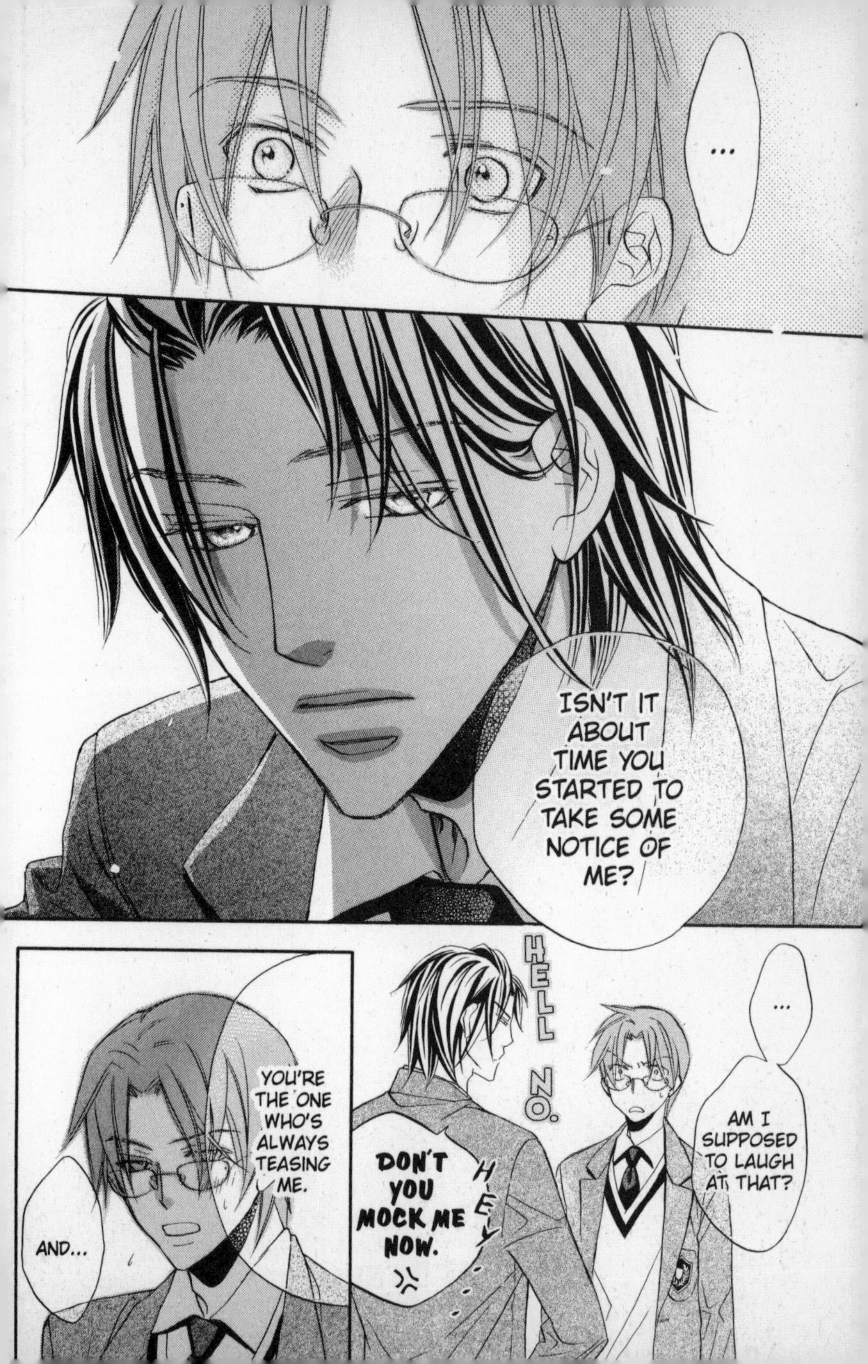
...
ISN'T IT ABOUT TIME YOU STARTED TO TAKE SOME NOTICE OF ME?
...
AM I SUPPOSED TO LAUGH AT THAT?
HELL NO.
HEY...
DON'T YOU MOCK ME NOW.
YOU'RE THE ONE WHO'S ALWAYS TEASING ME.
AND...

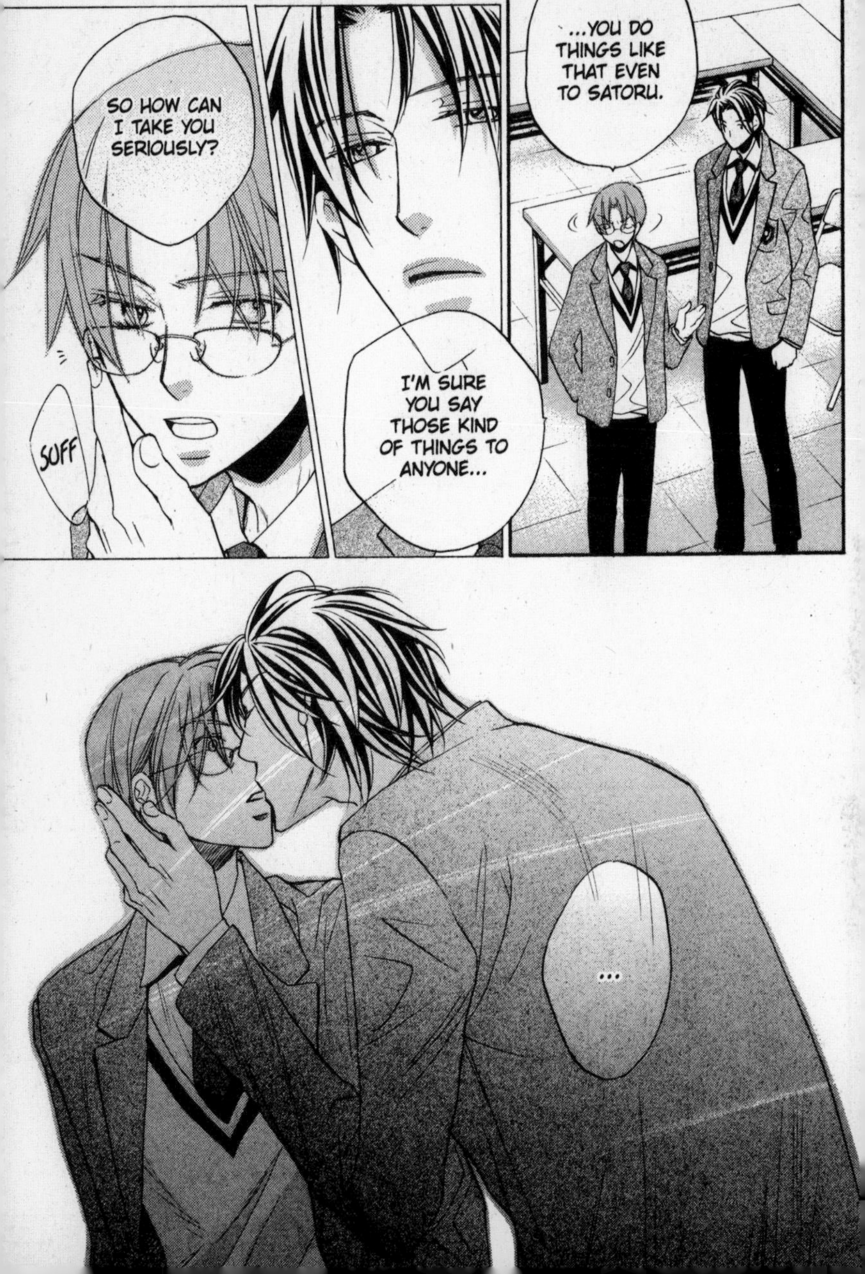
...YOU DO THINGS LIKE THAT EVEN TO SATORU.
I'M SURE YOU SAY THOSE KIND OF THINGS TO ANYONE...
SO HOW CAN I TAKE YOU SERIOUSLY?
SUFF
...

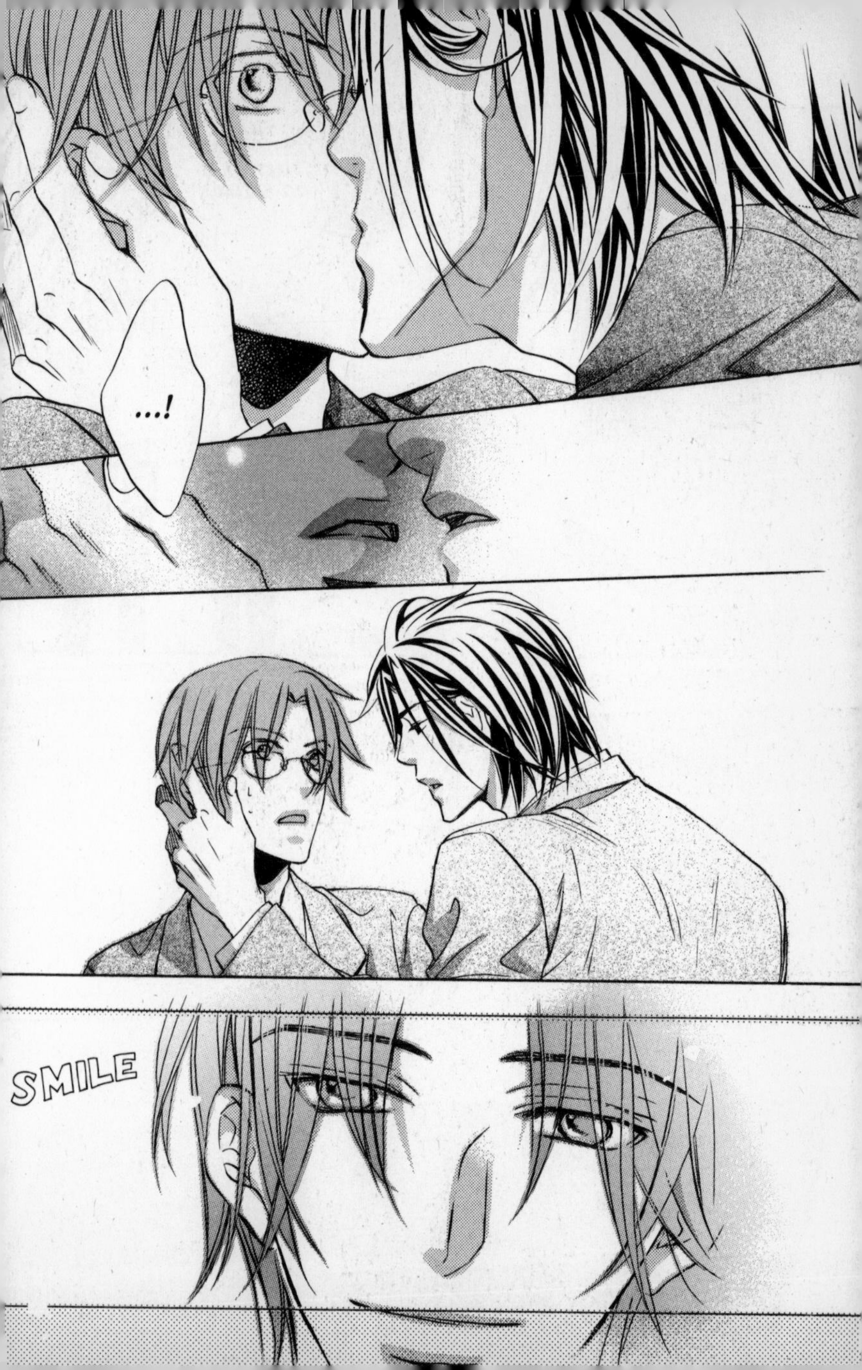
...!
SMILE

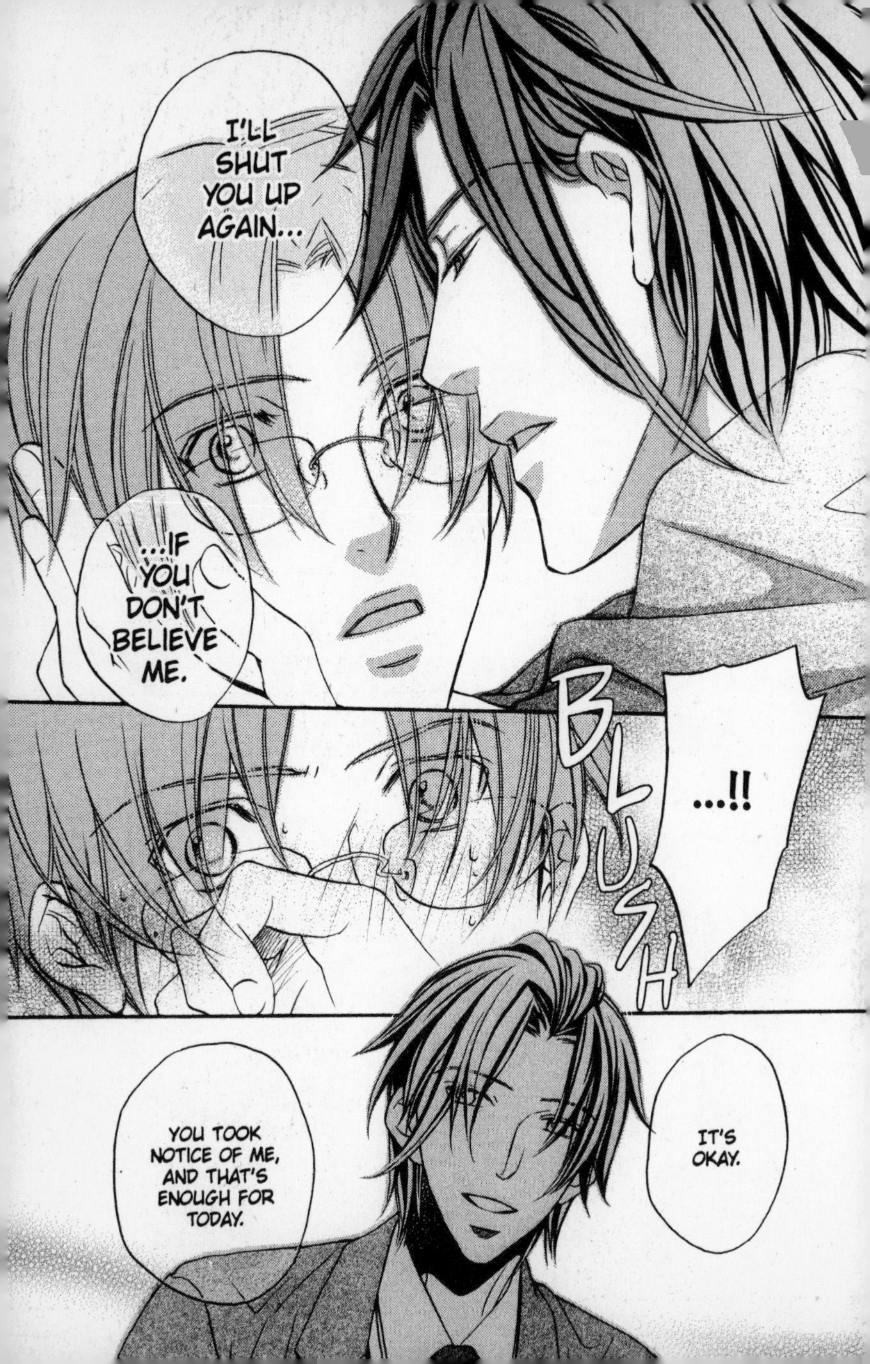
I'LL SHUT YOU UP AGAIN...
...IF YOU DON'T BELIEVE ME.
...!!
BLUSH
IT'S OKAY.
YOU TOOK NOTICE OF ME, AND THAT'S ENOUGH FOR TODAY.

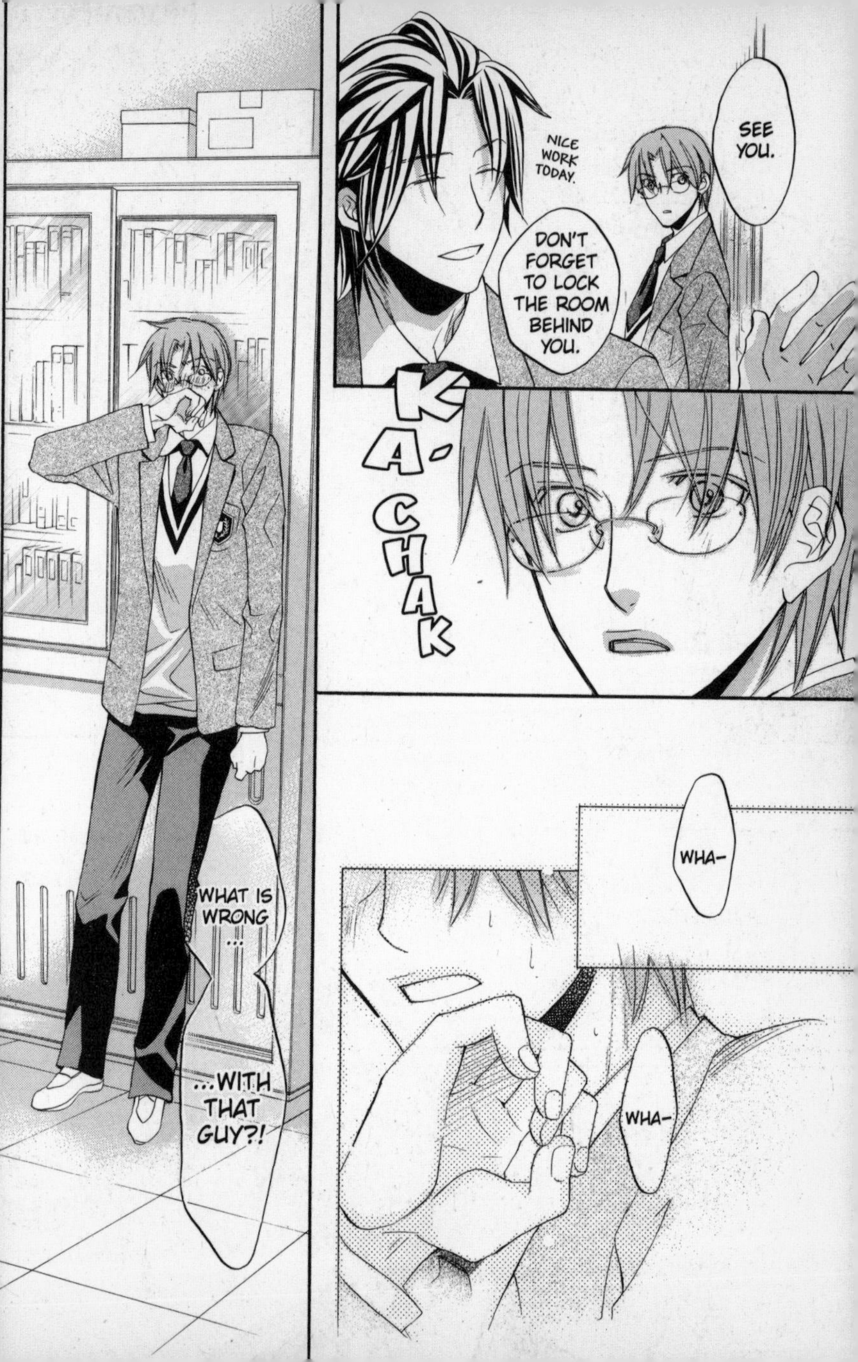
SEE YOU.
NICE WORK TODAY.
DON'T FORGET TO LOCK THE ROOM BEHIND YOU.
K-A-CHAK
WHA-
WHA-
WHAT IS WRONG ...
...WITH THAT GUY?!

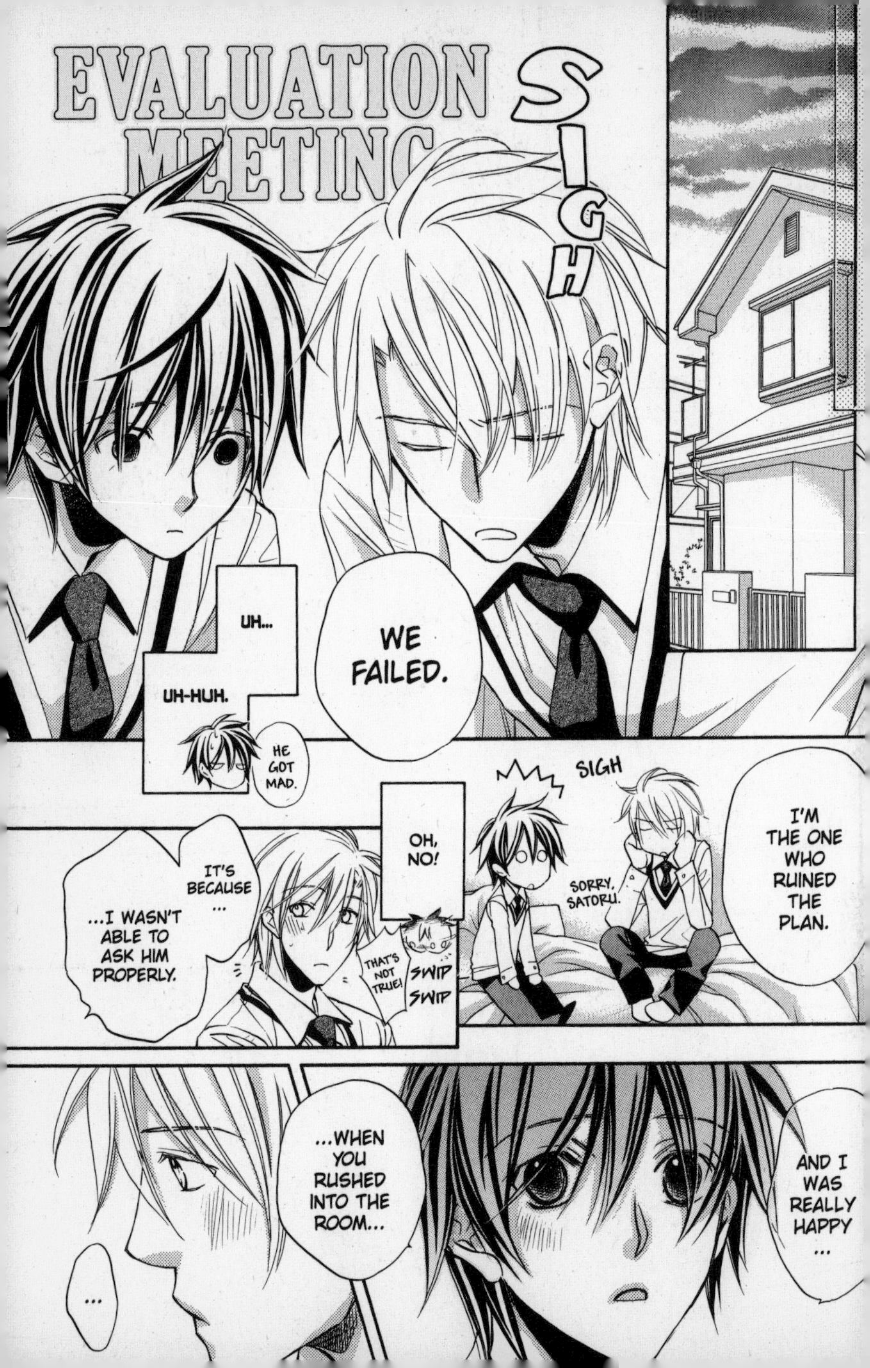
SIGH
EVALUATION MEETING
WE FAILED.
UH...
UH-HUH.
HE GOT MAD.
I'M THE ONE WHO RUINED THE PLAN.
SIGH
SORRY, SATORU.
OH, NO!
THAT'S NOT TRUE!
SWIP SWIP
IT'S BECAUSE...
...I WASN'T ABLE TO ASK HIM PROPERLY.
AND I WAS REALLY HAPPY...
...WHEN YOU RUSHED INTO THE ROOM...
...

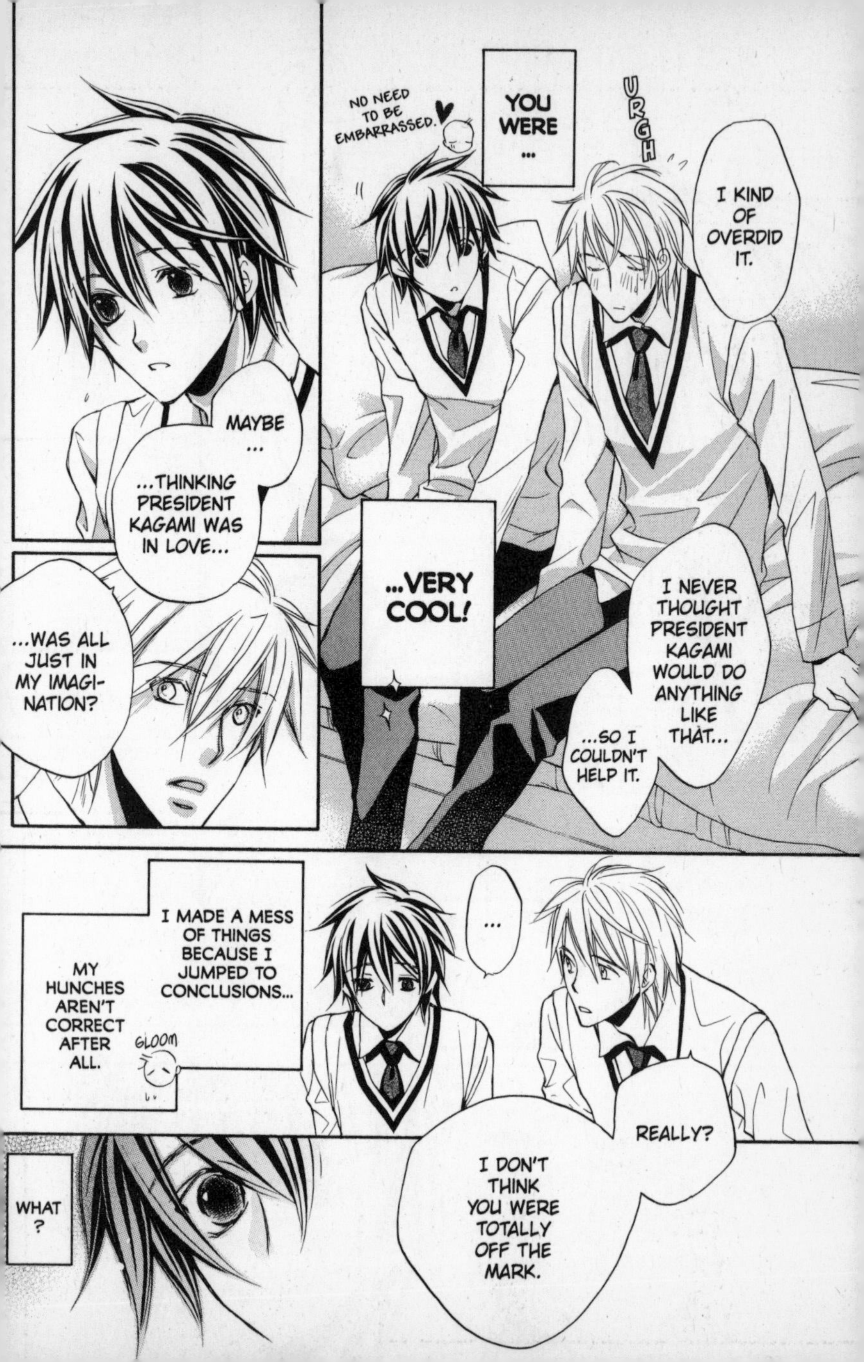
I KIND OF OVERDID IT.
URGH
YOU WERE...
NO NEED TO BE EMBARRASSED.
...VERY COOL!
I NEVER THOUGHT PRESIDENT KAGAMI WOULD DO ANYTHING LIKE THAT...
...SO I COULDN'T HELP IT.
MAYBE...
...THINKING PRESIDENT KAGAMI WAS IN LOVE...
...WAS ALL JUST IN MY IMAGI-NATION?
...
I MADE A MESS OF THINGS BECAUSE I JUMPED TO CONCLUSIONS...
MY HUNCHES AREN'T CORRECT AFTER ALL.
GLOOM
REALLY?
I DON'T THINK YOU WERE TOTALLY OFF THE MARK.
WHAT?

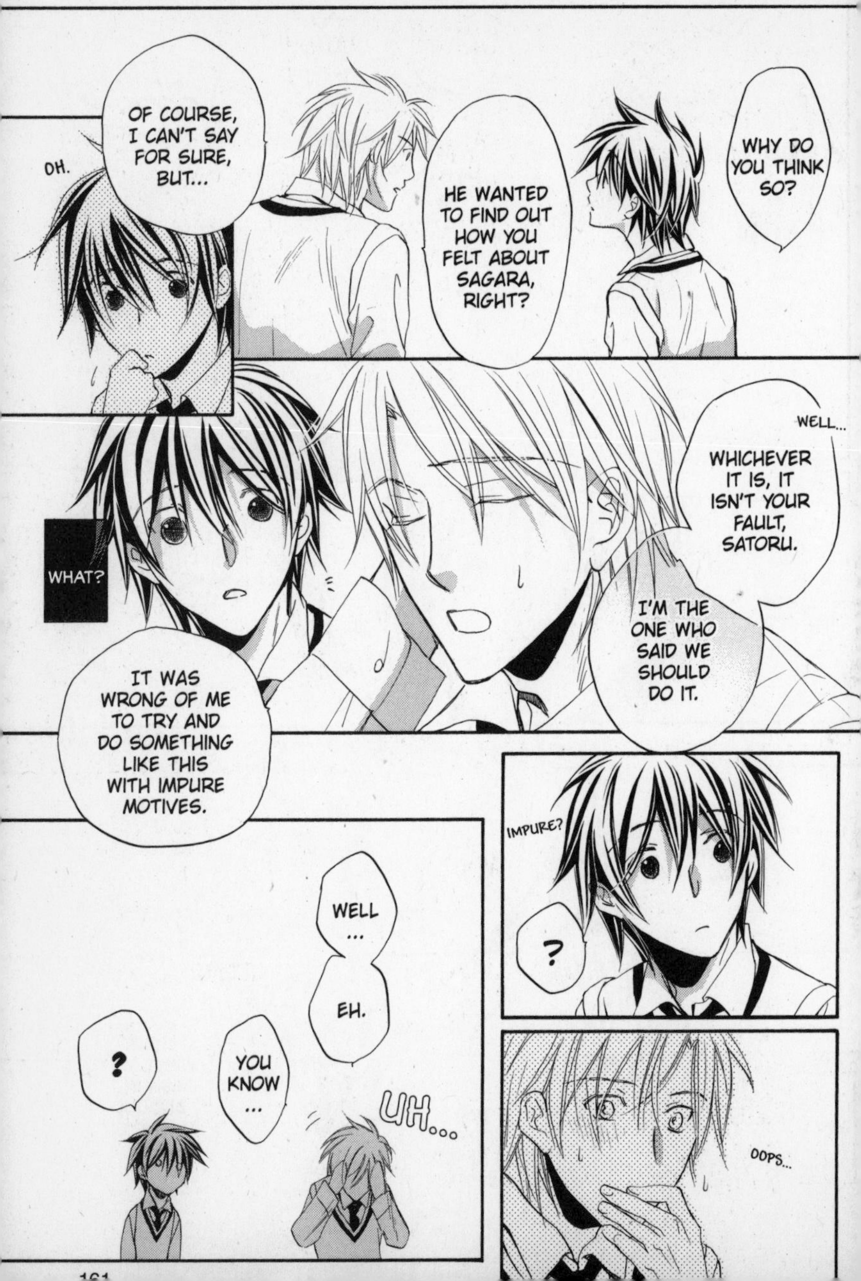
WHY DO YOU THINK SO?
HE WANTED TO FIND OUT HOW YOU FELT ABOUT SAGARA, RIGHT?
OF COURSE, I CAN'T SAY FOR SURE, BUT...
OH.
WELL...
WHICHEVER IT IS, IT ISN'T YOUR FAULT, SATORU.
I'M THE ONE WHO SAID WE SHOULD DO IT.
WHAT?
IT WAS WRONG OF ME TO TRY AND DO SOMETHING LIKE THIS WITH IMPURE MOTIVES.
IMPURE?
?
OOPS...
WELL ...
EH.
YOU KNOW ...
?
UH...

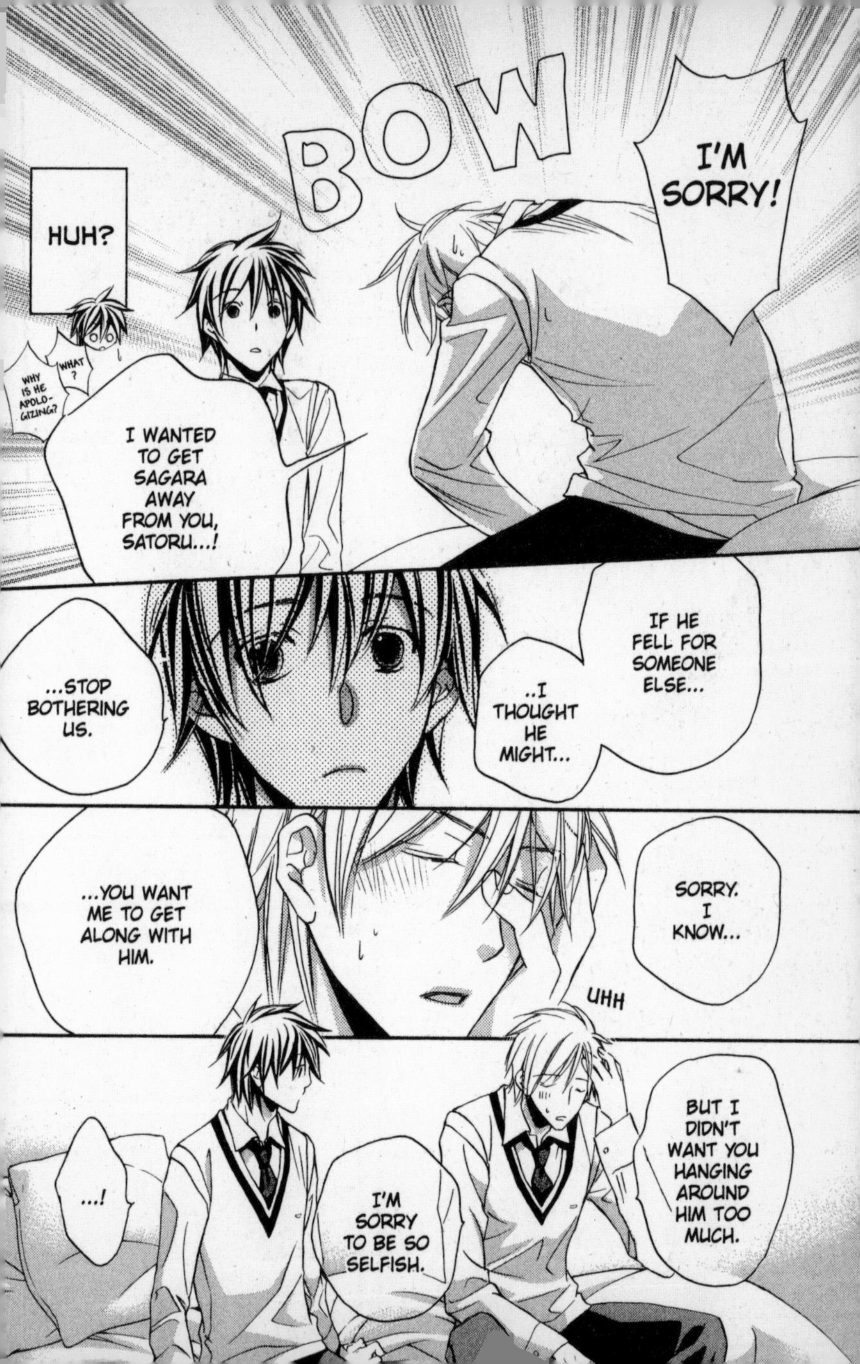
I'M SORRY!
BOW
HUH?
WHAT?
WHY IS HE APOLOGIZING?
I WANTED TO GET SAGARA AWAY FROM YOU, SATORU...!
IF HE FELL FOR SOMEONE ELSE...
..I THOUGHT HE MIGHT...
...STOP BOTHERING US.
SORRY. I KNOW...
UHH
...YOU WANT ME TO GET ALONG WITH HIM.
BUT I DIDN'T WANT YOU HANGING AROUND HIM TOO MUCH.
I'M SORRY TO BE SO SELFISH.
...!

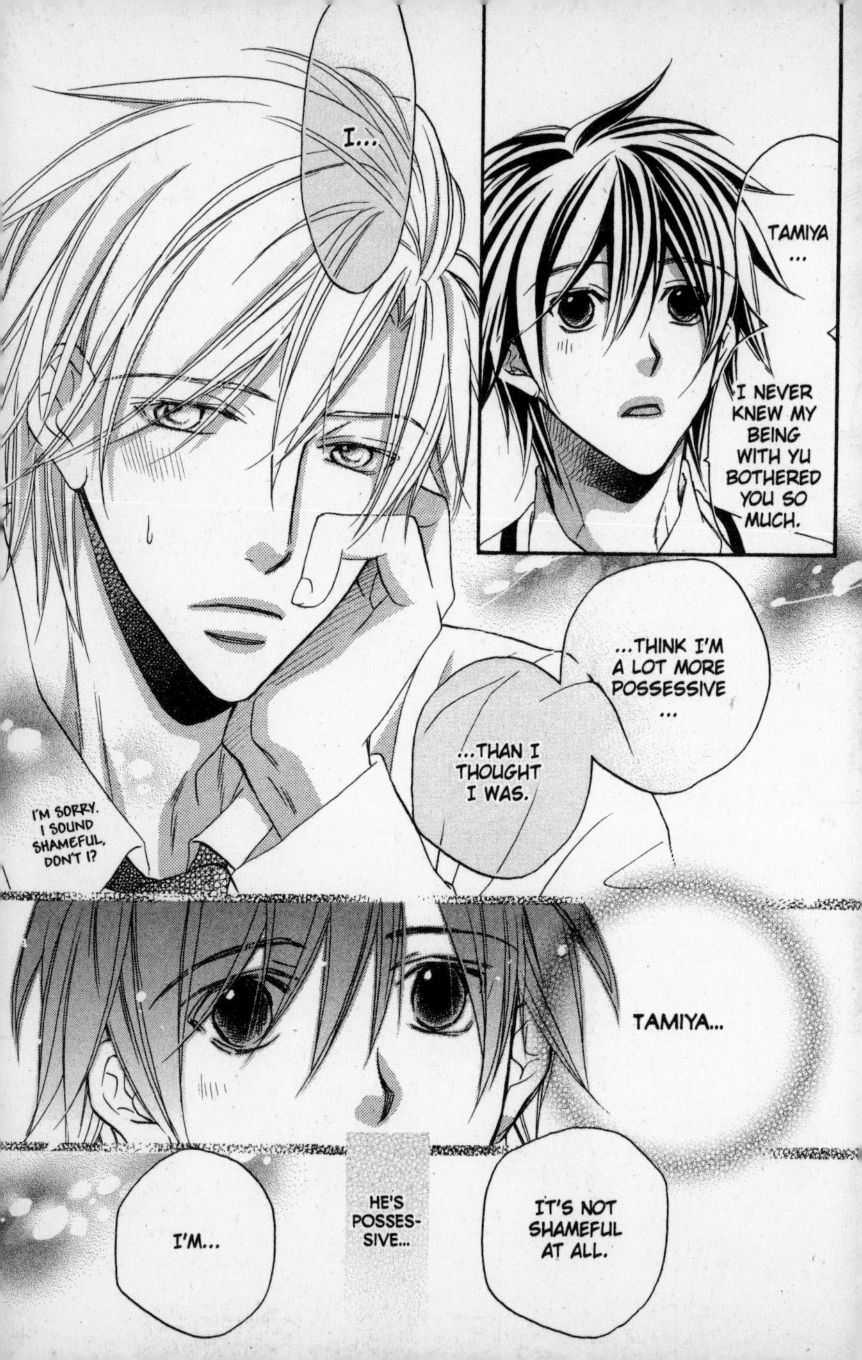
TAMIYA...
I NEVER KNEW MY BEING WITH YU BOTHERED YOU SO MUCH.
I...
...THINK I'M A LOT MORE POSSESSIVE...
...THAN I THOUGHT I WAS.
I'M SORRY. I SOUND SHAMEFUL, DON'T I?
TAMIYA...
IT'S NOT SHAMEFUL AT ALL.
HE'S POSSES-SIVE...
I'M...

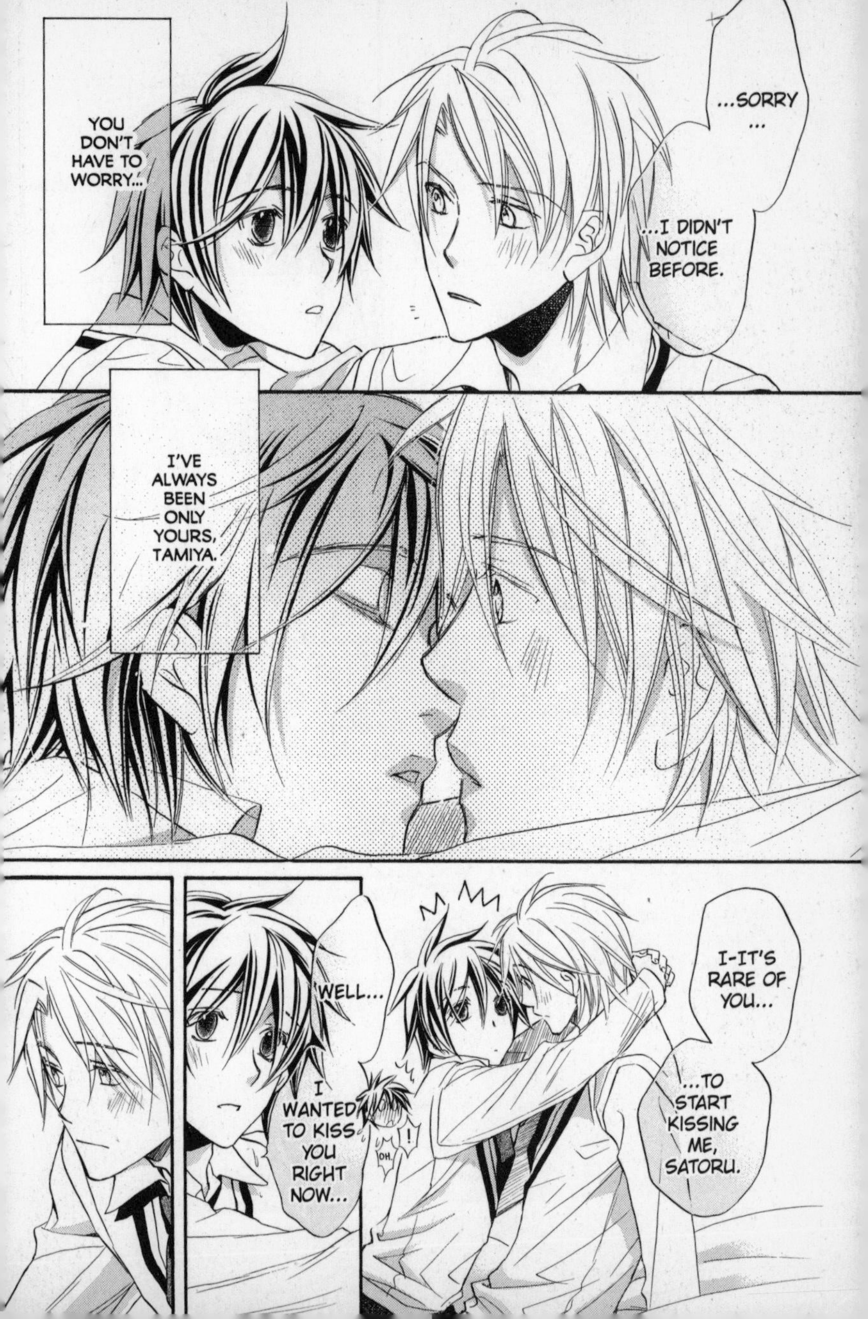
...SORRY ...
...I DIDN'T NOTICE BEFORE.
YOU DON'T HAVE TO WORRY...
I'VE ALWAYS BEEN ONLY YOURS, TAMIYA.
I-IT'S RARE OF YOU...
...TO START KISSING ME, SATORU.
!
OH.
WELL...
I WANTED TO KISS YOU RIGHT NOW...

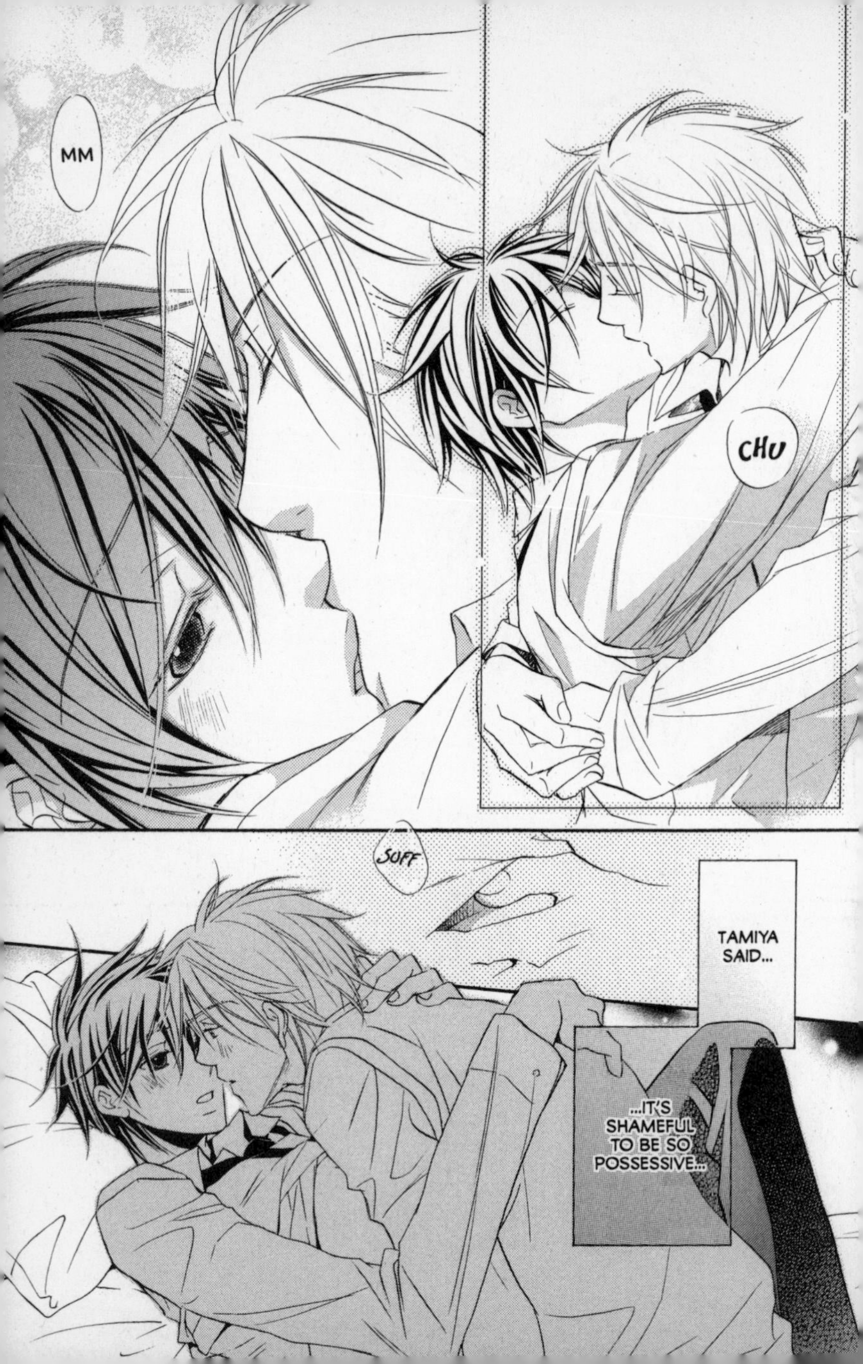
CHU
MM
SUFF
TAMIYA SAID...
...IT'S SHAMEFUL TO BE SO POSSESSIVE...

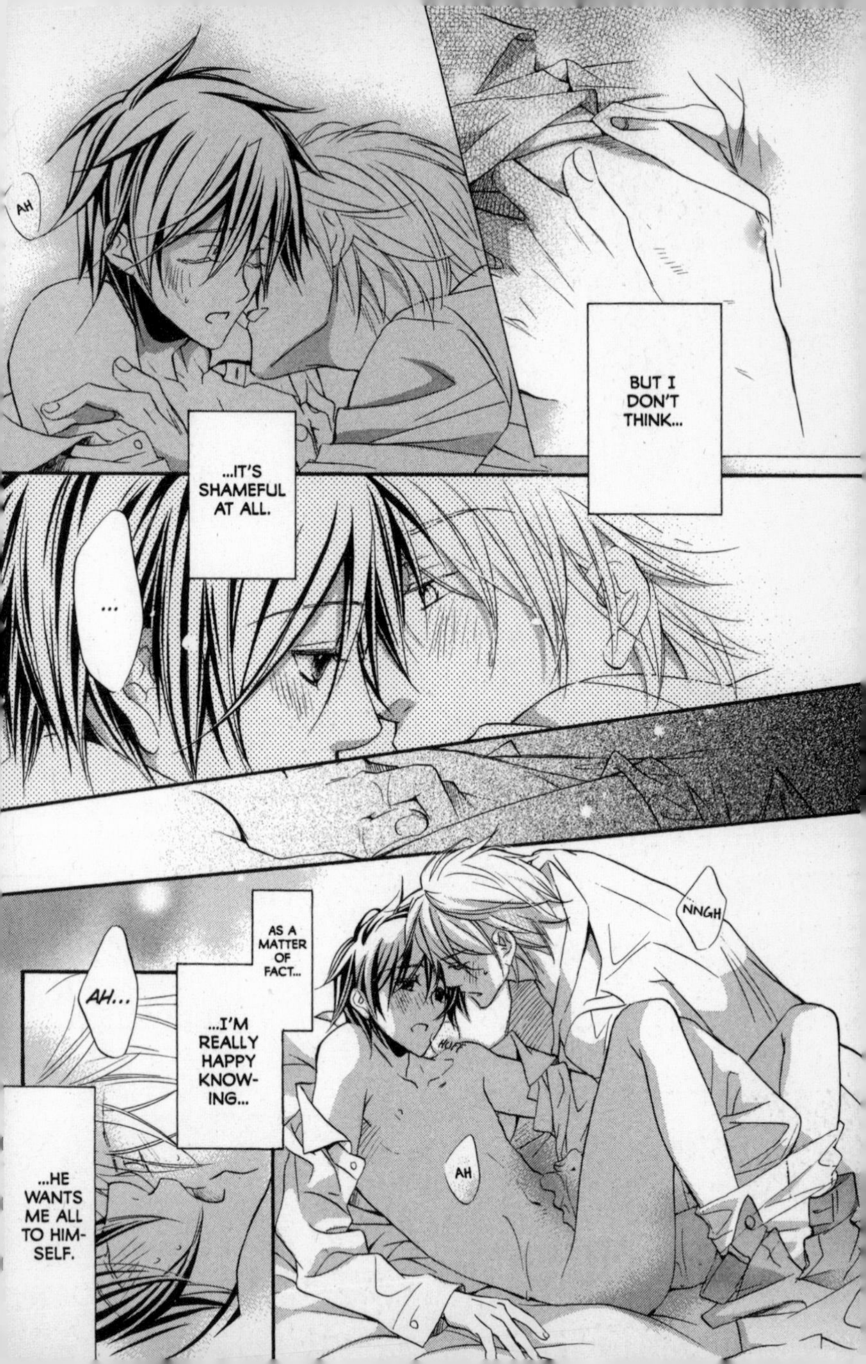
BUT I DON'T THINK...
AH
...IT'S SHAMEFUL AT ALL.
...
NNGH
AS A MATTER OF FACT...
HUFF
...I'M REALLY HAPPY KNOW-ING...
AH
AH...
...HE WANTS ME ALL TO HIM-SELF.

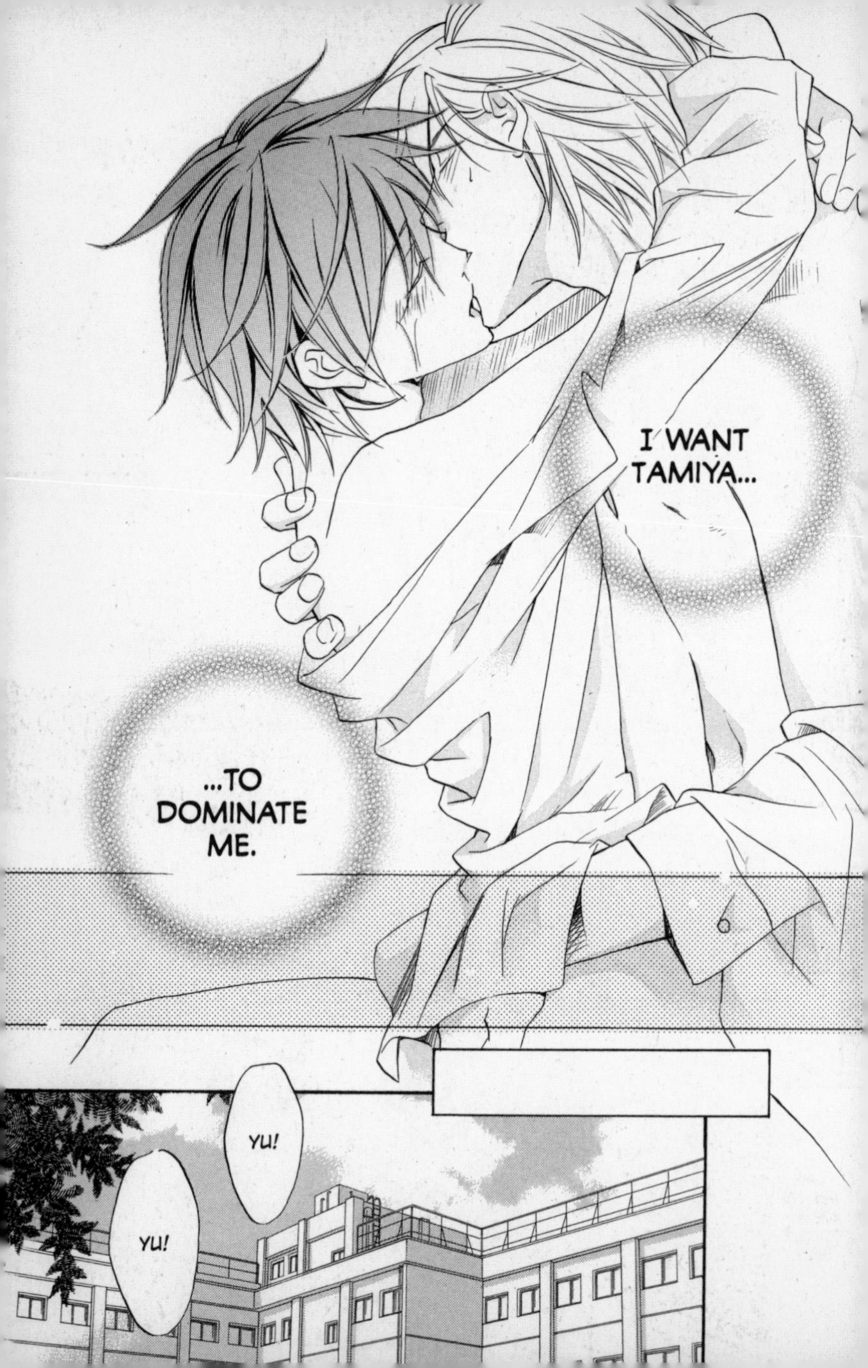
I WANT TAMIYA...
...TO DOMINATE ME.
YU!
YU!

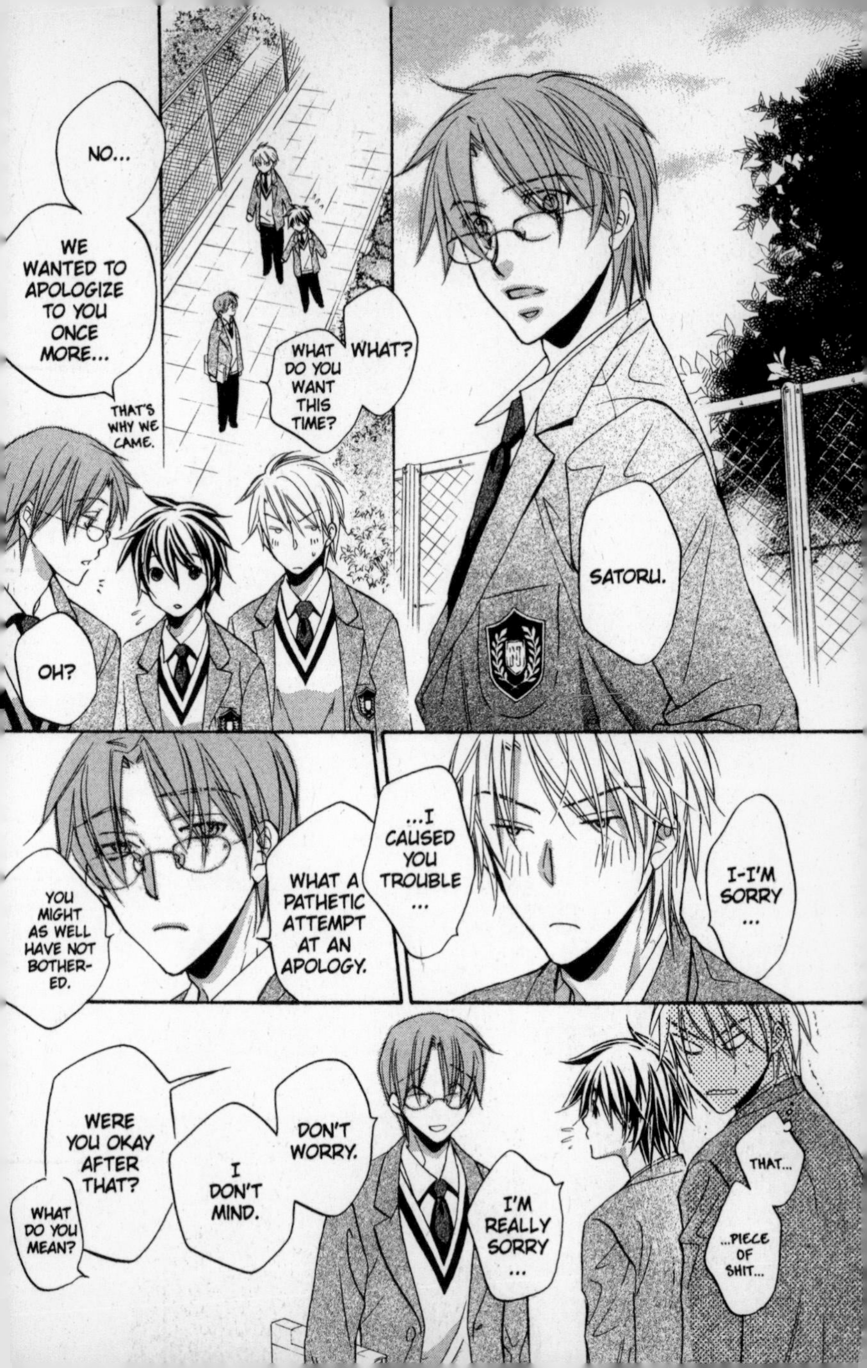
SATORU.
WHAT?
WHAT DO YOU WANT THIS TIME?
NO...
WE WANTED TO APOLOGIZE TO YOU ONCE MORE...
THAT'S WHY WE CAME.
OH?
I-I'M SORRY ...
...I CAUSED YOU TROUBLE ...
WHAT A PATHETIC ATTEMPT AT AN APOLOGY.
YOU MIGHT AS WELL HAVE NOT BOTHER-ED.
THAT...
...PIECE OF SHIT...
I'M REALLY SORRY ...
DON'T WORRY.
I DON'T MIND.
WERE YOU OKAY AFTER THAT?
WHAT DO YOU MEAN?

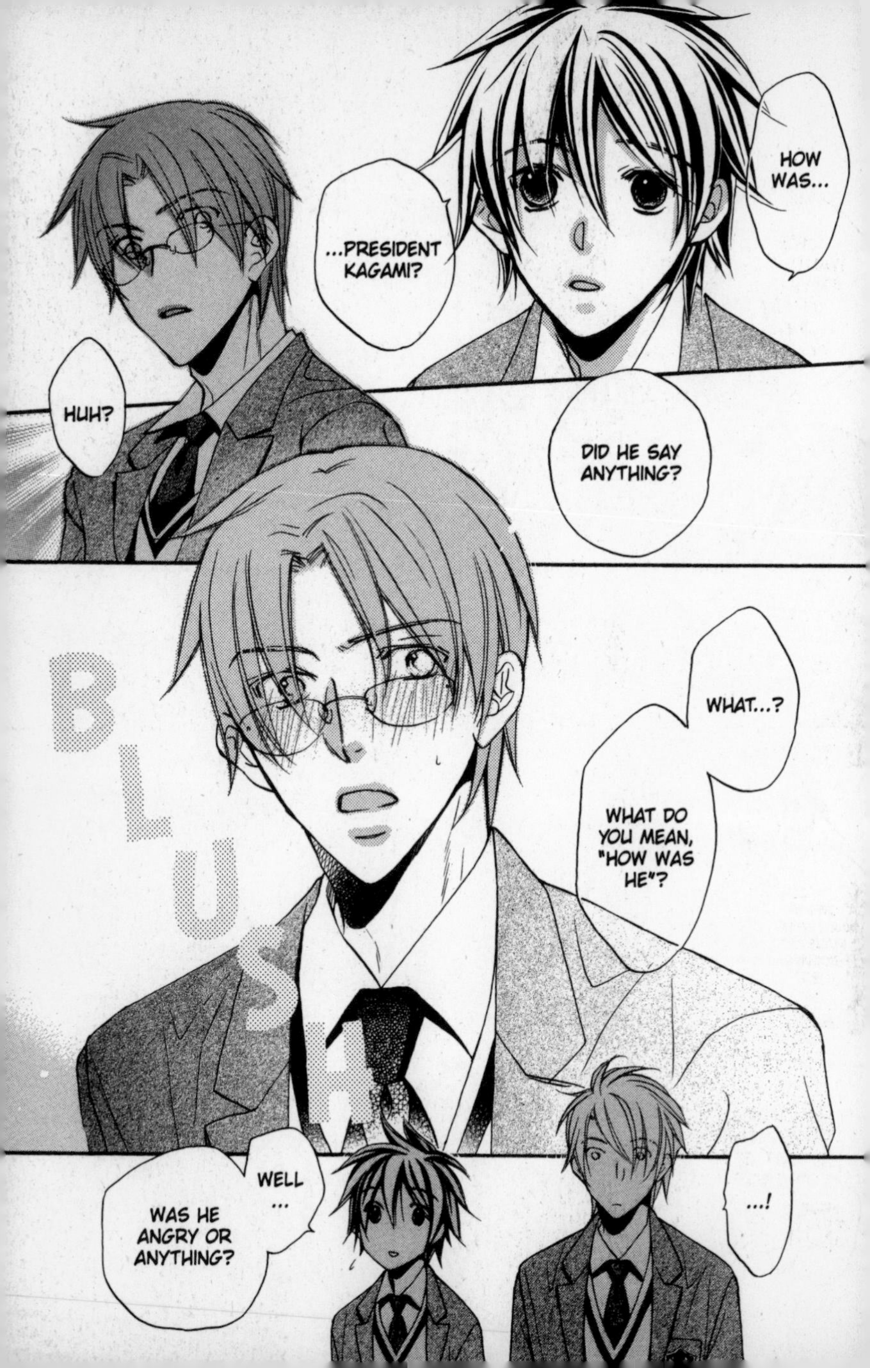
HOW WAS...
...PRESIDENT KAGAMI?
DID HE SAY ANYTHING?
HUH?
WHAT...?
WHAT DO YOU MEAN, "HOW WAS HE"?
BLUSH
...!
WELL ...
WAS HE ANGRY OR ANYTHING?

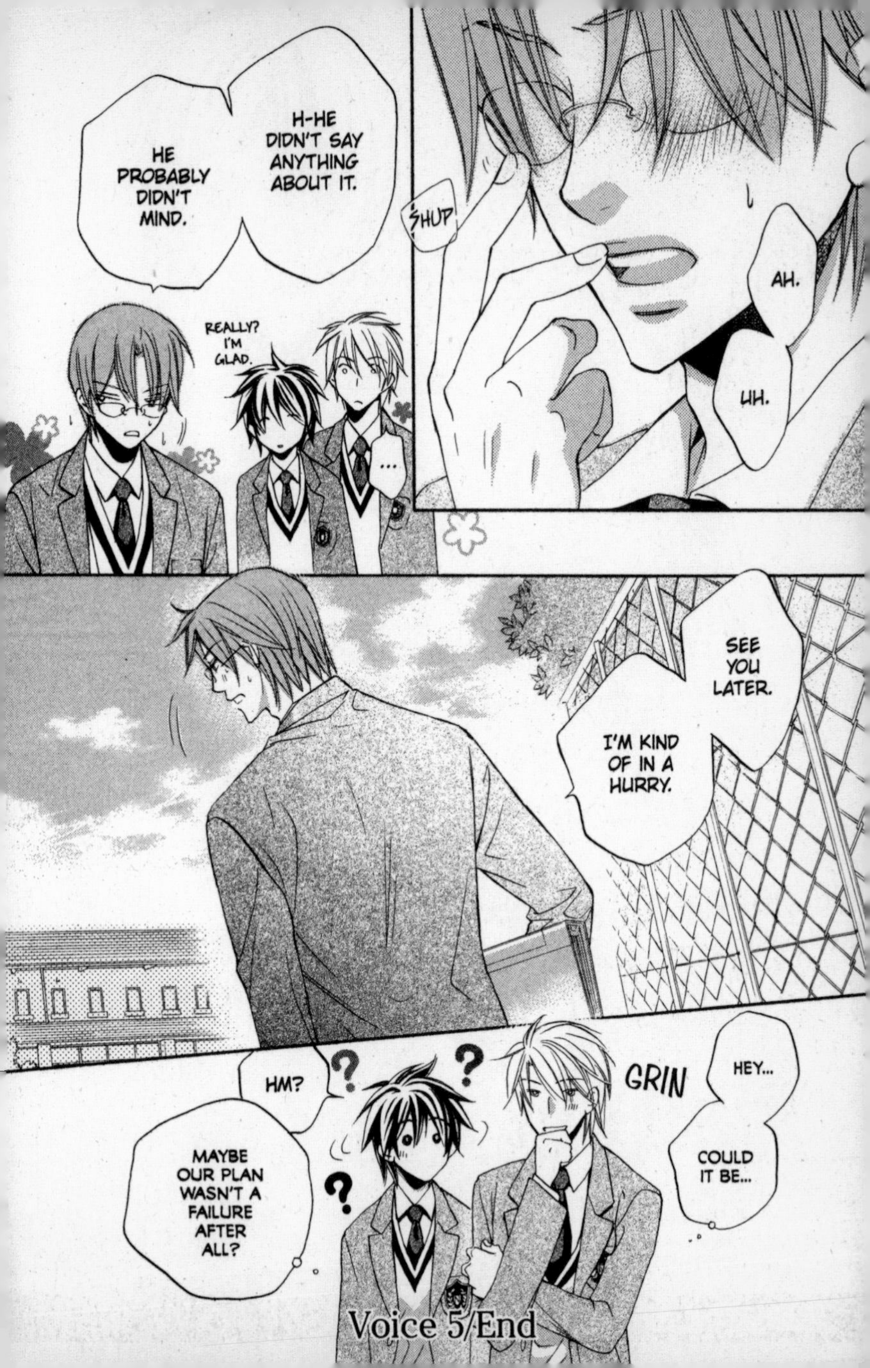
SHUP
AH.
UH.
H-HE DIDN'T SAY ANYTHING ABOUT IT.
HE PROBABLY DIDN'T MIND.
REALLY? I'M GLAD.
...
SEE YOU LATER.
I'M KIND OF IN A HURRY.
GRIN
HEY...
COULD IT BE...
HM?
MAYBE OUR PLAN WASN'T A FAILURE AFTER ALL?
?
?
?

Voice 5/End

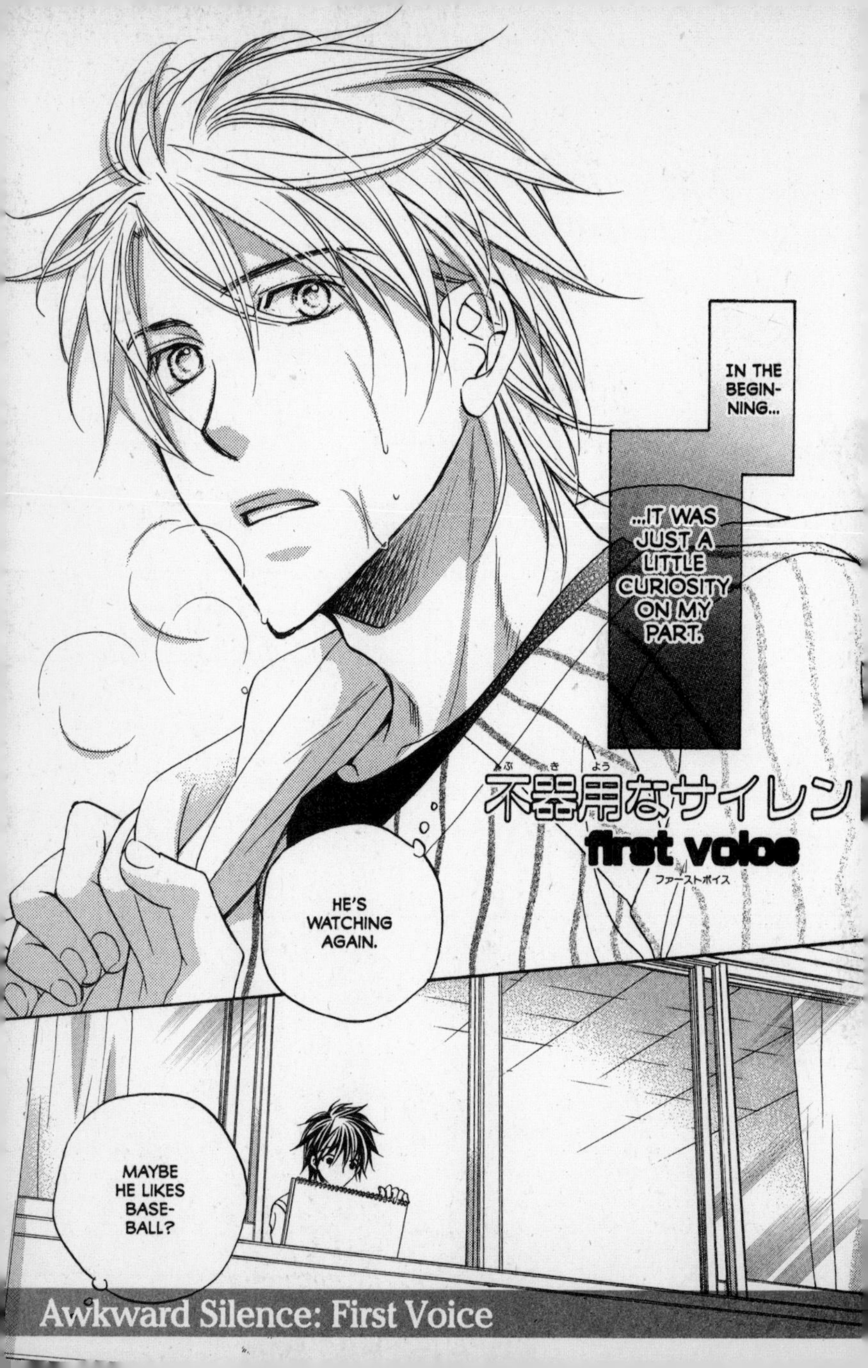
IN THE BEGIN-NING...
...IT WAS JUST A LITTLE CURIOSITY ON MY PART.
不器用なサイレン
first voice
ファーストボイス
HE'S WATCHING AGAIN.
MAYBE HE LIKES BASE-BALL?

Awkward Silence: First Voice

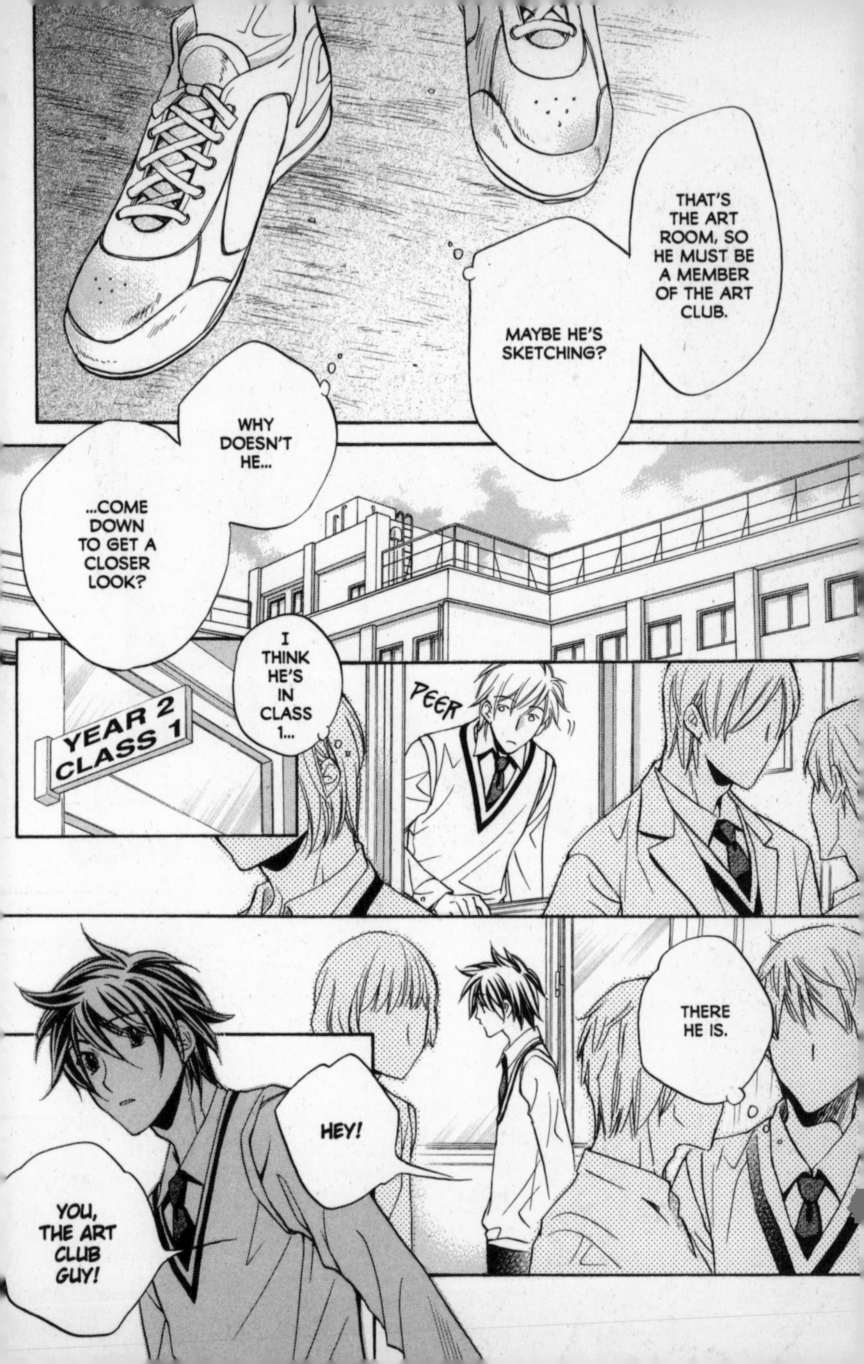
THAT'S THE ART ROOM, SO HE MUST BE A MEMBER OF THE ART CLUB.
MAYBE HE'S SKETCHING?
WHY DOESN'T HE...
...COME DOWN TO GET A CLOSER LOOK?
PEER
YEAR 2 CLASS 1
I THINK HE'S IN CLASS 1...
THERE HE IS.
HEY!
YOU, THE ART CLUB GUY!

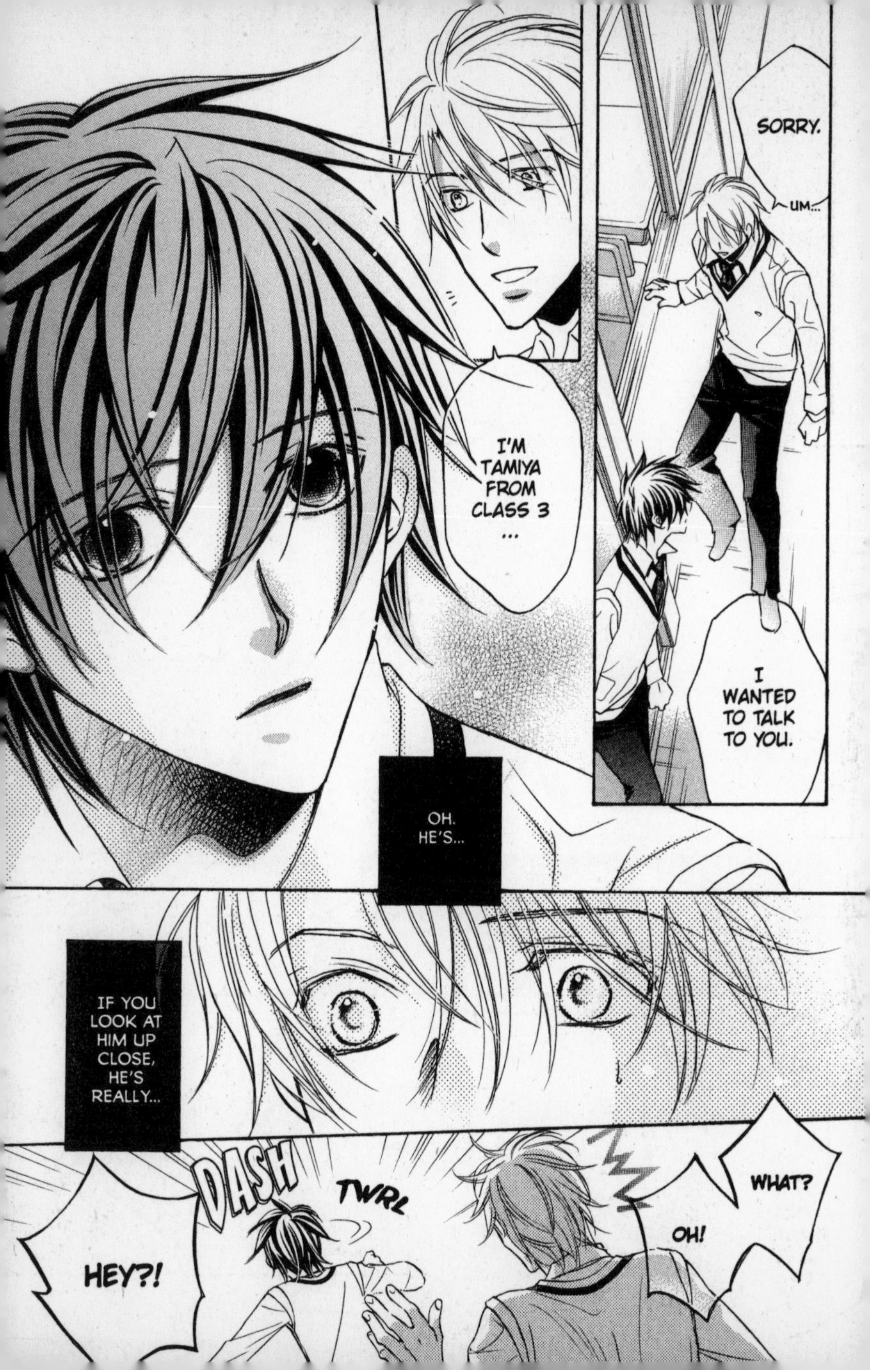
SORRY.
UM...
I WANTED TO TALK TO YOU.
I'M TAMIYA FROM CLASS 3 ...
OH. HE'S...
IF YOU LOOK AT HIM UP CLOSE, HE'S REALLY...
WHAT?
OH!
TWRL
DASH
HEY?!

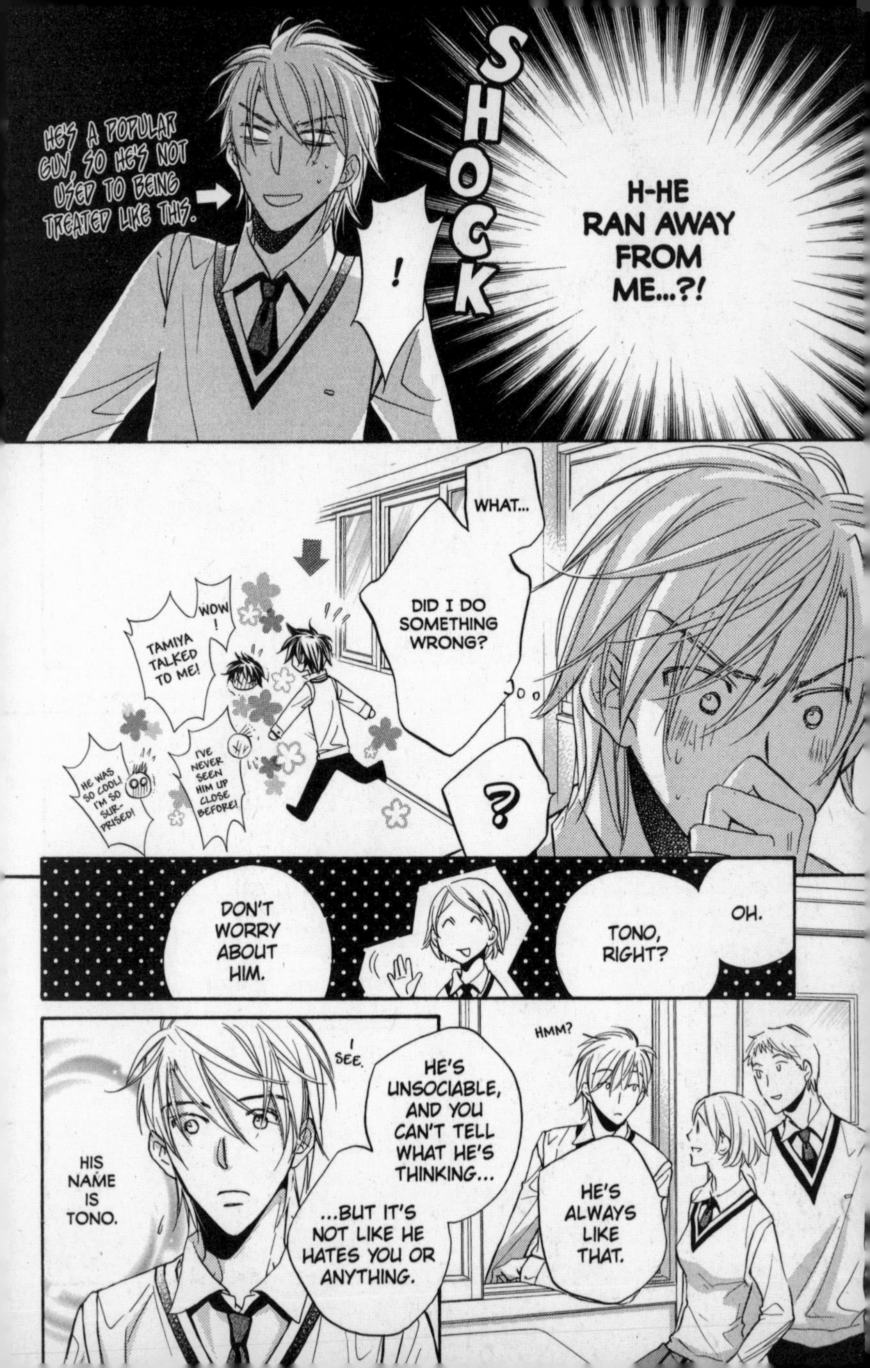
H-HE RAN AWAY FROM ME...?!
SHOCK
!
HE'S A POPULAR GUY, SO HE'S NOT USED TO BEING TREATED LIKE THIS.
WHAT...
DID I DO SOMETHING WRONG?
?
WOW!
TAMIYA TALKED TO ME!
I'VE NEVER SEEN HIM UP CLOSE BEFORE!
HE WAS SO COOL! I'M SO SURPRISED!
OH.
TONO, RIGHT?
DON'T WORRY ABOUT HIM.
HMM?
HE'S ALWAYS LIKE THAT.
HE'S UNSOCIABLE, AND YOU CAN'T TELL WHAT HE'S THINKING...
...BUT IT'S NOT LIKE HE HATES YOU OR ANYTHING.
I SEE.
HIS NAME IS TONO.

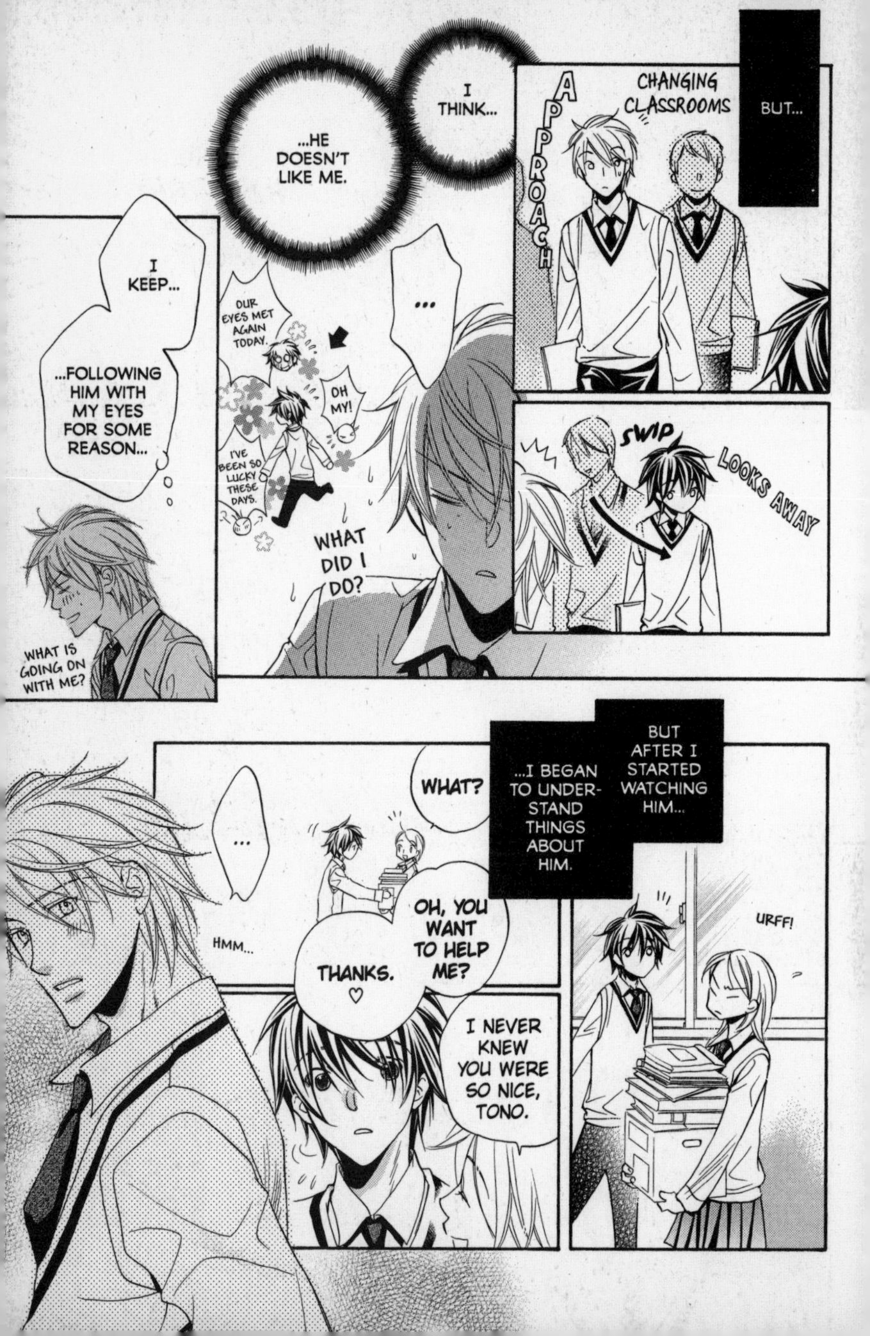
BUT...
CHANGING CLASSROOMS
APPROACH
I THINK...
...HE DOESN'T LIKE ME.
SWIP
LOOKS AWAY
...
OUR EYES MET AGAIN TODAY.
OH MY!
I'VE BEEN SO LUCKY THESE DAYS.
WHAT DID I DO?
I KEEP...
...FOLLOWING HIM WITH MY EYES FOR SOME REASON...
WHAT IS GOING ON WITH ME?
BUT AFTER I STARTED WATCHING HIM...
...I BEGAN TO UNDERSTAND THINGS ABOUT HIM.
URFF!
WHAT?
OH, YOU WANT TO HELP ME?
THANKS. ♡
...
HMM...
I NEVER KNEW YOU WERE SO NICE, TONO.

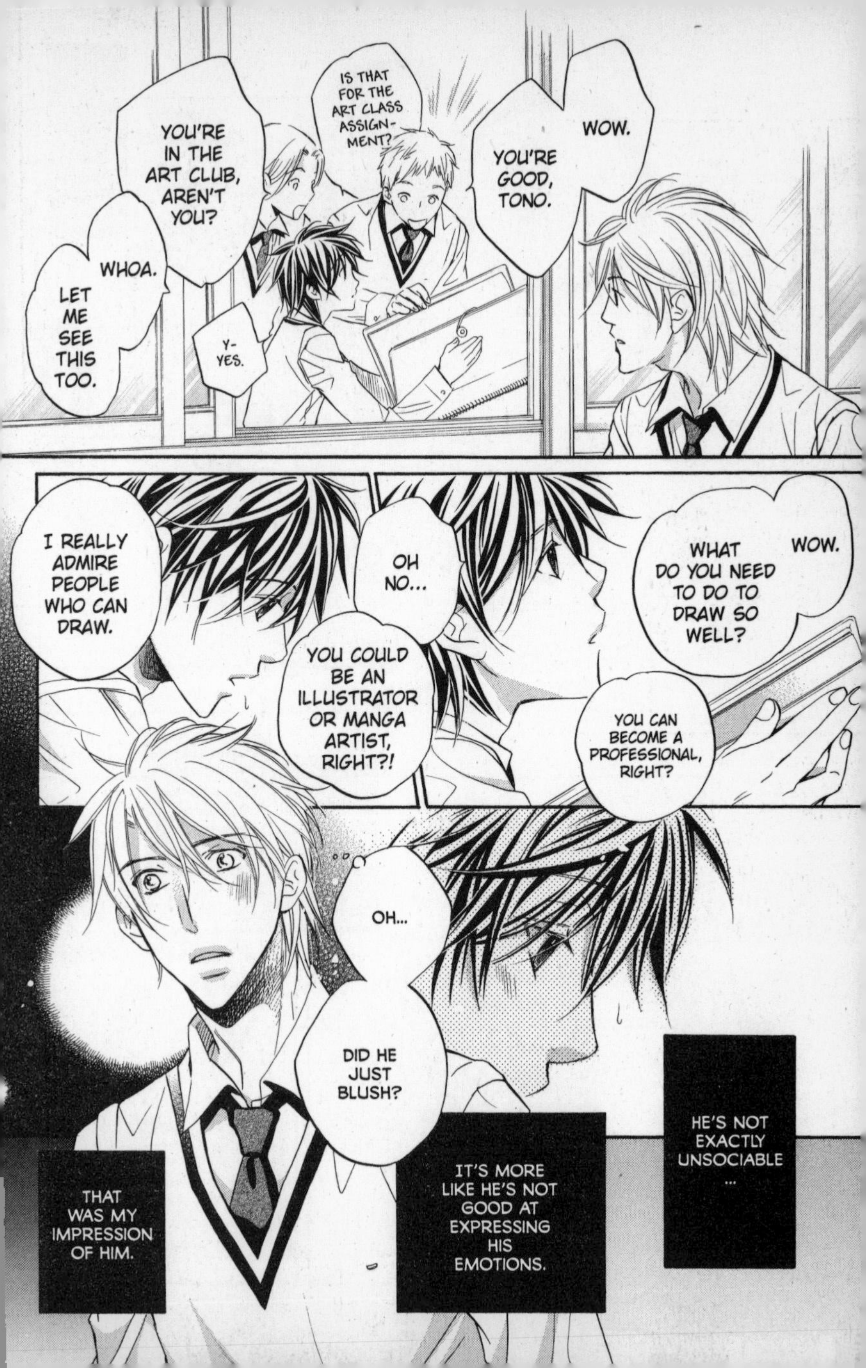
WOW.
YOU'RE GOOD, TONO.
IS THAT FOR THE ART CLASS ASSIGNMENT?
YOU'RE IN THE ART CLUB, AREN'T YOU?
WHOA.
LET ME SEE THIS TOO.
Y-YES.
WOW.
WHAT DO YOU NEED TO DO TO DRAW SO WELL?
YOU CAN BECOME A PROFESSIONAL, RIGHT?
OH NO...
I REALLY ADMIRE PEOPLE WHO CAN DRAW.
YOU COULD BE AN ILLUSTRATOR OR MANGA ARTIST, RIGHT?!
OH...
DID HE JUST BLUSH?
HE'S NOT EXACTLY UNSOCIABLE...
IT'S MORE LIKE HE'S NOT GOOD AT EXPRESSING HIS EMOTIONS.
THAT WAS MY IMPRESSION OF HIM.

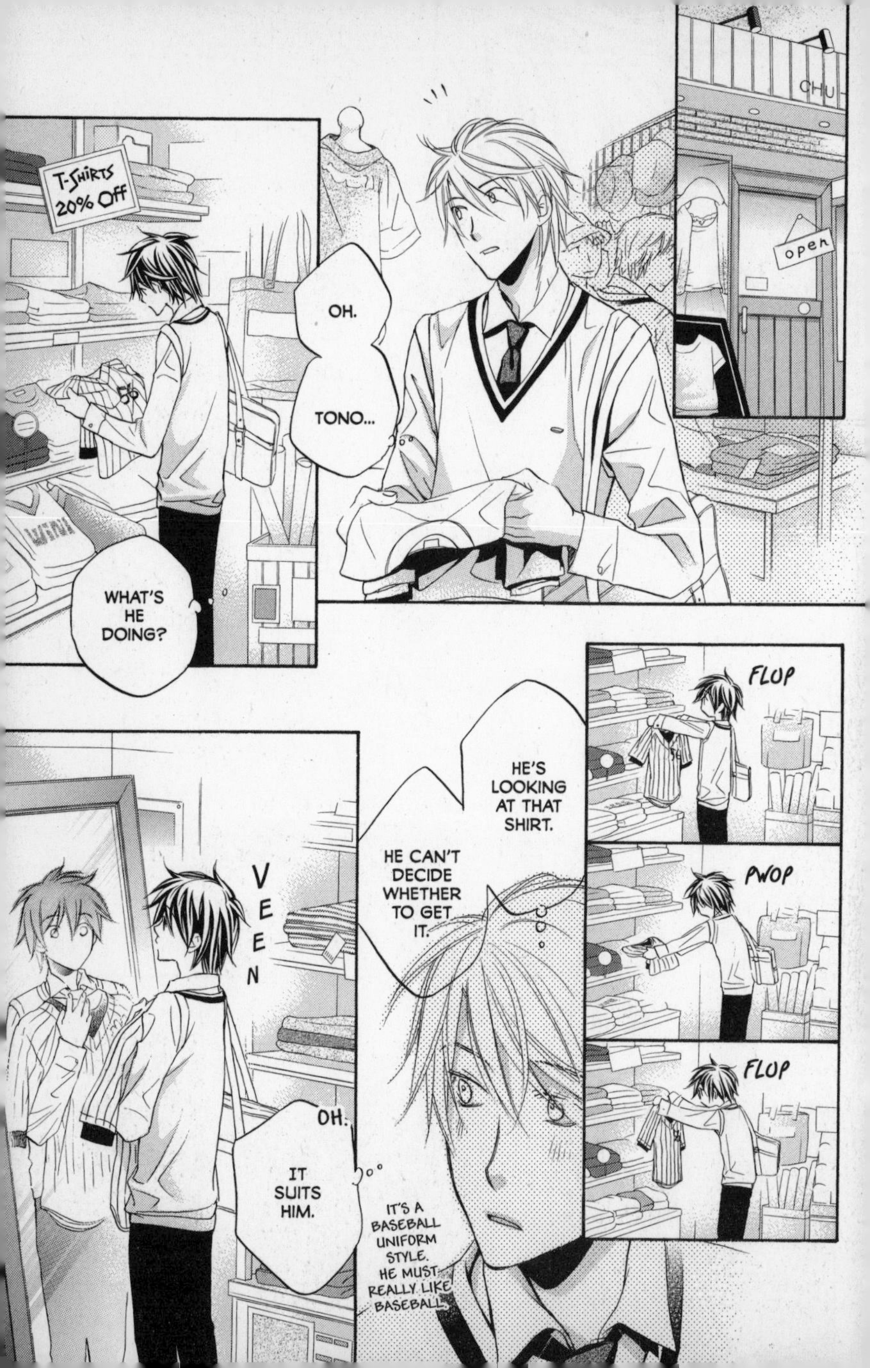
CHU
open
OH.
TONO...
T-SHIRTS 20% OFF
WHAT'S HE DOING?
FLOP
PWOP
FLOP
HE'S LOOKING AT THAT SHIRT.
HE CAN'T DECIDE WHETHER TO GET IT.
IT'S A BASEBALL UNIFORM STYLE. HE MUST REALLY LIKE BASEBALL.
VEEN
OH.
IT SUITS HIM.

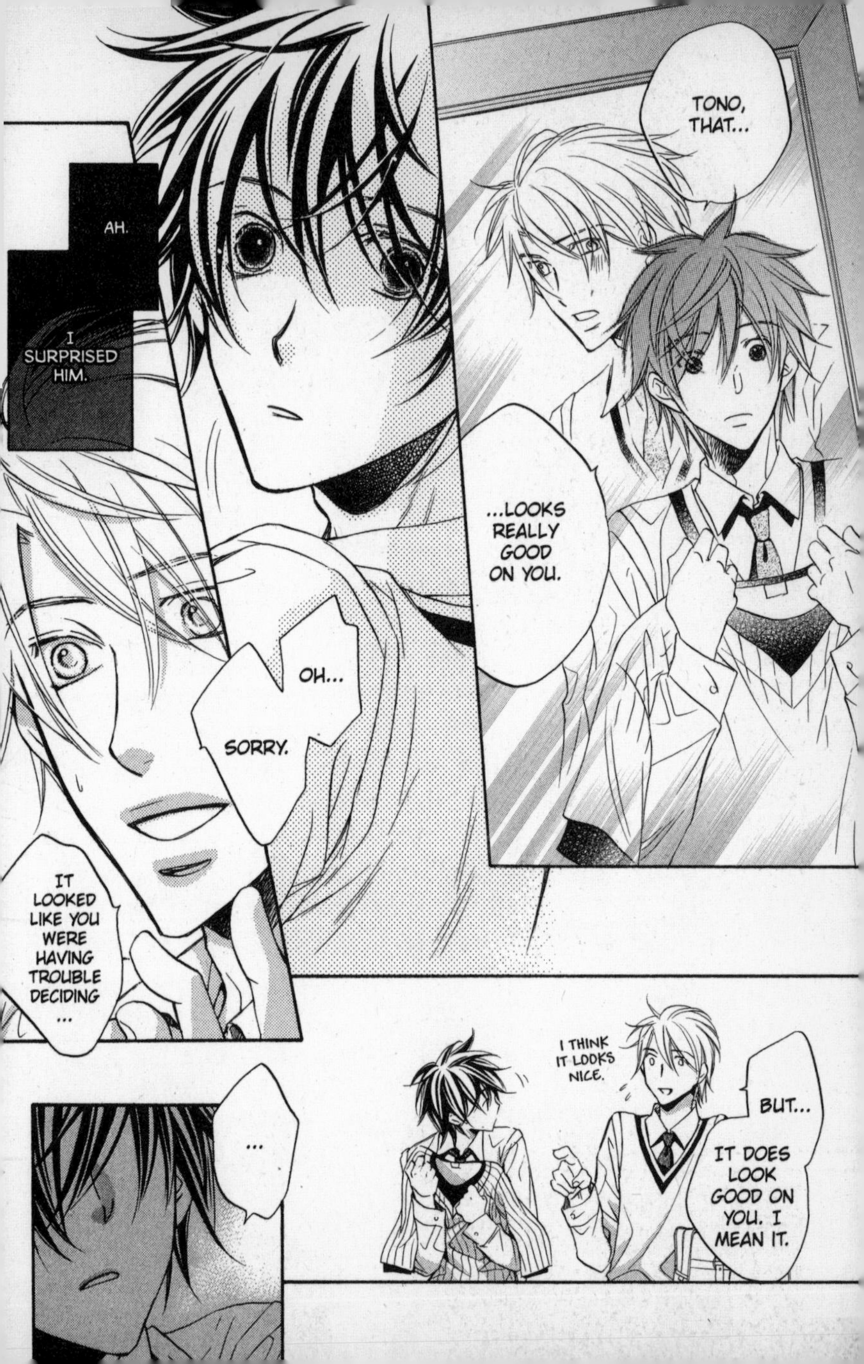
TONO, THAT...
...LOOKS REALLY GOOD ON YOU.
OH...
SORRY.
AH.
I SURPRISED HIM.
IT LOOKED LIKE YOU WERE HAVING TROUBLE DECIDING...
I THINK IT LOOKS NICE.
BUT...
IT DOES LOOK GOOD ON YOU. I MEAN IT.
...

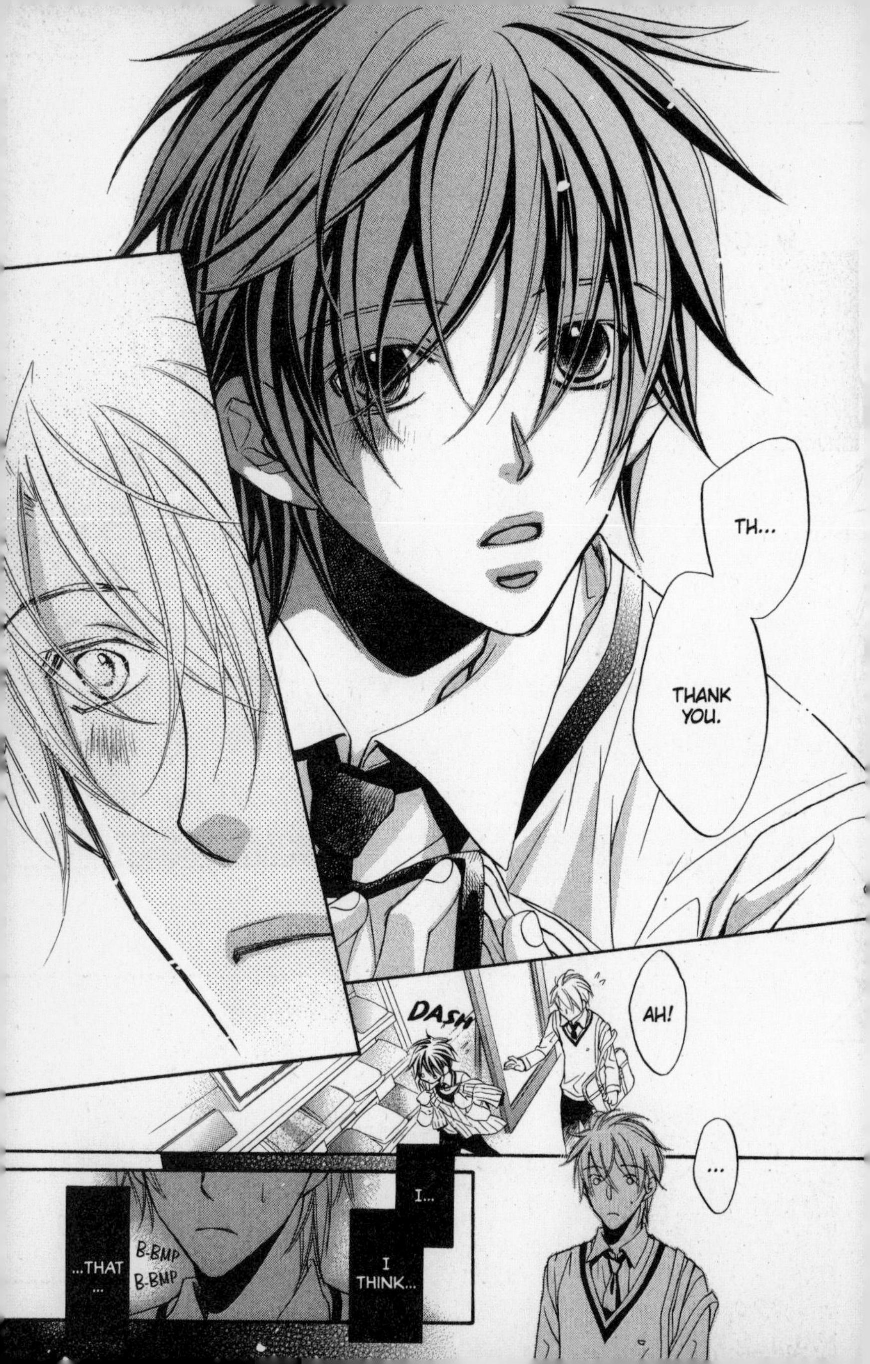
TH...
THANK YOU.
AH!
DASH
...
I...
I THINK...
B-BMP
B-BMP
...THAT ...

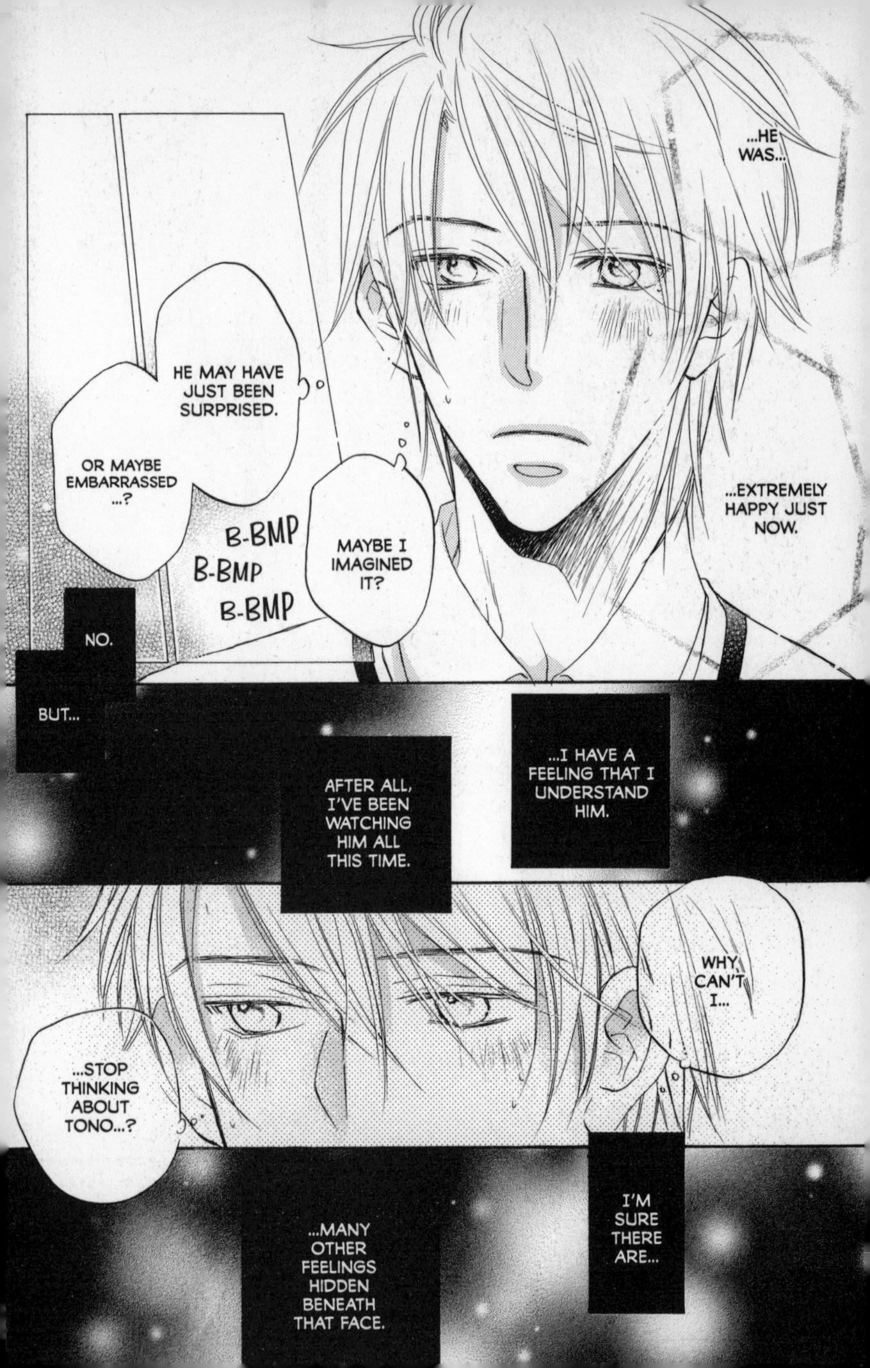
...HE WAS...
...EXTREMELY HAPPY JUST NOW.
MAYBE I IMAGINED IT?
HE MAY HAVE JUST BEEN SURPRISED.
OR MAYBE EMBARRASSED ...?
B-BMP
B-BMP
B-BMP
NO.
BUT...
...I HAVE A FEELING THAT I UNDERSTAND HIM.
AFTER ALL, I'VE BEEN WATCHING HIM ALL THIS TIME.
WHY CAN'T I...
...STOP THINKING ABOUT TONO...?
I'M SURE THERE ARE...
...MANY OTHER FEELINGS HIDDEN BENEATH THAT FACE.

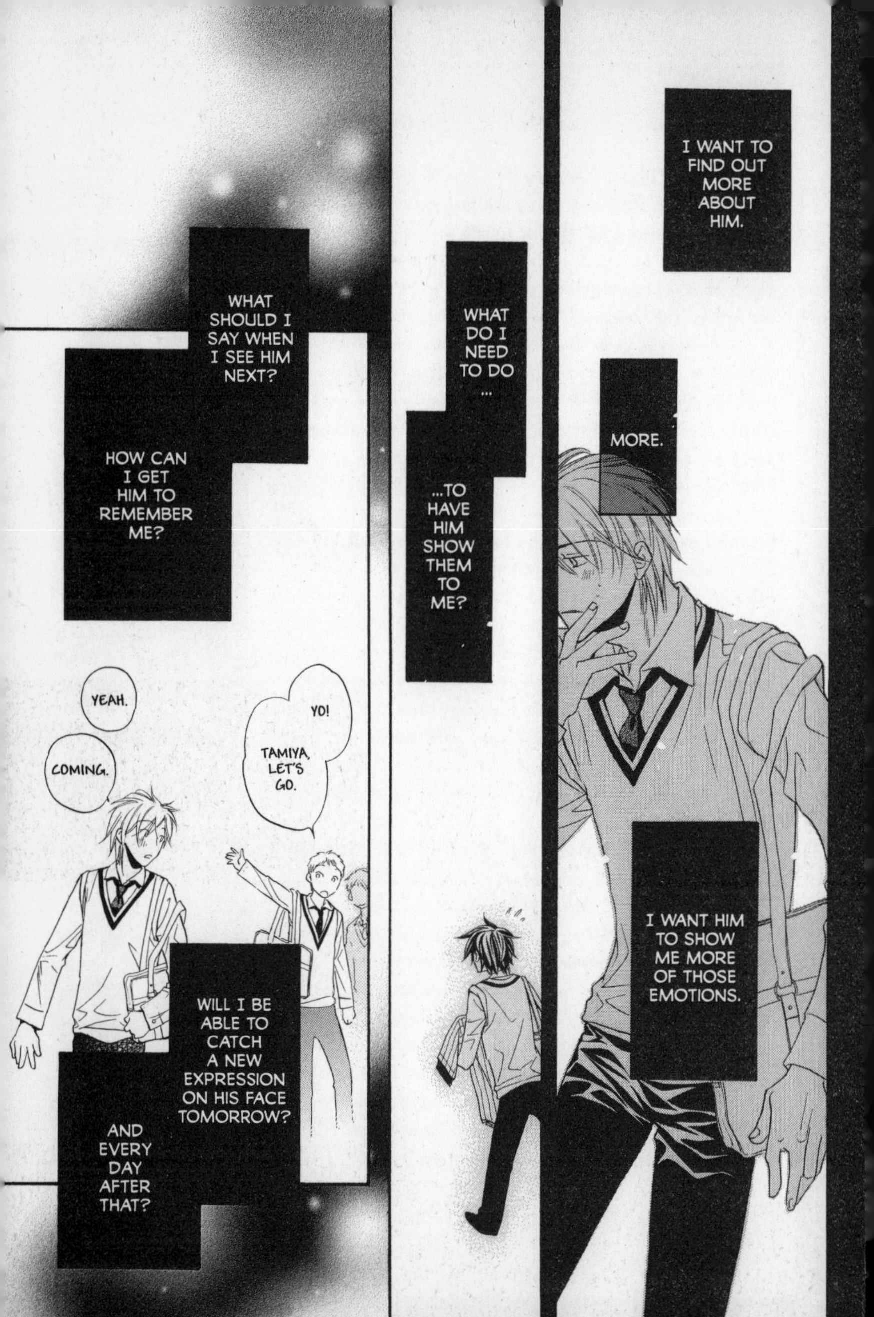
I WANT TO FIND OUT MORE ABOUT HIM.
MORE.
I WANT HIM TO SHOW ME MORE OF THOSE EMOTIONS.
WHAT DO I NEED TO DO ...
...TO HAVE HIM SHOW THEM TO ME?
WHAT SHOULD I SAY WHEN I SEE HIM NEXT?
HOW CAN I GET HIM TO REMEMBER ME?
YO!
TAMIYA, LET'S GO.
YEAH.
COMING.
WILL I BE ABLE TO CATCH A NEW EXPRESSION ON HIS FACE TOMORROW?
AND EVERY DAY AFTER THAT?

First Voice/End

Hello. I'm Hinako Takanaga. Hello to all readers new to this series, and thank you very much for picking up this volume if you read volume 1. The second volume of *Awkward Silence* is out... It says 2 on the cover, but I have a feeling that not many people picked up volume 1, so I'm sorry if you are new to the series and bought this volume by mistake. If you do happen to be that kind of person, please read volume 1 as well...! I—If you have time, that is. Thank you very much. B-BMP B-BMP Well then, I bring you volume 2. When I started the first chapter of the series, it was meant to be a one-shot, so I am very grateful I have been able to create volume 2. But we are now having some problems because this was not meant to be a long-running series, and also because I had fun in making this volume the way I wanted to. So the atmosphere seems different compared to volume 1. In volume 1, the two had just started their relationship, so there was something wriggly (hard to understand) about it. You could sense the remnants of the excitement of love in that volume, but this whole volume is about a doting lovey-dovey couple... It contains two stories that may seem like "Ah, just stay in your own world"... Then again, I like stories like that, but I am slightly worried if the people who liked volume 1 will like volume 2. So the publishing of this volume makes me very happy, but at the same time, the thought of this volume being stacked up in the bookstores gets me so worried that I can feel my stomach fluids rising up. Gurgh, gurgh. And so... I put Yu in charge of that itchy excitement of love, and I added some humor by introducing a funny family. I like the mother a lot. Also, since *Awkward Silence* started off with Tamiya suddenly confessing to Tono, I had received many letters saying, "How did Tamiya fall in love with Tono?" I decided to draw a one-shot showing this to bring in that excitement of falling in love that was lacking in this volume. Tono was much more expressionless in volume 1, and when I drew him again for this I got the idea that his beauty level (beauty level?) should be slightly higher than that of the current Tono.

✸ This series is starting to go all over the place. But I still have Yu's romance to take care of, so it is scheduled to continue on a little longer. It will take some time, so please take a look at the magazine or my homepage if you cannot wait for the next volume.

✸ ANAGURANZ ✸
http://anaguranz.com/
(as of August 2012)

You can check my work schedule and blog at the site above. I update the site with stupid diary entries too, so please drop by to take a peek when you have time. I'll be waiting for you. Thank you. ♪   ✸   ✸   ✸

✸ The editorial office has put together a small gift for readers who apply [Japan only]. There was a cat-ear feature some time ago in the magazine, and I created a short one-shot using the topic of "Tono cat and Tamiya dog." It isn't going to be placed in the graphic novel, but we've decided to add new illustrations and offer it as a gift. It will look like a picture book, and it will be in color. You don't often get the chance to see somebody else color your illustrations for you, so I'm looking forward to that. ↪ Please apply for it if you feel like it. Please.

✸ I apologize to my editor...for causing so much trouble again. I know I'm far from being a perfect manga artist, but I hope you'll continue to supervise me. Thank you very much to all of the assistants who help me. ↪ You make the lonely work so much more delightful to do. And most of all, I would like to thank all the people who picked up a volume of this book! I would be very grateful if you enjoy the manga. Please send me your messages telling me how you feel about it! I would be happy if you sent your letters to the editorial office, and I would be overjoyed if you sent me an email via my homepage. ↪ Well then, thank you very much for reading this. I hope we will meet again somewhere. ↪↪✸✸

Hinako Takanaga XXX

*The picture book gift offer ended in August 2008.

About the Author

Hinako Takanaga was born on
September 16th in Nagoya, Japan.
She is the creator of many popular
series, including *The Tyrant Falls in Love*,
which was also adapted into an anime
series. She is a Virgo, blood type O,
and a self-proclaimed coffee addict
who can get violent if she doesn't get
her daily dose. A fortune-teller once
told her she wasn't suited to be a
manga artist, but she doesn't believe
in fortune-telling anyway. She currently
lives with her vicious cat Choro.

Awkward Silence
Volume 2
SuBLime Manga Edition

Story and Art by **Hinako Takanaga**

Translation—**Tetsuichiro Miyaki**
Touch-up Art and Lettering—**NRP Studios**
Cover and Graphic Design—**Fawn Lau**
Editor—**Nancy Thistlethwaite**

Bukiyou na Silent 2 © 2008 Hinako Takanaga
Originally published in Japan in 2008 by Libre Publishing Co.,
Ltd. Tokyo.
English translation rights arranged with Libre Publishing Co.,
Ltd. Tokyo.

Printed in the U.S.A.

Published by SuBLime Manga
P.O. Box 77010
San Francisco, CA 94107

10 9 8 7 6 5 4 3 2 1
First printing, October 2012

www.SuBLimeManga.com

For more information

on all our products, along with the most up-to-date news on releases, series announcements, and contests, please visit us at:

 SuBLimeManga.com

 twitter.com/**SuBLimeManga**

 facebook.com/**SuBLimeManga**